DIAMONDS, GOLD, AND WAR

DIAMONDS, GOLD, AND WAR

The British, the Boers, and the Making of South Africa

MARTIN MEREDITH

PublicAffairs

NEW YORK

First published in Great Britain in 2007
by Simon & Schuster UK Ltd. A CBS COMPANY.

Published in the United States by PublicAffairs™,
a member of the Perseus Books Group.

Typeset in Bembo by M Rules

Cataloging-in-Publication Data is available from the Library of Congress
ISBN-13: 978-1-58648-641-9
ISBN-10: 1-58648-641-1

First Edition

10 9 8 7 6 5 4 3 2 1

I speak of Africa, and golden joys ...

Shakespeare
Henry IV, Part 2, Act v, Sc. iii

CONTENTS

PART VIII

PART IX

PART X

15°E   20°E

20°S

Namib

G E R M A N

B E C

20°S

*Kalahari
Desert*

Walvis Bay

•Windhoek

Desert

Tropic of Capricorn

S O U T H   W E S T

P R O T E C

25°S

N

•Angra Pequena

A F R I C A

B R I T I S H
Kur

BECHUANALAN
(to Cape Colony 1895)

Orange R.

Gr

ATLANTIC

N A M A Q U A L A N D

30°S

OCEAN

C A P E

Great Ka

Cape Town
Simonstown
Cape of Good Hope

•Paarl
•Stellenbosch

Mossel

15°E   20°E

25.°E   30.°E   35.°E

R

H

O

D   MASHONALAND

E   Salisbury

S   PORTUGUESE

I

A

Zambezi R.

Zambezi R.

Fort Victoria   Beira   20°S

Bulawayo

Matopo Hills

MATABELELAND

EAST

ALAND

Táti
Goldfields

AFRICA

Shoshong.   Limpopo R.   ZOUTPANSBERG

ATE   Pietersburg   V E N D A   PEDI   Oliphants R.

Gaberones   T R A N S V A A L

Pitsani   Rustenburg   Lydenburg   Nelspruit

OSHEN Mafeking WITWATERSRAND   Pretoria   Middelburg   Lourenço Marques

LLA Magaliesberg Hills   Barberton   Delagoa Bay

Vryburg   Vereeniging   Johannesburg   SWAZI

Potchefstroom   SWAZI-
LAND

Vaal R.   ORANGE   Majuba Hill   ×Laing's Nek   Kosi Bay

Fourteen Streams   FREE STATE   (to Natal 1902)

arkly West   ×Isandlwana ×   Z U L U (to Natal 1897)

y Modder R.   Ladysmith

emfontein   BASUTOLAND   NATAL   Tugela R.

Caledon   ×Spion Kop

berg   Orange R.   Pietermaritzburg   Durban   30°S

INDIAN

OCEAN

OLONY

aaff Reinet   X H O S A   Gt Kei R.

Gt Fish R.

rahamstown.   East London

Algoa Bay

Port Elizabeth

SOUTHERN AFRICA

1870—1910

Main railways completed by 1910   ×Battles

0   100   200   300 miles

0   100   200   300   400   500 km

AUTHOR'S NOTE

During my travels around southern Africa over the past forty years I have often been struck by the long-term repercussions that came from the making of the modern state of South Africa. Actions taken in the late nineteenth century continued to reverberate for more than a hundred years. One notable legacy is the multitude of battlefields that still arouse keen public interest – places such as Blood River, Isandlwana, Majuba and Spion Kop. But much else of modern South Africa was shaped by events of that time, in particular the rise of its fortunes from diamonds and gold and the steady dispossession of African land. It was also a time which saw the determined enforcement of segregation measures that culminated eventually in the apartheid system.

This book has been written in more auspicious circumstances. Despite their tortuous history, South Africans have managed to fashion for themselves a stable democracy with a robust constitution – one of the great triumphs of the late twentieth century. Witnessing this transformation has been a heartening experience. My thanks are due to a host of South African friends and acquaintances who over the years have given me such generous help and hospitality.

DIAMONDS, GOLD AND WAR

INTRODUCTION

When Britain took possession of the Cape Colony in 1806 during the course of the Napoleonic Wars it was a slave-owning outpost, three months' sailing distance from London, previously run as a Dutch commercial enterprise that had teetered on the edge of bankruptcy for years. Britain's only interest in the Cape was its use as a naval base at the foot of Africa halfway along the vital trade route between Europe and Asia – a stepping stone that the British government was determined to keep out of French hands. Its wartime occupation was not expected to be permanent.

The white colonial population, descendants of Dutch, German and French Huguenot settlers, was small, no more than 25,000 in all, scattered across a territory of 100,000 square miles. Most lived in Cape Town and the surrounding farming districts of the Boland, an area favoured with rich soils, a Mediterranean climate and reliable rainfall, renowned for its vineyards and gracious living. The prosperity of the Colony depended heavily on the labour of foreign slaves imported from other enclaves in Africa and from Asia. Almost every European family of standing in the western Cape owned slaves. Cape Town's population of 16,000 included some 10,000 slaves. White burghers also acted as overlords of the indigenous Khoikhoi, aboriginal pastoralists commonly called Hottentots, who had lost most of their land during 150 years of white occupation and who now served the white community as a labouring class treated no better than the slave population. The total population of the Cape Colony was no more than 75,000.

Beyond the fertile valleys and mountains of the Cape peninsular region lay a vast hinterland of scrub and semi-desert known to the Khoikhoi as the Karoo – the 'dry country'. Dutch stock farmers – 'trekboers', as they were called – had spread across this interior, herding sheep and cattle, living simply in ox-wagons or crude dwellings on farms they had staked out, trading in elephant ivory and animal hides and often clashing with indigenous pastoralists and hunters. In the north, the trekboers had reached the Orange River, 400 miles from the peninsula; a journey by wagon from their frontier farms to Cape Town and back took up to three months. In the east, they had collided with Bantu-speaking Xhosa chiefdoms expanding westwards across the Fish River into the Zuurveld grasslands, 450 miles from Cape Town. Parts of the frontier frequently degenerated into a turmoil of cattle raids and intermittent warfare.

As the Colony's new rulers, the British set out to impose some form of law and order on the turbulent eastern frontier, despatching regular troops there in 1811 to help burgher militias – commandos, as they were known – expel the Xhosa from the Zuurveld. In his report to London on the success of the mission, the governor, Sir John Cradock, remarked: 'I am happy to add that in the course of this service there has not been shed more Kaffir blood than would seem necessary to impress on the minds of these savages a proper degree of terror and respect.' In 1819, in a desperate bid to regain their land, 10,000 Xhosa warriors descended on the frontier village of Graham's Town intent on driving out the whites. But, once again, they were defeated, losing yet more land to the colonists.

In an attempt to provide the eastern frontier with greater security, the British government devised a plan to populate the area with immigrant settlers from Britain. The plan was presented to Parliament in London as an 'economy measure' that would help reduce unemployment and alleviate social unrest prevalent after the end of the Napoleonic Wars. Parliament duly voted £50,000 to transport volunteers to the Zuurveld and set them up as agricultural farmers on allotments of about a hundred acres. Some 4,000 men, women and

children were chosen from among 80,000 applicants. The majority of
the men were urban artisans with no farming experience. What none
of them was told, until their arrival in Algoa Bay in 1820, was that the
land they had been allocated was in fiercely disputed territory where
five frontier wars had previously occurred. The new settlers also discovered that the sour-grass farms of the Zuurveld were unsuitable for
cultivation. Within a few years, more than half had abandoned the
land and retreated to villages.

Having sponsored the 1820 settlers, the British government was
then obliged to ensure their protection in this highly volatile area. To
the consternation of the Colonial Office, as the succession of frontier
wars with the Xhosa continued, this became an increasingly costly
exercise. In his review of the history of British policy at the Cape published in 1853, a former colonial secretary, Earl Grey, concluded that
the government's commitment to British settlement made in 1819 on
the grounds of being an economy measure proved to be among the
most expensive in the annals of the British empire. What British officials found especially aggravating was that Britain had no vital interest
in the Cape other than its naval facilities on the peninsula. 'Few persons would probably dissent from the opinion that it would be far
better for this country if the British territory in South Africa were
confined to Cape Town and Simon's Bay,' observed Earl Grey. A
long-serving senior Colonial Office official, James Stephen, described
the Cape interior as 'the most sterile and worthless in the whole
Empire', with no commercial significance.

Despite the lack of enthusiasm for its colonial charge, the British
government introduced a series of substantial reforms designed to
bring the Cape into line with British practice elsewhere. Though
preoccupied principally with minimising colonial expenditure, it
nevertheless felt duty-bound to establish a stronger framework of
administration that took greater account of the interests of indigenous populations. British missionaries newly arrived at the Cape
campaigned vociferously for civil rights for the Khoikhoi, citing
examples of their ill-treatment at the hands of Dutch-speaking trekboers. In 1828, the Cape authorities promulgated Ordinance 50
making 'Hottentots and other free people of colour' equal before the

law with whites and removing legal restrictions on their movements. In 1834, slavery in the Cape was abolished, in common with the rest of the empire, and some 38,000 slaves were set free, though they were still required to serve four more years of bondage as 'apprentices'. A new court system was installed using English instead of Dutch as the only official language. What the Colonial Office intended henceforth was to convert the Cape into an English-speaking colony.

These changes aroused deep resentment among the colonists, notably among the Boer population in frontier districts who were long accustomed to living according to their own rules, largely beyond the reach of government authority. Many colonists found the idea that Khoikhoi and slaves could be placed on an equal footing with white Christians repugnant, 'contrary to the laws of God and the natural distinction of race and religion'. Though slave-owners were entitled to claim compensation for loss of 'property', they discovered that the compensation arrangements left them far short of the previous market value of their slaves. They were further aggrieved when the changes led not only to a shortage of labour but also to an outbreak of pilfering and theft. Demanding a new law against vagrancy to deal with it, they were outraged when the British authorities countermanded the legislation they introduced.

Frontier Boers had additional grievances. Once used to expanding eastwards at will to meet their demand for land, they were now blocked by the stubborn resistance of the Xhosa beyond the Fish River. The frontier region, moreover, was still plagued by insecurity. At the end of 1834, Xhosa warriors invaded the Colony, destroying white farms and seizing vast herds of cattle in another attempt to recover land lost in earlier wars. Once more, they were driven back. The British governor in Cape Town, Sir Benjamin D'Urban, a veteran of the Napoleonic Wars, castigated them as 'treacherous and irreclaimable savages' and took it upon himself to annex more Xhosa land in reprisal, intending to make it available for white settlement. But to the fury of the colonists, the British government in London, spurred on by missionary activists, repudiated the annexation and blamed white encroachment as the cause of the conflict. 'The Caffres had ample justification for the war,' concluded the colonial secretary, Lord Glenelg.

Determined to cast off British authority, Boer leaders organised the exodus of groups of families across the Orange River border into the highveld beyond, intending to set up their own state and recreate the society of the frontier trekboers as it was before the coming of the British. Reconnaissance parties reported there was land suitable for settlement in two areas to the north: the vast grasslands around the Vaal River; and the coastal hills below the escarpment of the Drakensberg mountains in an area that later became known as Natal. In a 'Manifesto' sent to the *Graham's Town Journal*, Piet Retief, an emigrant leader, cited a list of grievances including 'severe losses' resulting from the emancipation of slaves; and 'the unjustified odium which has been cast upon us by interested and dishonest persons, under the cloak of religion [missionary activists], whose testimony is believed in England'. He said he hoped that the British government would 'allow us to govern ourselves without its interference in future'. To forestall British concerns, he disclaimed all practice of slavery, but added, 'It is our determination to maintain such regulations as may suppress crime, and preserve proper relations between master and servant.'

The first group of 'emigrants', as they were called, crossed the Orange River drifts in 1836. By 1840, some 6,000 men, women and children, nearly one tenth of the total white population of the Cape Colony, had trekked northwards in their wagons, accompanied by their servants, cattle, sheep and moveable property. Most came from eastern frontier districts. Their departure received no acclaim from the rest of the Boer population. The Dutch church was critical of the emigrants and refused to appoint a *predikant*. The British authorities too opposed the exodus, fearful that it would cause yet more wars in the interior requiring their intervention. But they had no means to stop it.

The emigrants clashed first with Mzilikazi's Ndebele kingdom on the highveld, then with Dingane's Zulu kingdom. In 1839 they endeavoured to set up their own embryonic republic on coastal terrain adjacent to Zulu territory, laying claim to all fertile land between the Tugela and Mzimkulu rivers and incorporating a small trading post on the coast set up by British traders in 1824. At first named Port Natal, the trading post was renamed Durban in honour of the Cape Colony's governor in 1835 in the hope that it might help them win British recognition.

The Republic of Natalia lasted for little more than three years. When trekker leaders attacked neighbouring African chiefdoms to the south, capturing 'apprentices', and then extended their territorial claims there, the British government felt obliged to step in and annex Natal, thus acquiring a second colony in southern Africa – though with considerable reluctance. The Colonial Office official James Stephen considered Natal to be as worthless as the Cape. The only strategic interest the British had in Natal was to prevent the port of Durban from falling into the hands of a rival European power. Rather than submit to British rule once more, most of the trekkers streamed back across the Drakensberg to link up with other Boer groups that had remained on the highveld.

As trekker communities on the highveld sought to establish their own states, they fought repeatedly with African adversaries – the Basotho, the Griqua, the Tswana and the Ndebele. Britain intervened, signing treaties with the Basotho and the Griqua, considering itself responsible for the protection of native tribes beyond the colonial border and hoping to maintain peace in the area. But it soon tired of the exercise. Britain's own frontier problems with the Xhosa were costly enough: a Xhosa war in 1846–47 cost the British Treasury almost £2 million; another Xhosa war in 1851–52 cost a further £3 million. In 1852, William Gladstone, shortly before being appointed chancellor of the exchequer, told the House of Commons:

> The tales of our frontier policy at the Cape, and the losses which that policy has brought upon this country, when they are recounted to those who come after us, will appear all but fabulous. It will appear the height of extravagance that this country should have gone ahunting, as it were, to the uttermost ends of the earth to find means and opportunities of squandering its treasure and the lives of its subjects for no conceivable purpose of policy.

Determined to check the drain of imperial revenues into southern Africa, Britain abandoned the idea of intervention; humanitarianism on the cheap seemed to lead only to recurrent wars and mounting expense; it was no longer considered a viable policy. At a convention at Sand River in 1852, British officials recognised the independence of 'the Emigrant Farmers' in territory north of the Vaal River – the Transvaal, or the Zuid-Afrikaansche Republiek, as they called it. In exchange for a promise that there would be no slavery in the Transvaal, Britain disclaimed all alliances with 'coloured nations' there. At the Bloemfontein Convention in 1854, Britain similarly recognised the independence of the Orange Free State.

The two miniature republics were states in little more than name. The small trekker communities there claimed vast areas of land for themselves but were greatly outnumbered by the indigenous black population that occupied much of it. The administrations they set up were weak and disorganised and, unable to raise taxes, were constantly short of funds. The Transvaal, with a white population of 20,000, survived almost entirely on subsistence farming. Officials were often paid for their services in land grants instead of cash. The quest for more land continued relentlessly. African chiefs were often tricked into ceding territory, signing documents without realising the full implications, some believing they had merely entered into 'alliances'. Tswana chiefdoms were subjected to years of raids and harassment. A Boer commando raiding Tswana country in 1852 attacked David Livingstone's mission station at Kolobeng, destroying his store of Bibles and medicines. In the Orange Free State, Boer commandos fought a prolonged campaign to wrest the fertile Caledon River valley from the Basotho.

To satisfy the white demand for labour, commandos frequently abducted African children, describing them as 'apprentices' – *inboeke-lings* – to avoid accusation of overt slavery. The practice was sanctioned in the Transvaal by an Apprentice Act passed by the governing body, the Volksraad. In the 1860s missionaries considered *inboekelings* provided the main source of labour in the eastern Transvaal. A German missionary at Makapanspoort reported that wagonloads of children were regularly brought to the settlement. In the far north, in the Zoutpansberg district, the trade was known as 'black ivory', and soon outstripped the trade in white ivory once the elephant herds there had been decimated.

Both republics remained unstable. The Transvaal's difficulties were compounded by persistent quarrels between rival Boer factions that threatened to split the republic apart. Under attack from the Venda, the trekker settlements in the Zoutpansberg had to be evacuated, then abandoned. In the Orange Free State, the first president, Josias Hoffman, was ousted by a mob after he gave the Basotho king, Moshoeshoe, a small keg of gunpowder as a diplomatic gesture. Twelve years after the republic's founding, the Bloemfontein journal *De Tijd* spelled out how vulnerable the Orange Free State's population of 25,000 whites remained: 'Simple people find themselves in a vast land, surrounded in all quarters by enemies, without judges, without soldiers, without money, divided through ignorance and derided by a Colony adjacent to it [the Cape].'

The Cape Colony itself was in dire straits. During the 1860s, it was afflicted by drought, locusts, a slump in wine exports, a fall in the price of wool and a banking crisis. Railway-building ground to a halt seventy miles from Cape Town for lack of money. In Natal, the small white population lived in constant fear of the possibility of an uprising of the local Nguni population or an invasion from Zululand on the other side of the Tugela River. In general, the two southern African colonies were regarded as among the most troublesome, expensive and unprofitable possessions of the British empire.

Then, in 1871, prospectors exploring a remote area of sun-scorched scrubland in Griqualand, just outside the Cape's borders, discovered the world's richest deposits of diamonds. Britain promptly snatched the territory from the Orange Free State. Fifteen years later, an itinerant English digger, George Harrison, stumbled across the rocky outcrop of a gold-bearing reef on a ridge named by Transvaal farmers as the Witwatersrand. Beneath the reef lay the richest deposits of gold ever discovered. The gold strike transformed the Transvaal from an impoverished rural republic into a glittering prize.

What followed was a titanic struggle fought by the British to gain supremacy throughout southern Africa and by the Boers to preserve the independence of their republics. It culminated in the costliest, bloodiest and most humiliating war that Britain had waged in nearly a century. Britain provoked the war expecting it to be over within a few months, but it turned into a gruelling campaign lasting two and a half years; required half a million imperial troops to finish it; and left the two Boer republics devastated.

Faced with guerrilla warfare for which they were unprepared, British military commanders resorted to scorched-earth tactics, destroying thousands of farmsteads, razing villages to the ground and slaughtering livestock on a massive scale. Women and children were rounded up and placed in what the British called concentration camps, where conditions were so appalling that some 26,000 died there from disease and malnutrition, most of them under the age of sixteen. All this produced a legacy of hatred and bitterness amongst Afrikaners that endured for generations.

Two men personified this struggle: Cecil Rhodes and Paul Kruger. Rhodes, the son of an English country parson, used his huge fortunes from diamonds and gold to promote the expansion of the British empire as well as his own business interests. A ruthless entrepreneur with command of private armies, he was described by a British editor at the time of his death as the first of a dynasty of 'money kings' who had emerged as 'the real rulers of the world'. Paul Kruger, the Boer leader and landowner, whose only education was the Bible and who believed the earth was flat, defied Britain's prime ministers and generals for nearly a quarter of a century. British politicians constantly underestimated him. Britain's colonial secretary, Joseph Chamberlain, a Birmingham screw manufacturer, who was one of the principal architects of the Anglo-Boer war of 1899–1902, referred to him as an 'ignorant, dirty and obstinate man who has known how to feather his nest'. British cartoonists delighted in portraying Kruger as a bigoted peasant, with a barrel chest and a sullen expression, dressed in an ill-fitting frock-coat. Britain's high commissioner in southern Africa, Sir Alfred Milner, the main architect of the war, predicted that Kruger and the Boers would put up no more than 'an apology' of a fight. But, as Britain's poet of empire, Rudyard Kipling, later observed, the war taught the British 'no end of a lesson'.

Having overcome Boer resistance at a cost in British lives of 22,000 men, the British government then concluded that self-government might be a better option for its two Boer colonies. By 1907, the Transvaal and the Orange Free State were again self-governing under the control of defeated Boer generals who had signed the terms of surrender five years before. Britain next decided to amalgamate its four colonies into a Union of South Africa in the hope that the Boers and the British might find a way of resolving their differences and merge into a single South African nation.

The black population fared badly from this arrangement. After a hundred years of wars and clashes against both British and Boers, all the African chiefdoms lying within South Africa had succumbed to white rule. Most of their land had been lost through conquest and settlement. Now Africans were excluded from negotiations leading to the founding of the Union of South Africa and denied political rights under its proposed constitution. An African delegation went to London to make representations, protesting at what they regarded as Britain's betrayal of their interests, but to no avail. The black quest for political rights was to last for the next eighty years.

This book covers the tumultuous period that began with the discovery of the main diamond field in 1871 and culminated in the founding of the modern state of South Africa in 1910. It is a tale of great wealth and raw power, of deceit and corruption, set at a time when Britain was at the height of its imperial might. Politicians and journalists, in London as well as in southern Africa, fell under the spell of Cecil Rhodes' money and readily lent themselves to the cause of empire and its entrepreneurs. It was all part of what Sir Alfred Milner called 'winning the great game for mastery in South Africa'. The war that Milner engineered to achieve that mastery and, as he put it, 'to knock the bottom out of the great Afrikaner nation for ever and ever, Amen', brought repercussions that lasted for nearly a century. Out of the turmoil came a virulent form of Afrikaner nationalism that eventually took hold of South Africa, setting off yet another titanic struggle, this time between white and black.

PART I

1

DIAMOND FEVER

As diamond fever spread throughout southern Africa and beyond, the rush to the diamond fields of Griqualand turned into a frantic escapade that one Cape Town newspaper likened to 'a dangerous madness'. In their thousands, shopkeepers, tradesmen, clerks and farmers, excited by the prospect of sudden riches, set out in ox-wagons and mule carts heading for the desolate patch of sun-baked scrubland in Griqualand where diamonds had been discovered. Some travelled on foot, walking from as far away as Cape Town, a journey of 700 miles across the great thirstland of the Karoo.

They were joined by a horde of foreign adventurers: seasoned diggers from the Australian goldfields; fortyniners from California; cockney traders from the backstreets of London; Irish dissidents; German speculators; army officers on furlough; ship's deserters; bogus aristocrats, rogue lawyers, and quack doctors. 'Each post-cart and bullock-wagon brought its load of sordid, impecunious humanity,' one diamond dealer remarked in his memoirs.

The stories told of fabulous wealth were real enough. In the early days, diggers using picks and shovels found diamonds lying close to the surface. A day's work for those in luck could provide them with as many as ten or twenty diamonds. Some made their fortunes before breakfast. A penniless Englishman uncovered a 175-carat stone valued at £33,000. Each big discovery reignited the enthusiasm of others for the hunt. Many having 'made their pile' decided to return home, celebrating their departure with gunfire and spreading word to the outside world of the bonanza they had won.

But the mining settlements of Griqualand soon came to be renowned as much for despair, disease and death as for the fortunes made there. New arrivals were immediately struck by the stench and squalor of the settlements. The approach roads were lined with the carcasses of exhausted pack animals left to rot where they had fallen. Open trenches served as public latrines, sited at random amid the haphazard jumble of diggers' tents. Flies swarmed everywhere. 'Dishes and drink choked with them,' wrote Frederick Boyle, a visitor from England who arrived in November 1871. The air was thick with fine dust stirred up by the constant digging, sifting and sorting of dirt that went on from morning until night. An acute shortage of water meant that most diggers were rarely able to wash; the nearest river for bathing was twenty miles away. In summer, the grey, cindery plains of Griqualand were like an oven; in winter, the nights were bitterly cold. When the rains came, 'camp fever' – mainly dysentery – took hold, striking down diggers by the score. Dust storms erupted with sudden fury, ripping tents from the ground and tossing sheets of corrugated roofing into the air. 'In a perfectly still air one could see a distant wall rise far away on the plain,' one resident remembered. 'In a few minutes it would be on us with a roar, darkening everything, filling one's eyes, nose and ears, stinging one's face, forcing one to turn one's back on it.' Layers of dust coated everything. 'The dust of the dry diggings,' moaned a journalist in the *Diamond News* in November 1871, 'is to be classed with plague, pestilence and famine, and if there is anything worse, with that also.'

Moreover, for most diggers the rewards were meagre. Some scraped away with picks and shovels for weeks on end but found nothing of value, and hundreds of claims were abandoned every month as diggers ran out of money to pay the required licence fee. Just as every day brought wagon-loads of new arrivals brimming with hope and expectation, so in the other direction destitute men in ragged clothes trudged dejectedly away from 'the Fields', unable to afford the fare back to their homes. Everything depended on luck.

Among those who listened avidly to tales of diamond riches was (seventeen-year-old Cecil John Rhodes,) who had been sent from England to Natal to join his brother Herbert in a cotton-farming venture in the colony. Shortly after his arrival in the Natal capital of Pietermaritzburg in September 1870, Rhodes encountered a British army officer, Captain Loftus Rolleston, who had recently returned from diamond diggings on the banks of the Vaal River. Rolleston had been a member of one of the first organised expeditions to the area where, in January 1870, they had discovered a gravel bed containing an extensive 'wash' of diamonds.

'To hear Rolleston talk and to see his diamonds makes one's mouth water,' Rhodes wrote to his mother in September 1870. He went on to tell of 'three whoppers' found by diggers, one worth £8,000, another £9,000 and another £10,000. 'The man who found the £10,000 diamond offered his claim for 15s. [shillings] the evening before, and no one would buy it!' Diamonds, he wrote, were being found in 'unheard-of numbers'. He related how Rolleston had told him of an African who had traded for a roll of tobacco a diamond which had subsequently been sold for £800. In another letter, he mentioned the story of 'a Dutchman who trekked in, outspanned [his oxen], found a diamond worth £14,000, inspanned and trekked out all in one day'.

Rhodes initially resisted the diamond fever sweeping Natal. 'Of course,' he wrote home, 'there is a chance of the diamonds turning out trumps; but I don't count much from them. You see it is all chance.' Cotton, he added, was more of 'a reality'. His brother Herbert, however, a restless adventurer, relished the gamble and soon forsook cotton-farming for the diamond fields of Griqualand.

A year later, Rhodes followed him there. In October 1871, he set out on horseback with a few possessions loaded into an ox-cart, and rode up the interior escarpment to the highveld, curving around the edge of the Drakensberg mountains. The journey of 400 miles took him more than a month. Along the way his horse died, so he continued on foot.

His first glimpse of the diamond fields he described in a letter to his mother written shortly after his arrival: 'Fancy an immense plain with right in its centre a great mass of white tents and iron stores, and on one side of it, all mixed up with the camp, mounds of lime like ant-hills; the country round is all flat with just thorn trees here and there: and you have some idea of Dutoitspan, the first spot where dry dig-gings for Diamonds was begun.'

This was the place that marked the beginning of an industrial rev-olution. It was also the place that was to make Cecil Rhodes one of the richest men in the world.

The first diamond was discovered by accident. It was picked up by a Boer farmer's son in 1866, close to the banks of the Orange River on a farm named 'De Kalk' in the Hopetown area of the Cape Colony, and used to play children's games of 'five-stones'. A neighbour, Schalk van Niekerk, spotted the stone several weeks later and, thinking it might have some value, offered to purchase it. The farmer's wife laughed at the idea of selling a stone and told him that if he took a fancy to it he could have it for nothing. Van Niekerk told her that if it proved to be a diamond, he would share the proceeds with her. It was later valued in London at £500.

The De Kalk diamond was regarded as a freak and aroused little lasting interest. Though smaller stones were occasionally discovered in the area, geologists confidently declared that the terrain in that part of southern Africa was not 'diamondiferous'. In 1867, Sir Roderick Murchison of the Museum of Practical Geology in London said he would stake his reputation on it. A leading London expert, James Gregory, who was sent by a London merchant to investigate the Hopetown area, dismissed the whole idea of diamond discoveries as a hoax – 'a bubble scheme' set up by land speculators to increase land prices; if any genuine diamonds had been found, he said, then they must have been deposited by ostriches migrating from areas far to the north.

Then, in March 1869, Schalk van Niekerk had his second stroke of luck. A Griqua farm employee brought him a large stone he had found on the banks of the Orange River in the vicinity of De Kalk.

Van Niekerk promptly bought it in exchange for 500 sheep, ten oxen and a horse and then sold it to a diamond merchant in Hopetown for £11,200. An 83-carat diamond, it was subsequently purchased in London for £25,000.

In the rush that followed, prospectors concentrated their efforts on diggings along the banks of the Vaal River, north of the Orange River. An eighty-mile stretch of the Vaal was soon crowded with prospectors and speculators wandering from claim to claim, establishing brief settlements – Delport's Hope, Cawood's Hope, Last Hope, Forlorn Hope, Fools Rush, Midnight Rush, Winter's Rush, Poorman's Kopje. The digging was largely haphazard. Most dug down through sand and gravel for only a few feet, believing that diamonds had been washed downstream from their original beds in distant mountains. If they found nothing, they moved quickly to another site in search of better luck or joined the latest 'rush' to some newly favoured spot. Few prospered.

Other diamond discoveries in 1869 aroused far less attention than the river diggings. Twenty miles south of the Vaal River, Boer prospectors found diamonds in a natural basin, or pan, on a 6,000-acre farm named Dorstfontein owned by Adriaan van Wyk; the farm was commonly called Du Toit's Pan after a previous owner, Abraham du Toit. Van Wyk charged diggers seven shillings and sixpence a week for each claim of thirty square feet. Further discoveries were made on an adjacent 14,434-acre farm, Bultfontein, owned by Cornelis du Plooy.

But these 'dry diggings', as they came to be known, were thought likely to offer only modest rewards. The common view at the time was that diamonds were alluvial deposits, as diamond mining in India and Brazil had shown, and most diggers soon drifted back to the river sites. Adriaan van Wyk sold Dorstfontein farm, or Dutoitspan, to merchant speculators for £2,600; Cornelis du Plooy sold Bultfontein for £2,000.

Beneath the farms, however, lay two diamond 'pipes' or necks of long-extinct volcanoes containing unimaginable riches. Just two miles away to the north, on an adjacent farm, Vooruitzigt, owned by Johannes de Beer and his brother, were two more diamond 'pipes', still undiscovered, with even greater deposits. Put together, the three farms covering an area of about fifty-eight square miles amounted to the most valuable piece of real estate in the world.

It was not until the end of 1870 that a new rush to Dutoitspan and Bultfontein erupted. Within weeks, Dutoitspan was transformed into a sprawling mass of tents, wagons, mud heaps and mining debris. In May 1871, diggers alighted upon one of the two 'pipes' on Vooruitzigt, not far from De Beer's original farmhouse; within two months, 10,000 men were working there. Then in July, a group of diggers from Colesberg found diamonds on a hillock on Vooruitzigt that they named Colesberg Kopje. The rush there turned into a stampede. Diggers from De Beer's, Bultfontein and the river diggings joined the chaotic scramble for claims.

No one yet understood the geology of the mines. Diggers still assumed that all their finds would be near the surface, as had happened at the river diggings, requiring little more than the use of a pick and shovel to unearth. Beneath an upper layer of limestone, however, they found 'yellow ground' – a yellowish, decomposed breccia, often resembling dried mud, which proved to contain diamond deposits richer than those closer to the surface.

At Colesberg Kopje, the yellow ground extended as far as sixty feet below the surface. Diamonds found there, though mainly of low quality, existed in vast profusion. By August, an average of £50,000 worth of diamonds was being recovered each week. With such rich pickings, the price of claims at Colesberg Kopje soon soared to £100 each, then to £1,000, then to £4,000. But so frantic was the digging there that by November 1871 the yellow ground in some claims was all but exhausted. Beneath, lay a hard, compact, blue-coloured ground believed to contain no diamonds. To many diggers it seemed that 'the party was over'. Taking advantage of an offer from a syndicate of Port Elizabeth merchants, Johannes de Beer sold his 16,400-acre farm, Vooruitzigt, for £6,000.

After arriving in Dutoitspan in November 1871, Rhodes made his way to Colesberg Kopje where his brother Herbert had acquired three claims and had set up camp on a rise a few hundreds yards from the western end of the mine. Together with a small group of colleagues, Herbert belonged to a bachelors' 'mess', popularly known as the West End, run by Major Drury, an army officer formerly of the Cape Mounted Riflemen. The Rhodes brothers briefly shared a large tent but, as restless as ever, Herbert took off for England two weeks later, leaving Cecil to fend for himself.

At the age of eighteen, Rhodes quickly adapted to the routine of mining life at Colesberg Kopje – the diamond pipe that later became known as the 'Big Hole' of Kimberley. The mine itself covered a relatively small area, oval shaped and measuring at the time no more than 220 yards by 180 yards. The last of the four mines discovered, Colesberg Kopje had been laid out in a more orderly fashion than the earlier ones: it was divided into 470 claims, each one a square of 31 feet, with fourteen parallel roadways running the full length of the mine. With the price of claims so high, many had been split up into half-claims and quarter-claims, then into eighths and sixteenths. Thousands were at work there – white diggers together with their black labourers – crammed into a labyrinth of pits, endlessly filling buckets and sacks with broken ground and hauling them up and down ladders or on pulleys to the surface. The roadways above were permanently choked with carts and mules taking 'stuff' to sieves and sorting tables on the edge of the mine. Every day, some tumbled down into the pits below.

'I should like you to have a peep at the kopje from my tent door at the present moment,' Rhodes wrote to his mother on 4 January 1872. 'It is like an immense number of ant-heaps covered with black ants, as thick as can be, the latter represented by human beings.' Working on one of his brother's claims, he was finding on average thirty carats a week, he said, bringing him a weekly income of about £100. 'You will understand how enormously rich it is when I say that a good claim would certainly average a diamond to every load of stuff that was sorted – a load being about 50 buckets.'

A week later, the diamond fields were gripped by sudden crisis. The enormous output of the mines there had led to a collapse in the price of rough diamonds in London, prompting diamond buyers on the fields to shut up shop. Frederick Boyle recorded in his diary on January 13:

The Nemesis of our success has overtaken us today. A panic rules in the diamond market at home, and the reaction strikes us cruelly. There is no business doing in the Koopers' tents. Many have closed their doors. The diggers are half-angry, half-dismayed. They had encouraged each other to believe that since the market had borne so much, its patience must be inexhaustible. Sensible men know that catastrophe must come, but they had scarcely provided against it. I know that today there are acquaintances of my own who anticipated a heavy fall, but who will be obliged to sell at panic prices notwithstanding.

He described how later that day he was talking to a diamond buyer outside his tent when two English diggers approached.

Their great limbs were clad in corduroy; their faces were brown and bearded; their hands had not felt water since yesterday – not for a week if one should judge by looks – and they were covered with old scars and discolorations where the poisonous lime had festered in some trifling scratch. They had too the swollen lids and bloodshot eyes that 'sorting' entails.

One of the men produced a tin box wrapped in a scrap of rag. Inside were four diamonds – a spotless stone of fifteen carats and three fine white chips weighing together ten carats – the result perhaps of weeks of weary labour. He asked £50 for them, but the buyer declined to make an offer. 'If I can't get fifty pounds for all my sweat an' the health I've lost, I'll just pitch them stones into the Vaal!' the digger said, and left disconsolately.

Boyle himself, after a series of misfortunes, decided to leave. After examining a dozen locations, in December 1871, he had purchased for £365 a quarter-claim in Colesberg Kopje together with a two-wheeled cart in bad repair, two mules and a harness, and had found three partners to work the claim on shares with all finds to be split evenly. On the first day of working, an adjoining roadway collapsed, throwing tons of surface soil into his claim. In January, one of his two mules fell into a pit and he had to buy two more. Five days later, his cart was wrecked in a collision with an ox-wagon. Five days after that his two new mules bolted, never to be seen again, and his black labourers, after being paid, left in search of a better-paying employer. After two months of work, Boyle's partners had found diamonds worth only £42. When accounts were drawn up, Boyle calculated that he had made a working profit of only £5; and since the finds on his claim had been so meagre, his investment in the property itself was virtually worthless. He left the diamond fields convinced that diamond digging was a lottery in which there were very few winners.

2

BLUE GROUND

The discovery of diamonds in Griqualand precipitated a tussle between Britain, the Orange Free State and the Transvaal for control of the territory. Hitherto a backwater of little interest to any of its neighbours, its borders and status had remained ill-defined. At the beginning of the nineteenth century the area had been colonised by groups of mixed-race emigrants from the Cape Colony who proudly called themselves 'Bastaards' and who attempted to set up their own statelets north of the Orange River and establish their authority over the local inhabitants, indigenous Kora Khoikhoi and the Tswana-speaking Tlhaping. In order to maintain their credentials as a Christian community, they invited British missionaries to their capital at Klaarwater, asking them to build a mission station there. It was at the behest of the missionaries that they agreed to change their name to Griquas and to rename their capital Griquatown.

In a treaty signed in 1834, the Cape Colony accorded due recognition to the Griqua *kaptyn*, Andries Waterboer, as an independent chief and agreed to pay him a salary of £100 a year for protecting the colonial frontier, warning the authorities of possible attacks and sending back fugitives. A similar treaty was signed in 1843 with another Griqua leader, Adam Kok, who had established a statelet based on Philippolis, a mission station to the east of Waterboer's territory.

But Griqua lands were soon threatened by the arrival of hundreds of Boer emigrants from the Cape Colony. The Philippolis area, lying in the path of the main Boer exodus, soon passed into the hands of Boer owners and became part of the Orange Free State; the Griqua population there moved eastwards, establishing a new territory near Natal known as Griqualand East. Boer farmers also began to obtain farm leases in Waterboer's territory of Griqualand West, registering their titles there in the Free State. Waterboer's authority steadily waned. His son, Nicholas Waterboer, became embroiled in a complex land dispute with the Free State government which claimed for itself a large part of Griqualand West known as the Campbell Lands. In the 1860s, British officials in the Cape Colony were drawn into the dispute, asked to act as arbitrators.

When the rush to the alluvial diggings on the Vaal River began in 1869, a host of claims were made about ownership of the area. On the south bank of the Vaal, missionaries at the Berlin Mission station at Pniel maintained that they had bought the district from Kora Khoikhoi and tried to charge diggers licence fees. Other claims to the south bank were announced by Waterboer and by a Tlhaping chief, Mahura. The Orange Free State, for its part, proclaimed sovereignty – not just over the Vaal River diggings but over the whole of the Campbell Lands which stretched beyond. To demonstrate the point, President Johannes Brand appointed a *landrost* to preside at Pniel. The task was given to Olof Truter, a Swede with experience of the goldfields of Australia and California and a former policeman who proved well able to handle 'the rougher elements of the community'. A school, a courthouse and a prison were built at Pniel. The Free State Volksraad passed legislation regulating diggers' activities. When the dry diggings subsequently opened at Dutoitspan, Truter moved there to supervise diggers' committees and collect a portion of licence fees.

Although the river diggings lay well outside the Transvaal's recognised boundaries, President Marthinus Wessels Pretorius also claimed rights there and sent mounted police and a magistrate to the north bank. The diggers themselves were divided between supporters of the Transvaal's claims and those who favoured autonomy. But Pretorius, an inept, impetuous man who had acquired his own stake in the diamond fields, then tried to force the issue. In 1870 he provoked uproar by seeking to award an exclusive concession at the diamond fields to three of his friends. Diggers at the mining settlement at Klipdrift, on the north bank of the Vaal, declared an independent republic, choosing as president Stafford Parker, a former able seaman and owner of the local music hall. A flamboyant figure, with magnificent whiskers and a penchant for elegant clothes and dark glasses, Parker kept order by enforcing a bizarre set of punishments: diamond thieves were flogged; prostitutes and drunks were put in stocks; and card cheats were ducked in the river. More serious offenders were spreadeagled on the ground, tied to stakes and left under a searing sun to the mercy of the flies. Taxes were often collected at gunpoint.

Britain's interest in the diamond fields was equally keen. Officials in Cape Town welcomed the prospect of a new source of revenue and economic activity that the diamond trade would bring to the impoverished Cape Colony. But they were also concerned about the territorial ambitions of the Free State and the Transvaal that the diamond discoveries had inspired. Griqualand and, in particular, the Campbell Lands lay across the only 'road to the north' outside the two Boer republics that colonial hunters and traders used to gain access to the African interior. The volume of trade with the interior was substantial. In exchange for ivory, ostrich feathers and animal hides, traders sold to tribesmen guns and ammunition worth £75,000 a year. There was a danger that if the Free State acquired the Campbell Lands, the road to the north and its trade would be lost. Furthermore, British hegemony would be threatened by the growing power of neighbouring states.

The Cape's then colonial secretary, Richard Southey, was a fervent advocate of British expansion. He had arrived in the Colony as a boy, with his parents, along with other 1820 Settlers, and had since risen to become one of the most influential figures in the Cape administration. Known for his overt dislike of the Boers, Southey was determined that Britain should gain possession of the diamond fields. Acting in collusion with Waterboer's agent, David Arnot, an ambitious Cape Coloured (mixed race) lawyer with large land interests, Southey prompted Waterboer to appeal to the Cape government for 'protection'. The Cape government duly responded, agreeing to take up his case, issuing a statement of support for British subjects on the diamond fields and despatching a magistrate to Klipdrift to take control from Stafford Parker.

In London, the Colonial Office, mindful of past experience, viewed the dispute as part of the Boer tradition of expanding their own territory at the expense of native inhabitants. 'Her Majesty's Government,' the colonial secretary, the Earl of Kimberley, wrote to Cape Town officials in November 1870, 'would see with great dissatisfaction any encroachment on Griqua territory by those republics, which would open to the Boers an extended field for their slave-dealing operations.' What Kimberley favoured was the annexation of Griqualand and its diamond fields not by the British government but by the Cape Colony, which would thus be obliged to bear the burden and costs of administering it.

On a tour of the diamond fields in February 1871, the new British high commissioner and governor of the Cape, Sir Henry Barkly, a brisk authoritarian, quickly realised that what was at stake was not just a frontier dispute over land ownership but the whole issue of political leadership in southern Africa. He resolved that Waterboer's claims to the diamond fields needed to be supported, regardless of their merit, so as to ensure the supremacy of British interests. 'It was quite clear,' he reported to the Earl of Kimberley in March, 'that any appearance of faltering on my part would only encourage the Free State and Transvaal in upholding their claims.'

To decide the matter of ownership, Barkly proposed arbitration by the governor of Natal, Robert Keate. After considerable wrangling, Pretorius accepted the proposal, but Brand insisted on independent foreign arbitration and refused to participate. The Transvaal case was palpably weak and poorly presented. In September, Keate ruled in favour of Waterboer's claims and Waterboer promptly asked Barkly to take over the territory. Without waiting for approval from London, Barkly proclaimed the annexation of Griqualand West on 27 October 1871, not by the Cape Colony but in the name of the British Crown. Griqualand's eastern border with the Orange Free State was realigned to ensure that the whole of the diamond fields fell within its jurisdiction.

In London, Kimberley was furious that Barkly had annexed Griqualand West as a British colony without waiting until arrangements could be made for it to be incorporated into the Cape Colony. 'I never doubted,' Kimberley wrote, 'that Sir Henry Barkly made a mistake in annexing the diamond fields before the Cape Parliament had passed the Bill. He exceeded his instructions and departed from the line of policy which I believe would have succeeded, but which requires more patience than he seems to possess. However, we had no alternative but to approve his conduct.'

On the diamond fields, diggers' reaction to the announcement of British rule was mixed. A local newspaper reported 'much *éclat* and rejoicing' in the mining camps, but many seemed indifferent; some worried that British rule might bring new restrictions to their activities. A prisoner held by the Free State police claimed protection from the new British authorities and was removed from their custody by Cape police, whereupon the Free State magistrate, Olof Truter, solemnly arose from his bench, vigorously protested against such interference and closed down his court.

Resentment about Britain's annexation of Griqualand festered for years. In the Transvaal, the Volksraad blamed Pretorius for accepting arbitration in the first place, forced his resignation, and refused to consider itself bound by Keate's award. In Bloemfontein, President Brand issued a counter-proclamation and continued to protest year after year at the dispossession of territory he considered rightly belonged to the Free State. As a sop to the Free State, the British government eventually agreed in 1876 to make a payment of £90,000, but the issue still rankled.

Under British control, the diggers continued to ride a rollercoaster of mixed fortunes. Blue ground, initially feared to herald the end of mining, was found to be not rock-hard but friable, decomposing rapidly once exposed to weather. Moreover, it contained an even higher density of diamonds than yellow ground. But the hazards of mining deep pits reaching down without support more than eighty feet below ground-level became increasingly severe; roadways linking the pits to the mine edge frequently collapsed, leaving claims buried under tons of soil.

Cecil Rhodes, however, persevered, showing dogged persistence and gaining a reputation for managing his claims with vigour. His brother Herbert returned briefly to Colesberg Kopje in 1872, bringing with him another brother, Frank, who recalled: 'We found Cecil down in the claim, measuring his ground with his lawyer and in a tremendous rage with another man in the next claim to him, who had encroached on his ground.'

From the accounts given later by friends and acquaintances of Rhodes at Colesberg Kopje, he emerges as a shy, awkward youth, occasionally talkative – given to speaking abruptly in short, staccato bursts – but otherwise a dreamer, frequently preoccupied with his own thoughts and often to be seen supervising black labourers while sitting on an upturned bucket reading a volume of the classics, deaf to the noise about him. He was regarded as somewhat eccentric, notably careless about his dress.

Before deciding on a career as an artist, Norman Garstin spent a year at the diamond fields. On the day of his arrival there in 1872, while searching for a friend amid the maze of tents, wagons and debris heaps that surrounded the mine at Colesberg Kopje, he encountered Rhodes:

> After following many distracting directions, I lit upon a little cluster of tents and beehive huts set around an old and gnarled mimosa tree: a Zulu was chopping wood and an Indian cook was coming out of the mess tent with a pile of plates: and here it was I found my friend.
>
> Alongside of him was a tall fair boy, blue-eyed and with somewhat aquiline features, wearing flannels of the school playing field, somewhat shrunken with strenuous rather than effectual washings, that still left the colour of red veld dust.

Garstin pitched his tent next to Rhodes' and saw much of him in the following months. Years later he strove to recall his first impressions:

As I search my memory for the Rhodes of the early seventies, I seem to see a fair young man, frequently sunk in deep thoughts, his hands buried in his trousers pockets, his legs crossed and possibly twisted together, quite oblivious of the talk around him; then without a word he would get up and go out with some set purpose in his mind which he was at no pains to communicate . . . He was a compound of moody silence and impulsive action. He was hot and even violent at times, but in working towards his ends he laid his plans with care and circumspection . . . The duality of his nature, the contemplative and the executive, had a curious counterpart in his voice, which broke, when he was excited, into a sort of falsetto, unusual in a man of his make; his laugh also had this falsetto note.

Another of Rhodes' companions at Colesberg Kopje – or 'New Rush', as it became known – was William Scully, who had arrived at the diamond fields in 1871 at the age of sixteen just before the Colesberg deposits were discovered. One of the tasks he was given was to herd oxen and, by chance, he often took them to a pasturage in a shallow basin on the site of the Colesberg deposits. 'Within the perimeter was a low, oblong rise covered with long grass, and at the eastern end of which stood a grove of exceptionally large camel-thorn trees.' The rise, he noted, was full of holes dug by ant-bears and jackals.

Scully eventually joined Major Drury's 'West End' mess at Colesberg Kopje and spent many months sharing the Rhodes brothers' tent. He found Rhodes an aloof figure, intolerant in discussion, with solitary habits. Scully wrote:

I can very clearly picture Cecil Rhodes in one of his characteristic attitudes. After dinner it was his wont to lean forward with both elbows on the table and his mouth slightly open. He had a habit, when thinking, of rubbing his chin gently with his forefinger. Very often he would sit in the attitude described for a very long time, without joining in whatever conversation happened to be going on. His manner and expression suggested that his thoughts were far away, but occasionally some interjection would indicate that, to a certain extent, he was keeping in touch with the current topic.

Despite his solitary nature, Rhodes made several lasting friendships at 'New Rush'. He struck up a close business partnership with Charles Rudd, an English digger educated at Harrow and Trinity College, Cambridge, who had arrived at the Vaal River diggings in 1870. Rudd's first ventures there were not successful. He lived in a ragged tent and spent his time hauling buckets of gravel 300 yards from his claim to the river's edge to wash and sieve the 'stuff', finding few diamonds and eventually succumbing to typhoid. After recovering in Cape Town, he tried his luck at the dry diggings, working both as a digger and diamond-buyer and importing supplies to the diamond fields. Nine years older than Rhodes, once a champion rackets player, he was then described as tall, erect, slender, 'having fine dark eyes, a wispy moustache, and thick fair hair, with a well-trimmed black beard', and characteristically dressed in moleskin trousers, flannel shirt and an untidy hat.

Neither Rhodes nor Rudd enjoyed the business of digging. Rudd complained to a friend years later about the hard labour he and Rhodes endured, carrying 'pay dirt' in bags, boxes and buckets to the sorting tables for days on end when black labour was scarce; and he described how during this work Rhodes had broken the little finger of his right hand, preventing him from ever again being able to give a firm grip in a handshake.

They tried a number of other business ventures. One of them was to order from Britain an ice-making machine. On hot summer days, at one of the corners of the Diamond Market, they did a brisk trade in ice-cream, Rhodes turning the handle of the ice-cream bucket while Rudd sold it from a packing case. They charged sixpence a wineglass, with an extra sixpence for a slab of cake. 'The machine paid for itself in three months,' Rudd recalled, 'and we sold it at the end of the summer for more than it cost.'

Another firm friend of Rhodes was John Xavier Merriman, the son of an Anglican bishop and a serving member of the Cape parliament, an unpaid position that required him to make a living elsewhere. A tall, patrician figure, twelve years older than Rhodes, Merriman loathed the rough camp life of the diamond fields and, despite numerous opportunities there, failed to make much money. He enjoyed Rhodes' company and warmly praised his business skills. In a letter that Rhodes' brother Frank wrote home in April 1872, he mentioned Merriman's high opinion of Cecil. 'He says Cecil is such an excellent man in business; that he has managed all the business in Herbert's absence wonderfully well, and that they are all so very fond of him . . . He says most young fellows when they get up here and do well get so very bumptious, but that Cecil was just the contrary.' The two used to take long rides across the veld together, Rhodes on a rusty-brown pony named Brandersnatch, discussing the affairs of the Fields, the classics and world history.

What many of his contemporaries also remarked upon was Rhodes' lack of interest in girls. 'For the fair sex he cared nothing,' wrote Louis Cohen, who arrived in the diamond fields in 1872. 'I have many times seen him in the Main Street dressed in white flannels and leaning moodily with hands in his pockets against the street wall. He hardly ever had a companion, and seemingly took no interest in anything but his own thoughts, and I do not believe if a flock of the most adorable women passed through the street he would have gone across the road to see them . . . It is a fact that Rhodes was never seen to give the glad-eye to a barmaid or tripping beauty, however succulent.'

Occasionally, Rhodes would accompany friends to local dances. But it was noticed that he tended to pick out the plainest girl around, perhaps because they were as shy as himself. When his friends teased him about his taste in women, he would blush and flash back: 'Just an enjoyable exercise . . . just an enjoyable exercise.'

What preoccupied Rhodes at the time, certainly far more than girls but even more than diamonds, was the idea of obtaining a professional qualification. As a schoolboy, his ambition had been to train as a barrister or, failing that, as a clergyman, like his father. His father, Francis Rhodes, the Anglican vicar of Bishop's Stortford in Hertfordshire, an austere, remote figure, had intended that all seven of his sons should follow him into the church. But Cecil, his fifth son, had left secondary school at the age of sixteen without qualifying for the university education necessary to enter either profession. According to Rhodes' friend and banker, Lewis Michell, Rhodes' father 'recognised that he was unfitted for a routine life in England, and resolved to ship him to one of the Colonies', like so many thousands of other younger sons. Thus had Rhodes duly set out to join Herbert in Natal provided with the tidy sum of £2,000 by his aunt Sophia.

Despite the wealth he had accumulated from diamonds, Rhodes still hankered for a university education. 'Many young men would have been content to float on this easy tide of good fortune, but it was not so with Cecil Rhodes,' Norman Garstin recalled.

> I remember his telling me that he had made up his mind to go to the University, it would help with his career; also it might be wise if he were to eat his dinners, the position of a barrister 'was always useful'. Then in his abrupt way he said, 'I dare say you think I am keen about money; I assure you I wouldn't greatly care if I lost all I have tomorrow, it's the game I like.'

Shortly after his nineteenth birthday, however, Rhodes suffered what was described as a 'mild heart attack'; it was said to have been brought on by 'overwork'. In later life Rhodes was indeed troubled by heart problems, but his earlier years were marked more by vigorous activity than by signs of ill-health. Once he had sufficiently recovered, he made a long journey by ox-wagon northwards, accompanying Herbert who was keen to investigate rumours of gold finds in the northern Transvaal. Along the way, Rhodes decided to purchase a 3,000-acre farm in the Transvaal, though shortly afterwards he described it as 'no earthly good and only sunk money'.

Soon after their return to the diamond fields some four months later, Herbert sold his claims in New Rush and took off once more for the north. The two brothers were never to see each other again. After a three-year spell of prospecting for gold in the eastern Transvaal and a prison term in Mozambique for gun-running, Herbert came to an untimely end on the banks of the Shire River in southern Malawi in 1879 when an ember from his pipe ignited a demi-john of home-brewed gin that he was pouring, setting his clothes alight; he rushed to the river and jumped in but died of his injuries shortly afterwards.

Rhodes meanwhile pursued his own course. In July 1873, leaving his business interests in the hands of his partner, Charles Rudd, he set sail for England, intending to gain admission to Oxford.

3

KIMBERLEY

Dressed in full imperial regalia, Britain's first governor of Griqualand, Sir Richard Southey, was given a tumultuous reception on his arrival in the diamond fields in January 1873. In accordance with local tradition, crowds on horseback and in carriages gathered at a rendezvous on the road several miles outside the mining settlements to give him a resounding cheer and escort him into town. Preceded by brass bands, the governor, wearing a plumed hat and embroidered tunic, rode in state with his wife through triumphal arches specially erected for him. In the evening, residents entertained him with a fireworks display and a banquet.

With the coming of British rule, names were changed. The colonial secretary, Lord Kimberley, complained that he could neither spell 'Vooruitzigt' ('Foresight'), the former De Beer's farm where the two richest mines – New Rush (Colesberg Kopje) and 'Old' De Beer's – were located; nor did he consider that 'New Rush' was a sufficiently dignified title for the latest addition to Queen Victoria's empire. What was needed, said Kimberley, were 'English-sounding names'. Accordingly, a proclamation was issued, declaring: 'The encampment and town heretofore known as De Beer's New Rush, the Colesberg Kopje No 2, or Vooruitzigt, shall henceforth be designated the town of Kimberley.' New Rush became known as Kimberley mine;

and its diamond-bearing blue ground was now technically called
kimberlite.

Kimberley by 1873 was fast growing into the second-largest town
in southern Africa, boasting a population of some 13,000 whites and
30,000 blacks, with Dutoitspan two miles away adding a further 6,000
to the total. At the town centre, amid a chaotic jumble of tents and
canvas-covered frame houses, stood Market Square, a vast open space
crowded by day with wagons and Cape carts, where diggers, their
families, diamond dealers, tradesmen and merchants gathered to
peruse piles of goods for sale and exchange gossip and rumours. Each
morning, Boer farmers drove wagonloads of produce to the square –
springbok at a shilling each; blesbok and wildebeest at half-a-crown;
vegetables and firewood. Other wagons, piled with mining equipment, building materials, household utensils, provisions and liquor
arrived from Cape Town and other coastal ports, having survived the
journey of hundreds of miles over rough tracks.

At one side of the square stood the 'Griqualand Share and Claim
Exchange', where claims were bought and sold. On Saturdays, auc-
tions in Market Square attracted large crowds, looking as much for a
bit of entertainment as for products on offer; a brisk trade was done in
second-hand mining equipment, sold by diggers on their departure,
some leaving jubilantly, others ruing their ill-fortune.

Adjoining Market Square was Main Street, a business thoroughfare
lined with stores, canteens, bars and the frame tents of diamond
'koopers'. Diamond-buying was as important to Kimberley as
diamond-digging and often far more profitable. At the top end of the
trade were agents for leading diamond firms in Europe with large
financial resources who rarely deigned to leave their offices. As aristocrats of the diamond market, many affected a flamboyant style of
dress, wearing velvet jackets, white cord or buckskin breeches, long,
tight-fitting, highly polished boots and glittering spurs. Other diamond buyers with Main Street offices ventured out to the mining
camps, bars and canteens on the lookout for promising items. At the
bottom end of the trade were the 'kopje-wallopers', itinerant diamond
buyers too poor to establish their own offices, who scoured the mines
each day in search of diggers selling small, cheap diamonds they could

purchase on the spot. 'Many of these were young men who were averse to manual labour but whose business instincts were acute,' William Scully wrote. 'The equipment of a "kopje-walloper" consisted of a cheque-book, a wallet – known as a "poverty bag" – a set of scales, a magnifying glass, and a persuasive tongue. In the course of a morning one's sorting table might be visited by a dozen of them.'

Scattered around Kimberley was an array of rough hotels, boarding houses, billiard halls and gambling 'hells'. Drinking, gambling and sex were the town's main diversions. For every one hundred tents or so, there were two or three drinking saloons with their regular daily and nightly clientele. 'Nothing is more common than to see the canteens adorned with a row of dead-drunk corpses at ten a.m.,' complained John Merriman. Vast quantities of champagne were consumed to celebrate success. The most popular drink was 'Cape Smoke', a powerful brandy, never matured and frequently adulterated by unscrupulous canteen keepers and illicit liquor dealers. A Scottish doctor, Josiah Matthews, who set up a medical practice in Kimberley in 1872, estimated that at least two-thirds of his caseload could be traced to 'excessive indulgence in alcohol'.

Gambling hells abounded, ranging from semi-private luxuriously fitted houses to squalid shacks. Dr Matthews ventured into one in early 1873, 'a corrugated iron building of no great architectural pretensions, from whence came sounds of lively music and the hum of many voices'. An eager throng of players was crowded around the tables. 'Some, clad in decent clothes, but many in shirt sleeves and rough garb, just as they had come from the mine, had notes of large amounts in their hands, whilst bundles of them protruded from their pockets.'

While Matthews watched, a newcomer was admitted to the croupier's table.

He was addressed as Captain H. by surrounding friends and we watched his play with considerable interest, as despite a calm exterior his anxiety to win was evidently most intense. Play continued with varying success for some time, until his rolls having dwindled away, it seemed that H. had come down to his last £10 note. This he flung on the 'red' with a look of sheer despair, and awaited the issue with an agony of expression that was painful to witness. 'Red' would have proved his salvation, but alas! Once more 'black' was in the ascendant, and H. was 'played out'. With a muttered oath, but without any words intelligible to the bystanders, he darted outside the saloon into the open. Those absorbed in play merely jeered at his sudden departure.

From outside the gambling hell, a pistol shot rang out through the midnight air. Then a passer-by rushed in excitedly with the news that Captain H had shot himself and was lying smothered in blood, dead in the road.

Suicide was common; the main beneficiaries of the gambling hells were the proprietors, though occasionally some players prospered. A 19-year-old lad from north London, David Harris, who was lured reluctantly into Dodd's Canteen by a friend one night and eventually induced to stake £1 at roulette, left with £1,400 of winnings which formed the basis of his fortune. Harris returned briefly to London extolling the virtues of Kimberley as a place of limitless opportunity, before going back.

The same lure of money attracted a host of prostitutes – white, mixed-race 'Coloureds' and blacks. At first, the white women, unsure of their ground, stayed quietly in boarding houses, made a pretence of respectability and invented unconvincing pretexts for their presence before gravitating towards bars and saloons. Later visitors were less circumspect. In his *Reminiscences of Kimberley*, Louis Cohen described the arrival of a well-known octoroon who, from the moment she stepped down from the post-cart from Cape Town, 'did not conceal the fact she desired to be better known':

> She joked freely with the surrounding miners, and after absorbing a brandy and soda or two, hopped into a Cape cart that was waiting for her, shouting as she went, 'I'll be at Graybittel's canteen to-night.' And at Graybittel's she was, and the boys turned up fine. Some of them had dressed for the occasion, and when

the lady entered there was some disturbance. Quiet men got restless, restless men got thirsty, vain men posed, and quarrelsome men fought – but the saffron-coloured woman drank with all. The quiet, the restless, the bibulous, the vain, the quarrelsome were alike to her. She frolicked with the lot.

Standing on a champagne case, she offered herself for auction. The bidding started at £5 and a case of champagne and ended when a Dutch diamond merchant offered £25 and three cases of champagne. He took her to his frame tent across the road. 'But after half an hour had elapsed, "the boys" got round the tent and carried it bodily away, thus exposing to view the amorous pair.'

By late 1873, however, Kimberley was facing another period of crisis. A severe drought in Griqualand West drove up the cost of staple foods. Simultaneously, the price of rough diamonds in London fell by one third, driven in part by recession in Europe but affected as well by the sheer volume of Kimberley's output. The more that Kimberley produced, the lower the price went. In 1869, the diamond fields had exported £24,800 worth of diamonds; in 1872, the first full year of mining at Colesberg Kopje, the figure rose to £1,618,000; in 1873, despite the increase in production, it stood at £1,649,450. At 30 shillings a carat, diggers made a reasonable profit; at 20 shillings a carat, many could not survive. In the ensuing depression, canteen and hotel keepers suffered the worst; auctioneers were kept busy selling off everything from household furniture to store goods.

The difficulties of mining at Kimberley also worsened. By 1873, all the roadways at the mine had collapsed. Claims at the centre were left stranded. To overcome the problem, diggers constructed an elaborate system of cable transport held in place by a series of massive timber stagings erected around the margin of the mine. Each staging carried two or three platforms, one above the other, that were linked to the claims below by fixed ropes, made at first of hemp or rawhide, but later of wire. Hauling ropes attached to windlasses were used to lift buckets up from the claims. On reaching the platforms, the buckets were emptied via chutes into bags that were carted away to floors, sieves and sorting tables. By 1874, there were 1,000 windlasses on the stagings. The cable system provided visitors with an awe-inspiring sight.

> So thickly together were these lines set that the whole face of the vast pit seemed to be covered by a monstrous cobweb, shining in the moonlight as if every filament was a silver strand . . .
>
> Hide buckets were flying like shuttles in a loom up and down the vast warp of wires, twanging like dissonant harp-strings, with a deafening din of rattling wheels and falling ground . . .

But no sooner had the cable system been devised than more severe problems occurred. As the digging went deeper, the outside walls of the mine, consisting predominantly of black shale or 'reef' extending downwards for 300 feet or more, began to disintegrate. Summer storms regularly set off avalanches. Usually there was sufficient warning that an avalanche was coming. Great cracks appeared on top of the reef which diggers carefully measured to estimate when it was due to fall. The collapse of reef was a spectacular sight, as Lionel Phillips, a Londoner, described:

> Along the towering face at various points little bits of rock broke away, increasing rapidly in number and quantity during the next hour or so. The gaps between the solid ground and the doomed section increased visibly as one watched, and the gigantic body rolled over, crashed, and like an enormous tidal wave swept everything away in its path.

Occasionally, huge chunks of reef came away without warning. A claim-holder recalled:

> One morning, riding up to our west-end ground, I saw all our standing wires were slack. I raced up to the point of vantage, conscious of the probable cause. Hundreds of tons of ground had given way. The situation below was appalling. Most of our men had jumped down into the claims next to ours – sixty feet below . . . It took hours to get the dead and injured to the surface.

Apart from the loss of life caused by avalanches, the disruption to mining lasted for months while the debris was cleared away. In the first five years of production at Kimberley, one load of reef was extracted to every seven loads of blue ground.

Flooding added to the diggers' woes. In January 1874 torrential rains made mining in many parts impossible; six months later, some forty per cent of Kimberley mine was still under water. In the hope of clearing the water, the Kimberley mining board issued pumping contracts.

This was an area of business that attracted Cecil Rhodes and his partner Charles Rudd.

Rhodes' first sojourn at Oxford was brief. In October 1873 he was admitted as a student of Oriel College. In November he caught a severe chill while rowing on the Isis. The college doctor was sufficiently concerned to seek an opinion from Dr Morell Mackenzie, a London chest and throat specialist, who found 'his heart and lungs' affected and advised Rhodes to return to the hot, dry climate of Kimberley forthwith. In his casebook, Mackenzie wrote: 'Not six months to live.' Rhodes was also depressed at the time by the death of his mother to whom he had been deeply attached. In December he set sail for Cape Town.

In Kimberley, Rhodes and Rudd, though lacking any pumping equipment of their own, put in a bid to win the pumping contract at Kimberley mine. They failed there, so turned their attention to the smaller Dutoitspan mine where Rudd had business links with the chairman of the mining board. Amid accusations in the local press of jobbery, Rhodes and Rudd won the pumping contract worth £500 a month. The problem was that they still had no pumping equipment of their own and the board expected pumping to start at once.

The story of what happened next became one of the many legends about Rhodes cited as evidence of his early commercial genius. Hearing that a farmer in Victoria West possessed a pumping engine suitable for his needs, Rhodes hired a Boer transport driver to take him to the farm eight days' ride away. The farmer, however, proved reluctant to part with his engine, wanting it for irrigation. But Rhodes persisted, camping for days on the farmer's doorstep, cajoling him, charming his wife, gradually raising his offer and eventually getting him to agree to sell the engine for £1,000. 'Every man,' Rhodes claimed to have learned, 'has his price.' He returned to Kimberley in triumph, his reputation intact. 'We're a force, Rudd; a force to reckon with!' he is said to have told his partner.

What confounds the story is that the farmer had previously advertised the engine for sale for £1,000 in Kimberley. All Rhodes had to do was collect it. Nevertheless, Rhodes managed the Dutoitspan pumping contract successfully, making a substantial profit from it, which provided him with sufficient working capital for further mining ventures.

It was while Rhodes was busy manning the pumps in Dutoitspan in 1875 that dissident diggers rose in rebellion against Sir Richard Southey's administration in Kimberley.

4

THE DIGGERS' REVOLT

Long before Sir Richard Southey arrived on the diamond fields in 1873, white diggers had established a tradition of airing their grievances in a loud and boisterous manner that sometimes culminated in violence and riot. Since the early days, they had formed 'diggers' committees' to regulate their own affairs, relishing the freedom from state authority and taxation. The idea of 'diggers democracy', as it was known, was firmly entrenched. Members of diggers' committees were popularly elected and quick to defend the interests of their community. In clashes with landowners, diggers insisted that, on payment of an appropriate licence fee, they had the right to mine wherever diamonds and precious metals were found and had got their way. They had also placed a limit on claim-holders obtaining more than two claims each in order to protect small diggers and prevent mining from passing into the hands of large companies. Above all, they were determined to restrict the activities of blacks on the diamond fields: they wanted black labour but feared that black competition would undermine them. 'The difference between the general wants, character and position of the two races utterly forbid it.' Diggers' rights were thus confined to whites only.

Although Southey was given a warm welcome on his arrival in Kimberley, he was soon at loggerheads with the diggers. An autocrat, he set out to impose his own authority on the mining community and curb the independence of the diggers. A new constitution for Griqualand West in 1873 provided for an eight-member Legislative Council with four members elected, but left Southey with a casting vote and the right to veto legislation. Diggers' committees rejected the constitution but decided to participate in elections in November 1873 and put forward 'People's Candidates', hoping to wreck the work of the Legislative Council. But their candidates failed to win either of the two Kimberley seats. Though defeated at the polls, the diggers' committees continued to agitate for greater control, demanding that their remit should be extended from mining to municipal affairs.

Alarmed by the sheer belligerence of the diggers, the colonial secretary in Griqualand, John Blades Currey, feared that 'given sufficient encouragement they would take sole charge and constitute themselves a Republican government'. Currey's solution was to issue an ordinance setting up new mining boards with limited powers strictly confined to mining affairs. This, he recalled, was 'the best means of compassing my object of curbing or getting rid of the Diggers' Committees'. The diggers were given representation on the mining boards but felt aggrieved by their diminished status.

Another source of dissension was over the role of Africans on the diamond fields. While Southey agreed that the mines should remain in the hands of small independent diggers, favouring their interests over the demands of landowners and large companies, he was adamant that blacks and Coloureds should be given equal opportunity with white diggers as claim-owners and permitted to buy and sell claims for themselves on the same basis. 'As until recently nearly all the land in the Province belonged to persons of Colour,' he said, 'there is great injustice in attempting to deprive them.'

But white diggers were fiercely opposed to such notions. 'Ruin, financial ruin for the whites, moral ruin for the natives, these are the results of the attempt to elevate in one day the servant to an equality with his master,' thundered the *Diamond Field* newspaper in November 1874. 'Class legislation, restrictive laws and the holding in check of the native races till by education they are fit to be our equals, is the only policy that finds favour here.'

This contest between white and black on the diamond fields, coming at the start of southern Africa's industrial revolution, was to have lasting repercussions.

The diamond boom attracted a steady flow of black migrants from across southern Africa. Many travelled for weeks on foot to get to the diamond fields, arriving exhausted and emaciated. The largest number came from Pediland in the Transvaal region 500 miles away, encouraged by the Pedi paramount chief, Sekhukhune, to earn money for the purchase of guns. Tsonga migrants ('Shangaan') walked from Gaza territory north of the Limpopo nearly 1,000 miles away. Zulus arrived from Natal and 'Moshoeshoe's people' from Basutoland. In all, the mines drew more than 50,000 Africans each year in the early 1870s.

Most stayed for periods of between three and six months, working as labourers for white diggers or finding other work in the camps. They earned usually about 10 shillings a week and a further 10 shillings in the form of food, leaving for home once they had saved enough cash to buy cattle or a plough or a gun. An old muzzle-loading Enfield discarded by the British army could be bought for £3; a breach-loading Snider cost £12. Between April 1873 and June 1874, some 75,000 guns were sold in Kimberley. Gun sales provided a striking spectacle. 'At knock off time,' wrote one pioneer digger, 'our Kaffirs used to pass down streets of tented shops owned by white traders and presided over by yelling black salesmen whirling guns above their heads. These they discharged in the air crying: "*Reka, reka, mona mtskeka*" [Buy, buy, a gun]. A deafening din. A sight never to be forgotten.'

White diggers commonly complained about black labour, resorting frequently to abuse and violence. Black labour, the *Diamond News* argued in 1872, was both 'the most expensive in the world' and 'the most unmanageable'. With 5,000 independent diggers competing for their service, black labourers were able to move from one claim to the next in search of higher pay or a better employer. Without labour, diggers faced ruin. Time and again, they railed against their employees' tendency to 'desert', usually linking it to diamond theft, and demanded greater methods of control.

The problem of diamond theft became ever more prevalent from 1872. It was, wrote Dr Matthews, 'the curse of the Fields'. Large quantities of stolen diamonds were smuggled out of camps for sale in coastal towns or in foreign markets. Whites and blacks alike were involved in the trade. Diamonds were commonly stolen from claims or depositing grounds by black workers and sold on to white fences – illicit diamond buyers, as they were termed – operating from the myriad sleazy canteens and bars around Kimberley. Some bars – like The Red Light – became notorious as clearing houses.

Rough justice was meted out to both whites and blacks accused or suspected of involvement. In dealing with whites, the routine usually adopted was for a group of vigilante miners to confront their culprit before setting fire to his tent, shop or canteen, destroying all his property and then expelling him. In dealing with blacks, the usual punishment was flogging.

Added to diggers' anger over diamond theft was resentment at the way that some blacks and Coloureds from the Cape had managed to establish themselves as claim-holders, or share-workers managing claims in return for a percentage of profits. They were congregated mainly at Bultfontein, otherwise known as the 'poor man's diggings'. White diggers maintained that black diggers possessing the right to sell diamonds acted as conduits for the illegal traffic in the gems.

In March 1872, Kimberley's white residents demanded sweeping new laws enabling them to control and regulate black and Coloured workers. They wanted employees to be held to written contracts registered with a government official; to be subjected to searches at any time; and to be restricted by a night-time curfew. They also wanted a ban preventing blacks and Coloureds from holding a digging licence unless supported by fifty white claim-holders. In the following months, they resorted increasingly to sporadic violent protest, burning the tents of black claim-holders and attempting to lynch blacks suspected of stealing diamonds.

British officials, with few police at their disposal, struggled to impose their authority. In July 1872, a white digger who flogged two of his black workers, accusing them of diamond theft, then left them naked and bound in the open air on a winter's night, causing the death of one of them, was brought before the magistrate's court. He was found guilty by the jury only of common assault, committed, it was said, under 'great provocation'. The shock for Kimberley's residents was that the magistrate sentenced him to six months' hard labour without the option of a fine. Hitherto, crimes of violence against blacks had rarely been punished and even then sentences had been limited to small fines. The *Diamond Field* newspaper argued that the sentence had 'done more to defeat the ends of justice than uphold the dignity of the law'.

However, faced with increasing disorder, British officials capitulated to most of the diggers' demands. Using the terminology of 'masters' and 'servants', Proclamation 14 of August 1872 laid down a new regime for labour contracts, linking it to a system of pass laws that became the main device for controlling black labour throughout southern Africa for decades to come. On arrival in Kimberley, black migrants – 'servants' – were required to register at a depot and obtain a daily pass until they had secured employment. The labour contract they were given showed the name of the servant, his wages, his period of service and the name of his master. Once employed, the servant was required to carry a pass signed by his master. 'Any person who shall be found wandering or loitering about within the precincts of any camp – without a pass . . . and without being able to give a good and satisfactory account of himself' was liable to a £5 fine or imprisonment for up to three months or flogging. Masters were entitled to search the person, residence or property of their servants at any time without a warrant. In theory, the law was colour-blind, applying equally to all servants or employees. In practice it applied only to blacks.

Not all blacks, however, were subject to the pass system. Colonial officials saw fit to distinguish between civilised and uncivilised blacks:

There are many natives, half-castes, and others from the Colony, who are honest, intelligent and respectable men and these must of course be treated in every way similar to the whites, but the great mass of the labouring coloured population consists of raw Kaffirs, who come from the interior with every element of barbarism, and no touch of civilisation among them; in fact they must be treated as children incapable of governing themselves.

Thus, blacks who were their own masters, holding claims or cart licences, or engaged as independent traders, were granted 'protection passes' proving their exemption from pass laws – a pass to avoid a pass.

Despite these concessions, the diggers remained in a truculent mood, complaining of high tax impositions and continuing black disorder. They were further aggrieved by the demise of diggers' committees ordered by Southey's administration and their consequent lack of influence. Adding to this mix of grievances was dissension over rent increases in Kimberley demanded by private companies that owned the land on which the mines were located.

In August 1874, 500 whites gathered in Market Square to elect members to a Committee of Public Safety, a name chosen to signify revolutionary intent. Southey was left in no doubt that its members saw themselves as constituting potentially an alternative government. The Committee purchased editorial control of the *Diamond Field* and appointed as editor Alfred Aylward, a bearded Irish republican previously connected to the Fenian movement. A man of many talents, fluent in Dutch, he had worked as a medical orderly in Dutoitspan before becoming a digger. In 1872, he bought five claims in De Beer's mine, employed 75 labourers and became chairman of De Beer's diggers' committee, but he lost his claims and his position after being convicted of assault in November 1872 and sentenced to 18 months hard labour. Released in December 1873, he became a share-worker first in De Beer's then in Kimberley mine.

Aylward pursued his republican agenda relentlessly. In October 1874, he travelled to Bloemfontein for an audience with President Brand and five members of the Volksraad, exploring the possibility of linking Griqualand to the Orange Free State where the standard treatment of blacks was more to the diggers' liking. Brand told him he approved of the work of the Committee of Public Safety and, on his return to Kimberley, Aylward used this endorsement to support his campaign for a republican government. Aylward's enthusiasm for the republican cause, however, caused a rift with other members of the Committee who wanted reform rather than revolution. He consequently threw his energies instead into forming a Defence League and Protection Association which pledged not to pay taxes.

The issue that ignited this combustible cocktail of grievances and dissent was rent increases. In February 1875, after a prolonged dispute, the courts ruled that the owners of Vooruitzigt farm, a syndicate of Port Elizabeth merchants, were entitled to raise rents as they pleased. At a mass meeting of 800 people in Kimberley Hall on 3 March, Aylward urged diggers to take up arms. 'If I erect the English ensign with a black flag under it,' he declared, 'I expect to see you with your rifles and your revolvers . . . [ready] in the name of heaven and your country, to protect yourselves from injustice.'

Ten days later, a variety of dissident groups joined forces to form a Diggers' Protection Association, a paramilitary organisation consisting of seven armed companies, five at Kimberley and a burgher guard at Dutoitspan and De Beer's. At the head of the Protection Association was a *krygsraad* or war council. Its members included 'Captain' Alfred Aylward, given command of one of the infantry companies; 'Captain' Henry Tucker, a former member of the Cape parliament, claimholder and storekeeper; 'Captain' William Ling, a prominent claim-holder heavily in debt; and Conrad von Schlickmann, a former Prussian officer, given charge of the 'German company'. A manifesto signed by Tucker and Ling declared that as 'the rights, property and liberty of the diggers' were threatened by a large number of Africans who were 'not gaining their living by honest labour', nor subject to adequate police control, the Association's members would henceforth be responsible for the security of Europeans on the diamond fields. With some 800 men under arms, rebel militias took to drilling openly in Market Square and on the cricket ground. Witnessing these events, Louis Cohen recorded: 'Sometimes, when ordered to "right about face", they would, in a menacing and derisive manner, point their rifles at the Government Offices.'

Southey issued a proclamation warning all and sundry against 'taking illegal oaths or assembling in arms' and gave orders to protect public buildings with sandbags. But he had only a minuscule police force – nine officers, twenty-four white constables and a variable number of black auxiliaries – on whom to depend. Despite his precarious position, he decided to act.

In April, William Cowie, a dissident hotel keeper, was charged with supplying guns to Alfred Aylward without a permit. On the day of Cowie's trial, demonstrators gathered at the courthouse to demand his release. Showing considerable courage, the magistrate convicted Cowie, fined him £50 and denied him bail pending confirmation of his verdict.

No sooner had the verdict been announced than Aylward rode off to Kimberley mine to raise the black flag of revolt. On the way, he passed Louis Cohen who recorded the incident in characteristically flamboyant prose:

> I shall never forget on this memorable revolutionary occasion being in the Main Street, when suddenly I saw a man of Satanic bearing come galloping down it, waving a black flag in one hand and shouting valorously as if he were leading a heroic charge of cavalry. By his side a huge General Boom sabre dangled . . . This burlesque of Murat was a fair-sized man with luxuriant black curly hair and beard and moustache, which brought into prominence his thick sensual red lips and bright, though dissipated, bloodshot eyes. The Rouge et Noir on horseback was none other than the redoubtable Irish Fenian, Alfred Aylward . . .

That afternoon, one of Aylward's colleagues hoisted the black flag on a whim on a debris mound known as Mount Ararat, the signal for rebellion. Some 300 armed men rushed to the magistrate's court where a handful of constables, with drawn revolvers, managed to hold them in check.

Under police escort, Cowie was taken from the courthouse and marched 250 yards to the prison. But the prison entrance was by now blocked by a group of 150 armed men. Police reinforcements arrived. In the tense stand-off that followed, with a crowd of several thousand milling about outside the prison, rebel leaders and colonial officials negotiated a compromise. Cowie was released after Tucker signed a cheque for £50 that was to be cashed only if the sentence was confirmed.

The following day, Southey declared 'certain evil disposed persons' were in rebellion, requested British troops to be sent from the Cape Colony, and called for volunteers to enrol as special constables to protect government property. One of those who came forward was Cecil Rhodes. For ten weeks, while an expeditionary force was assembled in the Cape, rebel leaders ruled the streets of the mining camps but dithered over whether to overthrow the government by force of arms. When British redcoats finally arrived in Kimberley on 30 June 1875, after a journey of 700 miles, they met no resistance. Louis Cohen witnessed their arrival:

> I well remember seeing the men march up Du Toit's Pan Road, tired and dusty, straining their eyes for the sight of the diamonds they expected no doubt to see in heaps. They were led right into the heart of town . . .The next morning five of the loud-voiced rebels were arrested, an operation effected on them as easily as if they were goats. A bleat or two, and all was over.

With government authority restored, seven rebel leaders were put on trial. Three of them – Aylward, Ling and Schlickmann – faced charges of sedition, conspiracy and riot. After three days of hearing evidence, a local jury took twenty-three minutes to return a verdict of not guilty. The other four accused were also acquitted.

Southey, however, fared less well. His handling of the crisis was severely criticised. Military intervention had cost the imperial government in London £20,000. In a despatch to Lord Carnarvon, the colonial secretary in London, Sir Henry Barkly, the Cape governor, made it clear that he did not consider morality and justice to be worth such a high price. In August, Southey was relieved of his post.

The 'Black Flag Revolt', as it was called, marked a significant watershed. It represented a clear victory for white interests above all others. But it also led to the demise of the era of independent diggers and the consequent rise of Kimberley's diamond magnates.

5

ENTER THE MAGNATES

In the aftermath of the rebellion, the British government installed a new regime in Kimberley, determined to ensure that Griqualand and its turbulent mining community brought no further trouble or expense. In place of a governor, it appointed an 'administrator', Major Owen Lanyon, a tall, swarthy Irish martinet who made no attempt to hide his distaste for the primitive living conditions or his impatience with local dignitaries. To resolve disputes over land, the British administration purchased for the sum of £100,000 the Vooruitzigt farm, containing Kimberley mine, De Beer's mine and Kimberley town, becoming, in effect, the 'proprietor'.

Kimberley soon developed a more staid character. Banished were the grog shops and black prostitutes that had made Saturday nights in Kimberley the stuff of legend. The town now boasted churches, chapels, a synagogue, schools, temperance societies and a public library. Streets were regularly watered to keep down the dust. On Main Street, the Craven Club, with its reading room, card and billiard rooms, provided a convenient rendezvous for well-to-do diggers. Nearby, the Varieties Theatre offered entertainment in elegant surroundings. 'It looks exceedingly neat and comfortable,' reported the *Diamond News* when the theatre opened in November 1874. 'The walls are papered and decorated with handsome pictures. The stage has been erected upon the latest principles, so as to afford everyone present a full view of the actors. On either side of the stage is a splendid mirror seven feet in height, draped with red and damask curtains.'

A new residential suburb named Belgravia was laid out in 1875, attracting 'leading merchants and men of leisure' who built brick houses with all the trappings and comfort expected of a Victorian bourgeois lifestyle. A telegraph office opened in 1876, providing a direct link to Cape Town. Census figures in 1877 showed Kimberley to be the second-largest town in southern Africa, with a population of 13,500. When Dutoitspan and Bultfontein were added, the total population of the diamond fields was set at 18,000 – 8,000 whites and some 10,000 non-whites.

With the aim of sorting out the grievances that had led up to the Black Flag revolt, a royal commissioner, Colonel William Crossman, was appointed to examine the workings and finances of the mining industry. Crossman concluded in 1876 that the system of restricting the number of claims that claim-holders could possess, put in place to protect the interests of individual diggers and prevent mining companies from gaining control, was no longer viable. The future of diamond mining, he argued, belonged to capitalists and companies; and he recommended that no limit should be imposed on the size of holdings. Lanyon concurred with these findings. His interest, above all else, was to make sure that Griqualand was solvent.

A new breed of mining entrepreneur emerged. Some came from the ranks of the more successful diggers; some were Kimberley traders who had made their fortunes importing equipment and supplies; the most active group in purchasing claims were diamond merchants. All relied heavily on international connections. A slump in the price of diamonds in 1876 brought work on many claims to a standstill and enabled men with capital backing to pick up claims cheaply from forced sales. Within the space of four years, the number of claim-owners in Kimberley mine halved.

In the first four months of 1877, Jules Porges, a Paris-based diamond merchant, spent £90,000 buying up low-priced claims, giving him a 10 per cent interest in the Kimberley mine. Porges later teamed up with two Kimberley dealers, Sammy Marks and his brother-in-law,

Isaac Lewis, who had turned their small trading business into a sub-stantial mining company. In 1880 they merged their claims to form a joint-stock company, Compagnie Française des Mines des Diamants du Cap du Bon Espérance, otherwise known as the French Company. It controlled one-quarter of the Kimberley mine and was by far the largest mining operation on the diamond fields.

Another major player was Joseph B. Robinson, a cold, cantanker-ous claim-owner notorious for his ill-temper, meanness, and proclivity for seducing other men's wives and daughters. The son of 1820 set-tlers, he had been among the first diggers at the Vaal River before moving to Colesberg Kopje. By the time the British took control of Griqualand, he had become one of Kimberley's leading figures; he owned the only brick residence then there and provided the carriage for Governor Southey to make his grand entrance into the town in 1873. He also bought a newspaper, the *Independent*, to promote his political standing. Tall, with piercing blue eyes, he was renowned for his sour, tight-lipped expression and his habit of wearing a white pith-helmet. Successful as a lone operator, Robinson had interests in several mining ventures, but his principal vehicle was the Standard Diamond Mining Company which gained control of substantial parts of Kimberley mine.

The most colourful of the new entrepreneurs was Barney Barnato, a Jewish kopje-walloper born in the East End of London and known in Kimberley more for his performance as a music-hall entertainer than for his talent for business. A cousin of David Harris, who had won £1,400 in an hour playing roulette in a Kimberley bar, Barnato had arrived in the diamond fields in 1873 carrying a box of poor-quality cigars in the hope of starting a business career there. 'He was a strongly built young fellow,' wrote Louis Cohen, who first met him in a canteen, 'wore a pair of spectacles on his uninviting dust-stained face, and had the ugliest snub nose you could imagine, but as good a pair of large grey blue eyes as ever flashed through a pair of glasses.'

Barnato found it difficult, however, to make any headway as either a digger or a diamond buyer. He survived by working as an actor, appearing in various roles at the Theatre Royal, a one-storeyed cor-rugated iron building with a bar running the length of one side.

Facing hard times, he moved into a back room in a sleazy hotel, a notorious rendezvous for illicit diamond dealers, that was owned by his brother Harry. Together they managed to accumulate enough money to buy four claims in Kimberley in 1876, risking their entire capital. From such precarious beginnings, the mining interests of the Barnato Brothers began to prosper, albeit under a cloud of suspicion about the origin of their wealth. By 1878, their claims were bringing in an estimated £1,800 a week. By 1880, they had become major players in the diamond trade, with offices in London.

Amid this rising galaxy, Cecil Rhodes was no more than a minor contender. In partnership with Rudd, he began to build up a group of claims in a part of De Beer's mine known as Baxter's Gully. De Beer's was considered to be one of the poorer mines; claims could be purchased there more cheaply than in Kimberley mine. Whereas Kimberley's claims were officially valued at over £1 million in 1877, those of De Beer's were worth only £200,000; of Dutoitspan, £76,000; and of Bultfontein, £30,000. Nevertheless, De Beer's mine, reaching only one quarter of the depth of Kimberley, was cheaper to dig and less prone to reef falls.

Rhodes' personal standing in the mining community, moreover, was at a low ebb. His reputation had been severely damaged as a result of his handling of pumping contracts. As well as his contract in Dutoitspan, Rhodes had won a bid at the end of 1874 to clear Kimberley mine of water in two months and to keep it dry for the following two months. Pumping was a hazardous business. Pumps frequently broke down; wood supplies for the steam engines were scarce; there were endless delays in bringing in new equipment. On one occasion, a boiler exploded after Rhodes, in a fit of absentmindedness, forgot to feed in water. By May 1875, to the intense frustration of claim-holders, parts of De Beer's remained flooded. But, by promising to order new pumps from England, Rhodes was given an additional contract, to begin once the pumps had arrived in Kimberley.

In the meantime, the De Beer's mining board employed a 35-year-old Mauritian engineer, E. Huteau, to supervise pumping operations at the mine. Huteau succeeded not only in keeping the mine dry when the rainy season began at the end of 1875, but he kept operating costs below Rhodes' contract price of £400 a month, making Rhodes' contract appear unnecessary. On 26 December, however, Huteau's pumping operation failed spectacularly and the mine flooded. On inspection, it was discovered that an engine had been sabotaged. Rumours abounded that Huteau had previously been approached by a man offering a bribe of £300 to sabotage his pumping equipment. Angry diggers with claims under water insisted that Huteau identify the culprit.

By chance, the royal commissioner, Colonel Crossman, appointed to investigate diggers' grievances, opened his first session in Kimberley Hall on 5 January 1876 and was swiftly drawn into the furore. Crossman sent for Huteau who confirmed, under oath, that he had been offered a bribe, but he refused to name the culprit. Threatened with legal action, Huteau suggested a compromise: he would write the name on a piece of paper and hand it to the royal commissioner. Crossman read the paper, then immediately called out for Mr Cecil Rhodes to appear before him. As Rhodes could not be found – he was at Dutoitspan – the matter was adjourned.

Two days later, Rhodes told Crossman that the story was 'fictitious' and announced that on legal advice he had decided to ask the attorney-general, Sidney Shippard, to prosecute Huteau for perjury, thus preventing Crossman from pursuing his own enquiries and effectively ending public discussion of Rhodes' conduct. Shippard, an Oxford-educated lawyer, was part of Rhodes' circle of friends. Though a preliminary hearing was held six days later, at the following hearing Shippard announced that he would not proceed with the prosecution. Without giving any reason, Rhodes dropped the case. Nor did he make any further attempt to clear his name.

In March 1876, Rhodes left Kimberley for Oxford. 'My character was so battered at the Diamond Fields,' he wrote from Oxford, 'that I like to preserve the few remnants.'

Paying a visit to Kimberley in 1877, the English novelist and travel writer Anthony Trollope was impressed by the riches it produced but complained of the heat, the dust, the flies, the food, the living conditions, the high prices and the barren landscape. 'There are places to which men are attracted by the desire of gain which seem to be so repulsive that no gain can compensate the miseries incidental to such an habitation.'

Kimberley's most notable feature, he wrote, was Market Square, mentioned by local residents with pride, but which boasted only one building higher than one storey. 'This is its only magnificence. There is no pavement. The roadway is all dust and holes. There is a market place in the midst which certainly is not magnificent. Around are the corrugated iron shops of the ordinary dealers in provisions. An uglier place I do not know how to imagine.'

The mean-looking corrugated iron houses, in which rich and poor alike lived, were bereft of comfort. The cost of transport made many materials prohibitively expensive. Trollope continued:

It is difficult to conceive the existence of a town in which every plank used has had to be dragged five hundred miles by oxen; but such has been the case in Kimberley. Nor can bricks be made which will stand the weather because bricks require to be burned and cannot be burned without fuel. Fuel at Kimberley is so expensive a luxury that two thoughts have to be given to the boiling of a kettle . . . Lath and plaster for ceilings there is little or none. But a canvas ceiling does not remain long clean, or even rectilinear. The invincible dust settles upon it and bulges it. Wooden floors are absolutely necessary for comfort and cleanliness; but at Kimberley it will cost £40 to floor a moderate room. The consequence is that even people who are doing well with their diamonds live in comfortless houses, always meaning to pack up and run after this year, or next year, or perhaps the year after next. But if they have done ill with their diamonds they remain till they may do better; and if they have done well then there falls upon them the *Auri sacra fames*. When £30,000 have been so easily heaped together, why not £60,000; – and when £60,000 why not £100,000? And then why spend money largely in this state of trial, in a condition which is not intended to be prolonged, – but which is prolonged from year to year by the desire for more? Why try to enjoy life here, this wretched life, when so soon there is a life coming which is to be so infinitely better?

The surrounding countryside he found equally dreary, stripped of all timber. 'I do not think that there is a tree to be seen within five miles of the town.' A period of drought had turned the landscape brown. 'When I was there I doubt there was a blade of grass within twenty miles . . . Everything was brown, as though the dusty dry uncovered ugly earth never knew the blessing of verdure.'

Trollope was taken to Klipdrift – or Barkly, as it had been renamed – for a 'picnic' on the banks of the Vaal River and encountered there a solitary prospector, struggling to survive:

> As we rowed down the river we saw a white man with two Kafirs poking about his stones and gravel on a miner's rickety table under a little tent on the beach. He was a digger who had still clung to the 'river' business; a Frenchman who had come to try his luck there a few days since. On the Monday previous – we were told – he had found a 13 carat white stone without a flaw. This would be enough perhaps to keep him going and almost to satisfy him for a month. Had he missed that one stone he would probably have left the place after a week. Now he would go on through days and days without finding another sparkle. I can conceive no occupation on earth more dreary, – hardly any more demoralizing than this of perpetually turning over dirt in quest of a peculiar little stone which may turn up once a week or may not.

Yet, despite his dislike of the diamond fields, Trollope was enthusiastic about the way the diamond industry, far more than the efforts of missionaries or philanthropists, he said, had brought 'civilization' to the black population. 'The work of civilizing as it has been carried out by simple philanthropy or by religion is terribly slow. One is tempted to say that nothing is done by religion and very little by philanthropy. But love of money works very fast.'

While the teaching of religion had never brought large numbers of blacks to adopt European ways, said Trollope, he was convinced that European habits would bring about religion. 'When I have looked down into the Kimberley mine and seen three or four thousand of them at work . . . I have felt that I was looking at three or four thousand growing Christians.'

It was for this reason, said Trollope, that he regarded Kimberley as 'one of the most interesting places on the face of the earth'.

Rhodes returned to Oxford in 1876, still harbouring ambitions of becoming a barrister. At the age of twenty-two, he was already wealthy, worth about £40,000, but believed that a professional qualification would give him greater standing and advance his career. 'On calmly reviewing last year,' he wrote to Rudd from Oriel College in 1876, 'I find we lost £3,000 owing to my having no profession. I lacked pluck on three occasions through fearing that one might lose and I had nothing to fall back on in the shape of a profession.' He referred specifically to missed opportunities at Dutoitspan and De Beer's. 'If I had not funked collapse,' he said, none of those failures would have occurred. 'You will find me a most perfect speculator if I have two years and obtain a profession. I am slightly too cautious now.'

During the seven terms that Rhodes spent at Oxford between 1876 and 1878, he made little impression. The Dean at Oriel, the Rev. Arthur Gray Butler, who became a friend and advisor, described his career at Oxford as 'uneventful' and recalled: 'He belonged to a set of men like himself, not caring for distinctions in the schools and not working for them, but of refined tastes, dining and living for the most part together, and doubtless discussing passing events in life and politics with interest and ability.'

He rarely attended lectures and tutorials, appearing to be easily distracted. A fellow student recalled that he carried diamonds in a little box in his waistcoat pocket. 'When he condescended to attend a lecture, which proved uninteresting to him, he pulled out his box and showed the gems to his friends, and then it was upset, and diamonds were scattered on the floor, and the lecturer looked up and asking what was the cause of the disturbance received the reply, "It is only

Rhodes and his diamonds.'" His frequent failure to attend lectures involved him in what he described as 'tremendous skirmishes' with Oriel's dons.

He was a more familiar figure among a group of wealthy bon vivants. He took up hunting and polo and joined the Bullingdon, a drinking club whose members enjoyed parading in the High Street with horsewhips and hunting cries on festive evenings. Another of his favourite pastimes was to attend horse races.

Nor did Rhodes make much effort to pursue a legal career. He paid fees to enrol at the Inner Temple in London and attended a number of dinners, but never sought any instruction in law. 'My law experiences, up to the present time,' he wrote in 1877, 'consist of eating dinners and the theatre.'

Indeed, his attention was more often focused on events in Kimberley than on gaining a professional qualification. He followed the fluctuating fortunes of the diamond trade with avid interest, keeping in close touch with Rudd by correspondence, offering him advice and encouragement. During a slump in 1876, he wrote: 'If bad times have got you in a mess, do not funk. They are temporary. Diamonds in themselves are more liked than ever, all the swells now wear them in preference to anything but the people hit in foreign loans have been as you can understand selling their houses and diamonds, dropping their carriages and horses in town.' He was nevertheless cautious about acquiring more claims or property. 'Do not plunge for much more at the Fields. We have sufficient block at De Beers to make a fortune if diamonds last and have enough property in Kimberley. If we make more money I would sooner say lend it or go in for a nest egg here at home.'

Rhodes returned to Kimberley during the long vacations of 1876 and 1877. He returned again in 1878, intending to stay for only six months, before completing his final term at Oxford, but he was soon caught up in a hectic bout of mining activity. The introduction of steam engines to cope with the growing depth of Kimberley mine had created boom conditions. 'Steam is rampant, and steam engines are *the* investment of the day,' reported the *Diamond News* in 1877. Diamond output and labour productivity grew by leaps and bounds. Even though diamonds fetched only two-thirds of the price they had in the early 1870s, profits soared. By 1879, the average rate of profit of private companies in Kimberley reached 30 per cent. The surge in profits set off a scramble for claims. By 1879, just twelve private companies or partnerships controlled three-quarters of Kimberley. The same process of consolidation occurred in De Beer's.

Combining with other claim-holders, the Rhodes–Rudd partnership built up a syndicate with the second-largest holding in De Beer's and set their sights on gaining control of the entire mine. Following the lead of the French Company in Kimberley mine, they launched a joint-stock company on 1 April 1880, naming it De Beers Mining Company.

Late one night, as he walked past the office of a German diamond merchant, Alfred Beit, and noticing he was still at work, Rhodes decided to look in on him.

'Hallo,' said Rhodes, 'do you never take a rest, Mr Beit?'

'Not often,' replied Beit.

'Well, what's your game?' asked Rhodes.

'I am going to control the whole diamond output before I am much older,' said Beit.

'That's funny,' said Rhodes. 'I have made up my mind to do the same.'

PART II

6

THE IMPERIAL FACTOR

While Kimberley's magnates were manoeuvring for advantage, Britain's imperial ambitions were also on the march. In 1874, a new Tory government led by Benjamin Disraeli had come to power with aims of extending the realms of the British empire and reversing the years of fiscal rectitude and frugality overseas pursued by the previous Gladstone administration. Disraeli proudly called himself 'an Imperialist' and appointed as colonial secretary a like-minded expansionist, the Earl of Carnarvon. Carnarvon's main preoccupation was imperial defence. He regarded the Cape and its naval facilities at Simon's Bay as being the most important link in the imperial network outside Britain itself, upon which the safety of the whole empire might one day depend. In the words of a Royal Commission on Colonial Defence chaired by Carnarvon, the Cape route was 'essential to the retention by Great Britain of her possessions in India, Mauritius, Ceylon, Singapore, China and even Australasia'. It needed to be 'maintained at all hazards and irrespective of cost'. Strategic considerations overrode financial concerns. Furthermore, the Cape provided a vital commercial link. Despite the opening of the Suez Canal in 1869, one seventh of all British trade annually passed the Cape. In the event of a war affecting the Mediterranean and the Suez Canal, the Cape route would become even more important.

What concerned Carnarvon was the chaotic character of the interior of southern Africa, which offered opportunities for other European powers to meddle and undermine British supremacy in the region. In sum, southern Africa consisted of three separate British colonies, two Boer republics and a troublesome assortment of African chiefdoms, notably the Xhosa, the Zulu, the Swazi, the Pedi, the Venda, the Tswana and the Sotho. It was an area of ill-defined borders where armed conflict appeared to be endemic. Carnarvon was alarmed in particular by the Transvaal's determined efforts to expand eastwards and gain access to the sea at Delagoa Bay, which would enable it to escape from commercial dependence on colonial ports and break away from British domination. He was adamant that the security of the Cape could not be assured unless Britain controlled the interior.

To forestall the Transvaal's moves, Britain claimed possession of Delagoa Bay for itself. But when the matter was put to arbitration, Britain lost to Portugal. The Transvaal meanwhile sought to involve other European powers. In 1875, President Thomas Burgers toured Europe in search of German and Dutch aid to build a railway joining Pretoria to Delagoa Bay. Carnarvon concluded that the sooner the Transvaal was incorporated into the British orbit the better.

As colonial secretary in a previous British administration, Carnarvon had gained the credit for launching Canada as a self-governing dominion by amalgamating seven independent provinces inhabited by French-speaking and English-speaking colonists with different traditions and mutual distrust; and he assumed that a similar feat could be accomplished in southern Africa. Carnarvon's plan was to construct a confederation of its disparate peoples that would serve as a bastion of the British empire and protect both its strategic and commercial interests.

The advantages of confederation, Carnavon told the cabinet, were 'very obvious'. It would encourage the flow of European immigration and capital; provide a more effective administration at less expense; and reduce the likelihood of demands for aid in the form of money or troops. Furthermore, it would assist the development of 'a uniform, wise and strong policy' towards 'the native question'. In sum, confederation would ensure a great leap forward.

Carnarvon found few willing accomplices in the region, however. There were too many old grievances, too much distrust. For the Boer republics, cooperation with Britain meant only '*die juk van Engeland*' – 'the yoke of England'. Carnarvon managed to cobble together a conference in London in August 1876 attended by a variety of delegates from southern Africa, but made no headway.

But just when the cause of confederation seemed hopeless, it was suddenly given new life by a dramatic turn of events in the Transvaal. A war that President Burgers launched against the Pedi leader, Sekhukhune, in the eastern Transvaal went badly awry. On 14 September 1876, the Colonial Office received a telegram from the British high commissioner in Cape Town, Sir Henry Barkly, warning of the Transvaal's imminent collapse.

Army of President totally routed[.] Deserters pouring into Pretoria[.] Sickakuni pursuing in force[.] Meeting at Landrosts office Lydenburg agreed to ask British government to take over Transvaal[.] Volksraad summoned fourth September[.] Am I to accept the proposed cession[?]

Burgers' decision to attack Sekhukhune carried high risks. The Transvaal was barely a functioning state. Its government was virtually bankrupt; its burghers refused to pay taxes; banks refused to approve any more advances; public officials went unpaid, and land pledged for public and private debt was unsaleable. The Transvaal possessed no army. Its security depended on a commando system that required widely dispersed farming settlements to provide volunteers, arms and ammunition. The reservoir of white manpower was limited: the total population of about 40,000 whites was scattered over a vast terrain, outnumbered at every turn by indigenous Africans and constantly worried about the possibility of a black alliance rising against them. At most, only about 8,000 men, mostly farmers, were available for military service.

President Burgers had come to office in 1872, aspiring to establish the Transvaal as a modern state. A liberal *predikant* from the Cape, educated in Utrecht in Holland and married to a Scots girl, he launched a number of ambitious schemes but lacked the means to implement them. He introduced a new code of laws but had few magistrates or courts to enforce them. He borrowed heavily hoping to build a railway link to Delagoa Bay incurring loan commitments at exorbitant rates of interest that ruined state finances. Moreover, Burgers soon clashed with conservative factions. His attempts to establish a secular system of education were attacked for 'taking the Bible out of schools'. When alluvial gold deposits were found in the Lydenburg district of the eastern Transvaal in 1873, he encouraged *uit-landers* (foreigners), mainly English-speaking prospectors, to settle there, awarding them two seats in the Volksraad; one of the seats was taken up by Herbert Rhodes, Cecil's brother. To capitalise on the gold discoveries, Burgers had gold sovereigns struck bearing an image of himself, causing further outrage among conservatives.

His efforts at reform, furthermore, were overshadowed by a series of prolonged disputes over land, labour and taxation with Sekhukhune's Pedi state, the most powerful chiefdom in the Transvaal region. Sekhukhune's army was fully equipped with guns purchased by Pedi migrant labourers with earnings from the diamond fields of Griqualand. His capital at Tsate in the Leolu mountains was heavily fortified. Nevertheless, responding to clamour from eastern Transvaal settlers for action against Sekhukhune, the Volksraad voted for war. Aware of the risks, Burgers assembled the largest expeditionary force the Transvaal had ever mobilised – 2,000 burghers, 2,400 Swazi warriors and 600 Transvaal African auxiliaries – and led it into the field himself, wearing a top hat and presidential sash.

Burgers' campaign soon disintegrated. From the outset, morale amongst the burghers was low. The bulk came from commandos outside eastern Transvaal – from Pretoria, Potchefstroom and Rustenberg – areas facing their own problems. Within days, the Swazi contingent deserted, complaining of the lack of burgher support. An initial attack on the Pedi capital quickly collapsed and burghers refused to advance further. 'We are all entirely unwilling to storm Secoecoeni's Mountain for the reason that we see no chance of safeguarding our lives or of conquering the kaffer,' they declared in a petition. As the commandos streamed home, Burgers was obliged to leave the campaign in the hands of a mercenary force – the Lydenburg Volunteers – recruited from 'very rough characters' from the diamond fields and the gold fields with promises of pay, booty and land. Its first commander was the German officer Conrad von Schlickmann, who had participated in the Black Flag revolt in Kimberley; after his death, the Irish republican Alfred Aylward, also of Kimberley fame, was chosen as commander. The Lydenburg Volunteers were soon notorious for atrocities against the black civilian population.

News of the Boer retreat, though not in fact as dramatic as described in Barkly's telegram, galvanised Carnarvon into action. He immediately scribbled a note to Disraeli seeking permission to take control of the Transvaal. 'My hope is that by acting at once we may prevent war [over southern Africa] & acquire at a stroke the whole of the Transvaal republic after which the Orange Free State must soon follow and the whole policy in S. Africa for wh. we have been labouring fully and completely justified,' he said.

With Disraeli's approval – 'Do what you think wisest' – Carnarvon appointed Sir Theophilus Shepstone to act as special commissioner to the Transvaal. Ostensibly, Shepstone's remit was to report on the state of affairs there and to assess the threat that native wars posed to British territories in southern Africa. In secret, he was given instructions to annex the Transvaal if 'a sufficient number' of its residents were willing, or even if they were not willing, and to install himself as the first British governor.

For thirty years, Shepstone had served as a Natal administrator, first as Diplomatic Agent to Native Tribes then as secretary for native affairs, exercising a paternal overlordship over Natal's Nguni population. An austere, secretive man, the son of a Wesleyan missionary who landed in the Cape with 1820 Settlers, he was regarded as the foremost authority on the Zulu and a general expert on African matters, fluent in several Nguni dialects. He was known by the Zulu honorific of Somtseu meaning 'Father of the Nation'. Though he had less experience of dealing with the truculent Boers of the Transvaal, Carnarvon regarded him, according to Disraeli, as 'heaven-born for the object in view'. He was a committed imperialist, keen to extend British paramountcy to the highveld and convinced of the merits of Carnarvon's confederation scheme. Knowing his views, Carnarvon had invited Shepstone to attend the London conference, hoping his involvement would help boost the case for confederation, and had arranged for him to receive a knighthood while there. Now he was despatched back to southern Africa in haste, leaving on 23 September, having no time 'to say goodbye to any one'. To support Shepstone on his mission, Carnarvon promised a battalion of troops would be sent from Britain under the guise of relieving a regiment already stationed in the Cape.

To underpin the whole operation, Carnarvon prevailed upon Sir Bartle Frere, one of the empire's elder statesmen, to take up the post of high commissioner and governor of the Cape, giving him greatly increased powers. Frere's distinguished career included forty-one years of service in India; he had also led a successful mission to Zanzibar to persuade the Sultan to ban the slave trade. He was a personal friend of the royal family, a Privy Councillor, a former president of the Royal Geographical Society and a fervent evangelical Christian. Though he knew next to nothing about southern Africa and had no experience of dealing with pugnacious white colonists, he shared Carnarvon's vision of pushing forward the frontiers of empire, admired Carnarvon for his feat in uniting the Canadian states in a single dominion, and believed firmly in the goal of establishing a southern African confederation under British control.

Carnarvon provided Frere with a wide remit. He proposed that Frere should go out to the Cape 'nominally as Governor, but really as the Statesman who seems to me most capable of carrying my scheme of Confederation into effect'. Frere's reward was to be appointed the first governor-general of a new British dominion.

But Carnarvon's ambition did not stop there. He began to fashion the idea of a 'Cape to Cairo' policy, envisaging even greater swathes of Africa coming under British control, out of reach of other European powers. In a letter to Frere on 12 December 1876, he wrote:

I should not like anyone to come too near us either on the South towards the Transvaal, which must be ours; or on the North too near to Egypt and the country which belongs to Egypt.

In fact when I speak of geographical limits I am not expressing my real opinion. We cannot admit rivals in the East or even the central parts of Africa: and I do not see why, looking to the experience that we have now of English life within the tropics – the Zambesi should be considered to be without the range of our colonisation.

On 15 December 1876, Sir Theophilus Shepstone, accompanied by an escort of twenty-five troopers from the Natal Mounted Police, a small band of officials and an assortment of African grooms and servants, set out from the Natal capital of Pietermaritzburg, heading for the Transvaal highveld. His staff included Melmoth Osborn, Captain Marshal Clarke and a 20-year-old junior official, Rider Haggard. Haggard's venture into the African interior was to provide him with a wealth of material for his novels *King Solomon's Mines*, *She* and *Allan Quatermain*.

Their journey to Pretoria was conducted at a leisurely pace. In his autobiography, *The Days of My Life*, Haggard recalled spending 'moonlit nights of surpassing brilliancy' sitting around a roaring camp fire, listening to tales of 'savage Africa', many of them told by Shepstone himself. Though Shepstone had the reputation of being a saturnine figure, silent and self-contained, Haggard found him more approachable. 'He had the power of silence, but he observed everything and forgot little. To me, however, when the mood was on him, he would talk a great deal.'

Among the servants was Umslopogaas, Shepstone's head attendant, a son of the Swazi king, who made several appearances in Haggard's novels. Describing him in *The Days of My Life*, Haggard wrote: 'He was a tall, thin, fierce-faced fellow with a great hole above the left temple over which the skin pulsated, that he had come by in some battle. He said that he had killed ten men in single combat . . . always making use of a battle-axe!'

On 27 January 1877, Shepstone and his party arrived in Pretoria. The Boer capital had begun its existence in 1854 as a *kerkplaas*, a place where a travelling *dominee* (priest) called at intervals to offici-ate at weddings and baptisms. It was still little more than a village, with a white population of only 2,000, notable for its simple cot-tages surrounded by gardens full of roses, willow trees and rows of vegetables. An avenue of blue gum trees led into the town from the south. At the centre was Church Square around which stood the Dutch Reformed Church and public buildings. It was here every three months that far-flung farming families and local residents would gather for *nagmaal*, a religious and social event when babies were baptised, marriages were celebrated and the square was clut-tered with market stalls, tents and wagons. On the south side of the square stood the Raadsaal, a simple, single-storeyed thatched build-ing where parliament assembled.

Visiting Pretoria in 1877, Anthony Trollope recorded its charm but also noticed 'a certain flavour of untidiness':

> Brandy bottles and sardine boxes meet the eye everywhere. Tins in which pickled good things have been conveyed accumulate themselves at the corners. The straw receptacles in which wine is nowadays conveyed meet the eye constantly, as do paper shirt-collars, rags, old boots, and fragments of wooden cases. There are no dust holes and no scavengers, and all the unseemly relics of a hungry and thirsty race of pioneers are left open to inspection.
>
> And yet in spite of the mud, in spite of the brandy bottles, in spite of the ubiquitous rags, Pretoria is both picturesque and promising.

To Shepstone's relief, he was given a cordial reception. The arrival of the British was seen as a welcome defence against the possibility of an attack by Sekhukhune's army. Moreover, the British affirmed publicly that they intended to respect the Transvaal's independence. In discus-sions between the two sides, however, it soon became evident that Shepstone was bent on annexation. Though British citizens living in towns like Pretoria, numbering in all about 5,000, welcomed the prospect of British rule, opposition to the British presence among the Boer population began to grow.

A further complication arose when reports reached Pretoria claiming that on 16 February Sekhukhune had signed a peace treaty with the Boers, thus removing the threat of war that was the main justification for British intervention. According to Pretoria's negotiators, Sekhukhune had agreed to become a subject of the Transvaal state and submit to its laws, and had signed a document to that effect. The following week, however, a German missionary involved in the peace negotiations, Alexander Merensky, sent a letter to Shepstone denying that a peace treaty had been signed and insisting that there were still areas of dispute; Sekhukhune, he said, had specifically refused to become a Transvaal subject. Accompanying Merensky's letter was a note from Sekhukhune addressed directly to Shepstone: 'I beg you, Chief, come help me, the Boers are killing me and I don't know the reasons why they should be angry with me.'

To ascertain the facts, Burgers and Shepstone agreed to despatch a commission to Sekhukhune's territory, consisting of two representatives of the Transvaal government and two from Shepstone's staff. Osborn and Clarke were selected; Haggard was chosen as secretary.

Riding in the heat of summer, Haggard's small party made their way through the 'fever country' of the eastern Transvaal, reaching Sekhukhune's mountain stronghold at Tsate on 27 March. 'It was an uncanny kind of place,' wrote Haggard. 'If you got up at night, if you moved anywhere, you became aware that dozens or hundreds of eyes were watching you.' After a restless night, they were taken to meet Sekhukhune, 'a man of middle age with twinkling black eyes and a flat nose, very repulsive to look on'. As Haggard sat on a log taking notes, Sekhukhune dismissed the treaty as a fraud. 'I will not stand under the law. I am unwilling to pay taxes. I have to live by my people and any tax payable by them should come to me as their chief.'

Back in Pretoria, meanwhile, Shepstone manoeuvred to deliver the *coup de grâce*. He brushed aside a Volksraad resolution angrily rejecting annexation and claimed in a letter to Carnarvon in March that he had received petitions from 2,500 residents supporting annexation. 'To this number must be added many who were prevented from signing by the terrorism that is exercised in some districts, and especially in Pretoria.' He further claimed that a million natives 'placed like a dark fringe round a widely spread white population' resented Boer rule. Moreover, not only did Sekhukhune still pose a threat to the republic, but the Zulu king, Cetshwayo, 'is known to entertain a great antipathy towards this State'. Cetshwayo was keen, said Shepstone, to 'wash his spears' in white blood. In discussion with Burgers and his officials, Shepstone raised the spectre of a Zulu invasion.

On 9 April, Shepstone informed Burgers that he intended to annex the Transvaal, whereupon Burgers informed Shepstone that he intended to issue a public protest. Two days later, at eleven in the morning, a group of eight British officials assembled in Church Square amid the jumble of oxen and ox-wagons to announce the decision, nervous about the reaction that might come. 'In a country so full of desperadoes and fanatical haters of anything English,' wrote Haggard, 'it was more than possible that . . . a number of men could easily be found who would think they were doing a righteous act in greeting the "annexationists" with an ovation of bullets.'

Putting on his spectacles, Melmoth Osborn, secretary to the mission, proceeded to read Shepstone's proclamation, listing a host of reasons for annexation: the country was bankrupt; commerce was destroyed; the white inhabitants were divided into factions; the government had fallen into paralysis; 'neighbouring native powers' were tempted to intervene.

> And whereas the ravaging of an adjoining friendly State by warlike savage tribes cannot for a moment be contemplated by Her Majesty's Government without the most earnest and painful solicitude . . .

Osborn's voice faltered and his hands trembled so violently that Rider Haggard had to take the printed text from him and continue reading the proclamation.

> And whereas I have been satisfied by numerous addresses, cere-

monials and letters . . . that a large proportion of the inhabitants of the Transvaal see . . . the ruined condition of the country . . . and therefore earnestly desire the establishment within and over it of Her Majesty's authority and rule . . .

A small crowd, mostly English, gave a few cheers and the officials, breathing a sigh of relief, departed. There was no flag-raising ceremony to mark this latest acquisition of the British empire. Shepstone thought it prudent to await the arrival of British troops from Natal.

Immediately afterwards, Burgers' counter-proclamation was read out in Church Square by a member of the executive council. To avoid violence, he declared, the Transvaal government had agreed under protest to submit to British rule. He advised burghers to remain calm. Addressing his officials in the Volksraad Zaal, he told them: 'We bow only to the superior power. We submit because we cannot successfully draw the sword against this superior power, because by doing so we could only plunge the country into deeper miseries and disasters.'

Promised a pension by Shepstone, Burgers left the Transvaal by ox-wagon, complaining bitterly that during his term of office he had been 'driven almost to despair by betrayal and corruption on all sides, ruined in my private estate as well as in health'.

7

OOM PAUL

Though the Transvaal's Boers accepted British rule in 1877 without resistance, Boer resentment at the arbitrary annexation of
their republic ran deep. The Transvaal had been founded by trekboers
determined to break away from British control and to regulate their
own affairs. One of their principal grievances in the Cape Colony had
been what they called *gelykstelling*, the social levelling between whites
and blacks which they claimed that Britain supported. The constitution they drew up in 1858 declared: 'The people are not prepared to
allow any equality of the non-white with the white inhabitants, either
in Church or State.' Now British rule had been imposed on them
once more, uninvited and unwanted, bringing the same agenda of
reform.

The key figure in organising resistance was Paul Kruger. A legendary commando leader, tall and broad-shouldered, Kruger
epitomised the stubborn, resilient and resourceful character of the
trekboers. Born in 1825 on a farm at Bulhoek on the northern frontier of the Cape Colony, he had been taught the Bible but otherwise
his formal education had been limited to a course of instruction, lasting three months, given by an itinerant tutor in a schoolroom built of
grass and reeds. He became instead a master of the frontier crafts – an
expert hunter, horseman and guerrilla fighter. At the age of ten, he

trekked northwards with his family joining an emigrant group led by
Hendrik Potgieter, a wealthy frontier farmer overtly hostile to British
rule. Six months later, he witnessed the battle of Vegkop where 4,000
Ndebele warriors stormed Potgieter's laager, a fortress of fifty wagons
drawn up in squares, chained together and secured with leather
thongs. Along with his family, he followed Potgieter's group to
Natalia, experiencing the shock of the murder in 1838 of Piet Retief's
party at the hands of the Zulu king Dingane and the subsequent massacre of trekker families at Weenen by Zulu impis. Returning to the
highveld, Kruger participated in Potgieter's expedition against the
Ndebele chief, Mzilikazi, in the Magaliesberg area of the western
Transvaal. And it was there, at the foot of the Magaliesberg hills, that
he and his father Caspar decided to settle.

In accordance with Boer tradition, on reaching the age of sixteen,
Paul Kruger was entitled to choose two 6,000-acre farms, one for
grazing and one for growing crops. His main residence became his
farm at Waterkloof near Rustenburg, but he also spent much time
hunting, making many narrow escapes. At the age of twenty, while
hunting rhinoceros along the Steelpoort River, near Sekhukhune's
capital, his heavy old four-pounder elephant gun blew up in his hand.
Bleeding profusely, he treated the wound with turpentine and cut
away the remnants of his thumb with a jack-knife. When gangrene set
in, he tried an old Boer remedy, plunging his hand into the warm
stomach of a goat. The wound took six months to heal.

His first wife and their baby died of fever. His second wife, Gezina,
whom he married in 1847, bore him nine sons and seven daughters.
For a period of twenty years, he mixed farming with fighting, taking
part in nine major campaigns against African chiefdoms, rising to the
rank of the Transvaal's commandant-general. In 1852 he participated
in the commando raid on the Kwena stronghold at Kolobeng when
David Livingstone's house was destroyed, along with his medical
equipment and library. Away at the time, Livingstone accused the
Magaliesberg Boers of atrocities; they accused him of supplying arms
and ammunition to the Kwena.

Kruger also featured increasingly in the Transvaal's political affairs.
He was present at the signing of the Sand River Convention in 1852

when the British government recognised the Transvaal's independence, and participated as a member of the commission set up to devise a Transvaal constitution. He helped to resolve factional disputes between the Transvaal and the Orange Free State and to negotiate a settlement between the Basotho king, Moshoeshoe, and the Free State. He retired as commandant-general in 1873, a respected elder commonly referred to as Oom Paul – Uncle Paul – and went to live in a new homestead built on his farm at Boekenhoutfontein.

His guide throughout his life, he maintained, was God and the Bible. He never read any book other than the Bible, knowing much of it by heart. He was convinced of the literal truth of biblical texts and constantly referred to them when making decisions and in everyday life. To Kruger, the earth was flat because of what the Bible said. So sure was he that the earth was flat that when an American traveller was introduced to him as being on a voyage around the world, Kruger retorted: 'You don't mean round the world . . . It is impossible! You mean *in* the world.' In many ways, he resembled a seventeenth-century zealot rather than a nineteenth-century politician.

He belonged to the 'Dopper' Church, the *Gereformeerde Kerk van Suid-Afrika*, the smallest and most conservative of the Dutch Reformed churches in southern Africa, whose members saw themselves as closer to God than other groups and believed they possessed a special understanding of God's purpose. They were known as Doppers, it was said, because they believed in extinguishing the light of the Enlightenment, the Dutch word *domper* meaning an extinguisher.

Kruger himself played a leading role in breaking away from the Transvaal's main church, the *Nederduits Hervormde Kerk*, to establish the Dopper Church. Together with a few like-minded colleagues, he recruited a new minister from the *Christelike Afgescheiden Gereformeerde Kerk* in Holland, a splinter group which had seceded from the state church in 1834, rejecting its liberal theology and its evangelical emphasis on personal devotion and experience. Shortly after the minister's arrival in the Transvaal in 1858, Kruger joined other dissidents in denouncing the *Nederduits Hervormde Kerk* as a 'deluded' and 'false' church and left.

The core of Dopper theology, based almost exclusively on the Old Testament, was the Calvinist conception of the sovereignty of God in every aspect of life and acceptance of the Bible as the only source of belief and practice. Its followers preached a gospel of an omnipotent God who intervened directly in the lives of individuals and communities; they upheld the doctrine of predestination; and they believed in the notion of the Elect, of a people chosen by God. They exerted strict control over the moral behaviour of their members; to fail God knowingly was to leave oneself and one's nation liable to punishment. To be certain that only God's pure word was heard, they forbade the singing of hymns; the Psalms were considered proper texts but the rest were 'man-made'. They also rejected the use of church organs and frivolities such as dancing. Their manner of dress was unique: objecting to long coats, men wore short jackets and broad-brimmed hats with wide trousers pinched up at the back; women always wore hoods or bonnets with their hair behind their ears. Outside their own circles, the term 'Dopper' was synonymous with extreme conservatism and uncouth manners.

When the liberal Cape *predikant* Thomas Burgers was elected as the Transvaal's president in 1872, a group of Doppers was so appalled that a 'Godless' person had become head of state that they decided to emigrate, choosing Damaraland and Ovamboland in south-west Africa as suitable destinations. Kruger was asked to lead the exodus, but declined. Many subsequently perished trying to cross the Kalahari desert in what was later called the Thirstland Trek. Among the victims was Kruger's stepmother.

When Burgers decided to go to war with Sekhukhune in 1876, he asked Kruger to come out of retirement to join the expedition. But Kruger refused. 'I cannot lead the commando if you come,' Kruger replied, according to his memoirs, 'for, with your merry evenings in laager and your Sunday dances, the enemy will even shoot me behind the wall, for God's blessing will not rest on your expedition.'

Kruger blamed the failure of the Pedi campaign and all the other ills affecting the Transvaal on Burgers' leadership, using customary biblical references:

How is this regression to be explained? The word of God gives us the key to it. Look to the case of Israel; if the people have a devout King, everything is prosperous; but under an ungodly ruler the land goes backward and all the people must suffer thereby. Read Leviticus 26 with attention and see how literally its words have been fulfilled. In the days of the voortrekkers, a handful of people put thousands of Kaffirs to flight . . . But see how when Burgers is President – he knows no Sabbath; he rides through every part of the country on Sundays; of Church and religion he knows nothing (Leviticus 26.17).

With similar fervour, Kruger attacked the coming of the British, telling Shepstone that he would never consent to annexation. 'I was bound by my oath to uphold the independence of the Republic.'

From the outset of their dealings with him, the British underestimated Kruger. They regarded him as an uneducated, ill-mannered backveld peasant steeped in bigotry – a *takhaar*, to use the Afrikaans word. They were particularly struck by his ugliness, mentioning it so often that it became shorthand for his whole personality, and, indeed, his objectives. In middle age, his face had coarsened; baggy pouches had begun to appear under his eyes; his nose had broadened; his mouth seemed set in grim disapproval; his hair, parted on the left and neatly slicked down, was turning grey. His broad shoulders showed a slight sag. His Dopper dress – a short-cut black jacket, baggy trousers and black hat – gave him a rather quaint appearance. His body and clothes reeked of the odour of Magaliesberg tobacco, a weed so potent that younger men blanched when he offered them his pouch. Added to this was his habit, so disagreeable to the English, of spitting profusely.

In one of the first descriptions of Kruger sent by British officials from Pretoria, Shepstone's legal adviser, W. Morcom, wrote in February 1877: 'Paul Kruger is an elderly man, decidedly ugly, with a countenance denoting extreme obstinacy, and also great cruelty.' He went on:

His conduct at the public luncheon on Tuesday was as the Belgian consul described it 'gigantically horrible'. His dirty wooden pipe was visible, for it stuck out of his breast pocket; his scanty hair was in such a condition of greasiness that it lay in streaks across his head, the drops of rancid cocoanut oil gathering at the ends of each streak of hair, and thus rendering necessary the use of the pocket comb during lunch. The napkin was turned to strange use during lunch.

A more perceptive assessment was made by Sir Bartle Frere, the new high commissioner in southern Africa: 'I am assured by those who know him well that he is a very shrewd fellow who veils under an assumed clownish manner and affectation of ignorance, considerable ability, that he has great natural eloquence and powers of persuasion.' Frere concluded, however: 'There is nothing in what is visible to a stranger to indicate a possible regenerator of the Transvaal.'

Kruger's first tactic was to try to persuade the British government to hold a plebiscite testing Shepstone's claim that a majority of whites favoured annexation. In May 1877 he set off for England at the head of a three-man delegation, travelling by coach to Bloemfontein, then to Kimberley, then to Worcester where he boarded a train for the first time in his life for the journey to Cape Town. The sea voyage to Plymouth took twenty-six days.

His meetings with Carnarvon at the Colonial Office were cordial but fruitless. 'I should only be misleading you,' Carnarvon told him at their first encounter in July, 'if I were to hold out to you the slightest expectation that the policy which has been adopted could now be altered, or that the annexation of the Transvaal could be undone.' At their second encounter, when Kruger pressed the case for a plebiscite, Carnarvon replied that it was 'impossible' and would call into question 'the act which Sir Theophilus Shepstone did with the sanction of the Queen and in her Name'. At their third encounter, the same barren exchange was repeated. Outside their formal sessions, Carnarvon invited Kruger and his associates to lunch at his family seat at Highclere near Newbury. Kruger was in a grumpy mood and only cheered up when he was shown the horses and stables.

By the time he returned to the Transvaal in November, the groundswell of Boer opposition to British rule had gained considerable momentum. Britain's action in annexing the Transvaal had united a collection of squabbling Boer factions, hitherto preoccupied with church and family, in a common cause to defeat the British. Kruger himself, having spent several months at 'enemy' headquarters, was initially suspected of succumbing to British bribes and had to manoeuvre deftly to gain leadership of the resistance. In January 1878, accompanied by an escort of armed horsemen, Kruger rode into the centre of Pretoria to address a mass meeting. The mood was rebellious. When Kruger related how Carnarvon had told him that he had no intention of revoking annexation, one old Boer warrior, Henning Pretorius, rose to declare, 'Rather than submit to the English, I will give my blood for the country.' But Kruger called for patience. He proposed that delegates should gather support for a petition asking Carnarvon to 'restore us our country' with the warning that it was 'the last means to obtain our end by peaceable means'. In a letter to Melmoth Osborn written from Boekenhoutfontein he pledged: 'In case the majority should be for annexation I have openly stated that I am prepared to stoop under and obey the authority of the Queen of England.' He expressed his hope for a peaceful outcome. Although there was popular agitation for action, he said, 'it appears to me that I shall succeed to convince my countrymen to reach their independence by a peaceful course'. By April 1878, Kruger's supporters had collected 157 petitions with more than 7,000 signatures; a total of 587 were in favour of annexation; 6,591 were against.

Armed with this result, Kruger made a second trip to London in June 1878. His discussions with the new colonial secretary, Sir Michael Hicks Beach, however, were just as fruitless as they had been with Carnarvon. The most the British were willing to offer him was a form of self-rule similar to that enjoyed by the Cape Colony. Kruger later described the offer to his supporters. 'I will try to explain to you what this self-government, in my opinion, means. They say to you, "First put your head quietly in the noose, so that I can hang you up: then you may kick your legs about as much as you please!" That is what they call self-government.'

The highlight of Kruger's second visit to London came when an Englishman presented him with a gold ring engraved with the words:

'Take courage, your cause is just and must triumph in the end.' Kruger wore the ring for the rest of his life.

Meanwhile the wave of anger over Britain's annexation of the Transvaal spread further afield to the Boer communities of the Orange Free State and the Cape Colony, stimulating old grievances. In the Free State there was lingering resentment over the way the British had intervened in 1868 to annex Basutoland in response to Moshoeshoe's plea for help, just as it was about to be overrun by their own commandos; there had been further outrage when the British snatched the diamond fields of Griqualand from its grasp in 1871. The Free State now found itself surrounded by British-run territories, imperilling its own independence. Members of the Volksraad spoke up in favour of returning the Transvaal to Boer rule.

In the Cape, it gave a huge boost to a nascent cultural and political movement led by Boer intellectuals calling themselves Afrikaners. In Paarl, a small market town thirty-five miles from Cape Town, a Dutch Reformed Church minister, Stephanus du Toit, joined several associates in 1875 to found a society named *Die Genootskap Van Regte Afrikaners* – the Fellowship of True Afrikaners – dedicated to promoting the use of Afrikaans, a colloquial language commonly used in Boer farming communities throughout southern Africa. It had diverged from Dutch over the years, changing vowel sounds, adopting simplified syntax and incorporating loan words from languages that were spoken by slaves in the Cape in the seventeenth century – Malay, Portuguese creole and Khoikhoi. It was the language used between masters and servants and amongst the poorer sections of the Boer community. Upper and middle-class Boers, particularly those living in the western Cape, spoke 'High Dutch', the language of the church and the Bible, and regarded the *Zuid-Afrikaansche taal* with disdain, dismissing it as *Hotnotstaal*, a 'Hottentot' language, or a *kombuistaal* – a kitchen language. They also used English to a considerable extent, the only official language of the Colony and thus the language of commerce, law, administration and – increasingly – culture.

What Du Toit and his colleagues feared and resented most was the growing cultural domination of the British colonial regime, aided and abetted by Boers themselves. In a lecture given in 1876, the chief justice, Sir Henry de Villiers, described Afrikaans as being 'poor in the number of its words, weak in its inflections, wanting in accuracy of meaning and incapable of expressing ideas connected with the higher spheres of thought'. The energy of colonists, he said, would be far better spent in appropriating English, 'that rich and glorious language', that ultimately would become 'the language of South Africa'. Du Toit argued that a mother tongue was a person's most precious possession: 'The language of a nation expresses the character of that nation. Deprive a nation of the vehicle of its thoughts and you deprive it of the wisdom of its ancestors.' He wanted to develop Afrikaans as a *landstaal* – a national language.

To spell out this message, in 1876 Du Toit launched *Di Afrikaanse Patriot*, the first newspaper to use an early form of Afrikaans. The following year he was the main author of a history entitled *Die Geskiedenis van Ons Land in die Taal van Ons Volk – The History of Our Land in the Language of Our People*. It was the first book to treat all Afrikaners, dispersed as they were among British colonies and independent republics, as a distinct people, occupying a distinct fatherland; and it linked them to a common destiny endowed by God: to rule over southern Africa and civilise its heathen inhabitants.

The book marked the beginning of a new historiography that would eventually take hold of Afrikanerdom, portraying Afrikaners as a valiant nation wrongfully oppressed by decades of British rule. On page one, it stated: 'In this way we can see that the English have been scoundrels from the earliest times.' In what was to become a standard interpretation of Afrikaner history, one episode after another from the past was cited as evidence of British oppression, starting from the moment the British took possession of the Cape in 1806. The exodus of emigrant farmers from the Cape in the 1830s now became known as the Great Trek, a defiant gesture against imperial Britain on behalf of the Boer nation. The emigrants were now called *voortrekkers*, pioneers endowed with heroic qualities, steadfast in their determination to protect Afrikaner freedom and solidarity, guided by a deeply religious sense of purpose, and courageously heading into the unknown interior only to find the British in relentless pursuit. In their quest for supremacy, the British had annexed the first Boer state, the Republic of Natalia; then they had seized the diamond fields of the Free State.

Such ideas had limited circulation. A leading Cape Afrikaner editor, Jan Hofmeyr, wrote in 1876 that 'the men of the *Patriot* were waging a hopeless battle'. But Britain's annexation of the Transvaal, riding roughshod over the pleas of its Boer inhabitants, seemed to confirm their validity and gave them new impetus. 'The annexation of the Transvaal has had its good side,' wrote Jan Hofmeyr. 'It has taught the people of South Africa that blood is thicker than water. It has filled the Africanders, otherwise grovelling in the mud of materialism, with a national glow of sympathy for their brothers across the Vaal, which we look upon as one of the most hopeful signs of the future.'

What the British action had set in motion were the stirrings of a nationalist movement.

The trouble mounting for the British in the Transvaal was aggravated by a weak and incompetent administration there. Shepstone was given few staff and limited funds for reviving it from bankruptcy. When congratulating Shepstone on annexation in a despatch from London in May 1877, Carnarvon reminded him of the need for fiscal restraint:

> I know that you must somehow have the means to pay your way and to carry on Govt. effectively, and no economy would be so unwise as one which would involve a real risk of misrule and of fresh disorder: but I need not remind you how very desirable it is not to come upon Imperial assistance in point of money more than is necessary. Your object must be to bear in mind these two opposite considerations – effective government and economy.

What made matters infinitely worse was that Shepstone turned out to be, in the words of an official report, 'an execrably bad manager'. He soon used up a grant of £100,000 in paying out large sums to burghers who lodged claims against the state, many of them bogus. After but six months of British rule the financial affairs of the Transvaal were in such a state of chaos that years afterwards Treasury officials were still vainly trying to discover in what manner and to what ends Shepstone had spent much of his money. 'A colony that had been annexed because it was bankrupt was permitted to sink into a still more inexcusable bankruptcy,' wrote the eminent historian Cornelis de Kiewiet.

British officials conceded meanwhile that there was 'no visible government', nor any form of representation. The Volksraad building was used as an English club. To compound Shepstone's difficulties, a campaign launched in 1878 to force Sekhukhune into submission ended in stalemate. Shepstone became so unpopular with Transvaalers that in August 1878 Frere asked for him to be recalled and replaced by another official.

Thus, on his return home in December 1878, after an absence of six months, Kruger found the Boer mood even more belligerent. At a meeting at Wonderfontein in the Potchefstroom district on 10 January 1879, a crowd of several thousand burghers turned up to listen to Kruger give an account of his travels. Many there favoured war. 'Mr Kruger,' one burgher declared, 'We have been talking long enough; you must now let us shoot the English.' But Kruger argued that the time was not yet ripe; for one thing, there was a serious shortage of arms and ammunition.

Twelve days later, British forces in neighbouring Zululand suffered a catastrophic military defeat.

8

THE WASHING OF SPEARS

Surveying his southern African domain on his arrival at Government House in Cape Town in March 1877, Britain's new high commissioner, Sir Bartle Frere, felt confident that he was within reach of establishing a new British dominion. It was to be the crowning glory of his illustrious career. The outlook seemed auspicious. The Cape Colony in the 1870s was enjoying increased prosperity, driven in large part by the boom of the diamond industry in Griqualand West; investment in railways, harbours and roads grew apace. The white population reached 250,000. The ambitions of the Cape, moreover, largely coincided with the objectives of imperial Britain. Cape politicians advocated the expansion of Cape influence in southern Africa as a means of ensuring law, order and development. During the 1870s, the Cape government took on administrative responsibility for Basutoland and much of the Transkei territories lying between the Cape and Natal. Despite differences over the merits of confederation, the Cape was regarded as a reliable ally in working for British supremacy in the region.

But to Frere's frustration, he was soon diverted by a series of African revolts erupting over the steady encroachment of white rule and its many manifestations – magistrates, missionaries, farmers, labour agents, taxation and land-grabbing. Instead of stamping his authority on the region as he had intended, Frere discovered the outer reaches of his realm were under threat.

In September 1877, in what marked the start of the ninth Xhosa war, Gcaleka Xhosa attacked a Cape police post. They were joined later by Ngqika Xhosa based in the Cape. It took colonial forces and British reinforcements seven months to suppress the revolt, at a cost of £1.75 million. In February 1878, there was a rising by Griqua in Griqualand East. This was followed by a Griqua rebellion in Griqualand West that spread to aggrieved Khoikhoi, Tlhaping and Kora groups, affecting most areas of the Colony as well as territories to the north and west of it.

Frere interpreted this tide of events as a 'general and simultaneous rising of Kaffirdom against white civilisation' that blocked the way to confederation and needed to be stamped out altogether. Along with his Cape officials, he took the view that as long as independent African chiefdoms were allowed to exist, the danger of a 'black conspiracy' against white authority would be ever present. The most powerful of them all was Zululand. Once British forces − using new breech-loading Martini-Henry rifles − had suppressed the Xhosa rebellion, Frere set his sights on forcing Zululand into submission. In promoting this new strategy, he received the full support of his Transvaal consul, Sir Theophilus Shepstone, Britain's leading authority on the Zulu people.

For nearly fifty years, Zululand had functioned as a militarised state with a powerful army, wreaking havoc among neighbouring African chiefdoms during the 1820s and clashing with Boer trekkers during the 1830s. Although suffering a major defeat at the Ncome River in 1838, in a battle the Boers called Blood River, the Zulu army remained a formidable force; new age-regiments were regularly recruited, trained for close combat and stationed at barracks around the country. Every young Zulu was keen to 'wash his spear' in the blood of his enemies to prove his manhood. In internal disputes, mass slaughter and arbitrary executions were commonplace.

When Britain established the colony of Natal in 1843, the Zulu

king, Mpande, agreed to a border between Zululand and Natal running along the line of the Tugela and Buffalo Rivers. The border
remained relatively tranquil. Mpande sought to avoid direct confrontation with white power and established a cordial relationship
with Shepstone, Natal's secretary for native affairs.

On Zululand's north-west frontier with the Transvaal, however,
there was constant friction as Boer settlers infiltrated on to land the
British authorities recognised as Zulu territory. Rather than go to war,
Mpande ceded to the Boers in 1854 a wedge of fertile land between
the Buffalo and Blood Rivers that became known as the Utrecht district. But Boer farmers continued their infiltration further east into
adjacent areas on the north-west border, claiming yet more Zulu territory. Mpande repeatedly asked Shepstone for assistance in mediating
in the frontier struggle; in 1869 he even suggested the creation of a
'neutral' British buffer zone to halt Boer encroachments. Shepstone
supported the Zulu case; the British government was opposed to
Boer expansion, yet the dispute rumbled on with the threat of war
ever present.

When Mpande died in 1872, he was succeeded by his 40-year-old
son Cetshwayo, a tall, broad-chested man of regal bearing, with
immense thighs typical of the Zulu royal house. Troubled by internal
rivalry, Cetshwayo invited Shepstone to attend his 'coronation',
hoping that a show of British support would strengthen his hand.
Shepstone duly accepted, keen to use the opportunity to extend
British influence over Cetshwayo. He explained later: 'I felt bound,
representing as I did the Government of a civilised race, to take advantage of the opportunity by endeavouring to ameliorate the condition
of a people under one of the most oppressive despotisms in the world.'

Accompanied by an escort of 110 white troopers and 300 African
auxiliaries, Shepstone crossed into Zululand in August 1873. During
two days of discussion at a military kraal on the Mahlabathini Plain,
Shepstone found Cetshwayo to be a skilful negotiator:

Cetwayo is a man of considerable ability, much force of character, and has a dignified manner; in all conversations with him he
was remarkably frank and straightforward, and he ranks in every

respect far above any Native Chief I have ever had to do with. I do not think that his disposition is very warlike; even if it is, his obesity will impose prudence; but he is naturally proud of the military traditions of his family, especially the policy and deeds of his uncle and predecessor, Chaka, to which he made frequent reference. His sagacity enables him, however, to see clearly the bearing of the new circumstances by which he is surrounded, and the necessity for so adjusting his policy as to suit them.

Cetshwayo insisted that all Boer settlements below the Drakensberg, including the whole of the Utrecht district, rightfully belonged to Zululand. To prevent further Boer encroachment, he offered to cede all the disputed territory to the British. But Shepstone, knowing how such a move would antagonise the Boers, felt unable to accept.

Cetshwayo's coronation followed on 1 September. Shepstone opened the proceedings with an address in perfect Zulu to a large gathering of chiefs and councillors, setting out the terms of British support. These included an end to indiscriminate bloodshed and arbitrary execution. Then he led Cetshwayo into a marquee that British troops had erected and placed on his head a gaudy crown run up by the master tailor of the 75th Foot and on his shoulders a scarlet and gold mantle also provided by the British mission. Outside, a military band struck up and an artillery detachment fired a seventeen-gun salute.

When Britain took control of the Transvaal four years later, Cetshwayo assumed, in view of previous British pledges, that he would be able to regain lost territory. The border dispute by now had festered for sixteen years. During that time, while Boers had seized Zulu land and cattle, Shepstone had urged them to show moderation and restraint. They had duly complied. They had provided a full statement of their case in writing. Now Cetshwayo wanted the matter resolved.

Now the Transvaal is English ground, I want Somtseu to send the Boers away from the lower part of the Transvaal, that near my country. The Boers are a nation of liars; they are bad people, they lie, they claim what is not theirs, and ill-use my people.

But Shepstone proved to be a fickle friend. Once he had been installed as grand-overlord of the Transvaal highveld, he advocated 'a more thorough control of the Zulu Country', whether this was gained 'by means of annexation or otherwise'. He was more concerned to appease his disaffected Boer subjects than to pursue Zulu land claims.

Alarmed by talk of annexation, Cetshwayo became increasingly distrustful of Shepstone's intentions, telling a missionary: 'I love the English. I am not Mpande's son. I am the child of Queen Victoria. But I am also a king in my own country and must be treated as such. Somtseu must speak gently to me. I shall not hear dictation . . . I shall perish first.'

In October 1877, Shepstone attended an ill-tempered meeting with a Zulu delegation near the Blood River, infuriating them by suggesting a compromise with the Boers over the land issue. The meeting broke up in disarray. Livid that his authority should be challenged, Shepstone told London that the Zulu delegation had been 'exacting and unreasonable in their demands, and the tone they exhibited was very self-asserting, almost defiant and in every way unsatisfactory. At no moment during the whole interview was there apparent the smallest hope of any reasonable arrangement.'

Shepstone now turned against Cetshwayo with a vengeance. Insisting that he had come into possession of 'the most incontrovertible, overwhelming and clear evidence', never previously disclosed, he threw his weight into supporting Boer claims to the disputed territory and dismissed the Zulu case as 'characterised by lying and treachery to an extent that I could not have believed even savages capable of'.

In despatches to London, Shepstone railed against the disruptive effect of allowing Cetshwayo's regime to remain in place. 'Zulu power,' he said, 'is the root and real strength of all native difficulties in South Africa.' In December 1877, he told Carnarvon:

> Cetshwayo is the secret hope of every petty independent chief hundreds of miles from him who feels a desire that his colour shall prevail, and it will not be until this hope is destroyed that they will make up their minds to submit to the rule of civilization.

The outbreak of the Xhosa war in the Cape, he argued, had been inspired by the Zulu king. 'I am fully satisfied,' he told Frere in January 1878, 'that no permanent peace can be hoped for until the Zulu power has been broken up.' Frere, already convinced of the need for war, readily concurred. The overthrow of Cetshwayo, he believed, would be a salutary lesson for all African chiefdoms.

The British government had no objection to annexing Zululand at an appropriate moment, but was nervous that Shepstone's warmongering might lead to precipitate action before proper preparations had been made, and wanted to avoid war. To gain time, Britain authorised a boundary commission to investigate the dispute. In view of assurances that Shepstone had given about the rightful ownership of the disputed territory, Frere fully expected the boundary commission would find in favour of Boer claims and thus precipitate a Zulu uprising. But in July 1878, the boundary commission upheld Zulu claims. 'The evidence shows,' said their report, 'that this so-called "disputed territory" has never been occupied by the Boers, but has always been inhabited by the border clans, who have never moved their kraals, and that the only use ever made of the land by the Boers has been for grazing purposes, which in itself proves nothing.' The Transvaal government had never exercised any jurisdiction, civil or criminal, nor had it ever governed any of the natives resident on the land. It had never received taxes or land rent from the Zulu inhabitants and had never appointed a government official there. For five months after receiving the report, Frere delayed any announcement about its findings while he worked out another way to bring on a war.

Using the pretext that Natal was threatened by a Zulu invasion, Frere sent British troop reinforcements there from the Cape. Cetshwayo was quick to express his concern to British officials:

> I hear of troops arriving in Natal, that they are coming to attack the Zulus, and to seize me; in what have I done wrong that I should be seized like an 'Umtakata' [wrongdoer]? The English are my fathers, I do not wish to quarrel with them, but to live as I have always done, at peace with them.

Frere brushed aside such protestations and continued to talk up the danger of a Zulu invasion, claiming in his reports to the Colonial Office that Cetshwayo had 60,000 warriors under his command, ready to strike across the border; the people of Natal, he insisted, were 'slumbering on a volcano'.

Alarmed by his warnings, the British government authorised the despatch of two more British battalions to Natal, but still hoped that war could be avoided. The difficulty that British ministers faced was that they had no immediate means of controlling Frere. There was as yet no direct telegraph link to the Cape or Natal. The telegraph cable from London reached only as far as the Cape Verde islands; from there messages had to be carried to Cape Town by ship, taking at least sixteen days; letters and despatches spent up to a month en route from London. The time lag enabled Frere to argue that he needed to respond to events on the ground without waiting for government approval of every decision he made and provided him with an excuse to ignore government instructions altogether.

But in any case, neither Frere nor his army commander, Lord Chelmsford, expected anything more than a short, sharp action before Zulu resistance collapsed. Having recently thrashed the Xhosa, Chelmsford was in a confident mood. 'I am inclined to think,' Chelmsford wrote to a subordinate in November, 'that the first experience of the power of the Martini-Henrys will be such a surprise to the Zulus that they will not be formidable after the first effort.'

When Paul Kruger passed through Durban in December on his way back to the Transvaal from his second visit to London, Frere asked him whether he would be willing to join the campaign as an adviser, suggesting he could name his own reward. 'The independence of my country and people,' replied Kruger and turned down the request. Kruger nevertheless agreed to talk to Chelmsford about the best ways and means of waging war against the Zulus. He warned that whenever British forces set up camp they should form their wagons into a laager as the Boers were accustomed to do and send out scouts and spies to inform them of Zulu movements. It was advice that went unheeded.

The device that Frere used to provoke a war was an ultimatum he sent to Cetshwayo on 11 December incorporating demands that he knew were unacceptable. Frere told Cetshwayo to disband his army and abolish his military system, in effect to remove his principal source of power, or face the consequences. Cetshwayo was given thirty days to comply. To ensure that there was no interference from London, Frere delayed informing the Colonial Office about his ultimatum until it was too late for it to be countermanded. The full text of his demands did not reach London until 2 January 1879. By then, Chelmsford had assembled an army of 18,000 men – redcoats, colonial volunteers and Natal African auxiliaries – along the Zululand border, ready for invasion.

On 11 January, Chelmsford crossed the Buffalo River at Rorke's Drift, an old Irish trader's post that had become a mission station, placing himself in command of the main expeditionary force of 4,700 men, which included 1,900 white troops and 2,400 African auxiliaries. His intention was to advance along a wagon track that ran from Rorke's Drift to Cetshwayo's capital at Ondini, sixty miles to the east. As the track was in bad condition, he decided to set up an intermediate camp along the way. After making a personal reconnaissance of the area, he selected a site beneath a giant rocky outcrop called Isandlwana, twelve miles from Rorke's Drift, shrugging off the misgivings of several members of his staff. No trenches or any other kind of defences were built around the camp because Chelmsford considered it would take too much time. Nor did he order sufficient reconnaissance, dismissing the likelihood of a Zulu frontal assault on a force of heavily armed British soldiers, even though the Zulu were renowned for that type of warfare.

At dawn on 22 January, Chelmsford led the main part of his column out of the camp to make a sweep of country to the south-east, ignoring reports of Zulu bands moving towards Isandlwana. At nine-thirty a.m., a messenger galloped up to Chelmsford's group with a note from the camp commander, written at eight a.m., warning that 'Zulus are advancing in force from the left front of the camp.' When a staff officer asked Chelmsford, 'What is to be done on the subject?', Chelmsford replied: 'There is nothing to be done on that.' Despite other bits of intelligence reaching him in the following hours,

Chelmsford remained in the field, taking no action to send back reinforcements to Isandlwana.

The British army that day suffered one of the worst disasters in its history. A Zulu force of 20,000 warriors swept into the camp at Isandlwana, annihilating six companies of the 24th regiment. In all, some 1,360 men died – 870 white soldiers and 490 black auxiliaries and non-combatants. Out of a total garrison of 1,760 troops, only 55 whites and 350 auxiliaries survived. An estimated 1,000 Zulus were killed.

Later that afternoon, another Zulu force attacked the mission station at Rorke's Drift which the British had converted into a makeshift hospital. Forewarned that the Zulus were coming, a British detachment of a hundred men improvised defences by throwing up barricades of wooden biscuit boxes and bags of maize cobs and managed to hold out against a ferocious assault lasting twelve hours.

The shock waves from a British army's defeat at the hands of spear-carrying tribesmen spread across southern Africa. All over Natal, white communities were gripped by panic, fearing a Zulu invasion would soon overwhelm them. In London, Disraeli was not only mortified by the blow to Britain's military prestige, but livid that Frere had started the war without his sanction. No one doubted that the British army would eventually prevail in Zululand, but its defeat at Isandlwana left Britain humiliated in the eyes of rival European powers. The only glimmer of light was the gallant defence of Rorke's Drift. At a time of disaster, Britain wanted to hear of heroes. A total of eleven Victoria Crosses were awarded for the defence of Rorke's Drift. Chelmsford meanwhile was quick to cover up his own catastrophic failure of command at Isandlwana, blaming it on subordinate officers.

Needing to restore its authority in southern Africa, Britain set out not just to crush resistance but to dismantle the Zulu state. Cetshwayo sent a series of envoys to Frere: 'What have I done? I want peace. I ask for peace.' But Frere was in no mood to listen. Bolstered by reinforcements and armed with rockets, artillery and Gatling machine guns, British forces, after a ponderous five-month campaign, routed the last of Cetshwayo's impis at the battle of Ulundi. More than 1,500 warriors died for the loss of thirteen on the British side.

A new British proconsul, General Sir Garnet Wolseley, was

despatched to deal with this troublesome part of south-east Africa, with powers to act as 'supreme civil and military authority' not only over Natal and Zululand but also over the Transvaal; what the British cabinet wanted was a 'dictator' to sort out the mess. Wolseley was the most famous British general of his time, with a record of reckless daring combined with a talent for organisation. He had served in the Crimea, Burma, India and China. More recently, he had led the British campaign to subdue the Ashanti in West Africa and served briefly as governor of Natal. He was also vain, outspoken and frequently contemptuous of other people.

In short order, Wolseley packed Cetshwayo off to prison in Cape Town and broke up his kingdom into thirteen 'kinglets', stripping Cetshwayo's Usuthu clan of their status, land and cattle and rewarding Zulus who had sided with the British, or who had capitulated early, in a ruthless display of divide-and-rule tactics. A sizeable chunk of southern Zululand was given to a white gun-runner, John Dunn, once an ally of Cetshwayo, who had deserted him at the beginning of the war to join the British camp. The entire 'disputed territories' were ceded to the Transvaal. Wolseley claimed that his 'settlement' had laid 'enduring foundations of peace, happiness and prosperity' but it resulted only in years of bitter strife amongst rival Zulu factions.

Next, Wolseley turned his attention to smashing Sekhukhune's Pedi state in eastern Transvaal. In November 1879, he mustered a motley army of British troops, colonial volunteers, Transvaal African auxiliaries and 8,000 Swazi warriors to destroy Sekhukhune's capital at Tsate. While Wolseley led the main column along the valley to the town, the Swazi regiments descended from the heights that lay behind it. It was all over in a few hours. Sekhukhune was taken prisoner and incarcerated in Pretoria; his followers were dispersed into new settlements, losing much of their land.

Wolseley assumed that such a demonstration of imperial might would have a salutary effect on the restless mood of the Transvaal Boers. But, by crushing both Cetshwayo and Sekhukhune, the British had liberated the Transvaal Boers from the two greatest threats to their security. They now saw a new opportunity to get rid of the British.

9

MAJUBA

Two weeks after Wolseley's assault on Sekhukhune's capital, a mass meeting of angry Boers was held at Wonderfontein to decide what action to take to rid the Transvaal of British rule. Since Wolseley's arrival in September 1879 as the new overlord of the Transvaal, their mood had become increasingly rebellious. From the outset Wolseley had done little to hide his contempt for the Boers and their campaign for independence, both privately and publicly. In his diary on 18 October, he jotted down a few reflections.

A Boer's idea of life is, that he should pay no taxes of any sort or kind, that he should be amenable to no sort of law he disliked, that there should be no police to keep order, that he should be allowed to kill or punish the Natives as he thought fit, that no progress towards civilization should be attempted, that all foreigners should be kept out of the country & that he should be surrounded by a waste of land many miles of extent each way which he called his farm, in fact that he should have no neighbours as the smoke of another man's fire was an abomination to him. These Transvaal Boers are the only white race I know of that has steadily been going back towards barbarism. They seem to be influenced by some savage instinct which causes them to

fly from civilization . . . Altogether I regard them as the lowest in
the scale of white men & to be also the very most interesting
people I have ever known or studied.

In a despatch to London in October 1879, Wolseley wrote that the
Boers had 'all the cunning and cruelty of the Kaffir without his
courage or honesty . . . they could not stand up against our troops for
an hour'. They were, he said, 'utterly incapable of governing themselves'.

In public, Wolseley derided all notion of independence. In a proclamation issued shortly after his arrival in Pretoria, he declared: 'It is
the will and determination of Her Majesty's Government that this
Transvaal territory shall be, and shall continue to be for ever, an integral portion of Her Majesty's dominions in South Africa.' Using more
graphic language during a tour of the Transvaal, he told an audience
in Standerton: 'So long as the sun shines, the Transvaal will be British
Territory; and the Vaal shall flow back to its sources before the
Transvaal is again independent.'

When Wolseley heard that Boer dissidents intended to hold a mass
meeting at Wonderfontein, he issued a proclamation warning that
those taking part and their families might face prosecution for treason.
Ignoring the threat some 2,000 Boers gathered at Wonderfontein,
parading with the Vierkleur, the Transvaal flag, in front of Paul
Kruger's tent. Once again, Kruger advocated caution. 'The steps you
wish to take are a matter of life and death,' he said. 'You know that
England is a mighty power, while our forces are small and insignificant
in comparison with what she can bring into the field . . . Consider
carefully before you shout "Yes! Yes! We want to fight!"'

On 15 December 1879, after five days of deliberation, the meeting
unanimously approved a *Volks-Besluit* – a Decision of the People –
declaring that Transvaal burghers had no wish to be British citizens.
Nothing less than independence would suffice. 'We solemnly declare
that we are prepared to sacrifice our life and shed our blood for it.'
When two delegates – one of them a former president, Marthinus
Pretorius – paid a call on Wolseley to inform him of the resolution,
Wolseley promptly had them arrested on charges of high treason,

then released them, believing he had called their bluff. 'Poor silly creatures,' he wrote in his diary, 'they go on playing at soldiers & blustering, knowing in their hearts they would bolt at the sight of the first troop of our Dragoons.'

Yet sympathy for the Transvaalers' cause was gaining momentum. In November, Gladstone, in opposition, described the whole idea of British rule as folly. 'The Transvaal, a country where we have chosen most unwisely – I am tempted to say insanely – to place ourselves in the strange predicament of the free subjects of a Monarchy going to coerce the free subjects of a Republic, and to compel them to accept a citizenship which they decline and refuse . . .' In January 1880, the London *Times* referred to 'a very serious and determined spirit of disaffection among the Boers'. It was evident, said the paper, that a majority of white inhabitants were opposed to British rule. During an election campaign in March, Gladstone continued his attacks, describing annexation as 'the invasion of a free people'. The Transvaal, he said, had been obtained 'by means dishonourable to our country' and, if elected, he would 'repudiate' annexation.

There was also growing support for the Transvaalers' cause amongst Afrikaner communities in the Cape and the Orange Free State. The Afrikaner press there expressed strong solidarity. Hoping to mobilise opinion against confederation, Kruger travelled southwards in April, addressing meetings in Paarl, Stellenbosch, Worcester and Malmesbury. In Cape Town he canvassed members of parliament, pleading: 'Do not wash your hands in the blood of your brothers.' Afrikaner MPs subsequently helped defeat proposals favouring confederation, dealing it a fatal blow. The Cape parliamentarian John Merriman recorded: 'There is hardly a farmhouse in the country in which this matter of the Transvaal annexation is not talked about, and there is a strong and bitter feeling growing up against the British government.' What British officials now began to fear was the emergence of a pan-Afrikaner movement challenging British hegemony.

Despite all this, Britain stuck to the same old policy of confederation. For all the vehement opposition he had expressed on the campaign trail, Gladstone, having won the election, decided to make no change, persuaded that what was needed was a strong hand to uphold the imperial image in southern Africa. Both Gladstone and his colonial secretary, Lord Kimberley, were influenced in particular by a report from Wolseley outlining the Transvaal's prospects. He pointed out that gold had already been found in the Transvaal and that 'there can be little doubt that larger and still more valuable goldfields will sooner or later be discovered', bringing British immigrants in such numbers that they would soon swamp the Boer population. It would surely be very short-sighted, he said, to give up the Transvaal merely to save the cost of keeping a British garrison there.

In a letter Gladstone sent to Kruger in June, he wrote: 'Looking to all the circumstances both of the Transvaal and the rest of South Africa, and to the necessity of preventing a renewal of disorders [a Zulu uprising] which might lead to disastrous consequences, not only to the Transvaal, but to the whole of South Africa, our judgement is that the Queen cannot be advised to relinquish her sovereignty over the Transvaal.' All that he was prepared to offer was a form of 'self-government'.

Kruger concluded that war was now inevitable. 'The general conviction was now arrived at that further meetings and friendly protests were useless,' he said in his memoirs. 'The best course appeared to be to set quietly to work and to prepare for the worst by the purchase of arms and ammunition. The great prudence and the strictest secrecy had to be observed in order to avoid suspicion.'

Oblivious of the danger and convinced of British superiority, Wolseley recommended that the British garrison in the Transvaal and Natal could safely be reduced from six to four battalions. On leaving Pretoria in April 1880 at the end of a brief tour of duty, he wrote that his one regret was that the Boers had shown themselves unwilling to fight, as that would have enabled him to put an end to all their nonsense.

British officials meanwhile continued to stamp their authority on the Transvaal. The Transvaal's administrator, Colonel Owen Lanyon, previously the administrator of Griqualand West, held the Boers in as much contempt as Wolseley had done and was determined to enforce tax-collection measures that they had hitherto largely avoided. Boer resistance to paying taxes was commonplace even during the days of

Boer rule. Now British taxation demands became the trigger for full-scale rebellion.

In November 1880, a Potchefstroom magistrate, A. M. Goetz, seized a farm wagon belonging to Piet Bezuidenhout and put it up for auction as punishment for his refusal to pay the tax dues on his farms. The tax authorities had demanded £27. 5s. After a long wrangle with Goetz, Bezuidenhout had offered to pay £13. 5s, but only on condition that the money be put aside for the coffers of a future Boer republic. The magistrate had then referred the matter to Pretoria, at which point Lanyon decided to make an example of Bezuidenhout, ordering his prosecution.

On the day of the auction – 11 November – a prominent Boer activist, Piet Cronjé, rode into Potchefstroom with a hundred armed supporters, seized the wagon and camped provocatively on the outskirts of the town. Lanyon despatched a contingent of British troops to Potchefstroom and ordered arrests, but had no means to effect them. The tax rebellion spread. With Boers massing on his farm, Cronjé sent a message to Kruger on his farm at Boekenhoutfontein near Rustenburg telling him that they were now ready to start the war for independence. Kruger made haste to Potchefstroom where he encountered the local British commander, Colonel R. W. C. Winsloe. Winsloe put it to Kruger that Cronjé's action amounted to open rebellion.

'I should agree with you, if we had acknowledged the annexation,' replied Kruger. 'But that is not the case. We do not look upon ourselves as British subjects, and the question of the tax is not a private question of Bezuidenhout's but a question of principle which concerns the whole country.'

Like Wolseley, Lanyon was convinced that the Boers would never actually take action. In a despatch to General Sir George Colley, the new high commissioner who was based in Natal, he wrote: 'I don't think that we shall have to do much more than show that we are ready and sit quiet.' The Boers, he said, were not only 'inflated toads', they were 'incapable of any united action, and . . . mortal cowards, so anything they may do will be but a spark in the pan'. Lanyon neither ordered any further troop dispositions, nor called for reinforcements until it was too late. The number of British troops in the Transvaal was no more than 1,750, scattered in seven isolated garrisons.

Observing the difficulties the British had in asserting their authority in Potchefstroom, the Boers recognised that the time had come to strike. On 8 December, some 5,000 burghers assembled at a farm called Paardekraal, near present-day Krugersdorp, in a defiant and determined mood. After three days of deliberation, with a pause in the proceedings on the Sabbath, they resolved on 13 December to proclaim the Transvaal's independence, to reconstitute the old Volksraad and to establish a republican government. At its head was an executive triumvirate that included Kruger and the commandant-general, Piet Joubert. Before the burghers left, they built a memorial to the new unity of the *volk*. Each man gathered a stone from the hillside and one by one, walking by in single file, laid the stone to form a huge cairn around a pole bearing the old republican flag, the Vierkleur, each stone a symbol that the burghers had sworn loyalty to each other to fight to the death in the republic's defence.

A copy of the proclamation declaring a republic was sent to Lanyon, together with a covering letter couched in diplomatic terms.

> We declare in the most solemn manner that we have no desire to spill blood, and that from our side we do not wish war. It lies in your hands to force us to appeal to arms in self-defence, which may God forbid. If it comes so far, we will do so with the deepest reverence for Her Majesty the Queen of England and her flag. Should it come so far, we will defend ourselves with a knowledge that we are struggling for the honour of Her Majesty, for we fight for the sanctity of the treaties sworn by her, but broken by her officials . . .

The Boer plan was to establish a new temporary capital at the small highveld town of Heidelberg, sixty miles south of Pretoria, guard the frontier with Natal, and lay siege to British garrisons across the Transvaal. Boer commanders estimated that they could count on 7,000 mounted burghers. Kruger hoped that volunteers from the

Orange Free State would also enlist and wrote to President Brand and the Volksraad in Bloemfontein appealing for support. 'Whether we conquer or die, freedom will come to Africa as surely as the sun rises through tomorrow's clouds – as freedom reigns in the United States. Then shall it be from the Zambesi to Simon's Bay, Africa for the Afrikanders.'

The war of independence, as the Boers called it, amounted to little more than one ambush and three skirmishes. But it left the British army humiliated once more, brought an end to Britain's 'forward' policy and gave a massive boost to the nationalist movement burgeoning among the Afrikaner populations of southern Africa.

The first action occurred on 20 December as a column of troops from the 94th Regiment, on its way from Lydenburg to help guard Pretoria, approached a small stream called the Bronkhorstspruit, thirty-eight miles from the capital. Since setting out on 5 December, the column had made slow progress over the rough tracks and swollen rivers of the eastern Transvaal. Though the commanding officer, Colonel Philip Anstruther, had been warned to expect trouble, his train of wagons was spread out over half a mile, the ammunition boxes were screwed down, and the 250 men, in their scarlet and blue uniforms, marched at ease, eating peaches, cheered on by a medley of popular tunes from the band.

Catching sight of a body of Boer horsemen near Bronkhorstspruit, the band abruptly stopped playing. A Boer despatch rider approached with a message warning Anstruther to order a halt. Anstruther replied that he had no wish for a hostile confrontation but that he intended to proceed to Pretoria. In the ensuing engagement, the column lost 56 men dead and 92 wounded. Mortally wounded and realising his position was hopeless, Anstruther ordered his men to throw their hats in the air and wave handkerchiefs as a signal of surrender.

Determined to avenge Bronkhorstspruit and put down the rebellion, General Colley assembled a field force from units in Natal, sending it to the northern border with the Transvaal and establishing headquarters for himself at Fort Amiel near Newcastle. Colley was a distinguished academic soldier, a former professor at Sandhurst, but his active service had been limited and his command of the Natal Field

Force was to prove disastrous. His priority was to cross the border and relieve besieged garrisons in the Transvaal. In a notable display of arrogance, for which British officers had become renowned, Colley sent a message on 23 January 1881 to the commandant-general, Piet Joubert, calling on him to disband his forces or face the full might of imperial Britain, suggesting that although he might understand the consequences, his backveld followers surely did not:

> The men who follow you are, many of them, ignorant, and know and understand little of anything outside their own coun-try. But you, who are well educated and have travelled, cannot but be aware how hopeless is the struggle you have embarked upon, and how little any accidental success gained can affect the ultimate result.

Without waiting for a reply, Colley led his Natal Field Force – con-sisting of 1,400 men, an 80-strong naval brigade, artillery and Gatling guns – to a strategic pass in the hills on the Natal–Transvaal border called Laing's Nek. Colley's assault on Boer positions at Laing's Nek on 28 January ended in disarray, with heavy casualties; Colley himself admitted 'failure' but claimed the reverse was 'not serious'. An engagement that he led at Ingogo inside the Natal border on 8 February to protect his supply lines resulted in more heavy casualties; as Colley retreated under cover of darkness to avoid defeat, he left behind many of the wounded to die of exposure. In the space of ten days, he lost one quarter of his field force, either dead or wounded. 'One or two more Pyrrhic victories like this and we shan't have any army left at all,' Lieutenant Percival Marling wrote at the time.

Hoping to retrieve his reputation, Colley ignored the chance of an armistice and conceived the idea of seizing the summit of a massive flat-topped hill called Majuba that overlooked Laing's Nek and com-manded the country for miles around. He prepared his plan largely in secret, informing only two officers, and made no proper reconnais-sance of the area. Bolstered by reinforcements, he put together a scratch force of 600 men that included three companies from the

92nd Highlanders and a naval brigade, and led them out on the night of 26 February 1881 to the base of Majuba hill, taking no artillery or Gatling guns.

The climb up the southern slopes of Majuba was steep, but Colley's force managed to reach the summit just before dawn without difficulty. Colley was elated. The position seemed impregnable. Far below on the northern side he could see three Boer laagers, unaware of the British presence. Colley deployed a line of troops to defend the perimeter of the summit and kept others in reserve, but again made no proper reconnaissance of the area, nor saw any need for entrenchments. The mood of the men was relaxed. At first light, a group of Highlanders advertised their presence by standing on the skyline, shaking their fists and yelling at the Boers below. The Boers were astounded and began to panic, expecting an artillery bombardment. But nothing happened. Colley had brought no artillery.

Largely unseen by the British, Boer groups began scaling the northern slopes of Majuba. By midday, some had reached the edge of the summit, from where they opened fire on the Highlanders' position. On two occasions, a Highlander lieutenant made a hazardous run to report in person to Colley the growing danger posed by the Boer assault, but Colley took little notice. On a third occasion, the lieutenant was told that the general was asleep. The British perimeter began to crumble then collapsed. As panic took hold, terrified soldiers sprinted for the rear, then fled down the hillside. While trying to rally his men, Colley was fatally shot in the head. Within thirty minutes, the British were swept off the summit.

At his headquarters at Heidelberg, Kruger saw the Boer victory at Majuba as a sign of God's support for their fight for freedom. 'We glory not in human power,' he declared in an Order of the Day. 'It is God the Lord who has helped us – the God of our fathers, to whom for the last five years, we have addressed our prayers and supplications.'

For the British, the shame of Majuba was even more intense than that of Isandlwana. Elite units like the 92nd Highlanders had cut and run in the face of Boer irregulars. There were no heartening stories to be told like the heroic stand made at Rorke's Drift. Nearly a hundred men had died, 132 had been wounded, and 56 had surrendered to men dressed in civilian corduroy trousers and floppy-brimmed hats. Boer losses amounted to one man killed and six wounded.

News of the calamity shocked Britain. The War Office prepared to send reinforcements. The clamour began to 'Avenge Majuba'. Queen Victoria and the Conservative opposition demanded that Britain restore its authority. But Gladstone had no appetite for more conflict. He feared, moreover, that further British military action might precipitate an Afrikaner uprising across southern Africa. In March he reached a preliminary agreement with Kruger, conceding independence subject only to a vague and ill-defined reservation about 'the suzerainty of Her Majesty'. A final agreement was publicly announced on 3 August 1881 by the new British high commissioner, Sir Hercules Robinson, speaking at a ceremony in Church Square, Pretoria, perched on a hastily made platform of planks and straw bales, dressed in full proconsular dress and plumed hat. Despite the pomp, all that it amounted to was a device to extricate Britain from the Transvaal with minimum embarrassment.

Buoyed up by their defeat of imperial Britain, the Transvaal Boers now set out to expand the borders of their state to the east and to the west, and to impose their will on African chiefdoms around them.

PART III

10

THE DIAMOND BUBBLE

A new bout of diamond fever struck southern Africa in 1881, prompted by the formation of a host of joint-stock companies in the diamond fields as the era of independent diggers came to an end. The rush to invest in joint-stock companies was as hectic as the original diamond rush of the 1870s. Speculators thronged the main diamond market in Ebden Street in Kimberley, where a new stock exchange was established to accommodate the huge increase in business:

> Ebden Street [wrote Dr Matthews] was filled from morning to night with a tumultuous and maddened crowd. The various offices of companies in formation were simply stormed, and those who could not get in at the door from the pressure of the crowd, threw their applications for shares (to which were attached cheques and bank notes) through the windows, trusting to chance that they might be picked up . . .
>
> It was astonishing how the mania seized on all classes in Kimberley, from the highest to the lowest . . . how everyone, doctors and lawyers, masters and servants, shop-keepers and workmen, men of the pen and men of the sword, magistrates and I.D.B.s [illicit diamond buyers], Englishmen and foreigners, rushed wildly into the wonderful game of speculation.

Following the launch of De Beers Mining Company in April 1880, more than seventy joint-stock companies made their debut on the market within a year. Claim-holders forming joint-stock companies made their own valuation of their assets, set the capital of the new enterprises, took shares equivalent to the value they claimed for their holdings and then offered the remainder to the public. As merchants and bankers in Cape Town and Port Elizabeth scrambled to join the buying frenzy, the competition for shares became so intense that stock in 1881 traded at premiums ranging as high as 300 per cent.

In the case of De Beers, the claim-holders valued their ninety claims at £200,000, floated the company with a nominal capital of two thousand £100 shares, divided 1,900 shares among themselves, and offered the remaining 100 shares to the public. Rhodes and Rudd each acquired 280 shares. When the Barnato Company was floated on the share market in March 1881, at the height of the diamond boom, its four claims were valued at £25,000 each; within an hour the £75,000 worth of shares on offer were subscribed twice over and after two days they were selling at a premium of 25 per cent.

Some claim-holders made huge fortunes. One former digger, William Knight, whose claims were valued at £12,000 in 1880, sold out for £120,000 and left for England. J. B. Robinson sold 913 Standard £100 shares in March 1881 for £194,640, more than double their nominal value. One financial agent in Kimberley, involved in floating five companies requiring a capital of £496,000, took in £1,230,000 over a three-week period.

As well as promoting viable companies, some claim-holders owning worthless or poor ground took advantage of the clamour for dia-mond scrip to launch new ventures, knowing that they had little or no chance of success. Indeed, the greatest volume of dealing took place in shares not of well-known companies but of dubious new ones. 'It was evident,' wrote Dr Matthews, 'that it mattered very little to the general public, or the majority at all events, what the company was, what the value of the claims might be or where they were situated; so long as it was a diamond-mining company it was quite sufficient to commend public favour.' Claim-holders in the two richest mines, Kimberley and De Beer's, tended to hold on to their most valuable claims there but to use cash they had raised from limited sales to buy up poorer claims in the other two mines, Dutoitspan and Bultfontein, and then sell them to colonial investors at inflated prices. By the end of 1880, claim prices had risen by 50 per cent in Dutoitspan and 75 per cent in Bultfontein. Some claim-holders with capital often invested everything they had in a single company to boost its share price, secure a quick profit, and then reinvest in a new venture.

Another scam involved claim-holders acting in collusion with each other to force prices higher. The *Diamond News* reported in March 1881:

> There appears to be a 'ring' here, and every person in it has received an allotment of shares from each company, while the capital of the general public is received and politely returned. Immediately the shares are quoted at a premium and the outsiders are glad to pay it to get into what is apparently a good thing, but which has only been made to appear such by the chicanery of the promoters and their supporters.

Some leading Kimberley figures engaged in dubious dealings. The town's mayor, J. B. Robinson, endeavoured to offload some poor ground he owned in Kimberley mine by floating a new venture, the Crystal Diamond Mining Company, with a capital of £160,000, three times its assessed value. In a review of new companies published in September 1880, the *Dutoitspan Herald* pointed out that some of the Crystal claims were 'worse than valueless'.

Cecil Rhodes was also heavily involved in company promotion. Not only did he become director of seven diamond-mining companies, he also sat on the board of water, coal, tramway, loan, steam laundry and theatre companies. Like Robinson, he helped set up new ventures stuffed with claims of little value selling shares at a high premium. Poor claims shed by De Beers were put into the International. The claims were floated at £3,700 each and the company was capitalised at £131,700. The International slipped into debt, failed to pay dividends, was put into liquidation and then sold back to De Beers for the knock-down price of £18,974. Another company promoted by

Rhodes was the London and South African, which became a hold-all for poor ground in the West End of De Beer's mine. Its 96 claims were valued at £1,500 each, but it was a bogus operation. It never went into production, but lent its funds to another mining company for a fixed rate of interest. De Beers subsequently bought one third of the company at a bargain price and then absorbed it altogether.

The most notorious of Rhodes' ventures was the Beaconsfield Diamond Mining Company. It was formed out of twelve claims discarded by Jules Porges' Compagnie Française. The assessed value of the Beaconsfield claims, according to an Inspection Report subsequently made in November 1881 by the Standard Bank, was £40,395. But the promoters valued the claims at £10,000 each and they were paid three-quarters of the £132,000 capital. 'Such companies should be sorted out as soon as possible,' said Inspector Rennie of the Standard Bank, 'and an example made of a promoter here and there.'

The boom, however, was short-lived. The values placed on Kimberley's mining companies had soared far beyond their production capacity. By the middle of 1881, the total nominal capital of £7 million was more than twice the officially assessed value of the mines in 1880. Not only had claim-holders floated companies at excessively high values, they had then spent the proceeds on further speculation in other companies or on paying out dividends to impatient investors demanding a quick return on their money; no more than 10 per cent of the total capital of the companies floated was retained for investment. None of the companies possessed reserve funds.

Moreover, the boom had been fuelled largely by credit. Initially, all share transactions were for cash, but the spectacular leaps in prices encouraged speculators to buy on credit. At the outset, banks willingly made advances for the purchase of scrip, but then began to take fright. In April 1881, the Standard Bank said it found it 'necessary to check the speculative mania before it assumed greater dimensions' and refused to accept company scrip as collateral for loans. As the bubble burst, Kimberley's mining magnates looked to foreign investors in England and Europe for salvation. They were the only sources of capital that remained; local sources of capital in Kimberley and the

Cape Colony had long been exhausted. But foreign investors steered clear.

The collapse was precipitate, ruining hundreds of investors. Shares that had traded at £400 each in March 1881 fell to as low as £25. One of the casualties was Andrew McKenzie, a prominent Cape Town dock agent and building contractor who in early 1881 had begun speculating in diamond shares on a 'gigantic scale':

> It appears to have been his misfortune that his first speculations proved successful [wrote his liquidator] for . . . misled thereby or prompted by a natural love of speculation he plunged madly into the excitement. He appears to have bought into every company . . . in many instances beyond the highest market rates giving his bills with pledges of shares in payment of his purchases which altogether amounted to £300,000.

McKenzie's bankruptcy in December 1881 detonated a commercial crisis in the Cape Colony that lasted for several years.

Rhodes, Rudd, and most other Kimberley magnates managed to weather the storm. In March 1881, De Beers merged its shares in a deal with an even larger group of claim-holders led by Frederic Philipson Stow, giving it an unassailable hold on the mine and enabling it to withstand the fall-out from the crash more readily.

But Kimberley's reputation around the world was wrecked. 'It may be safely said,' wrote Dr Matthews, 'that in its rash and reckless speculation Kimberley was almost guilty of financial suicide, for not only was an all but fatal blow given to the industry which supported the place, but all confidence in its resources was for a time destroyed in the minds of its colonial neighbours and the home investing public.'

The general manager of the Standard Bank concurred: 'No immediate improvement can be expected,' he wrote in November 1881, 'as the diamond share market is now thoroughly discredited.' An editorial in the *Griqualand West Investors Guardian* commented at the end of the year: 'There is no use denying that we have botched our own affairs to a very considerable extent.'

The dire straits into which the mining industry had fallen were compounded by a host of other problems. Independent companies operating in the same mine produced the same kind of difficulties that small claim-holders had faced – only on a much larger scale; working at different depths, they undercut each other's operations. Open-cast mining also became increasingly hazardous. As a result of fallen reef, only one-third of the claims in Kimberley mine were workable in 1881. Neither the companies nor the Kimberley mining board could raise sufficient funds to remove the reef. Then the price of diamonds collapsed. In 1882, a depression in the European diamond market, caused in part by overproduction in Kimberley, nearly halved carat prices and sent one-third of Kimberley's companies to the wall.

The big players once again survived, profiting from the demise of smaller competitors. They also acquired an appetite for political action to promote their own interests.

11

THE STRIPPING CLAUSE

A fter nine years as a British Crown Colony, Griqualand West was incorporated in 1880 as a new province of the Cape Colony. No longer were British officials directly responsible for its administration. In place of a local council, the electorate was entitled to send four members to the Cape parliament, two representing the constituency of Kimberley and two representing Barkly West district.

Standing as a candidate in Kimberley for election in March 1881, at the height of the bubble boom, the mining magnate J. B. Robinson campaigned for stricter enforcement of laws to control black labour – a popular issue in the white community. 'One of the first lessons to be instilled into them will be respect for the laws of *meum* and *tuum*' he said.

Cecil Rhodes, at the age of twenty-seven, chose to stand in Barkly West, formerly known as Klipdrift. It was a raw rural constituency, where most of the voters were Boer farmers who shared little of Rhodes' preoccupation with the needs of the mining industry. Rhodes' purpose was to get the Cape government to build a railway line linking Kimberley to the ports to alleviate mining costs. The Barkly West constituency afforded him the opportunity to gain a seat in parliament without having to compete against Robinson in Kimberley or another popular figure, Dr Josiah

Matthews. Only one other candidate showed an interest in representing Barkly West, so Rhodes was duly elected unopposed as one of its two members.

Rhodes made an immediate impact on his arrival in parliament in April 1881, if only by dressing 'without the least consideration for fashion', causing consternation among its conservative members. 'I am still in Oxford tweeds,' he declared defiantly, 'and I think I can legislate as well in them as in sable clothing.' He also earned a rebuke from the Speaker by referring to other members by their names instead of their constituencies. A parliamentary reporter described his maiden speech as 'bluff and untutored in style, with no graces of oratory' and noted that Rhodes was 'boyishly nervous and uncouth in gesture'. His constant fidgeting drove other members to distraction. 'He is in a continued state of restlessness, whether sitting in his seat or standing on his legs,' one observer remarked. 'He is never still from the time he enters the House until he leaves it.'

Thomas Fuller, then one of the leaders of the parliamentary opposition, remembered Rhodes in 1881 as a 'tall, broad-shouldered man, with face and figure of somewhat loose formation':

> His hair was auburn, carelessly flung over his forehead, his eyes of bluish–grey, dreamy but kindly. But the mouth – aye, that was the 'unruly member' of his face. With deep lines following the curve of the moustache, it had a determined, masterful and sometimes scornful expression. Men cannot, of course, think or feel with their mouths, but the thoughts and feelings of Cecil Rhodes soon found their way to that part of his face. At its best it expressed determined purpose – at its worst, well, I have seen storms of passion gather about it and twist it into unlovely shapes.

Rhodes openly expressed impatience with the speeches of other members. During long-winded discussion, he became restless, sitting on his hands and bouncing up and down to the embarrassment of other members. When speaking himself, he went straight to the point, weighing in with dogmatic pronouncements, not bothering with an introduction, his voice breaking every now and then into a high falsetto. He used few gestures, noted Fuller:

> He often kept his hands behind him, or thrust one forward towards the person or persons he was especially addressing, or passed it over his brow in a pausing way. When he considered his argument especially convincing, he would conclude by flopping down on the seat with an expressive jerk, as much to say, 'Answer that if you can!'

To ensure that his speeches were well reported and hoping to influence public opinion, Rhodes bought a controlling interest in the *Cape Argus*, the main newspaper in the Colony. The deal cost him £6,000, and was concluded in the utmost secrecy. Rhodes wanted the *Argus* to support him but to retain the semblance of an independent newspaper. In negotiations with the editor, Francis Dormer, Rhodes made clear his own views on editorial policy. 'The bargain was concluded, with firmly fixed resolves on my part,' Dormer disclosed years later, 'but not, I fear, without certain mental reservations on the part of my young and eager friend.'

With a free and easy manner, Rhodes became a familiar figure in Cape Town society, relishing the talk and arguments of politicians who gathered at the Civil Service Club or at Poole's for lunch. He befriended the new governor and high commissioner, Sir Hercules Robinson, who had been chosen to inaugurate a less adventurous policy than Sir Bartle Frere, and cultivated him as a potential ally. He also struck up a close friendship with Captain Penfold, the harbour master, sharing quarters with him in Adderley Street; under Penfold's tuition, he became an enthusiastic yachtsman in Table Bay.

After parliament adjourned in July, Rhodes returned to Kimberley, but he did not stay long. With the fall-out from the diamond bubble under way, he took the opportunity to head for Oxford to complete his final term and obtain a degree – although, by now, he had lost all interest in gaining a professional qualification. The excitement of business deals, money-making and, more recently, political intrigue had forged different ambitions. But Rhodes still aspired to possess an

Oxford degree. It was the cachet of an Oxford degree, the sense of belonging to an elite group with the advantageous contacts to be made, that Rhodes had always sought, rather than the wider benefits of an Oxford education. 'Have you ever thought how it is that Oxford men figure so largely in all departments of public life?' he once remarked. 'The Oxford system in its most finished form looks very unpractical, yet, wherever you turn your eye – except in sciences – an Oxford man is at the top of the tree.' After seven weeks of 'dogged effort', he passed examinations for an ordinary B.A. degree, then returned to the Cape.

Back in parliament in Cape Town, Rhodes joined Robinson in pressing for new legislation to suit the needs of mine-owners. As well as campaigning for a railway linking Kimberley to the Cape, they sought measures to ensure both a constant supply of black labour for the mines and greater control over black workers once they had been recruited. They also demanded tough legislative curbs on illicit diamond dealing, claiming that between one-third and one-half of all diamonds were being stolen and smuggled out of the mines by illicit diamond buyers (I.D.B.s). Unless this evil was crushed, warned Robinson, 'the mining industry will be swept away altogether'. In April 1882, Rhodes was appointed chairman of a parliamentary committee to investigate the I.D.B. issue.

The outcome was the Diamond Trade Act of 1882 containing draconian provisions: suspects were presumed guilty until proven innocent; a special court was established to try offenders without a jury system; penalties were raised to include prison terms of up to fifteen years; and the police were given powers to search without warrants and to engage in 'trapping' operations, using agents provocateurs. Rhodes admitted that trapping operations were 'obnoxious', but argued that they were an essential weapon in dealing with diamond theft. He also fought hard to secure an additional punishment of flogging, but was thwarted by other members, including Dr Matthews. In Kimberley, Rhodes was acclaimed a hero; Matthews was eventually hounded out of office.

Kimberley's mine-owners also gained government approval for a new system of searching that affected both black and white workers.

All workers below the rank of manager were required to pass through search houses on entering the mines and leaving them. Separate search houses were set up for black and white workers. Blacks were ordered to strip naked and were subjected to degrading body searches. Whites did not have to take off their clothes and underwent only a limited visual inspection. They nevertheless regarded the new regulations as an assault on the respectability and dignity of their occupations. Many had previously been small claim-holders or share workers, now forced by changing circumstances to take up wage employment as overseers or skilled artisans. Searching placed them in the same category as black labourers. They were further aggrieved when the mine-owners decided to enforce an additional regulation requiring whites to change their clothes in search houses and don uniforms. Initially, only blacks had been ordered to wear uniforms – in their case, grain sacks. The new regulation was denounced as being in effect a 'stripping clause' for whites. In October 1883, white overseers went on strike, bringing the mines to a standstill. After a week, the mine-owners capitulated.

Six months later, in another attempt to impose industrial discipline on white workers, mine-owners reactivated the 'stripping' order, issuing instructions for search inspectors to examine the open mouths and boots of all white workers. Five employees – two overseers, a miner, an engine driver and a fitter in Kimberley mine – who refused to open their mouths for a finger search or to remove their boots were arrested and sent for trial. Others who refused to comply were dismissed.

A full-scale strike ensued. Led by a 28-year-old overseer, Frederick Holmes, a crowd of white and black workers marched on Kimberley mine to shut down the pumping gear. They were met by an armed contingent of police and special constables barricading the road with overturned trucks. Holmes sought to negotiate, calling out: 'Don't fire on us. We are not here to do any harm. Allow me to speak.' But the special constables opened fire, killing Holmes and five other whites. The strike petered out.

In parliament, Rhodes appealed to his colleagues not to investigate the shooting. The dispute, he argued, was not between capital and labour, or a contest between whites, but rather 'white men supported by natives in a struggle against whites' – white men, moreover, who

were resisting measures to stop diamond theft. In other words, white
strikers were not only thieves, they were betrayers of their race.
Parliament duly voted by a wide margin not to investigate the shooting.

As well as helping to force workers into line, Rhodes used his
political position to advance the interests of large mining companies
like De Beers and weaken their smaller competitors. In 1883, he
secured a change in the legislation governing mining boards to accord
representation on the boards on the basis of the size of the holdings of
mining companies. This effectively enabled large mining companies to
take control of the boards; hitherto, no company, regardless of the size
of its holdings, had been permitted to have more than one representative on each board. Now, with control of the boards, large
companies were able to determine what areas were given priority for
reef-removal work, invariably deciding to concentrate the work on
their own properties, thus ensuring the demise of smaller competitors.
In the case of the De Beer's mine, the De Beers Company used its
position on the board to restrict water and reef removal to its own
holdings, forcing several competitors into bankruptcy and then purchasing their properties at bargain prices.

Kimberley in these years was sunk in gloom. The depression, starting
in 1882, lasted through to 1885. The price of diamonds on the
London rough market over that period fell by 42 per cent. Output
valued at £4 million in 1882 was worth only £2.5 million in 1885.
The total capitalisation of the mines was reduced from £9.6 million to
£7.8 million. Mining profits scarcely reached 4 per cent of total capital. Most of the profits were made by only ten companies. To survive,
mining companies shed thousands of workers, white and black; white
employment fell by 61 per cent to 1,210; black employment by 47 per
cent to 9,000. Unemployed whites faced destitution; those still in
work faced company attempts to force down their wages. Unable to
collect dues from their members, the mining boards collapsed.

A spate of suicides hit the town. Hardly a week passed without the
local press reporting the death of a prominent businessman. So many
suicides occurred that newspaper editors lost all sympathy when

reporting them. 'This mania for suicide taints the whole moral atmosphere,' complained the *Diamond Times*, 'and it is questionable whether it is good for the safety and morality of Society that such acts be recorded with tenderness.' In a letter Rhodes wrote to John Merriman in Cape Town in April 1883, he lamented: 'The suicidal mania is seizing the community here . . . The doctors say it is almost like an epidemic.'

Two smallpox epidemics added to the malaise. The first, spreading northwards from Cape Town in 1882, was contained by a young, energetic Afrikaner doctor, Hans Sauer, newly graduated from Edinburgh University. He set up a quarantine camp at a crucial crossing point on the Modder River, thirty miles south along the main road from the Cape, and insisted that travellers were examined, vaccinated, fumigated and, if necessary, placed into quarantine. At times, Sauer's camp held as many as 1,800 detainees.

Sauer was employed by Kimberley's sanitary inspector and given a police detachment to help him, but, as he admitted, he possessed no legal authority to force travellers to comply. In his memoirs, he wrote:

> There were, of course, many who objected violently, but force was always employed to make them submit, with the result that at one time I had as many as nineteen actions for assault, battery and interference with persons on the Queen's highway, but somehow none of these actions came to anything; they all mysteriously faded away and died out.

Sauer subsequently discovered that behind the scenes Rhodes had acted to 'square' every case before it came to court:

> It was Rhodes, and Rhodes alone, who had conceived the plan, and who had persuaded all the important factors on the Fields to back the adventure. As always, Rhodes displayed his extraordinary ability for pulling the strings while keeping entirely out of sight.

The second outbreak, starting in October 1883, turned into disaster, however. Instead of dealing openly with the epidemic, Kimberley's mine-owners and other leading businessmen conspired to deny its existence, fearing that news of the outbreak would lead to mass desertion by the black labour force and require expensive counter-measures.

Black labourers arriving from Delagoa Bay in the north were sus-pected of carrying smallpox. They were immediately isolated at a quarantine station set up on a farm nine miles from Kimberley. A team of six doctors visited the quarantine station, three of them reporting that the disease was not smallpox but an aggravated form of chicken-pox. An Edinburgh-trained doctor, Edmond Sinclair Stevenson, was summoned from Cape Town to give his opinion. 'If it was smallpox, a quarantine would be called, the result being that the comparatively large population, mostly niggers and others, would be thrown out of work,' Sinclair Stevenson wrote in his memoirs. 'Needless to say we pronounced it chicken-pox, otherwise it might have led to serious trouble.' Pink slips were handed out to the town's residents, signed by doctors, stating that the disease was not smallpox but 'a bulbous dis-ease of the skin allied to pemphigus' – an extremely rare skin disease.

But Hans Sauer, returning from a long hunting trip in the Transvaal, was convinced the disease was smallpox and claimed the outbreak was being covered up. He was roundly condemned by all and sundry. 'It was not only the diamond magnates who were hostile,' wrote Sauer in his memoirs, 'but the vast majority of the population, who were in the same galley as the magnates, for should the mines shut down on account of this disease, they would starve just as cer-tainly as the magnates would lose their profits.'

While the wrangling continued, the disease took hold. Sauer was initially refused permission to inspect mine housing areas and had to turn to parliament in Cape Town for support. Parliament eventually passed a new Public Health Act, enabling Sauer to prove his diagno-sis was correct, but he was still vilified for his efforts. The new law, he wrote, 'made me the most unpopular man on the Diamond Fields. High Society turned its back on me, and as for the ruck of the pop-ulation, it simply spat when I passed.'

Proof of the disease, however, came too late for many of Kimberley's residents. The epidemic raged for two years before mass vaccinations and quarantine measures finally eradicated it. Officially, some 700 people died, including 51 whites; some 2,300 were infected. But the real figures were far higher and were deliberately obscured by officials trying to conceal the full extent of the epidemic.

Rhodes' life in Kimberley was meanwhile shaped by new friend-ships. Though Rhodes readily took part in social activity and had a large number of acquaintances, he did not make friends easily and appeared to remain aloof, disliking intimacy and preferring to keep people at a distance. His partnership with Charles Rudd was first and foremost a business arrangement. During the late 1870s, he 'messed' with a group of bachelors known as the 'Twelve Apostles' but regarded them as associates rather than as close friends. Nor did he have any women friends, openly expressing an aversion to marriage. Writing to an acquaintance in Kimberley from Oxford in 1876, he remarked: 'I hope you won't get married. I hate people getting mar-ried. They simply become machines and have no ideas beyond their respective spouses and offspring.'

But with a young Scottish doctor, Leander Starr Jameson, who arrived in Kimberley in 1878, Rhodes established a friendship that endured even through times of great personal disaster that Jameson brought upon him. It was a friendship, according to Jameson's biog-rapher, Ian Colvin, that became 'as strong as a marriage bond'. Five months older than Rhodes, short, slim and boyishly handsome, Jameson had trained at University College, London and seemed set on a glittering career as a London surgeon. But possessing a restless and reckless temperament, he threw it all up to join a medical practice in Kimberley. He quickly became a popular figure there, admired for his skill and charm as well as his love of poker and gambling. Though he never married, he greatly enjoyed the company of women.

'Hardly a more popular notability resided on the Diamond Fields than clever, well-fashioned Dr Jameson,' recorded Louis Cohen in his characteristically scurrilous prose. 'No matter what happened to be the trouble with matron, maid, or widow, a visit from the dextrous Doctor would always set things right.' Cohen related how he had advised one man who complained that he was childless to consult

Dr Jameson, 'with the result that, hey presto! Before the year was out, and on the first of April too, he became the proud pater of bouncing twins. The Doctor was, indeed, a life-giver.'

Jameson was none too scrupulous in other ways. During the small-pox epidemic, he was one of the doctors who, in line with the mine-owners' and businessmen's wishes, readily asserted that the disease was only chicken-pox. Like Rhodes' brother Herbert, Jameson was galvanised by the chance of adventure. And it was Rhodes' talk of his 'big schemes' that he found so attractive. Years later, he recalled, 'I soon admitted to myself that for sheer natural power I had never met a man to come near Cecil Rhodes.'

Another friendship that Rhodes cultivated was with Alfred Beit, one of Kimberley's leading experts on diamonds and a financial mastermind. A small, shy and unprepossessing figure with bulbous brown eyes and a receding chin, he had been posted to Kimberley in 1875 as the representative of a diamond merchant company. Born in Hamburg in 1853, six months before Rhodes, he came from a sophisticated German-Jewish family but performed poorly in school and was apprenticed to a diamond-broking firm in Amsterdam where he developed a talent for examining stones.

'When I reached Kimberley,' Beit told the journalist Frank Harris,

I found that very few people knew anything about diamonds: they bought and sold at haphazard, and a great many of them really believed that the Cape diamonds were of a very inferior quality. Of course, I saw at once that some of the Cape stones were as good as any in the world; and I saw, too, that the buyers protected themselves against their own ignorance by offering one-tenth part of what each stone was worth in Europe. It was plain that if one had a little money there was a fortune to be made.

Beit's first fortune, however, came not from diamonds but from property speculation. Responding to the demand for business premises, he bought a piece of land, built a dozen corrugated iron sheds for offices, kept one for himself and let out the rest for a monthly rent of £1,800. Twelve years later he sold the ground for £260,000.

Beit belonged to a group of German bachelors at Kimberley who set up their own 'German Mess', similar to Rhodes' 'English' mess. Among its members was Julius Wernher, a young German aristocrat whom Jules Porges had sent to Kimberley in 1873 to look after his company's interests. Beit and Wernher forged a lasting business partnership, but made an odd couple. Wernher was a huge, handsome, former Dragoon who had served in the Prussian cavalry in the Franco-German war of 1870–71; Beit was a dumpy figure, whose head appeared too large for his body; uncomfortable with strangers, he seemed a mass of nervous mannerisms, tugging at his collar, twisting his moustache and biting the corner of his handkerchief.

Beit's diamond interests were concentrated on Kimberley mine. Though dabbling in several company ventures there, he focused his attention in particular on the Kimberley Central Company, aiming to build it into a vehicle for expansion. His role in the rise of Kimberley Central impressed Rhodes and he set out to win over Beit 'on the personal'. Like Jameson, Beit was captivated by Rhodes' talk of 'big schemes'. He himself had no particular ambition, even though he was to achieve remarkable success. His tastes were simple. What moved him most, according to Rhodes, 'was to be rich enough to give his mother £1,000 a year'. When Beit first went back to Germany on a visit, he took his mother for a drive, enquired whether she liked the carriage, the horses and the coachman, and then gave them all to her. 'Mother,' he said, 'when I was a boy I always hoped that one day I should have enough money to give you a carriage and a pair of horses, and now my dream has come true.' Beit liked to gamble, and to win, but despite his success he remained a gentle, self-effacing magnate, renowned for many acts of kindness. 'At bottom, Beit was a sentimentalist,' reported Frank Harris. 'This was the fine side of the man, the side through which Rhodes used him.'

Using people who he thought could help further his schemes was Rhodes' usual motive in pursuing them. But in the case of Neville Pickering, a carefree youth with little personal ambition, Rhodes formed a relationship that differed from all others. The son of a Port Elizabeth parson and four years younger than Rhodes, Pickering had arrived in Kimberley to work for a property company before Rhodes recruited him in 1881 as secretary or chief clerk at De Beers. He was bright, efficient and gregarious with a sunny disposition and was much admired by the young ladies of Kimberley.

Rhodes became devoted to Pickering. Within a few months of his taking up the De Beers appointment, the two of them moved into a small, corrugated iron cottage facing the Kimberley cricket ground. Despite Rhodes' wealth and position, the cottage was sparsely furnished; it was a place of wooden chairs, bare tables, iron bedsteads and horsehair mattresses that lacked all comfort but suited Rhodes well enough. A Coloured manservant looked after them, acting as housekeeper, cook and valet. For Rhodes, it was a fulfilling experience. In the words of Ian Colvin, Rhodes had found a 'bosom friend' and 'confidant of all his dreams'. 'They shared the same office,' wrote Colvin, 'worked together, played together, rode together, shot together.'

But it was a friendship that was to be cut cruelly short.

12

DREAMS AND FANTASIES

Alongside his business interests, Rhodes' political horizons began to expand. As a youth, in common with many young men, he harboured grand dreams of power and glory. What was unusual in his case was the extent to which he held on to them. He grew up in an age when Victorian Britain regarded itself as the standard-bearer of civilisation, sending its colonists, missionaries, officials and engineers abroad to open up new continents, develop markets for its industrial products and spread the gospel of Christ. The expansion of empire was seen both as an economic necessity and a moral duty to the rest of humanity. In the words of David Livingstone, the missionary-explorer who became one of Victorian Britain's archetypal heroes, there were 'two pioneers of civilisation: Christianity and commerce'. Livingstone's lonely death in central Africa in 1873 while searching in vain for the source of the Nile unleashed a burst of imperial sentiment that mixed a world power's responsibility for trusteeship with a strong dose of economic opportunism. Disraeli's surge of imperial activity during the 1870s – acquiring Cyprus, Fiji and a large bulk of shares in the Suez Canal – won popular support. In a pamphlet written in 1876, Edwin Arnold, editor of the *Daily Telegraph*, used the phrase 'from the Cape to Cairo' to demonstrate the scale of imperial ambition.

Queen Victoria herself was particularly pleased when, at her own suggestion, Parliament in 1877 bestowed on her the title of Empress of India.

That same year, at the age of twenty-four, after completing his first full year at Oxford, Rhodes drew up what he later called 'a draft of some of my ideas', giving it the title 'Confession of Faith'. It was a strange, rambling document, full of fantasies and grievances, summing up in juvenile fashion his views of the ills afflicting mankind and his solutions for them. But Rhodes considered it sufficiently important to pass it on in 1891 to the London journalist W. T. Stead so that it could eventually be published. 'You will see,' he told Stead, 'that I have not altered much as to my feelings.'

In part, the 'confession' reflected his interest in the work of authors he admired: Aristotle's *Ethics*; Marcus Aurelius' *Meditations*; Gibbon's *The Decline and Fall of the Roman Empire*. But Rhodes was also influenced by two more recent publications: One was a book published in 1872, *The Martyrdom of Man* by Winwood Reade, an obscure British Darwinian who argued that man had no hope of an after-life or posthumous reward; the only reward to be found was in improving the human race. 'To develop to the utmost our genius and our love, that is the only true religion,' wrote Reade. Rhodes described *The Martyrdom of Man* as a 'creepy book', but added, mysteriously, that it 'made me what I am'.

The other publication, an inaugural lecture by John Ruskin as Slade Professor at Oxford, delivered in 1870, was brimful of imperial fervour:

> There is a destiny now possible to us, the highest ever set before a nation to be accepted or refused. We are still undegenerate in race; a race mingled with the best northern blood. We are not yet dissolute in temper, but still have the firmness to govern and the grace to obey . . .
>
> Will you youths of England make your country again a royal throne of kings, a sceptred isle, for all the world a source of light, a centre of peace; mistress of learning and of the Arts, faithful guardian of time-tried principles . . .?

This is what England must either do or perish: she must found colonies as fast and as far as she is able, formed of her most energetic and worthiest men; seizing every piece of fruitful waste grounds she can set her foot on, and there teaching these her colonists that their chief virtue is to be fidelity to their country, and their first aim is to be to advance the power of England by land and sea . . .

All that I ask of you is to have a fixed purpose of some kind for your country and for yourselves, no matter how restricted so that it be fixed and unselfish.

Rhodes' own 'draft of ideas', written in June 1877, drew heavily on such exhortations. Starting in an Aristotelian manner, he wrote:

It often strikes a man to inquire what is the chief good in life; to one the thought comes that it is a happy marriage, to another great wealth, to a third travel, and so on, and as each seizes on the idea, for that he more or less works for its attainment for the rest of his existence. To myself, thinking over the same question, the wish came to make myself useful to my country . . .

I contend that we are the first race in the world, and that the more of the world we inhabit the better it is for the human race. I contend that every acre added to our territory means the birth of more of the English race who otherwise would not be brought into existence. Added to which the absorption of the greater portion of the world under our rule simply means the end of all wars.

He pledged himself to work for: 'The furtherance of the British Empire, for the bringing of the whole uncivilised world under British rule, for the recovery of the United States, for the making of the Anglo-Saxon race into one Empire.' He was particularly exercised by the 'loss' of the United States, blaming it on 'two or three ignorant pig-headed statesmen' in the eighteenth century. 'Do you ever feel mad, do you ever feel murderous? I think I do with these men.' Nevertheless, there was Africa. 'Africa is still lying ready for us [and] it is our duty to take it . . . more territory simply means more of the Anglo–Saxon race, more of the best, the most human, most honourable race the world possesses.'

To accomplish this feat of empire-building, Rhodes proposed the formation of a secret society, similar to the Jesuit order, a society with 'members in every part of the British Empire working with one object and one idea'; in effect, a 'Church for the extension of the British Empire'. He described the kind of men who would make suitable recruits and outlined how they would work to 'advocate the closer union of England and her colonies, to crush all disloyalty and every movement for the severance of our Empire'. He also proposed that the society should purchase newspapers, 'for the press rules the mind of the people'.

These ideas found their way into a will that Rhodes drew up in Kimberley in September 1877 – one of many wills that he was to write. Nominating as executors of his entire estate the secretary of state for the colonies (then Lord Carnarvon) and Sidney Shippard, then attorney-general of Griqualand West, he instructed them to establish a secret society 'the true aim and object whereof shall be the extension of British rule throughout the world, the perfecting of a system of emigration from the United Kingdom and colonization by British subjects of all lands . . . especially the occupation by British settlers of the entire Continent of Africa', together with large parts of the rest of the world. A copy of this will was also passed to Stead in 1891 in a sealed envelope with instructions that it should not be opened until Rhodes' death.

Rhodes broached some of these ideas in open conversation, even with strangers. On a visit to Kimberley in 1877, Joseph Orpen, an Irish-born surveyor, magistrate and politician, recorded remarks Rhodes made at a dinner party he gave at his two-roomed corrugated iron cottage. Sitting at the head of the table, Rhodes began: 'Gentlemen, I have asked you to dine . . . because I want to tell you what I want to do with the remainder of my life.' He intended, he said, to devote it to the defence and extension of the British Empire. 'I think that object a worthy one because the British Empire stands for the protection of all the inhabitants of a country in life, liberty, property, fair play and happiness . . . Everything is now going on happily around us. The Transvaal is much happier [since annexation] and much better off than it was and is quietly settled under government. The Free State is perfectly friendly and can join us when and if it likes. It is mainly the extension of the empire northward that we have to watch and work for in South Africa.'

When he took up his seat in parliament in April 1881, Rhodes was preoccupied mainly with mining matters, in particular the need to get a railway built to Kimberley. But it was not long before he was drawn into his first foray into the problems of Africa – a crisis in Basutoland, once ruled by the legendary king, Moshoeshoe.

Fearful of the steady encroachment of Free State settlers into Basutoland, Moshoeshoe repeatedly asked for the protection of Queen Victoria, imploring that his people might be considered 'fleas in the Queen's blanket'. The British government eventually agreed to annex Basutoland in 1868, but three years later, keen to reduce imperial commitments and ignoring fierce protests among the Sotho, it decided to hand over responsibility for control to the Cape Colony.

As a result of the spate of insurrections in the Cape in 1877 and 1878, the prime minister, Gordon Sprigg, a vain and ambitious politician who favoured an aggressive approach to dealing with troublesome African territories, embarked on a policy of disarmament of black tribes. After a minor rebellion in the Quthing district of Basutoland in 1879, he decided to apply the same policy there. Addressing a Sotho *pitso* – council meeting – in 1879, he lectured his audience in abusive terms. 'The Government feels that, like the rest of the natives in South Africa, you possess very much the character of children, and the Government knows that children cannot at all times trust themselves.' Any attempt at resistance to disarmament, he warned, would simply be crushed. 'You know that the tribes which have gone to war with the Government in the Colony have been destroyed. The Gcalekas and Gaikas [Xhosa peoples] – where are they today? . . . In every case where the black man has attacked the white man, he has ultimately . . . gone before him.'

The Sotho, however, refused to hand over their firearms, most of which they had bought with money earned at the Kimberley diamond mines and which they needed in the constant struggle to retain their existing lands.

What followed was the 'Gun War' of 1880. It lasted eight months, cost the Cape £3 million and ended in stalemate. It also left the Sotho bitterly divided between 'loyal' and 'rebel' factions. Cape politicians themselves were at odds over what to do next. Some advocated outright 'scuttle', leaving the Sotho to their own devices; some hoped Britain might be persuaded to take back responsibility for the territory. Rhodes spoke in favour of imperial annexation. 'It is not as if white colonists could be settled in those territories,' he told parliament. 'The policy of the Imperial Government would not allow that. The Parliament would never allow Basutoland to be confiscated; no colonist could go there; the land would simply be peopled with the native races. How could this weak colony retain those territories?' The Cape, he said, lacked the necessary resources, reminding his colleagues that its white population was no greater than that of a 'third-rate English city, spread over a great country'.

Desperate to resolve the Basutoland quagmire, the Cape government recruited the services of General Charles Gordon, one of the foremost heroes of the Victorian age. A decorated veteran of the Crimean War and commander of the Chinese army that had crushed the Taiping rebellion in 1863–4, Gordon had spent six years in Khartoum during the 1870s serving as governor of Equatoria province in southern Sudan. Gordon saw himself as God's instrument and believed he possessed mesmeric power over primitive people. The British political establishment regarded him as half mad – 'inspired and mad', according to Gladstone. Despite his formidable record, on his return to London he was packed off to Mauritius, in his words to supervise 'the barracks and drains' there. He was thus keen for a new adventure.

After helping to reorganise the Cape's colonial army, Gordon ventured to Basutoland in 1882, arranging a series of *pitsos* with Sotho chiefs. Rhodes too ventured to Basutoland in 1882. He had agreed to serve on an official mission set up to evaluate claims for compensation from 'loyal' Sotho. In a memorable fragment of imperial history, Rhodes met General Gordon at a magistrate's headquarters at Thlotsi Heights, north of Maseru, and struck up a warm friendship with him.

They often went for long walks together. Gordon, twenty years older than Rhodes, chided the younger man for his independent opinions. 'You always contradict me,' he said on one occasion. 'I never met such a man for his own opinion. You think your views are always right and everyone else wrong.' On another occasion, Gordon complained, 'You are the sort of man who never approves of anything unless you have had the organising of it yourself.'

Gordon told Rhodes the story of how, after he had subdued the Taiping rebellion, the Chinese government had offered him a roomful of gold.

'What did you do?' asked Rhodes.

'Refused it, of course,' replied Gordon. 'What would you have done?'

'I would have taken it,' said Rhodes, 'and as many roomfuls as they would give me. It is no use for us to have big ideas if we have not got the money to carry them out.'

Gordon was sufficiently impressed with Rhodes to ask him to work with him in Basutoland, but Rhodes declined. 'There are very few men in the world to whom I would have made such an offer. Very few men, I can tell you; but of course you *will* have your way. I never met a man as strong for his opinion; you think your views are always right.'

Gordon soon fell out with the Cape government and returned to England. The Cape government itself, weakened and impoverished by the Gun War, soon tired of responsibility for Basutoland and passed it back to Britain. Gordon, however, did not forget Rhodes. When he was given a new assignment in Khartoum – this time to evacuate Egyptian troops threatened by the advance of the Mahdi's Dervish army – Gordon asked Rhodes to join him. Once again, Rhodes declined. When Rhodes heard the news of Gordon's death in 1885 on the steps of the governor's residence in Khartoum, dreaming of posthumous glory for himself he remarked: 'I am sorry I was not with him.'

By then, however, Rhodes was engaged in a new African adventure, one of far greater significance than Basutoland: a battle to secure 'the road to the north'.

13

THE ROAD TO THE NORTH

The road to the north had been pioneered by British missionaries pushing ever deeper into the interior of Africa, far beyond the limits of white settlement. After establishing a mission station at Griquatown, the London Missionary Society sent the Scottish missionary Robert Moffat northwards to set up a mission station among the Thlaping at Kuruman on the fringe of the Kalahari desert. For fifty years, Moffat's efforts 'to teach poor heathen to know the Saviour' achieved only limited success. But Kuruman nevertheless became not only a missionary outpost but also a base for exploration and a centre of learning. Moffat was the first to reduce the Tswana language to written form; he then translated the Bible into Tswana and produced copies from his own printing press. A market-gardener by training, he planted orchards and willow trees, taught the use of the plough and introduced irrigation projects.

Kuruman was soon renowned as the 'gateway' to the north. Hunters, traders and travellers passing through were invariably offered hospitality by the Moffat family. 'A warm autumnal beneficence oozed from Kuruman,' wrote James Chapman. 'It was the sort of place you came away from with a pomegranate, a pumpkin, quinces or a cabbage; and if you were trekking north it was the last place where you might recruit your oxen, bullocks, cows, sheep and goats.'

Though disdainful of African customs and traditions such as polygamy, Moffat befriended leading Tswana chiefs and opened a second mission station further north at Molepolole among the Kwena. He also struck up a friendship with Mzilikazi, the founder and leader of the Ndebele people, a former Zulu warrior chief who had carved out a new domain for himself in the Magaliesberg area of western Transvaal. They met only rarely, first in 1829, then again in 1835, but established a bond of trust that had lasting consequences. When Mzilikazi, after clashing with Boer commandos, moved northwards in 1837 and established a new capital across the Limpopo, Moffat visited him there in 1854 and again in 1857 to ask his permission to set up a mission station. Though Mzilikazi himself was never converted to Christianity, he gave Moffat his approval. Two years later, when Moffat set out from Kuruman, leading a small team of missionaries on a four-month journey to Matabeleland, Mzilikazi sent him a message of welcome: 'The king longs exceedingly to look on the face of Mtjete again.' The mission station that Moffat founded at Inyati on the banks of the Nkwinkwizi River was the first white settlement in the area north of the Limpopo then know as Zambesia.

Among the missionary recruits whom the London Missionary Society sent to Kuruman was David Livingstone. He arrived there in 1841 as a newly qualified doctor at the age of twenty-eight, serving as an apprentice to Moffat and later, while convalescing from a lion attack, marrying his daughter Mary. As a conventional missionary, Livingstone was a failure. He attached himself to the Kwena but remained with them for less than six years and in that time made but one convert who subsequently lapsed. He was far more influential as a traveller, writing about the depredations of the slave trade in southern Africa and advocating European settlement there. As a result of his experiences among the Kwena, however, he developed an abiding dislike of the Boers. In his writings, he stoked up anti-Boer sentiment, referring to them as 'white thieves' and complaining of their mendacity, greed and stinginess, thus adding to the mutual hatred between British missionaries and Boers. And he repeatedly called on Britain to prevent the Boers from closing 'the missionaries road' into the heartland of Africa.

Clashes between Tswana chiefdoms and encroaching Boer settlers became endemic from the 1850s. The Tswana chiefdoms occupied fertile lands and vital watering places along a 500-mile corridor of territory to the west of Boer settlements in the Transvaal and the Orange Free State that the Boers coveted for their own use. The position of Tswana chiefs was weakened by internecine quarrels over land and water-holes, and by succession disputes that frequently culminated in violent conflict. While missionaries sought to protect and defend Tswana interests, the Boers were quick to exploit Tswana rivalries, siding with one group against another, taking land as a reward.

But it was not only land that excited outside interest. In 1867, a German geologist, Carl Mauch, returned from travels to the north of the Limpopo to announce that he had discovered two gold-bearing reefs in Mashonaland, one of which he had traced for eighty miles, the other for twenty miles. In a letter to the *Transvaal Argus* in December 1867, Mauch wrote: 'The vast extent and beauty of these goldfields are such that at a particular spot I stood as if transfixed, riveted to the place, struck with wonder at the sight.'

Mauch suggested that what he had found was the land of Ophir, a city mentioned in the Bible as the place from which King Solomon's ships brought back gold. He also identified another gold-bearing reef located at Tati in Kalanga territory, an area between the Ngwato, a northern Tswana chiefdom, and Mzilikazi's Ndebele kingdom. On the strength of gold samples taken from Tati, the *Transvaal Argus* confidently announced in July 1868: 'We now declare, on the sacred word of our editor, that the said sample required but to be seen in order to dispel the strongest doubts of even the most sceptical. The "myth", as the gold discovery has been termed, has resolved itself into a stupendous fact.'

The gold rush that followed to Tati produced only disappointing results, but the belief that to the north of the Limpopo lay the land of Ophir held firm. Rider Haggard picked up the idea while he was stationed in the Transvaal and, on his return to England, turned it into a hugely successful novel, *King Solomon's Mines*.

As Boer encroachment on their land continued, a number of Tswana chiefs appealed to Britain for protection, encouraged to do so by British missionaries. Foremost among them was Kgama, the Ngwato chief, based at Shoshong. Sending greetings to 'Victoria, Great Queen of England', he asked her 'to preserve me and my country, it being in her hands':

> The Boers are coming into it, and I do not like them. Their actions are cruel among us black people. We are like money, they sell us and our children . . .
>
> I wish to hear upon what conditions Her Majesty will receive me, and my country and my people, under her protection. I am weary with fighting. I do not like war, and I ask Her Majesty to give me peace. I am very much distressed that my people are being destroyed by war, and I wish them to obtain peace . . .
>
> There are things which distress me very much – war, selling people, and drink. All these things I shall find in the Boers, and it is these things which destroy people to make an end of them in the country. The custom of the Boers has always been to cause people to be sold, and today they are still selling people . . .

When Britain annexed the Transvaal in 1877, the Tswana predicament was temporarily alleviated. But once the British had withdrawn four years later, humiliated by Boer victories, Transvaal settlers – 'freebooters' – flocked across the western border agreed with Britain in 1881, in violation of the terms of the Pretoria Convention, knowing that Britain would not intervene. Many enlisted as mercenaries – 'volunteers' – supporting rival Tswana factions in return for promises of land. One group of freebooters led by Gey van Pittius aided Moswete in his struggle against a pro-British chief, Montshiwa of the Rolong; a second group under Gerrit van Niekerk helped Mosweu against another pro-British chief, Mankurwane of the Tlhaping.

In May 1882, Mankurwane reported to a senior British official in Pretoria: 'I have the honour to inform you that there is a Commando of Free State and Transvaal subjects besieging my town of Taungs. I am told that those who form this Commando wish to take my country to form an independent Republic.' By the time his message reached Cape Town, the siege was over and the Boers had won. Mankurwane was obliged to watch as Boer freebooters divided up his land into farms of 6,000 acres each for themselves. He was also forced to sign a treaty agreeing to refer all future disputes to the Transvaal authorities and not to the British. No British assistance was forthcoming. Writing to the British high commissioner in Cape Town in August, Mankurwane complained: 'Seeing therefore that I had been deserted by the British Government . . . I have done that which I ought to have done long ago, namely made my peace with the Boers . . . and have had to give up a considerable portion of my country.'

With land taken from Mankurwane running for more than 100 miles westwards from the 1881 border, Van Niekerk and his freebooters – some 400 Boer families in all – proceeded to set up their own petty republic, calling it Stellaland, to mark the passing of a comet, and established a capital at Vryburg near Taungs. The capital was a modest affair, consisting of a score of brick houses, a few stores, a billiard room and a croquet ground.

Having disposed of Mankurwane, the freebooters turned on Montshiwa. Montshiwa held out for three months, but was eventually forced to surrender two-thirds of his land, losing everything south of the Molopo River. He too was obliged to acknowledge allegiance to the Transvaal. On Montshiwa's land, Van Pittius and his freebooters established the republic of Goshen, a name taken from Genesis – 'the best of the land of Egypt given to Joseph'. The capital of Goshen, Rooi Grond, was simply a fortified farm, near Mafikeng, one mile west of the Transvaal border, occupied by a few dozen adventurers.

Both 'republics', however, lay across the road to the north, blocking access to the interior. One of the first actions taken in Vryburg was to impose a tax of £3 a fortnight on all traders passing through Stellaland. Stellaland and Goshen thus represented a significant threat to the Cape's trade with the African interior, then worth a sizeable £250,000 a year. They were moreover an obstacle standing in the way of the only feasible rail route northwards to Zambesia and its fabled riches, outside the Boer republics. It seemed inevitable that they would eventually merge into a greater Transvaal, leaving the Cape out on a limb.

Preoccupied with more pressing issues than an obscure conflict on the edge of the Kalahari desert, the British government responded to Boer raids into Bechuanaland with studied indifference. 'A most miserable page in South African history,' a Colonial Office official noted in December 1882, 'but as we shall not attempt to coerce the Boers, Montsoia and Mankoroane must face starvation as best they can.'

But Cecil Rhodes was galvanised into action. Despairing of British help and infuriated by what he saw as the 'constant vacillation' of British policy, he campaigned relentlessly for the Cape to take control of the area, stressing the advantages of 'Cape colonialism'. In May 1883, he persuaded the Cape's prime minister, Thomas Scanlen, to send him north to investigate the state of affairs in Bechuanaland and, on his return to Barkly West, bombarded Scanlen with telegrams. 'If Transvaal get them [Stellaland and Goshen] we are shut out from interior trade, and our railway to Kimberley comparatively useless . . . Don't part with an inch of territory to the Transvaal. They are bouncing. The interior road runs at the present moment on the edge of the Transvaal country. Part with that, and you are driven into the desert . . . If you part with the road you part with everything.' Rhodes urged Scanlen to 'act at once', but Scanlen was not persuaded.

In a speech to parliament in Cape Town in August 1883, Rhodes went further, claiming that 'the whole future of this Colony' was at stake:

> I look upon this Bechuanaland territory as the Suez Canal of the trade of this country, the key of its road to the interior . . . The question before us really is this: whether this Colony is to be confined to its present borders, or whether it is to become the dominant state in South Africa – whether, in fact, it is to spread its civilization over the interior . . .

The land to the north lying beyond the Transvaal, he said, had great prospects. 'I claim the development of the interior as the birthright of this Colony.' If the Cape failed to secure control of the interior, then 'we shall fall from our position of the paramount State'.

Despite such rhetoric, Rhodes failed to win parliament's support for colonial expansion; the Basutoland fiasco served as a warning of the perils it involved. But he found Britain's high commissioner, Sir Hercules Robinson, more favourably disposed to the idea. Robinson was an outspoken advocate of colonial 'home rule' rather than imperial rule and considered that colonists rather than metropolitan officials were better suited as agents of African administration. He was amenable to using his influence with London. According to Rhodes, as a result of his own efforts, Robinson rapidly 'grasped the fact that, if Bechuanaland was lost to us, British development in Africa was at an end'. Robinson's version, given to the *Cape Times* in 1895, was different: 'Rhodes did tell me a story once about his taking me up an exceedingly high mountain and showing me all the wonders of the Northern Expansion; but the truth is, I saw the Northern Expansion before I ever saw Mr Rhodes.'

The missionary lobby was also effective in prodding the British government into taking a more active interest in the fate of Bechuanaland. While Rhodes' preoccupation was to safeguard a trade corridor to the north, the missionaries wanted Britain to exercise trusteeship on behalf of the Tswana and protect them from Boer depredations. The main champion of the Tswana cause was John Mackenzie, a grizzled Scottish missionary who had headed the London Missionary Society station at Shoshong for fourteen years before moving to Kuruman in 1876. While on home leave in 1882–3, Mackenzie toured England arousing public opinion with articulate attacks on the activities of Boer freebooters in the two republics.

The issue of Bechuanaland was thus high on the agenda when Paul Kruger arrived in London as the newly elected president of the Transvaal to discuss some unfinished business from the 1881 settlement. In ebullient mood, Kruger started by demanding a new western boundary incorporating the whole of the road to the north, making the Transvaal's critics all the more determined to stand firm. In a deal eventually concluded in February 1884, Britain made a number of concessions: it dropped all reference to imperial 'suzerainty' and reduced the Transvaal's outstanding debt. In return, Kruger agreed to a new border line with Bechuanaland, taking a slice of Tswana territory, but leaving the bulk of Tswana territory intact. The deal gave Britain overall responsibility for administering the troubled southern half of Bechuanaland, including the two republics of Stellaland and Goshen, thus securing the road to the north. Robinson claimed that his role at the London Convention had been crucial in obtaining the deal. 'The Northern Expansion could never have been if the road up to it had not been kept open,' he said in 1895, 'and the battle of opening the road was fought and won by me in London in the winter of 1883–4.' The records support his claim.

The task of administering southern Bechuanaland was assigned to a British commissioner. The first candidate selected for the post was John Mackenzie, the ardent defender of Tswana interests. In making this commitment, Britain fully expected that in due course, its protectorate over southern Bechuanaland would be handed to the Cape, relieving it of the burden and the cost.

Mackenzie's task was fraught with peril. He was asked to establish order in a region torn apart by years of strife and plunder and occupied by aggressive gangs of freebooters and land sharks who had no intention of submitting to British authority, least of all to a missionary with a record of defending Tswana interests and of open hostility to them. To accomplish his task, Mackenzie was allowed to recruit a police force of 'not more than twenty-five men'. Saying farewell to him in Cape Town, Robinson was hardly reassuring. 'I have only one anxiety,' he told Mackenzie, 'that some ruffian may "pot" you; otherwise I have no doubt of the result.'

Mackenzie nevertheless took to the task of establishing imperial protection with relish. He signed an agreement with Mankurwane promising him the return of his lands and declared the Goshen farms to be the property of the Crown pending a proper investigation of titles. But not only did his actions enrage the freebooters, they infuriated Rhodes and Robinson who wanted Cape expansion, not imperial trusteeship.

Rhodes' campaign to extend the Cape's boundaries gathered

momentum during 1884. Addressing parliament in July, he repeated his warning of the previous year:

> Is this House prepared to allow these petty republics to form a wall across our trade routes? Are we to allow the Transvaal and its allies to acquire the whole of the interior? Bechuanaland is the neck of the bottle and commands the route to the Zambesi. We must secure it, unless we are prepared to see the whole of the North pass out of our hands . . . I do not want to part with the key to the interior, leaving us settled just on this small peninsula. I want the Cape Colony to be able to deal with the question of confederation as the dominant state of South Africa.

If the Cape did not move to annex Bechuanaland, he said, then the British government would 'interfere' there, adding, 'We must not have the Imperial factor in Bechuanaland.' This time, Rhodes' views gained widespread support. He now manoeuvred to get Mackenzie removed.

Unaware of how precarious his position had become, Mackenzie decided that a flag-raising ceremony in Vryburg, the capital of Stellaland, would be an appropriate sign of the new British presence. In a despatch to Robinson in Cape Town, Mackenzie painted a rosy picture. 'As they hoisted the flag amid hearty cheers, I thought here is the answer to all unjust and silly remarks which have been made recently in Cape Town about "eliminating" the Imperial element from Bechuanaland, and especially concerning myself as a breeder of strife' – a clear gibe at Rhodes.

Robinson, however, was not amused. 'You are not authorised to hoist the British flag as that implies sovereignty and Bechuanaland is just a protectorate,' he replied. He told Mackenzie his actions were likely to provoke conflict, and ordered 'Come down here at once.'

To replace Mackenzie as commissioner, Robinson chose Rhodes. Rhodes often liked to tell the story of his appointment, dressing up what had in fact been a telegraphic exchange:

The Governor said, 'Oh, you can go up [to Bechuanaland] but I can give you no force to back you up. You must use your own judgement.'

I replied: 'Will you allow me to do what I like?'

'Yes,' said the Governor, 'but if you make a mess of it, I shan't back you.'

I said, 'That is good enough for me.'

On learning of the appointment, an official in the Colonial Office asked: 'What information have we respecting Mr Rhodes?' A colleague replied that Rhodes was 'a sensible man' although inexperienced and untrained in administrative work. The general view in London was that he would 'do very well as a stop gap'.

But Rhodes had hardly begun his mission to Bechuanaland when a new threat appeared on the horizon.

14

THE GERMAN SPECTRE

The semi-desert coastline of south-west Africa offered few attractions to colonists. Britain considered it to be of no value at all. When Sir Bartle Frere had suggested extending British control there, Carnarvon permitted him merely to annex Walfisch Bay, the only significant harbour between the Cape Colony and Portuguese Angola. Carnarvon was adamant that no further territory need be taken. 'Walfisch Bay and no more,' he decreed.

Apart from a trickle of missionaries, hunters and traders, few whites ventured into south-west Africa. In 1883, however, a young German adventurer, Heinrich Vogelsang, arrived in Angra Pequena, a small harbour 150 miles north of the Cape border, with dreams of establishing a German colony. Acting on behalf of Adolf Lüderitz, a leading merchant in the old Hanseatic port of Bremen, Vogelsang persuaded a local chief to exchange a cession of the harbour and the surrounding 215 square miles for £100 worth of gold and 60 rifles. Having gained his enclave in 1883, Lüderitz pressed the German chancellor, Prince Otto von Bismarck, for a monopoly of trade in the area and the 'protection' of the German flag.

Bismarck at the time had no interest in establishing German colonies in Africa. He made enquiries with the British government in London to ascertain the status of German traders in south-west Africa, suggesting that Britain itself might like to extend its 'protection' to them. The British replied that, although they considered the area part of the British 'sphere of interest', they had no official rights there and were thus not inclined to offer protection. No one in London saw any cause for concern. Bismarck duly instructed the German consul in Cape Town to accord Lüderitz all 'assistance' and to extend his consular 'protection' to Angra Pequena.

Cape trading firms, however, regarded the German presence as a potential threat to their business. In August 1883, the Cape decided to send its own gunboat to the area to investigate; the gunboat returned with the disturbing news that German traders at Angra Pequena were demanding annexation by the Reich or at least Reich 'protection'. Cape politicians insisted that the area traditionally had been under the Cape's control, though they could produce little evidence to support their claim. Apart from annexing some off-shore islands near Angra Pequena in 1866 to obtain guano deposits, the Cape's activities had been confined to trade. But while Cape politicians were keen to assert their rights to south-west Africa, they also wanted to avoid bearing the financial cost of administering the coast and hoped that Britain would annex it for them. The prime minister, Thomas Scanlen, remarked privately in November 1883: 'With our small population, [and] the impossibility to maintain forces necessary to ensure obedience and respect for our orders, a large expanse of territory is a source of weakness and humiliation. And just now our financial burdens and diminishing revenue forbid the incurring of grave risks. If the Imperial Government would aid, something might be done.'

Bismarck meanwhile, prompted by German commercial interests, began to adopt a bolder approach. In the autumn he sent a series of increasingly forceful despatches to London asking for an unequivocal statement on the status of any British or Cape rights to Angra Pequena and its adjacent territory. The British replied, as before, in vague terms. 'Although Her Majesty's Government have not proclaimed the Queen's sovereignty along the whole country, but only at certain points such as Walfisch Bay . . . they consider that any claim to sovereignty or jurisdiction at latitude 18° and the frontier of the Cape Colony, would infringe their legitimate rights.' Unaware that

Bismarck was beginning to change his mind over the merit of 'overseas projects', British ministers continued to assume that his primary concern was not colonies but protection for his traders and saw no reason to oppose the development of a German commercial enclave at Angra Pequena. 'I do not myself see why we should object to Germany . . . occupying other parts of the coastline,' said a senior British official. 'It is a long way from everywhere.'

What Britain hoped was that the Cape would annex south-west Africa and bear the cost involved. On 3 February 1884, the colonial secretary, Lord Derby, cabled the Cape government inviting it to annex the coast as far as Walfisch Bay. But the only answer he received was: 'Ministers ask matter to be kept open, pending Cabinet meeting here. Premier away.' No other reply was sent for months. According to one account, Scanlen read the official telegram while in Cradock, pocketed it and then promptly forgot it. The British too dawdled over the issue. Not until 7 May did the Colonial Office repeat the cable of 3 February. Again there was no reply, this time because Scanlen's government had fallen.

Infuriated by the months of obfuscation and delay, Bismarck became convinced that the British were preparing to thwart Germany and steal Angra Pequena for themselves, and decided to take unilateral action. In the first step towards establishing a German colony, he declared a *Reichshutz* on 24 April 1884, giving Lüderitz's commercial company the right to govern Angra Pequena under imperial charter.

With a new government in place, led by Thomas Upington, the Cape belatedly stirred itself. 'Yours 3rd February and 7th May,' cabled the high commissioner, Robinson, on 29 May. 'Ministers have decided to recommend Parliament to undertake control and cost of coast line from Orange River to Walfisch Bay.' The British government was delighted. Derby, still misunderstanding Bismarck's intentions, blithely informed him Britain would now be able to offer protection 'to any persons, German as well as English, who may have duly acquired concessions or established [factories] on the coast'.

The jubilation was short-lived. In June, Bismarck sent his son Herbert on a special mission to London to tell Gladstone in blunt terms to keep his hands off Angra Pequena. In a speech to the

Reichstag, Bismarck announced that he had decided that Germany should build its own empire in Africa, throwing in for good measure a warning that Britain and its colonial governments would be ill-advised to block German claims, unless they could prove their own sovereignty. Rather than provoke confrontation over a barren and worthless coastal enclave 'a long way from everywhere', the British government backed down over Angra Pequena. But its retreat caused fury in the Cape. Taking its own initiative, the Cape government cabled London on 17 July announcing that it had annexed the whole coast from the Orange River northwards to the Angola border – including Angra Pequena. Britain, however, refused to give it support.

Bismarck's next move shocked the British government and produced uproar in the Cape. On 7 August 1884, Germany declared Angra Pequena to be its sovereign territory. It followed this with an announcement that it had annexed the whole of south-west Africa, other than Walfisch Bay. Within the space of six months, a small commercial outpost had 'ballooned' into a huge semi-desert colony. Whereas, at the beginning of 1884, Britain had regarded Africa south of the Limpopo as its rightful sphere of interest, now, in Gladstone's words, the 'German spectre' had arisen.

On his way north in August as the newly appointed commissioner of Bechuanaland, Rhodes was accompanied by Frank Thompson, a native administrator who spoke Setswana and who had been engaged to act as his secretary and interpreter. The two stopped briefly at Thompson's farm on the northern border of Griqualand West for refreshment and a change of horses. Thompson, an admirer of Rhodes, recorded the incident in his autobiography:

> Rhodes stepped into my wife's sitting room, and taking a kit-bag swept into it as many of her books as he could find.
> 'Something to do if I am faced with a weary and boring wait in the veld,' he said.
> My wife, I remember, expostulated. He had a habit of reading a few chapters and then, if the book pleased him, tearing off the part he had finished and handing it on to me, while he read

the rest. He said this would make the book more interesting as we could share the pleasure of the story, and the discussions would be more intelligent. It was the action of a future millionaire, but hardly good for my wife's little library.

With fresh mounts, they set off for Stellaland. 'I often laughed at the sight of Rhodes on horseback,' wrote Thompson. 'He never learnt to ride well . . . He was too loosely knit to make a good ride, had a very careless seat, and no horse was fast enough for him.'

Rhodes' plan was to offer the Boer freebooters title for land they occupied on condition that they accepted Cape rule and dispensed with the Stellaland republic. While Rhodes waited at a camp outside the main Boer laager at Commando Drift, Thompson went on ahead to engage the Boers in preliminary discussions. After two days of heated argument, according to Thompson, they agreed provisionally to take British title.

Rhodes' account of what happened, told later to his constituents in Barkly West, cast himself in a more heroic light, as he was accustomed to do. Entering the Boer encampment at Commando Drift, he said, he found Adriaan de la Rey – a Transvaaler known as 'Groot' Adriaan because of his size and strength – frying chops over an open fire. De la Rey said nothing, and Rhodes sat down opposite him in silence. Eventually De la Rey looked up from the frying pan and declared, 'Blood must flow!' 'No,' said Rhodes, 'give me my breakfast, and then we can talk about blood.' According to Rhodes, he stayed at Commando Drift for a week, became godfather to De la Rey's grandchild and secured a settlement.

However it happened, a settlement giving Stellaland's Boers rights to land they had seized as booty was signed by Rhodes and Thompson on 8 September 1884. Tswana rights to the land were ignored. 'The occupation of Stellaland had gone too far to have been disturbed,' Rhodes subsequently explained.

From Stellaland, Rhodes and Thompson moved on to the republic of Goshen, travelling via the Transvaal to get there so as to avoid any incident. The Boers of Goshen – aided and abetted by Kruger, despite the London convention – were far more hostile to the idea of

British or Cape rule. Even as Rhodes and Thompson approached their 'capital' at Rooi Grond – a collection of mud huts close to the Transvaal border – they were engaged in running battles with Montshiwa around Mafikeng.

Once again, Thompson went on ahead, leaving Rhodes at the Transvaal border. He found the 'president' of Goshen, Gey van Pittius, in his tent. Thompson told him that he had brought a message from Rhodes, the commissioner of Bechuanaland. 'And who the hell is Mr Rhodes?' a Boer asked. Thompson was held prisoner and then released to take a message back to Rhodes telling him that he had no right to style himself commissioner as the land of Goshen had been won by conquest from Montshiwa, and demanding recognition as an independent state. After another round of fruitless messages, Rhodes sent Thompson back to Van Pittius to warn that force would now be used against him.

When darkness fell, Rhodes and Thompson started on their return journey to Stellaland, then rode onward to Barkly West. By changing horses seven times, they covered 120 miles in under ten hours. On arriving at Barkly West, Rhodes went straight to the telegraph office and conversed on the wire with Robinson in Cape Town, sitting there from nine o'clock at night until breakfast the next morning.

Just when British officials were beginning to grapple with the ramifications of Bismarck's move on south-west Africa, the fate of Bechuanaland suddenly aroused further alarm. On 16 September 1884, in defiance of the London convention, Kruger proclaimed the Transvaal's annexation of Goshen and of Montshiwa's remaining territory 'in the interests of humanity'. On 3 October, the Reverend Stephanus du Toit, who had been employed by Kruger as the Transvaal's director of education and who had attended the London convention as an official Transvaal delegate, turned up at Rooi Grond, made a fiery speech, renamed the place Heliopolis and hoisted the Vierkleur. Once more, it seemed, the road to the north was threatened.

But it was not only into Bechuanaland that Transvaal Boers were expanding. A similar process of colonisation was under way into northern Zululand from the Transvaal's eastern border. Boer mercenaries offering their services to rival Zulu factions in return for grants of land claimed vast stretches of Cetshwayo's former territory. On 16 August 1884, they had declared yet another Boer state, the *Nieuwe Republiek* – the New Republic – and then laid claim to St Lucia Bay, a coastal inlet above northern Natal on the Indian Ocean. Natal's governor, Sir Henry Bulwer, warned: 'The intention of the Boers is to take a strip of land about four farms deep, along the whole length of the [Zulu] Reserve . . . Their real object, no doubt, is to reach the sea, which has always been one of the cherished ideas of the Boers of the Transvaal.'

What British officials now feared possible was an alliance between the Transvaal and Germany, from its base in south-west Africa, that would endanger British supremacy in southern Africa. On 20 September, the London *Times* reported that Germany wanted to 'push on into the Transvaal, Bechuana and Zulu countries' as part of a '*mittel-Afrika*' strategy. From Durban, Bulwer reported that a German exploring party, led by an officer in Prussian military uniform, was marching openly through the St Lucia Bay area. From Cape Town, Robinson reported: 'For some time rumours have been circulating as to German designs on St Lucia Bay in Zululand. I need hardly say that a German port in that neighbourhood would be very inconvenient.' The War Office weighed in with a confidential memorandum warning that, as a result of Boer and German action, Britain's entire strategic interests in southern Africa were at risk.

Confronted by this array of threats, Britain adopted a new 'forward' policy in southern Africa, though with considerable misgivings about the risks and costs of becoming more deeply involved there. In short order, the British government told Kruger his annexation of Goshen was unacceptable and instructed an expeditionary force of 4,000 men to move into the area and clear out the Boer freebooters; it also despatched a warship to St Lucia Bay to plant the British flag there. 'Both Natal and the Cape Colony would be endangered,' said the colonial secretary, Lord Derby, 'if any foreign power chose to claim possession of the coast.'

Command of the Bechuanaland expedition was given to Sir

Charles Warren, an irascible and headstrong officer with previous experience of the region. Along with his military role, Warren was appointed special commissioner with political responsibility for working out a new dispensation. At a meeting with Warren, shortly after his arrival in Cape Town in December, Robinson impressed on him the need to accept the settlement that Rhodes had signed in Stellaland in September 1883. Acting in league with Rhodes, Robinson was determined to ensure an outcome that made Bechuanaland secure for white settlement under Cape rule. Warren had a different agenda. He was far more interested in restoring Tswana rights under imperial control. But, without understanding the implications, he agreed to send a telegram to Gerrit van Niekerk, the 'president' of Stellaland, pledging himself, in advance, to uphold Rhodes' 1883 agreement. At Robinson's suggestion, Warren also agreed to take Rhodes along with him as an adviser and asked Rhodes to go on ahead to Stellaland to establish a British presence and maintain order.

Rhodes duly set out by wagon from the railhead at Kimberley, accompanied by an aide, Harry Currey, and two servants. 'We drove in the cool hours of the morning and evening,' Currey recalled, 'getting out of the wagon to shoot partridges and koorhaan of which there was an abundance.' On arrival in Vryburg, Rhodes hired a corrugated iron hut, naming it 'Government House'. It was so small that at night the table had to be moved outside to make way for mattresses. Currey slept in the hut; Rhodes, as was his habit, slept in the wagon.

'The first thing we did,' recalled Currey, 'was to go in search of a pool in which we could bathe. When we found one we put a few natives on to enlarge it and to swim in it morning and evening was a great relaxation after listening to all the [motley crowd of ruffians] who claimed rights in the area in dispute.' Rhodes ordered supplies of whisky and Guinness stout from Kimberley, both for themselves and to entertain local Boers.

Rhodes found Van Niekerk only too willing to hand over Stellaland, for it had no funds and was close to collapse; he promised in return that all registered land titles would be recognised.

Back in Cape Town, Warren spent a month organising his expeditionary force. It moved slowly northwards towards Bechuanaland, digging deep water-wells every dozen miles, establishing fortified supply lines, setting up military bases, accompanied by three balloons for long-distance observation – never once sighting any 'enemy'. Most freebooters withdrew into the Transvaal to await Warren's departure. The more enterprising ones travelled southwards to Kimberley to hire themselves out as transport contractors to the British army, earning £2 a day.

Having established himself in a 'well-built and sightly fort' at Barkly West, Warren began to suspect that many of the land claims made by Stellalanders were 'fictitious' and proposed that an accurate survey should be carried out. He turned for help to Rhodes' old adversary John Mackenzie, whom he had first met in Kuruman in the late 1870s, telling Robinson that Mackenzie would be 'able to give me much information which I have been unable to obtain from other sources'. Robinson pointed out that Mackenzie's involvement would arouse Boer hostility.

Mackenzie arrived at Barkly West on 20 January. Rhodes came down from Stellaland the next day, in a sulky and taciturn mood. His appearance did not help matters. According to Ralph Williams, a British intelligence officer, he was dressed in 'a big slouch bush hat, the shabbiest and most ragged of coats, and a very dirty pair of white flannel trousers, with old tennis shoes as his footgear'. When asked his name and business, he merely stated 'Rhodes'.

Two days later, Warren set off for a meeting that Kruger had requested at Fourteen Streams on the Transvaal border, taking with him a large mounted escort and a screen of scouts, worried by rumours that Boer hotheads were determined to 'pot' him. Rhodes and Mackenzie accompanied him, sharing the same coach.

Kruger told Warren that there was no need for his military expedition – using four thousand men to drive out fifty or a hundred undesirables. The 'flag incident' at Rooi Grond, he said, had occurred without his consent. All he wanted was law and order.

The meeting achieved little, but was memorable as the first encounter between Rhodes and Kruger. Rhodes was thirty years old at the time, Kruger nearly sixty. Kruger remarked to an aide: 'That young man will cause me trouble if he doesn't leave politics alone and turn to something else.' Kruger compared Rhodes to a race horse: 'Well, the race horse is swifter than the ox, but the ox can draw the greater loads. We shall see.'

When Warren finally arrived in Vryburg from Fourteen Streams, he and Rhodes dined regularly, but were soon locked in a bitter dispute over the land issue. Warren made clear he intended to repudiate Rhodes' 1883 agreement and to restore land to the Thlaping and Rolong, despite his previous commitment to Van Niekerk. Rhodes was adamant that his agreement recognising Boer claims and ratified by the colonial secretary had to stand – 'otherwise Her Majesty's word is given and broken as occasion requires'. Resigning his post, Rhodes told Warren: 'The course you have pursued since your arrival in Stellaland has been most prejudicial to the peace not only of this district but of the whole of South Africa.'

Warren's army went on to take control of Bechuanaland without resistance. Most of the Boer freebooters slipped back across the border, duly warned by Kruger that he would not support them. 'Let there be no more talk of "Shoot the Englishman" or of "damned Englishmen,"' he said. 'Let the burghers of the Transvaal and Land of Goshen guard their tongues as well as their actions; otherwise they'll pay dearly for their words.'

The British government eventually settled the future of Bechuanaland, deciding on a limited annexation. As a gesture to Tswana chiefs, the southern half, up to the Molopo River, became a crown colony known as British Bechuanaland in 1885, established in the hope that it could soon be transferred to the Cape. The northern half, including Kgama's Ngwato chiefdom, was declared a British 'protectorate'. The Germans and the Boers were shut out. The road to the north had finally been secured.

15

THE MOST POWERFUL
COMPANY IN THE WORLD

A new phase in diamond mining opened in 1885 that was to transform the industry's prospects. After years of grappling with devastating reef falls in open-cast pits, mining companies began to experiment with underground operations, constructing shafts and tunnels to reach deep-level diggings. By the end of 1885, all three major companies in Kimberley mine – the Central, the French and the Standard – had moved to systematic underground mining; in the De Beer's mine, the De Beers company, its largest claim-holder, followed suit. Though the costs of establishing underground operations were high, production and profits soared. Whereas Kimberley Central's output in 1884 fell to as low as 600 loads a day, in 1887 it reached more than 6,000 loads a day. The deep-level diggings, moreover, proved to contain even richer diamond deposits. A recovery in the European market buoyed carat prices, further increasing profits. In 1887, Kimberley Central declared a dividend of 35 per cent. The opening of the railway line to Cape Town in 1885 provided another huge boost.

The success of underground operations, however, raised once more the spectre that had overshadowed the industry since the 1870s: increases in production eventually led to price falls and declining profitability. As companies competed to raise production to gain higher profits, so simultaneously did they increase the risks of wiping out profits altogether. The stakes by now were considerable: Kimberley Central had a fully paid-up capital of £750,000; De Beers, £1 million.

The solution had long been foreseen: a monopoly company in control of the entire industry. After returning from the diamond diggings in 1871, Frederick Boyle had observed:

> You cannot drown the market with an article only appertaining to the highest luxury – without swift and sudden catastrophe . . . By royal monopoly alone, or by means of great and powerful companies, can jewel digging be made a thriving industry. Into the hands of a company all these public fields must fall, and, thus used, they may benefit the country for generations to come.

Several attempts at amalgamation had since been made. In 1882, Rhodes and his partners in De Beers approached the Paris bankers Baron Erlanger and Company with a scheme to consolidate holdings in De Beer's mine; but the scheme foundered when claim-holders failed to agree on the valuation of their holdings. In 1883, the European merchant bankers N. M. Rothschild and Sons showed an interest in amalgamating holdings in Dutoitspan mine, but did not pursue it. In 1885, Rhodes' friend John Merriman acted for the Standard Bank in proposing amalgamation in Dutoitspan mine as a way of recovering advances it had made to mining companies there, but without success. In 1886, Charles Roulina, a wealthy Parisian diamond-cutting factory owner, and Charles Posno, a London-based speculator, formed a syndicate of banks and diamond merchants to promote the formation of a giant new company, Unified Diamond Mines, with the aim of merging the interests of all the major companies; that initiative also failed.

The only option left, following the failure of the Unified initiative, was for the major companies to fight it out amongst themselves for control. By 1885, the total number of companies had been reduced to about one hundred: nineteen in Kimberley mine; ten in De Beer's; thirty-seven in Dutoitspan; and thirty-two in Bultfontein.

Two companies had emerged by 1885 as the most likely nuclei for a diamond mining monopoly: Kimberley Central and De Beers. Both set about crushing smaller rivals by producing as many diamonds as possible; in the words of a Standard Bank report, by 'swamping them with production'. In 1886, Kimberley Central alone produced more stones than either the Dutoitspan or Bultfontein mines and almost as many as the entire De Beer's mine, boosting Central's revenues but keeping carat prices low. De Beers developed its operations at breakneck speed, doubling the amount of ground it excavated in the process and showing, according to the Standard Bank, 'a reckless disregard for human life'. With accidents multiplying and disease rife, the death rate in the mine reached 150 per thousand employed.

Appointed chairman of De Beers in 1886, Rhodes pursued the last surviving independent companies in the mine relentlessly. By the beginning of 1887, only one independent company remained: the Victoria headed by Francis Oats. With the backing of the merchant bankers J. H. Schröder, Oats refused to come to terms. Rhodes therefore turned for help to Alfred Beit, using his connections to Jules Porges and Company, Europe's leading importer of Cape diamonds, to carry out the *coup de main*. Instead of trying to take on Oats in Kimberley, Rhodes asked Porges to buy shares in the Victoria Company discreetly in London. 'We felt that if they were bought in the London market,' Rhodes subsequently explained, 'it would excite no remark.' At a cost of £57,000, De Beers acquired 3,000 shares and Beit and Porges a further 3,000 shares. After waiting for an opportune moment, Rhodes announced in April 1887 that, as the largest shareholder in the Victoria Company, he had decided the time had come to amalgamate with De Beers.

Thus De Beer's mine became the first mine in Griqualand West to come under the control of a single company. In his report to the De Beers annual meeting in May 1887, Rhodes declared that amalgamation would enable the diamond industry to gain the position it ought to occupy, 'that is, not at the mercy of the buyers, but the buyers under the control of the producers'.

The Victoria deal also marked the beginning of a highly effective collaboration between Rhodes and Beit. Rhodes came to depend increasingly upon Beit's financial advice. Any problem concerning diamonds would invariably be solved by Beit. 'Ask little Alfred' became a catch phrase among Rhodes' circle of friends. Beit himself prospered greatly by speculating in Victoria shares, clearing a profit of £100,000, doubling his own wealth.

While these company manoeuvres were under way, Hans Sauer often saw Rhodes seated on the edge of the De Beer's mine 'gazing intently down into its depths, absorbed in his reflections'. Later, Sauer asked him what he had been thinking about. '"I was calculating the amount of blue ground in sight and the power that this blue ground would confer on the man who obtained control of it," was his answer.'

As well as driving the pace of amalgamation, the introduction of underground mining, together with the increasing use of steam engines and other machinery, brought major changes to the organisation of the labour force. Rather than local white overseers, skilled miners were needed. They were recruited from the coal mines of Cumberland and the tin mines of Cornwall; shaft sinkers came from Lancashire; artisans from the factories of Scotland and England. The number of colonial whites employed in the mines fell to just 10 per cent of the white labour force. Kimberley now witnessed the emergence of a poor-white community. An Anglican priest reported that he knew of no Coloured family 'so low as the most degraded whites'.

New laws were approved introducing a legal colour bar between white and black employees. Whereas British administrators had previously resisted legal discrimination, the Mining Act of 1883 decreed that 'no native is to be permitted to manipulate explosives or prepare the same for blasting or other purposes'. Blasting had to be carried on 'under the supervision of a European'. Subsequent legislation ruled that: 'No native shall work or be allowed to work in any mine, whether in open or underground workings, excepting under the responsible charge of some particular white man as his master or "baas"'.

To ensure a more reliable supply of black labour, mining companies organised their own system of recruitment. Recruits were required to agree to contracts running for six to twelve months rather than three to six. Their living conditions also changed. Originally, diggers had accommodated black workers on their compounds or encampments in tents or sheds. Subsequently, they were housed in barracks. From 1885, mining companies required black workers to live in fenced and guarded compounds on their property for the entire term of their contract. Closed compounds had the advantage of preventing diamond theft. They also provided mine-owners with greater control of the labour force.

The model for the closed compound system that developed in Kimberley was a convict station built by De Beers as a base for employing cheap convict labour. In return for housing and feeding several hundred convicts, De Beers was given the right to use them as free compulsory labour, paying only a small fee to the Cape government. The government's inspector of mines considered 'these convict barracks . . . the perfecting of the compound system'. De Beers found the employment of convicts so advantageous that it continued to use them for nearly fifty years.

By 1889, all 10,000 black mineworkers in Kimberley were accommodated in closed compounds. Some discussion ensued about the idea of incorporating white employees into the compound system. In his annual report in 1884, the inspector of mines proposed that it should apply to all mineworkers, but the idea was not pursued. Whites were permitted to live in the town, leaving blacks confined to segregated compounds.

The lifestyle of Kimberley's magnates, meanwhile, was enhanced by the opening of the Kimberley Club. Like many other enterprises in the town, it was a venture launched as a joint-stock company, by a group of seventy-four well-known citizens, each of whom pledged to take one debenture share of £100. Among the shareholders were Rhodes, Rudd, Robinson, Jameson and Dr Matthews. When the double-storeyed building was completed in 1882, it was judged impressive: 'It beats anything of the kind I was ever in,' wrote young Neville Pickering. 'We have our dinners and dances – one finds oneself in evening dress every night. It's ruination to health and pocket.

And then our Club is such perfection. Electric bells wherever you like to touch. Velvet pile and Turkey carpets to walk upon and then one loses oneself in a luxurious lounge. This reminds me of an advertisement I remember seeing at home: Call a spade a spade, but call our new velvet lounges the very essence of luxury and extreme comfort.'

Rhodes and Beit were often seen at the Club together, sharing a customary drink to start the day; their favourite tipple was Black Velvet, a mixture of champagne and stout. 'Ah,' Rhodes would proclaim, 'it makes a man of you!' They played poker there, albeit badly. Occasionally, they attended a Bachelors' Ball, Rhodes vigorously twirling the plainest girl in the room, Beit indulging his penchant for tall girls.

In the final race to gain control of the diamond industry, their alliance was to prove decisive. Beit's involvement with Jules Porges and Company provided Rhodes with links to foreign banks needed to finance any takeover. But the opposition they faced was formidable.

At the beginning of 1886, four powerful companies dominated Kimberley mine: the Central, the French, the Standard and Barnato. The Barnato was the smallest of the four. At one stage, with his claims buried under reef falls, Barney Barnato had thought of selling up, but he resumed mining operations in 1885 and embarked on an aggressive amalgamation drive in Kimberley to rival Rhodes' acquisitions in De Beer's. His first victim was the Standard, once controlled by Robinson. He next gained control of the Central, retaining the name as a vehicle for further acquisitions. Only the French Company and a few minor players now stood in his way. Barnato's intention was to gain control of the French, expand output, push carat prices down to a level at which no other company could make a profit, and thereby force the closure of De Beer's, Dutoitspan and Bultfontein mines.

The future of the diamond industry thus hinged on the fate of the French Company. Rhodes made the first move. Using Beit's connections, Rhodes secured the promise of a loan of £750,000 from a syndicate of French and German financiers in exchange for a block of De Beers' shares. But as speculators continued to drive up the price of

French shares, Rhodes had need of far more funds. Through Beit, he obtained an introduction to Nathaniel de Rothschild, head of Europe's wealthiest financial house and an active speculator in diamond shares. While Barnato was in the throes of amalgamating the Central and the Standard, Rhodes set sail for England in July 1887, accompanied by Gardner Williams, an American mining engineer well known to the Rothschilds, whom he had hired in May 1887 as a new manager for De Beers. At Rhodes' behest, Williams had compiled a full report on the diamond industry, stressing the advantages of amalgamation under Rhodes.

Rhodes' meeting with Rothschild in London went well. Rhodes asked for a £1 million loan to help him purchase the French Company and Rothschild promised to support him if he could get the agreement of its directors and shareholders to sell. Rothschild looked to make a profit of at least £100,000 on the deal. Travelling on to Paris, Rhodes was given a similarly favourable reception by the directors of the French Company. Once again, Beit had prepared the way, persuading Jules Porges in advance that amalgamation of the mines was a sound financial objective and that Rhodes was the man to accomplish it. A price of £1.4 million was agreed, subject to the approval of shareholders at a meeting scheduled for October.

Rhodes subsequently liked to boast of his genius in pulling off the deal: 'You know the story of my getting on board the steamer at Cape Town, going home and buying the French Company within twenty-four hours,' he would say. But the real architect behind the deal was 'little Alfred'.

Barnato, however, was not so easily thwarted. He himself had previously acquired one fifth of the French Company's shares. On hearing of Rhodes' bid, he put in an offer of £1.7 million, hoping to raise sufficient funds from the Standard Bank. At a meeting of all the Kimberley shareholders in the French Company in September, he urged them to hold out for better terms than the Rhodes offer. As speculators on all sides joined the throng, the price of diamond shares continued to soar.

Though making massive gains from share speculation, both Rhodes and Barnato faced acute difficulties. Rothschild's warned Rhodes that the price of French shares had reached such heights that they could not hope to purchase enough of them to prevent a Central takeover. Rhodes feared that Rothschild's might abandon him altogether, preferring to 'make half a million' profit by selling the shares already purchased on behalf of De Beers to the Central instead. Rhodes' colleagues urged him to negotiate a settlement rather than enter a bidding war that De Beers might win, but at too high a cost. Barnato, meanwhile, ran into trouble when the Standard Bank refused to advance loan money.

In October 1887, a compromise settlement was reached. Rhodes agreed that if he was allowed to buy the French Company unhindered, he would resell it to the Central but retain a one-fifth stake in Central. The advantage of the scheme was that it would allow amalgamation to take place in Kimberley mine and then open the way for the amalgamation of Central and De Beers. This arrangement, supported by Barnato and Beit, was designed to ensure that amalgamation was achieved without a fall in any company's share value, thus satisfying industrialists and speculators alike. 'The great comfort I feel now is that the goal is reached,' Rhodes wrote in a private letter to Frederic Stow, one of his closest associates, on 22 October 1887. 'Barnato . . . is working in everything with me and has given his pledge to go to the end with me.'

Outwardly, the battle between Rhodes and Barnato was fought as aggressively as before. A host of legends later circulated about their struggle. Rhodes himself relished such tales. Certainly, there were protracted disputes over the valuation of their properties. While the disputes continued, speculators drove share prices in Central and De Beers ever higher. Borrowing heavily, Rhodes increased his holding in Central from one-fifth to three-fifths. By March 1888, the market value of the mines had soared to nearly £23 million. De Beers' shares worth £3. 10s in January 1885 reached £47.

But the original deal remained largely intact. Amid the hullabaloo, it was noticed that Rhodes and Beit had become increasingly friendly with Barnato. They met for drinks; Rhodes introduced Barnato into the Kimberley Club, despite the disdain with which other members regarded his flashy habits. After making huge profits from speculation, Barnato agreed in March 1888 to give up his shareholding in Central in exchange for gaining the largest shareholding in De Beers.

At Rhodes' behest, a new company was set up – De Beers Consolidated Mines Limited – with ambitions that far outstripped the original purposes of the old De Beers company. Instead of being limited to diamond mining, Rhodes wanted the new company to be able to engage in any business enterprise, annex land in any part of Africa, govern foreign territories and maintain standing armies.

Barnato objected to such grandiose notions and argued in favour of restricting the terms of the company's Trust Deed to business activity. A final meeting to discuss the Trust Deed was held in Rhodes' corrugated iron cottage. Barnato brought his nephew, Woolf Joel, with him; Rhodes was supported by Beit. The arguments went on all night. Rhodes produced facts, figures and maps to persuade Barnato about the fabulous wealth to be gained from exploiting other parts of Africa.

'Aren't those just dreams of the future?' asked Woolf Joel. 'Dreams don't pay dividends.'

'No, my friend,' replied Rhodes, 'they're not dreams, they're plans. There's a difference.'

Just before dawn, Barnato gave way. 'Some people have a fancy for *this* thing and some for *that*,' he said. '*You* have a fancy for making an empire. Well, I supposed I must give it to you.'

The first annual general meeting of De Beers Consolidated Mines was held on 31 March 1888. The company's assets were considerable. It owned the whole of the De Beer's mine, three-fifths of the shares in the Kimberley mine and a controlling interest in both Bultfontein and Dutoitspan. Barnato had 7,000 shares in the new company; Rhodes, 4,000. Rhodes called on the remaining shareholders to surrender and triumphantly proclaimed his determination to make De Beers 'the richest, the greatest, and the most powerful Company the world has ever seen'.

As rewards for their endeavours in founding the new De Beers, Rhodes, Beit, Barnato and Frederic Stow were made 'Life Governors' and given a generous package of financial benefits: each was entitled to a one-quarter share of the net profits remaining after distribution of a 36 per cent dividend. 'I feel with a Company that will be worth as much as the balance of Africa you must have four or five men to whom you make it worth their while to devote a great portion of their time to it,' explained Rhodes. The powers that Life Governors possessed were formidable. They were able to operate in almost every way as if there were no shareholders.

When minority shareholders in the Central Company objected to the terms of the takeover and won a court ruling in their favour, Rhodes put the Central into liquidation, then won a tender for its assets, paying with a De Beers cheque made out for £5,338,650.

The consequences of amalgamation were soon felt in other ways. As De Beers cut back production, hundreds of miners, black and white, lost their jobs. On 4 June, white demonstrators marched from Dutoitspan to the head office of De Beers, pushing a cart containing an effigy of Rhodes. Before proceeding to burn it, they declared:

> We will now commit to the flames the last mortal remains of Cecil John Rhodes, Amalgamator General, Diamond King and Monarch of De Beers, but not of the Pan [Dutoitspan], thank God! And in doing so let us not forget to give three cheers for a traitor to his adopted country, a panderer to the selfish greed of a few purse-proud speculators, and a public pest. May the Lord perish him. Amen.

Rhodes shrugged off such protests and proceeded to buy out the last remaining independent mine operators in Dutoitspan and Bultfontein. By September 1889 he had achieved a complete monopoly of all Kimberley's mines – 90 per cent of the world's production. Together with the world's principal diamond merchants, he then set out to achieve a marketing monopoly of the diamond trade to ensure that the market could be manipulated to the best advantage, keeping supply in line with the highest price available. By 1891 virtually all Kimberley's output was channelled to members of a syndicate based in London that controlled the system. Rhodes was well pleased with the result. De Beers' ranking as one of the most powerful companies in the world provided him with a solid platform from which to pursue other ambitions. 'Money is power,' said Rhodes, 'and what can one accomplish without power? That is why I must have money. Ideas are no good without money . . . For its own sake I do not care for money. I never tried it for its own sake but it is a power and I like power.'

PART IV

16

A CHOSEN PEOPLE

The Kruger household on Church Street, Pretoria, offered genial hospitality to all who called, friends and strangers alike, even after Paul Kruger became president of the Transvaal in 1883. During the day, the front door was kept wide open; there were no sentries posted there. To each visitor, Kruger extended his huge hand in welcome. From the kitchen, his wife, Gezina, provided an endless flow of coffee, rusks and other delicacies.

The house had been built by Charles Clark, an English-speaking builder who had settled in Pretoria during President Burgers' tenure in office and whom Kruger liked to describe as his tame Englishman. It was set back no more than six feet from the street but was largely concealed by tall shade trees. Along the front ran a wide stoep, or veranda, where much business was conducted. Inside was a large reception room furnished with settees, armchairs, two round tables and a collection of upright chairs. Volksraad committee meetings were sometimes held there. There was also a dining room, a bedroom, and a small private study. The back stoep was used to store biltong – dried meat. And in the back garden, Kruger kept cows.

Kruger's routine was to rise at daybreak, unlock the front door, and then retire to his private study to read a chapter from the Bible by the light of a paraffin lamp or tallow candle. After early morning coffee, in summer he would sit on the stoep, smoking his pipe, ready to receive his first callers; in winter, he remained in the reception room, with a large Bible placed nearby. At mealtimes, he said grace twice, speaking in High Dutch and at length. Women not wearing bonnets were required to place serviettes over their heads. Gezina was never seen without a bonnet. Partial to milk, Kruger always kept a bowl of milk and bread beside him. On a state visit to Germany in 1884, he insisted on toasting the Kaiser's health in milk.

He seldom read the morning papers, preferring to rely on a summary prepared for him by his aide, Dr Willem Leyds, a young attorney he recruited from Holland in 1884. After meeting his executive council, he presided over the Volksraad, dressed in an old frock-coat with a broad green sash of office bound over his shoulder. Debates in the Volksraad were often heated. Members were accustomed to expressing their views with great vehemence, gesticulating wildly and thumping the table. Kruger participated in similar manner, famous for his 'bellowing' and 'buffalo rushes'.

'On the first occasion upon which I visited the Raad,' wrote Captain Francis Younghusband, a special correspondent for the London *Times*,

> I saw Mr Kruger, almost before the original speaker had finished, rise and roar in his deep big voice at the meeting, and almost break the table with his violent thumps upon it. I thought that something very important must be under debate, but was told that they were merely debating whether some minor official's salary should be cut down or increased! Mr Kruger is always emphatic upon whatever subject he speaks. But when he wishes to really enforce a point he comes round to his great stock argument that the independence of the country would be endangered if what he wishes is not agreed to.

Kruger was usually successful in getting his own way through the use of such histrionics. Describing his official encounters with Kruger, in a tone of affectionate exasperation, General Nicolaas Smit, the hero of Majuba, recalled:

I do stand up to him, I know he is wrong and I tell him so; but first he argues with me, and if that is no good he gets in a rage and jumps around the room roaring at me like a wild beast . . . and if I do not give in then he fetches out the Bible and . . . quotes that to help him out. And if all that fails, he takes my hand and cries like a child and begs and prays me to give in . . . who can resist a man like that?

Kruger's ambitions for the Transvaal were modest. The government depended for revenue on a pastoral economy and a small gold-mining industry in the Lydenburg district of the eastern Transvaal, and its finances remained precarious. Short of funds, Kruger was persuaded by an enterprising Hungarian adventurer, Hugo Nellmapius, that a useful method for the state to raise money was to sell monopoly concessions to independent businessmen. Nellmapius had arrived in the eastern Transvaal in 1873, at the age of twenty-six, to try his hand at gold prospecting. Trained as a civil engineer, he had a working knowledge of the use of dynamite, introduced large-scale mining operations to the eastern Transvaal and set up a transport business along a new road he constructed to the sea at Delagoa Bay. Settling in Pretoria in 1878, he purchased a farm at Hatherley on the Pienaar's River, ten miles east of the capital, struck up a warm friendship with Kruger, financed a new house for him on his Church Street property, and looked around for business opportunities.

In September 1881, Nellmapius set out his plan for monopoly concessions in a four-page document he submitted to Kruger's executive council. He proposed only a small beginning, but the idea he put forward, once it took hold, was to have momentous consequences.

What the Transvaal needed, he said, was its own industries to produce basic products such as clothing, blankets, leather, flour and sugar, protected by high tariff walls to ensure their viability. What was lacking was entrepreneurial initiative. Any new enterprise involved high risk. But the government could overcome this by offering 'privileges, patents, monopolies, bonuses et cetera'.

As a start, Nellmapius asked for two monopolies, one for distilling liquor from local grain and other raw materials, the other for producing sugar from beets and maize. Since the cost of building and operating a factory would be at least £100,000, he said, his concession would have to last for at least fifteen years. In return, he was prepared to make an annual contribution to the Treasury of £1,000, paid in advance. Nellmapius' scheme for a fifteen-year liquor concession was duly approved by the executive council and the Volksraad. Once a contract was signed in October 1881, he took on as partners two other entrepreneurs, Sammy Marks and his brother-in-law, Isaac Lewis, and launched a company with a capital of £100,000 to manage the project – 'De Eerste Fabrieken' (The First Factory). Construction began on his farm at Hatherley.

In view of Kruger's abhorrence of liquor, it was ironic that the Transvaal's first factory was built to produce it. He nevertheless agreed to preside over the opening ceremony in 1883. While other guests indulged in champagne and sampled the distillery's first output – a rough, fiery gin – Kruger sipped milk. He remarked that although he himself disliked liquor, he did not regard its production as a sin. 'Drink is a gift from God,' he said, 'given to man for moderate consumption, and in that there is no sin.' He could well understand, he said, that a drink after a hard day's work could be refreshing and invigorating. What was reprehensible was drunkenness. He spoke of the factory as '*De Volks-Hoop*' – the people's hope – providing employment for burghers and encouragement for agricultural producers. A large poster decorating one of the walls read: 'A Concession Policy is the Making of the Country'.

Of more concern to Kruger was how to protect the Boer character of the Transvaal from foreign influence. He proposed restrictions on immigration 'in order to prevent the Boer nationality from being stifled', but recognised that, with only a limited pool of trained manpower available amongst Transvaalers, foreign recruitment was unavoidable. His solution was to appeal for immigrants from Holland. 'I apprehend the least danger from an invasion from Holland,' he said. Addressing a huge crowd in Amsterdam during a European tour in 1884, he declared: 'We have kept our own language, the language of the Netherlands people, who have fought eighty years for faith and freedom. Our people in the wilderness have kept their language and faith through every storm. Our whole struggle is bound up with this.' Over the course of the next fifteen years, more than 5,000 Dutch immigrants arrived in the Transvaal, reinforcing the ranks of civil servants and teachers.

Kruger also used his immense authority to promote the Calvinist concept of national calling and destiny. To celebrate the return of the Transvaal's independence in 1881, he organised a four-day 'festival of thanksgiving' at Paardekraal, where the year before burghers had vowed to defend the unity of the Volk and re-establish their republic. Speaking before a crowd of 12,000 Boers on the first day, 13 December, Kruger reminded them of the early struggle of the voortrekkers and of how each time God had guided them onward. The Great Trek, he said, was like the journey of the Israelites of the Old Testament leaving Egypt to escape the Pharaoh's yoke, and he cited it as evidence that God had summoned the Boers on a similar mission to establish a promised land in southern Africa. They were thus a chosen people.

The last day of the festival, 16 December, was used for the same purpose. It marked the forty-third anniversary of the Boer victory at Blood River in 1838 when a commando of 468 trekkers, three Englishmen and sixty blacks faced some 10,000 Zulu warriors. In a battle lasting two hours, three trekkers were slightly wounded and none killed, but 3,000 Zulus lay dead. For Kruger, the victory at Blood River was a miracle demonstrating God's support for the Boers and their special mission in Africa. Just as 16 December 1838 had been a turning point in the lives of the trekkers, said Kruger, so now 16 December 1881 was the beginning 'of still greater salvation'.

The festival at Paardekraal became a five-yearly event, presided over by Kruger, with ever greater emphasis being placed on the significance of the Blood River victory – Dingaan's Day, as it was called. The Transvaal government appointed a Dutch teacher to seek out survivors and record their memories. What became especially important was a pledge said to have been made by members of the commando a few days before the battle occurred that, if God granted them a victory, they would build a memorial church in his honour and commemorate the anniversary as a day of thanksgiving for ever more.

In his report of the battle, the commando leader, Andries Pretorius, did indeed refer to the covenant and, three years later, together with local people, he erected a church building at the Boer encampment at Pietermaritzburg in Natal. From 1861, however, the building was no longer used as a place of worship, but for commercial purposes. It became in turn a wagonmaker's shop, a mineral water factory, a tea room, a blacksmith's workshop, a school and, eventually, a woolshed. Nor, apparently, did most members of the commando take the covenant seriously. The covenant, in fact, fell rapidly into oblivion.

But facing the menace of British imperialism in the 1880s, Kruger and other prominent Afrikaners in the Transvaal sought to fortify morale by reviving public awareness of the covenant. Kruger argued that the setbacks the Boers had endured – from the British annexation of Natal in 1843 to the British annexation of the Transvaal in 1877 – were God's chastisements for their failure to honour their vow. The Boer victory in 1881 was a sign of God's continuing commitment.

Having regained independence, however, Kruger was allowed little respite from the attention of foreigners. In 1885, news arrived in Pretoria of a major gold discovery on the eastern border of the Transvaal. The editor of the *Pretoria Press*, Leo Weinthal, recorded Kruger's reaction. After remaining silent, lost in thought, Kruger remarked, with Old Testament fervour:

> Do not talk to me of gold, the element which brings more dis-
> sension, misfortune and unexpected plagues in its trails than
> benefits. Pray to God, as I am doing, that the curse connected
> with its coming may not overshadow our dear land just after it
> has come again to us and our children. Pray and implore Him
> who has stood by us that He will continue to do so, for I tell you
> today that every ounce of gold taken from the bowels of our soil
> will yet have to be weighed up with rivers of tears.

The first 'payable' gold discoveries in the Transvaal had been made in the early 1870s near the eastern escarpment, where the great Transvaal plateau breaks and drops away to the lowveld and the coast. Alluvial gold was found in the Lydenburg district in 1872 and at Pilgrim's Rest in the valley of the Blyde River in 1873. Diggers poured in from Delagoa Bay, the nearest port, traversing a stretch of wild, disease-ridden bushland to get there.

Further finds were made in 1882 in De Kaap, 'fever country' close to Swaziland. In 1883, a French prospector, August Robert, otherwise known as French Bob, struck the Pioneer Reef there. In June 1884, a Natal prospector, Graham Barber, reported a significant gold-bearing reef in the De Kaap valley; a small village known as Barberton sprang up nearby. New reefs were subsequently reported almost daily, prompting a rush of fortune-seekers from all over the world. Then, in 1885, a former Yorkshire coal miner, Edwin Bray struck 'Bray's Golden Quarry', part of the fabulously rich Sheba Reef. The first 13,000 tons of ore yielded 50,000 ounces of gold.

Barberton rapidly turned into a boom town, becoming the largest centre of population in the Transvaal. Thousands of claims were pegged; new companies were launched by the score, and millions of share certificates were sold. From dawn until late at night, the Barberton stock exchange was the scene of frantic activity. Investors in Britain scrambled to buy Barberton gold shares – *kaffirs*, as they were called. The £1 shares of Sheba Company rose to £105.

Kimberley's diamond contingent took an early interest in the De Kaap goldfields, sending out scouts and making periodic visits. Beit travelled there in 1884, accompanied by Jules Porges. 'Beit's energy when inspecting shafts and drives was really astonishing,' wrote Jim Taylor, his Barberton agent. 'From early dawn until dark he would ride and walk over the rougher country without showing signs of fatigue.' Beit plunged in with enthusiasm, buying shares in the French Bob Company and in Kimberley Imperial Company, becoming chair-man of both.

The young doctor Hans Sauer visited the goldfields during the course of a long hunting trip and toyed with the idea of giving up medicine for a more adventurous occupation. He arrived in Barberton amid a wave of excitement about the gold levels in the newly discov-ered Kimberley Imperial mine. 'Everyone on the Field was busy pegging out claims, and I did likewise.'

His dreams of a prospector's life, however, were soon dashed by the results of a poker game he played with Dr Jameson in Lydenburg:

> He was the dealer and gave me two kings. I bought three cards, amongst which he gave me two more kings, so that I had four of a kind in my hand. He also kept two and bought three more. With the four kings in my hand I bragged up to £800, which represented all my cash resources at the time. Jameson kept raising me until I was forced to put in my wagon and oxen, guns and outfit, and finally a pair of top-boots. Upon which he 'saw me' and beat me with a straight flush. I rose from the table broke to the wide world. Jameson kindly returned me the top-boots and my surgical instruments.

The Barberton boom soon turned to bust. Most companies never produced so much as an ounce of gold; many were straight swindles, set up to lure investors with bogus prospectuses. Though there were exceptionally rich pockets of gold scattered about the Barberton field, only five mines proved to be viable.

From his own investigations, Beit's agent, Jim Taylor, soon concluded that apart from such properties as Bray's Golden Quarry and the Sheba, Barberton was 'a flop'. Beit and Jules Porges hurried back to Barberton and sold out in time to avoid the worst of the crash, though not without loss.

Many others were ruined. Hundreds of fortune-seekers who had arrived with hope and enthusiasm trudged back penniless to Pretoria and Cape Town, some in rags. London investors lost huge sums. After such a disastrous debut on world markets, South African gold shares were viewed with deep distrust.

Then in 1886, an itinerant English prospector, George Harrison, who had worked in the goldfields of Australia as well as the eastern Transvaal, stumbled across a gold-bearing rocky outcrop on a farm called Langlaagte – Long Shallow Valley. Together with a colleague, George Walker, a former Lancashire coal miner, Harrison had been heading on foot to Barberton when he was offered work building a cottage on Langlaagte for a Boer widow, Petronella Oosthuizen. In

April, Harrison and Walker signed a contract with the Oosthuizen family permitting them to prospect for gold. In May, Harrison hurried to Pretoria to secure a prospecting licence, taking with him a sample of gold-bearing rock which he showed to President Kruger. He was duly named the '*zoeker*' – the discoverer – of the find and awarded a free claim. But Harrison decided to move on, selling his claim for £10. Beneath lay the richest gold field ever discovered.

17

JOHANNESBURG

The Witwatersrand – the Ridge of White Waters – was named by Boer farmers after the glistening streams that appeared to run from it after rainfall. It was a barren stretch of highveld, 6,000 feet above sea level, often swept by fires in the dry winter months. The gold reef that broke the surface there, running for some sixty miles from east to west, was different from all previous discoveries made in the Transvaal. Its gold deposits were contained not in quartz reefs but in a compressed water-worn gravel conglomerate of sedimentary origin. On outcrops on the surface, the conglomerate disintegrated into a mass of smooth quartz pebbles, of various shapes and sizes, white and red in colour. Boer farmers called the conglomerate *banquette* or banket, because it resembled a favourite type of sweet – nuts or almonds coated with sugar. Below the surface, the conglomerate dipped away at an angle, descending to unknown depths. The trace of gold contained within the reef was minute; what distinguished it was its vast extent.

The first prospectors to strike gold on the Witwatersrand were two German brothers, Fred and Harry Struben, who owned farms in the Roodepoort area. Both had participated briefly in the diamond rush in 1871 before returning home; Fred had also tried his luck at Barberton. In 1884, Fred broke off a piece of quartz surface rock, crushed and panned it, and came away with a teaspoon of gold. Further samples showed a high gold content. But the gold soon ran out. The Struben brothers were nevertheless convinced that 'payable' gold was to be found in the area, not in the form of alluvial deposits or quartz finds but as thin traces in hard rock. On 5 June 1885, Harry Struben disclosed their findings at a gathering of members of Kruger's executive council and the Volksraad assembled on a tennis court behind the Union Club in Pretoria. The Witwatersrand, he said, could prove to be richer in gold than any previous discovery in the Transvaal.

There was, however, considerable scepticism about such a notion. The Barberton bubble had left many mining men wary of such claims. One 'expert' sent by a prospective syndicate in Natal to investigate the Struben properties concluded after three months that there was more gold to be found in the streets of Pretoria than on the whole of the Witwatersrand.

When reports of new gold finds first reached Kimberley, the reaction was generally cynical. Only one of Kimberley's magnates, J. B. Robinson, decided to take a look for himself. Robinson had been 'squeezed out' during the amalgamation of the diamond mines and he now saw a chance to restore his fortunes. He was, however, heavily in debt; all his assets were held by the Cape of Good Hope Bank as collateral against loans advanced to him. Needing funds, he decided to approach Beit for help.

Beit's version of his encounter with Robinson was recorded by the journalist Frank Harris:

> One day he came into my office and said that he had lost all his money, that Rhodes and I had ruined him. He wanted to know if I would give him something to go to the Rand with and make a fresh start.
>
> I did not know what to say. At last I asked him how much he wanted. He said he would leave that to me.
>
> 'If I give you £20,000,' I said, 'will that do?' Of course I was not obliged to give him anything at all.
>
> 'Oh yes,' he said 'How good of you. I can win with that.'

So Beit gave Robinson a cheque for £20,000 in return for a one-third share in what was to be called the 'Robinson Syndicate'. Robinson took one-third for himself and gave one-third to his partner, Maurice Marcus.

Setting off for the Rand in July 1886, Robinson found himself sharing a coach with Hans Sauer. Sauer had received a letter from a medical colleague in Potchefstroom telling him of the gold finds. They arrived at the farm Langlaagte two days later and stayed the night with the owner, Petronella Oosthuizen. The next morning, they were shown the reef by an itinerant French prospector who had dug a small inclined shaft about thirty feet deep. They then moved on a mile to the east to an encampment on Turffontein farm set up by Colonel Ignatius Ferreira, a Boer adventurer from the Cape Colony. Ferreira had acquired a dozen claims in the vicinity and opened the reef in a cutting. The ore from both sites had a high gold content.

That night, Robinson, flush with Beit's money, made an offer to lease the widow's part of the farm and the next day began hunting for other properties, buying outright another part of Langlaagte. Sauer walked westwards for ten miles, accompanied by Mrs Oosthuizen's son, following the line of the reef outcrops, taking samples as he went, and becoming all the more convinced that a major goldfield lay beneath.

After two days of investigation, Sauer returned to Kimberley with his samples, in a state of considerable excitement. His brother-in-law, Harry Caldecott, advised him to approach Rhodes, whom he had met only a few times before.

> I went round next morning after breakfast to Rhodes's cottage, where I found him still in bed. He invited me in and asked me to sit down on the edge of his bed and state my business. He lis-tened to what I had to say . . . without much apparent interest.

Rhodes told Sauer to come back with his bag of samples at one o'clock. On his return, he found Rhodes, Rudd and two Australian miners waiting for him in the backyard of his cottage.

The miners had brought a pestle and mortar, a gold panning dish, and a small tub of water. Without delay, the Australians crushed and panned a large number of samples from my bag and in every instance got fine shows in the pan.

Rhodes still showed no excitement, but invited Sauer to call at the office of De Beers at four o'clock. There Rhodes asked him to return to the Witwatersrand the next day to act on his behalf:

After some hesitation I agreed to go the next day. He then said: 'What interest do you want in the venture?' I replied, 'Twenty per cent.' He said, 'Fifteen per cent', which I accepted. Whereupon he took up a sheet of paper, wrote out an agreement on these terms, signed it, and handed it to me. He then asked me whether any ready money would be of use to me. I said, 'Yes, £200 to start with, and to be accounted for.' He reached out for his cheque book, and wrote me a cheque for the amount. He then rose and bade me good-bye, telling me at the same time to draw on him for any reasonable amounts I might require for the adventure.

To his surprise, the next morning Sauer found that Rhodes and Rudd had decided to make the journey to the Witwatersrand themselves, taking the same coach. On arriving at Ferreira's camp, they stayed briefly at 'Walker's Hotel', a wattle-and-daub building that had been erected in the week since Sauer had left. Searching for a more suitable camping place, they first bought part of a Boer farm called Klein Paardekraal, about six miles west of Ferreira's camp, then moved headquarters to a farm called Roodepoort, making forays up and down the line of the reef, trying to decide what properties to buy.

Within a fortnight of Rhodes' arrival in July 1886, Ferreira's camp was crowded with tents and wagons as each day a stream of newcomers turned up from across southern Africa. Many came from the alluvial diggings in the eastern Transvaal, bringing with them their sluice boxes, pans, picks and shovels. But the Witwatersrand, with its mass of hard rock, offered few pickings for small-time diggers. What was needed was stamp batteries to crush the ore and steam engines to drive the batteries. The only stamp battery available on the Rand belonged to the Struben brothers and that was booked up for trial crushings for months ahead. New orders for stamp batteries took up to twelve months to be delivered. Consequently, for the first year after the gold rush began, the amount of actual mining carried out was negligible. Gold production in 1886 stood at £34,710.

The game instead was to acquire what looked like the most promising properties and claims along the line of the reef. Claim-holders formed syndicates, then floated companies, hoping to attract investors, frequently on the basis of flimsy evidence. No one was sure how deep the gold veins ran. An Australian mining engineer proclaimed that it was geologically impossible that conglomerate reefs could run deeper than 200 feet.

To Sauer's immense frustration, both Rhodes and Rudd adopted a highly cautious approach. 'Rhodes,' said Sauer, 'knew nothing of gold mining, and still less of gold-bearing ore bodies, and in the back of his mind was the fear that the whole thing might turn out to be a frost.' Sauer recalled one occasion, after he had tried unsuccessfully to persuade Rhodes to purchase a block of main-reef claims, how Rhodes had told him: 'It is all very well; but I cannot see or calculate the power in your claims.' When Sauer asked him to explain further, Rhodes replied:

> When I am in Kimberley, and I have nothing much to do, I often go and sit on the edge of the De Beers mine, and I look at the blue diamondiferous ground, reaching from the surface, a thousand feet down the open workings of the mine, and I reckon up the value of the diamonds in the 'blue' and the power conferred by them. In fact, every foot of blue ground means so much power. This I cannot do with your gold reefs.

But even mining engineers with gold-mining experience were sceptical about the Rand's prospects. One expert whom Rhodes asked to investigate was Gardner Williams, the American engineer whom he subsequently employed as general manager at De Beers. Williams

spent ten days on the Witwatersrand being given a guided tour by
Sauer of all existing strikes along the line of the main reef. At the end
of his trip, Sauer asked for his assessment. 'Doctor Sauer,' Williams
replied, 'if I rode over these reefs in America I would not get off my
horse to look at them. In my opinion they are not worth hell room.'

Rhodes and Rudd turned down a number of Sauer's suggestions,
missing opportunities that turned out subsequently to be of enormous
value. On one occasion, Sauer obtained an option to buy twenty-one
claims for £500 covering an area that became one of the Rand's richest mines. For ten days, while the option remained open, he struggled
in vain to persuade Rhodes and Rudd to act:

> The reef was so rich that Rudd could not bring himself to
> believe that the pannings were genuine, and persistently claimed
> that the reef was 'salted'. To convince him I managed to get,
> after some trouble, two white miners, who drilled holes in the
> reef and blasted out chunks of it with dynamite in our presence.
> We then panned some of the ore thus blasted out, and obtained
> the same phenomenally rich result. In spite of this absolute
> proof, Rudd stuck to his theory of the salting and refused to buy
> the property.

Rudd also turned down an opportunity to purchase at £40 each a
mile-long stretch of claims to the east of Ferreira's camp that also
proved to be fabulously rich in gold, supporting six highly profitable
mining companies.

Robinson, by contrast, bought heavily, picking up several properties
that Rhodes rejected, such as Randfontein; and he was spectacularly
lucky. Within weeks, the Robinson Syndicate had gained a leading
position on the Rand.

At this crucial juncture, Rhodes' venture into gold mining came to an
abrupt halt. Out of the blue, he received a telegram telling him that
his devoted friend Neville Pickering was dangerously ill and he
decided then and there to leave for Kimberley on the night coach.
Pickering had never properly recovered from a riding accident in

1882; he developed a chronic lung infection that sometimes left him hobbling on crutches. He had recently returned to Kimberley from a visit to his family in Port Elizabeth but had since relapsed.

To Rhodes' dismay, there were no seats available on the night coach to Kimberley; nor could he persuade any other traveller to give him theirs. He found a place instead on top of the coach with the mail bags, holding on grimly for a fifteen-hour ordeal over 300 miles of rough track. Recalling his own experience of riding with the mail bags across the Transvaal, Sauer wrote:

> The discomfort was so extreme and the fatigue produced by the continued effort of maintaining your position on top of the mail bags was such that I have seen strong men, used to knocking about the African veld, weep from sheer exhaustion . . . You constantly ran the risk of being flung from your perch on to the hard ground when the cart, going at a good speed, upset after striking a large boulder or a deep ditch at the side of the track . . . Your misery became acute during the night, the desire for sleep, the fatigue, and the feeling of insecurity becoming almost unbearable.

Rhodes stayed nursing Pickering for weeks on end, indifferent to anything other than his needs and comfort. 'Everyone knew that Pickering was Rhodes's greatest friend,' wrote Percy FitzPatrick, Sauer's brother-in-law, 'but until then nobody had any suspicion of the depth of affection and the character of that ideal friendship. Even those who knew Rhodes well would not have believed it possible that he could feel so deeply and be so tragically affected.'

When Sauer urged Rhodes by telegraph to respond to opportunities he had encountered on the Rand, notably an option to buy a part of Doornfontein farm for £250, he heard nothing. FitzPatrick recalled: 'Without irritation or impatience, but with utter indifference, he declined to see anyone on the urgent and important matters of business that always needed attention.'

The end came early in the morning of 16 October. As Pickering went into a sudden decline, Rhodes sent Pickering's brother William to fetch Jameson, but there was nothing that Jameson could do. In his last moments, Pickering whispered to Rhodes: 'You have been father, mother, brother and sister to me' and died in his arms. He was but twenty-nine.

Pickering's funeral was attended by a large gathering of miners and diamond buyers. According to Jameson's biographer, Ian Colvin, Rhodes, 'alternating hysterically between laughter and tears', turned to Barney Barnato and said in his high falsetto, 'Ah Barney, he will never sell you another parcel of diamonds!' A few days later, David Harris, a De Beers director, came across Rhodes and William Pickering sitting at a table in a back room at De Beers' offices, both crying. On the table between them was a gold watch and chain belonging to Neville that they were pushing back and forth. 'All I heard,' said Harris, 'was: "No, you are his brother." And again, "No, you are his greatest friend."'

Rhodes never returned to the cottage he had shared with Pickering and Pickering's name was never mentioned again in his presence. On the night of the funeral, he moved into Jameson's sparsely furnished cottage, making it his permanent Kimberley home. He quickly stifled further grief. 'Well, I must go on with my work,' he told Jameson that night. 'After all, a thing like this is only a big detail . . . only a big detail.'

For the Transvaal authorities, the sudden influx of a horde of unruly prospectors and miners thirty miles south of Pretoria required some hasty improvisation. A local official, veldkornet Johannes Meyer, made the first attempt to bring order, introducing a system for prospectors to peg out mine claims. In August, the minister of mines, Christiaan Johannes Joubert, and the surveyor-general, Johann Rissik, addressed a gathering of some 200 claim-holders on the farm Turffontein to outline the government's plans for the diggings. In September, the gold commissioner, Captain Carl von Brandis, an ex-Prussian cavalry officer, stood beside his wagon and read out in Dutch a proclamation signed by Kruger declaring the Witwatersrand 'a public digging'. In October, Von Brandis returned to proclaim a triangular stretch of land known as Randjeslaagte, already owned by the government, as the site for a new town. Randjeslaagte lay just north of the pegged claims on the main reef, not far from Ferreira's camp; it was enclosed by the boundaries of three other farms, Braamfontein, Doornfontein and Turffontein.

The name chosen for the new town was Johannesburg. But the origin of the name – though there were several obvious possibilities – was soon lost. Shortly after Von Brandis arrived, a blustery wind blew away his tent, and among the records to disappear that night were the plans and instructions from the surveyor-general believed to have contained an explanation.

Johannesburg was laid out on a rectangular plan, with wide streets cutting each other at right angles. At its centre was Market Square, a huge open space where wagons outspanned. The main thoroughfare, Commissioner Street, ran parallel to Market Square and marked a boundary between the government town and another district to the south known as Marshall's Town, formed from blocks of claims converted into freehold building land. Once the government started selling stands, a host of makeshift buildings sprang up – mud hovels, tin shanties, shacks and boarding houses. Commissioner Street was the favourite location, with one side belonging to the government, the other to Marshall's Town. Height's Hotel there did a roaring trade. On the other side of the road, the government hastily constructed a prison and a hospital, consisting entirely of mud bricks and wooden poles.

On his return from Kimberley in December, Rhodes was soon involved in choosing a site for a club, an amenity that he regarded as an essential part of a mining camp. After surveying the ground with Sauer, he selected four stands at the corner of Commissioner Street and Loveday Street in Marshall's Town. A single-storey building with a thatched roof was duly constructed.

As the new town took shape, President Kruger decided to pay a visit. Arriving in February 1887, four months after it was proclaimed, he was given a cordial reception. The gold commissioner read an address of welcome from a stand erected in front of the government offices on Market Square. But even on this first occasion, there were signs of the friction that was eventually to prove fatal. To Kruger's annoyance, he was presented with a number of petitions listing grievances. The diggers asked for a daily postal service; they wanted their own town council; their own concession-licensing court, and a reduction of customs duties and mining dues. They pointed out that they had no representation in the Volksraad to make their case heard.

Kruger responded by saying he wanted to make laws acceptable to all, but added that the Transvaal's laws had to be obeyed. 'I have secret agents in Johannesburg,' he said, 'and here, as elsewhere, there are scabby sheep among the flock who want to break the law. I would like everyone, of whatever nationality, to know that if there are any disturbances I will first call on you diggers to catch the diggers, but if this fails I will call out my burghers and treat you as rebels.'

The next morning, the President was in a more conciliatory mood, saying he would look into ways of making improvements to the gold laws. In the evening, he attended a banquet in his honour at which it was arranged that Rhodes should propose the principal toast of the evening: the President's health. Rhodes urged Kruger to regard the newcomers as friends and to extend to them – 'young burghers like myself' – the same privileges enjoyed by Transvaalers. Kruger replied with a brief word of thanks. This was to have been followed by another toast proposed by J. B. Robinson, but before Robinson could begin, Kruger rose to his feet saying abruptly, '*Myn tyd es op. Ech moet vertrek.*' – 'My time is up. I must be off.'

18

THE CORNER HOUSE

The focus of attention in Johannesburg's early days rested on two buildings that stood opposite each other on the corners of Commissioner and Simmonds Streets, a short distance from the site that Rhodes chose for his club. One was the stock exchange, a single-storey brick and iron building that attracted huge crowds at times of share excitement. Business was often so brisk that when the exchange closed its doors for the day, trading in shares continued on the street outside. The street market became such an integral part of share dealing that the mining commissioner eventually gave permission for a short section of Simmonds Street to be cordoned off with chains to facilitate after-hours trading.

Visitors from England were struck by the informality of the place. A disconcerted London stockbroker, E. E. Kennedy, wrote:

To a man fresh from the London Exchange where an individual is chaffed for the whole day if he wears a loud necktie, a gaudy pair of trousers, or something special in waistcoats, where it would be simply seeking for destruction of the offending article to walk in with any hat on your head but the time-honoured chimney-pot, the costumes of the Johannesburg Stock Exchange are a rude shock. These people wear every kind of headgear except the chimney-pot – helmets, deer stalkers, cricket caps, and even tam-o'shanters. The weather is cold in the early mornings, so there are many ulsters, some of remarkable design and colour; there are men in riding breeches and top boots, who carry a handsome crop and look as unlike stockbrokers as anything you could imagine. We found among members men who had been storekeepers, canteen keepers, lawyers, policemen, farmers, ostrich-feather dealers, clerks, bookmakers, one or two defaulting brokers from London, and even dealers in old clothes – which is what a good many of them appear to have had as their calling.

On the other side of Simmonds Street stood an unprepossessing wood-and-iron office with six windows and two doors. The windows bore the legend 'H. Eckstein' but gave no indication of what kind of business was carried out there. What was unusual about the building was that its windows were washed free of dust every day.

Hermann Eckstein was the son of a Lutheran pastor, born near Stuttgart in Germany in 1847, who had made his way to Kimberley in 1882 and become a mine manager, running the Phoenix Diamond Mining Company in Dutoitspan. As a member of the 'German mess', he struck up a close friendship with Alfred Beit. When Beit sought a representative to manage his interests on the Witwatersrand – his share in the Robinson Syndicate – he chose Eckstein for the job. Behind Eckstein, therefore, stood Beit; and behind Beit stood the diamond magnate Jules Porges and his partner Julius Wernher. At first, Eckstein's office in Johannesburg was called 'Beit's building'; but it later became known as Eckstein's Corner and then as the Corner House; and what it represented was the most powerful group of financiers in southern Africa.

To assist Eckstein, Beit recruited Jim Taylor, his agent at the time of the Barberton boom who had given him such valuable advice before the crash there. Born in Cape Town in 1860, Taylor had moved with his family to Kimberley in 1871 and had been employed in Beit's office sorting diamonds before trying his luck on the goldfields of the eastern Transvaal. Trusting their judgement, Beit gave Eckstein and

Taylor a free rein to buy promising properties. Most of their ventures proved highly rewarding. Using the expertise of American mining engineers, they were able to make astute purchases. Within two years, Beit, Porges and Wernher had obtained hundreds of valuable claims. In 1888 they bought Robinson's share of the Robinson Syndicate for £250,000. Needing further funds, they gained the support of key European financiers – the Rothschilds of Germany, Austria and France and Rodolphe Kann of Paris.

Rhodes took a different approach. Also in need of funds, he decided to float a new company in London to raise capital from British investors, using his reputation in the diamond industry as bait. Charles Rudd was despatched to London in November 1886 to organise its launch. The name given to the company – The Gold Fields of South Africa – sounded impressive. Its prospectus stated that Rhodes and Rudd had spent £25,000 on purchasing 'auriferous properties'. They had turned down many offers for them, it said, 'but opportunities for favourable investment of capital appears so greatly to exceed private means that the public are now invited to join in the enterprise'.

Though British investors had suffered badly from the Barberton collapse, there was still considerable appetite in the City for gold shares. The terms Rhodes offered seemed favourable. Whereas the promoters of other Transvaal mining companies typically asked for a 'vendors' interest' of up to 75 per cent of the money subscribed in cash and shares as their reward, Rhodes and Rudd allocated to themselves, as managing directors, only 200 Founders' shares of £100 each – less than 10 per cent – in exchange for passing to the company at cost the properties they had bought; which meant that they made no profit unless the company prospered. What was not made clear at the outset, however, was that, from their shares, Rhodes and Rudd were entitled to take three-fifteenths of any profits the company made and a further two-fifteenths in lieu of remuneration, amounting in all to one third of the profits.

The launch of Gold Fields was a great success. Within the first week after registration in February 1887, 70,000 £1 shares were sold; by the end of October, all 250,000 shares were taken. But the information available to shareholders was scarce. They were given no inventory of properties the company intended to acquire. Addressing the company's first meeting in London in March 1887, Rudd explained that it would be unwise to publish such details; to do so would give competitors in the Transvaal an advantage. He described Gold Fields as a 'personal' company, drawing on the experience and standing of its joint managing directors.

But it was, in fact, little more than a speculative venture based on guesswork. Through ill-luck and poor judgement, most of the properties Rhodes and Rudd had already acquired contained relatively low-grade ore. Neither their luck nor their judgement improved. Flush with shareholder funds, Rhodes went out and bought for £60,000 a farm called Luipaardsvlei containing the Botha Reef. 'The immense purchase was made on very shallow tests,' an independent observer remarked in 1887, 'and it remains to be seen whether this clever speculator has ventured too much on surface indications.' As it turned out, Luipaardsvlei was yet another low-grade property. When choosing a site for the headquarters of Gold Fields, Rudd decided to locate it not in the nerve centre of the mining industry around Commissioner Street and Simmonds Street, but in a new township at Doornfontein to the north-east of Randjeslaagte, a fifteen-minute drive by Cape cart from the stock exchange. Rudd and his staff were thus remote from all the hubbub, gossip and intelligence-gathering that went on there.

Indeed, so little aptitude for gold-mining did Rhodes and Rudd display that they began to divert Gold Fields funds into diamonds. By December 1887 Rhodes had spent £57,000 of unused capital and profit from gold share-dealings on De Beers and Kimberley Central shares. When the accounts for the year ended 30 June 1888 were presented, Gold Fields shareholders were astonished to find that the company had a larger holding in diamonds – £142,000 – than in gold.

The fortunes of the Corner House, by contrast, flourished. With the arrival of stamp batteries in 1887, gold mining began in earnest. By 1888, a boom was under way. Some of the Corner House properties produced gold at the rate of 10 ounces to the ton; one mine in November 1888 delivered a freak 4,000 ounces from 700 tons of ore.

In a despatch to Jules Porges early in 1889, Eckstein reported profits of £860,000 for the five-month period from August to December 1888. 'It could easily have been fixed at over £1,000,000 but I preferred following my usual rule by valuing everything at what I may term safe values.'

As if to crown the boom, Barney Barnato arrived belatedly from Kimberley, declared the Rand to be the future 'financial Gibraltar of South Africa', and went on a massive spending spree, investing nearly £2 million in property and mining shares. Within the space of three months he established a string of companies – Barnato Consolidated Mines; the Barnato Bank; Mining and Investment Corporation; and the Johannesburg Consolidated Investment Company – and started work on Barnato Buildings on Commissioner Street.

In an orgy of speculation, some 450 gold-mining companies were floated in 1888. 'Half the male population of Johannesburg is to be seen in animated conversation between the chains outside Eckstein's office,' wrote one chronicler of the day. 'If there is anyone in Johannesburg who does not own some scrip in a gold mine he is considered not quite right in the head. Half of the population of Kimberley is here. Barberton seems to have moved to Simmonds Street and some of the biggest men in Cape Town are buying.'

At the height of the boom in April 1889, J. B. Robinson took the opportunity to launch the Randfontein Estates Gold Mining Company. With a nominal capital of £2 million in £1 shares, it was the most ambitious project that Johannesburg had yet seen. In exchange for handing over to the company seven farms amounting to 29,000 acres, Robinson obtained a 'vendors' interest' of 1,809,000 shares. The price of the remaining shares soon reached £4 each. Rhodes and Rudd too caught the high tide of the boom, selling off parts of their low-grade holdings on Luipaardsvlei at a substantial profit.

Even the banks joined in the spree. Between January and April 1889, bank advances rose from £300,000 to more than £1 million. An investigation by the Standard Bank found that in the first quarter of 1889 the market value of the shares of some 400 companies stood at £100 million.

Then disaster struck. The first intimation of trouble was picked up by the Corner House. Miners working on one of its shafts on the main reef struck pyritic ore. In March, Jim Taylor cabled to Jules Porges & Co: 'Following is strictly private. Percy Company, Main Reef. Below level 120 feet reef changed from banket to quartz, blue, hard, no free gold but 10 dwts. in pyrites. Sunk 50 feet and there is no change.'

After inspecting the shaft, Taylor elaborated in a letter three days later:

> At 100 feet down the ore becomes lighter in colour and gradually changes at 115 feet to blue conglomerate; from 115 to 165 feet the reef continues getting harder and harder and shows in small veins the action of corrosion still going on where the water has percolated through cracks and on the contact side of the lodes with its walls.
>
> The reef is still there, of the same dimensions and appearance except that, instead of being a reddish colour through the rotting of sulphides, it is blue, with pyrites heavily charged all through the stone . . .
>
> I think the change is very unfortunate as it comes so much sooner than we expected.

The problem of pyritic ore was familiar to mining engineers with experience of the gold fields of the United States. Gardner Williams had warned both Beit and Rhodes that the Witwatersrand reefs would probably become pyritic below a depth of 100 feet and had accurately forecast what would then happen. It meant that gold could no longer be extracted simply by running milled ore over copper plates coated with mercury; it would have to be extracted from sulphides – the ore would have to be treated in chlorination plants. The cost of establishing chlorination plants, together with the extra expense of crushing harder rock, would affect all mining, making high-grade mines far less profitable and low-grade mines unviable. The implication was that every Rand share was overvalued, and many were worthless.

Before news leaked to the public, the Corner House took action to weather the storm and ordered chlorination equipment. Rhodes was in London at the time arranging the final stages of the amalgamation of the diamond mines with Lord Rothschild. At dinner at Rothschild's house one evening, Rhodes was placed next to an eminent American mining engineer and turned the conversation to the problem of sulphides. 'What do you do in America when you strike sulphide ores?' he asked. 'Mr Rhodes,' replied the American, 'then we say, "O God!"' Instead of trying to weather the storm, Rhodes decided to sell virtually all Gold Fields' properties; in effect, it ceased to be a gold-mining company altogether.

As, one by one, the Witwatersrand mines encountered pyritic ore, panic set in. Investors rushed to sell their shares and property; the share market collapsed; scores of companies closed; thousands were left bankrupt. Out of a white population of 25,000, some 8,000 packed up and left. By March 1890 the total market value of gold shares had dropped by more than 60 per cent. The ripple of disaster spread throughout southern Africa. Three banks in the Cape Colony failed, ruining some of the leading citizens of Cape Town.

Some observers freely predicted the end of gold mining on the Witwatersrand, but insiders in the Corner House thought differently. When Hermann Eckstein cabled Beit in London to ask whether it was advisable to proceed with plans to build an imposing new two-storey headquarters on the corner-house site, he replied, 'Yes, by all means'.

Amid the turmoil, the firm of H. Eckstein was quietly reorganised. At the end of 1889, without fanfare, Jules Porges retired and two new firms were launched: Wernher, Beit & Company based in London; and H. Eckstein & Company, its Johannesburg partner. Under the new dispensation, four-fifths of the profits made by the Johannesburg firm went to Beit, Wernher and two other London partners.

Even during the slump, Wernher, Beit & Co. made headway on the Witwatersrand, buying up properties along the main reef on the cheap. It was also the first firm to introduce a new cyanide process for treating gold ore, which had been developed in Glasgow. Initial tests between June and August 1890 proved highly successful. A small plant at Salisbury mine treated some 70,000 tons of ore and, to the astonishment of mining experts, achieved an extraction rate of up to 90 per cent, higher than the rate that had previously been won from mercury extraction. Using the same process to treat 10,000 tons of tailings on another mine, Wernher, Beit & Co. produced 6,000 ounces of gold missed by previous treatment. These results produced a rush to install cyanide plants, spurring a recovery on the Rand. The value of gold production soared from £1.7 million in 1890 to £4.2 million in 1892.

Wernher, Beit also led the way to a new phase of deep-level mining that transformed the Witwatersrand's long-term prospects. Mining companies had originally regarded land to the south of the main reef as worthless. They assumed that the main reef descended downwards at an angle and simply followed it. But Joseph Curtis, an American engineer working for Wernher, Beit, developed the theory that the main reef dipped out of the vertical confines of existing claims and headed south and was thus accessible via deep-level shafts.

Another Wernher, Beit employee, Lionel Phillips, a former Kimberley mine manager, became an ardent advocate of the deep-level theory. When Curtis experimented in December 1889 by drilling a borehole at a spot 1,000 feet south of the outcrop, he struck rich ores at 571 feet and the main reef at 635 feet. In great secrecy, Phillips and Curtis began to buy up farms south of the main reef, persuading Beit and Wernher to back them.

The scale of their achievement only became clear in later years. Some of the most famous mines in Johannesburg's history – Jumpers Deep, Nourse Deep, Glen Deep, Rose Deep, Village Deep, Crown Deep, Ferreira Deep, Geldenhuis Deep – were developed on properties they bought at the time of the slump.

19

A MARRIAGE OF CONVENIENCE

In the Cape, meanwhile, Rhodes, as well as pursuing his business interests, sought political power. As a member of the Cape parliament, he cultivated links with Afrikaner politicians who had begun to develop their own political organisations, far in advance of English-speaking politicians. His motive was largely opportunistic. Afrikaners constituted three-quarters of the Cape's population. They were, Rhodes told Jameson, 'the coming race'. By contrast, he was disparaging about the ability of English-speaking politicians, who lacked a political organisation of their own and operated on the basis of personal allegiance. 'The "English" party in the Cape Assembly was hopelessly divided and individually incapable,' Rhodes recalled. 'And it had nothing beyond that of serving office.' By collaborating with Afrikaner politicians, Rhodes aimed to establish a power base for himself from which he could promote his own scheme for Cape expansion to the north as well as his commercial interests. He was, moreover, impressed by the calibre of the Afrikaner leader, Jan Hendrik Hofmeyr – 'Onze Jan' – describing him as 'without doubt the most capable politician in South Africa'.

Hofmeyr was a talented journalist, the son of a wine farmer, born in Cape Town in 1845. At the age of twenty-six, he took over as editor of *De Zuid-Afrikaan*, a Dutch language newspaper, founded in

1830, that was read by the Afrikaner business and professional elite. An intellectual with broad interests, at ease in both English and Afrikaner circles, he possessed a library of 250 books ranging from religion to mathematics.

In 1878, when the Cape government decided to tax Cape brandy producers to raise extra funds for railway construction and to pay for the cost of the Xhosa war, Hofmeyr used *De Zuid-Afrikaan* to attack the measure and went on to found a farmers' protection association in the western Cape – *Zuid-Afrikaansche Boeren Beschermings Vereeniging* (BBV) – to promote and defend the interests of farmers who formed the vast bulk of the population. What Hofmeyr hoped to achieve was an organisation that would unite Afrikaner and English farmers. He saw no merit in the formation of an Afrikaner party on an ethnic basis. He was concerned about protecting Afrikaner culture but did not seek to elevate it to become a divisive issue. With similar purpose, he campaigned for the extension of Dutch language rights. Though he opposed Britain's annexation of the Transvaal, he urged Afrikaners in the Cape to remain loyal to the empire and the Colony. Cape Afrikaners, he said, were 'as loyal British subjects as any other people' but were not prepared to become Englishmen. In parliamentary elections in 1879, BBV candidates won nearly half of the upper-house seats and one-third of lower-house seats. Hofmeyr won the Stellenbosch seat.

Hardly had they taken their seats when a far more ambitious scheme was launched by the militant Paarl cleric Stephanus du Toit. In an editorial in the *Patriot* in June 1879, du Toit proposed the formation of an *Afrikaner Bond* with the slogan of '*Afrika voor de Afrikaners*' and with branches across southern Africa:

> An Afrikaner Bond, in which no nationality divides us from each other, but in which everyone who recognises Africa as his Fatherland can live together and work as brothers of a single house, be they of English, Dutch, French or German origin, with the exclusion of those who talk of England as their 'home' or of Holland and Germany as their 'Fatherland', and only want to fill their pockets with African wealth in order to go and spend it in Europe.

It would be the task of the Bond, he said, to prevent 'the sacrifice of Africa's interest to England, or those of the Farmer to the Merchant'; to develop trade and industry for the benefit of the land and 'not to fill the pockets of speculators'; to stop the money market from being dominated 'by English banks'. He also protested against the 'millions of pounds' spent on education for English-speakers, while the Afrikaner majority was 'totally neglected'. He proposed consumer boycotts, calling it the duty of 'every true Afrikaner not to spend a copper at an Englishman's shop if he can avoid it'.

Du Toit's Afrikaner Bond made a slow start, but benefited from an upsurge of nationalist sentiment inspired by the Boer victory at Majuba. Becoming even more radical, Du Toit tried to push the Bond into adopting an anti-liberal, neo-Calvinist platform, but only succeeded in arousing the wrath of more moderate Calvinists in the Dutch Reformed Church. In February 1882, he decided to throw in his lot with Kruger's Transvaal, accepting a position as head of its education department, and went on, in a fit of patriotic fervour, to raise the Vierkleur in the Land of Goshen, the incident that eventually provoked British intervention in Bechuanaland.

Hofmeyr had no liking for Du Toit's brand of politics, nor his objective of establishing an independent republic, but saw the Bond as a potentially useful vehicle for mobilising the Afrikaner community. As the tide of nationalist sentiment receded in the wake of the 1881 settlement that Britain reached with the Transvaal, Hofmeyr joined the Bond, seeking to moderate its aims. In a speech to parliament in October 1881, thanking the British government for the generous terms of peace with the Transvaal, he set out his position in clear terms:

It cannot be denied that since the annexation of the Transvaal, the feeling of Dutchmen towards the Crown has to some extent grown cool. All that feeling will now be done away with by the concessions accorded to the Transvaal. That will not only remove any momentary feeling of opposition towards British institutions and the British Government, but it will do more than this in establishing a new feeling in the hearts of Dutchmen which never existed before. Instead of resting upon simply a cool and calculating feeling as to the material advantages of British rule, they will now have a warm-hearted feeling of thorough attachment to the Crown, just such a feeling as animates the most loyal and patriotic Englishman. If this has been the result of the Transvaal war, then that war has not been in vain.

In May 1883, the BBV and the Afrikaner Bond amalgamated, using the occasion to display loyalty to the British crown. According to the official minutes of the congress in Richmond, three cheers were given to 'Our Honourable Queen' with 'the greatest enthusiasm'.

Though Hofmeyr was the Bond's acknowledged leader, he preferred to operate in the background, turning down the opportunity of becoming prime minister in 1884, supporting instead a succession of English prime ministers to avoid exacerbating tension between Afrikaners and the English minority. The parliamentarian John Merriman referred to him as 'the Mole' – 'You never see him at work, but every now and then a little mound of earth, thrown up here or there, will testify to his activities'. Hofmeyr's home in Camp Street, Cape Town – the White House – was used as a regular meeting place for the party caucus and considered to be the Bond's headquarters. 'The White House,' complained Merriman in 1884, 'are the arbiters of our destiny.'

When contemplating how best to advance his political career, Rhodes initially viewed the Afrikaner camp with deep resentment. Arriving in parliament as a political novice only six weeks after the Boer victory at Majuba, Rhodes felt humiliated that the British defeat had been met not by revenge but by concessions. According to Francis Dormer, the editor of the *Cape Argus*, Rhodes was 'one of those whom the stirring events of 1880–81 left in an attitude of violent antagonism towards a settlement which was based upon the undeniable defeat of British arms'. The paramount issue for the future, Rhodes believed, was whether the Dutch or the English would prevail. Dormer discussed the matter with Rhodes when he came to negotiate purchasing a controlling interest in the *Cape Argus*. Rhodes favoured a pro-

English line. Dormer advocated a more even-handed approach and refused to adopt an active anti-Afrikaner position.

According to Dormer, Rhodes, after pacing up and down, remarked:

> 'I suppose you are right . . . I think we understand one another. I don't dislike the Dutchmen. Your plan of working with Hofmeyr is the best – [Gordon] Sprigg impossible – [Saul] Solomon, he'd wreck an empire for what he is pleased to call his principles – and there's nobody else . . . But let us understand one another. We are not going to be trampled upon by these Dutchmen.'

Rhodes added: 'I don't pretend to have many fixed principles; but I do believe in doing to others as we would be done by, and I am sure that vengeance is no policy for a nation [the English] such as ours.'

Hofmeyr's first encounter with Rhodes came in the aftermath of Majuba. He recalled: 'When the war was over we had a talk with one another and I said: "It is an awful pity that war broke out." I was surprised when Mr Rhodes said, "No, it is not. I have quite changed my opinion. It is a good thing. It has made Englishmen respect Dutchmen and made them respect one another."' 'Well,' added Hofmeyr, 'when an Englishman could speak like that to a Dutchman, they are not far from making common cause with one another.'

During Rhodes' early years in parliament, he made a number of gestures to indicate his willingness to assist Bond causes, including support for Hofmeyr's bill to allow the use of Dutch in parliament. From 1886, as he became ever more determined to pursue northern expansion, he began a concerted campaign to court Cape Afrikaners as political allies, adopting positions he had once opposed to suit their interests. In discussion with Jameson, he was frank about his purpose:

> I mean to have the whole unmarked country north of the Colony for England, and I know I can only get it and develop it through the Cape Colony – that is, at present, through the Dutch majority.

One notable volte-face he performed was over the issue of agricultural protection. Afrikaner politicians had long favoured protection against external competition for Cape wine and grain farmers. Rhodes was an avowed free trader, telling parliament in 1884 that he would 'oppose anything that pandered to protection'. In 1886, however, he declared himself a protectionist, particularly with regard to wine and grain farmers. His old friend Merriman was outraged:

> Rhodes's apostasis has made me feel sicker than a stuck hog [he wrote to a friend in July 1886]. Here you have a fellow with the birth, the manner, the feelings and the education of an English gentleman offering himself publicly for sale to a crew composed of Venters and De Waals . . . and doing it so clumsily that he has spoiled his own market. The idea of Rhodes, who used to quote manuals of political economy with all the zeal of a lad fresh from the Oxford schools, taking his stand on the platform of protection whose sole *raison d'être* is extreme anti-British feeling.

Rhodes joined Hofmeyr in attempting to repeal a tax on locally produced brandy imposed in 1884. He supported Hofmeyr's motion in favour of compulsory religious instruction in government schools. He even spoke in favour of a Bond motion calling for a ban on Sunday 'pleasure' trains. The motion had been initiated by a Bond member incensed that special trains were allowed to run on Sundays between Kimberley and Modder River Junction, enabling people 'to spend their day in debauchery, drinking, gambling, dancing etc.', in direct contravention of the Ten Commandments. Rhodes described the Sunday trains from Kimberley as 'a public scandal'. Merriman thought Rhodes was making a fool of himself:

> The people he wants to conciliate laugh at him while they use him . . . What a curious farce it is that Rhodes, who took a leading part in starting the Empire League, should now be courting the advances of the Afrikaner Bond.

When the issue of 'native' policy and the extent of the 'native' franchise came under discussion, Rhodes again allied himself to the Bond camp, expressing his views even more vehemently than Bond politicians. The Bond were determined to reduce the political power accorded to non-whites under the 1853 constitution but felt constrained from making an outright attack for fear of mobilising the non-white vote against them at election times. Under the 1853 constitution, all male adult British subjects who owned property worth at least £25 or who received an income of more than £50 a year were entitled to vote, a relatively low qualification that enabled a significant number of non-whites to register. Many Bond opponents in the English-speaking community looked to the non-white electorate to support them at election time. 'We have continually expressed our conviction,' said the *Port Elizabeth Telegraph* in 1881, 'that if the Afrikaner Bond is to be well beaten it will have to be done by the assistance of the black vote. Look at the question as we may, we always come back to the fact that the Dutch in the colony are to the English as two to one, and that if they combine they can outvote us, and inflict upon us all the absurdities of their national and economic prejudices.' Rhodes had been one of those who urged native registration.

The franchise issue became increasingly important in 1885 when the Cape incorporated the Transkei, and with it some 80,000 potential new African voters and about 2,000 new white voters, increasing Afrikaner fears that eventually they might be swamped by the 'blanket' vote. The Bond urged higher qualifications and a literary test for voters, but was careful not to display racial prejudice. Rhodes, however, had no such inhibitions and made a frontal attack on the Cape's non-racial franchise, preferring, he said, 'to call a spade a spade'.

The 'native question', he said, was the 'big test question for South Africa'. He had arrived in the Colony, he said, as 'the most rabid Jingo', but he now considered that the Cape had allowed too many Africans the vote. 'As long as the natives remain in a state of barbarism we must treat them as a subject race and be lords over them . . . There would be no injustice in refusing the franchise to the natives as a whole in the Colony.' He even argued that 'the natives did not want the franchise'.

Rhodes endeavoured too to appeal to the *trek geest* – the trekking spirit – of the Afrikaners. 'I feel that it is the duty of this Colony, when, as it were, her younger and more fiery sons go out and take land, to follow in their steps with civilised government.' In line with this, he declared that 'what we want now is to annex land, not natives'. To wine farmers he offered a free-trade route to the interior for their products, seeking to harness Afrikaner support for northern expansion.

To his fellow Englishmen, he stressed the need for white colonial unity. 'You cannot have real prosperity . . . until you have first established complete confidence between the two races [English and Afrikaner].' And he offered his personal endorsement: 'I like the [Cape] Dutch, I like their homely courtesy and their tenacity of purpose.'

All this was music to the ears of the Bond. Rhodes also made a favourable impression with speeches to Afrikaner audiences. Recalling an address to wine farmers he made in Paarl, the Cape businessman Charles Kohler wrote:

> What a speech he made that day. Though he spoke in English, even the staunchest pro-Afrikaans farmer listened to him with rapt attention. I remember one old Boer patriot called Uys, who was sitting at the extreme end of a table, rising noiselessly and creeping nearer and nearer to Rhodes as he spoke. Like a bent ape, silently, the old fellow shuffled along . . . Finally, he crouched down right opposite Rhodes and sat there motionless, drinking in every word that was uttered, his eyes glued to the speaker's face.

The Cape's fortunes, meanwhile, were dramatically affected by the rise of the Witwatersrand gold industry. Accustomed to acting as the regional power, the Cape now faced a rival with immense resources behind it. In 1884, the annual revenues of the Transvaal amounted to £188,000; in 1886, the state was close to bankruptcy, failing to raise a loan of £5,000. By 1887, the Transvaal's output was equal to the Cape's. What ensued on one level was a tussle over railway construction and customs tariffs. But the wider issue at stake was whether the

Cape or the Transvaal would emerge as the dominant state, whether the colonial or the republican agenda for southern Africa would prevail.

Flush with new revenues, Kruger lost no time in pressing forward with his plan for a railway outlet to Delagoa Bay that would make the Transvaal independent of the Cape's customs and trading system. Hitherto, the Cape had enjoyed a virtual stranglehold on most goods imported into the interior. Kruger insisted that the Delagoa line would have to be completed before rival contenders from the Cape and from Natal were allowed into the Transvaal. 'Every railway that approaches me I look upon as an enemy on whatever side it comes. I must have my Delagoa Bay line first, and then the other lines may come.'

Rhodes argued that if the Delagoa line was completed first, then the Cape would effectively be shut out of the Transvaal's markets. 'If the Delagoa Bay railway is carried out we shall not get a continuation of the line from Kimberley to Pretoria. Commercial people will be always inspiring or instilling into the rulers of the Transvaal hostile action against the Cape Colony. In other words, if the Delagoa railway is carried out the real union of South Africa will be indefinitely deferred.' These were arguments with which Hofmeyr and the Bond readily concurred. Cape farmers, as well as businessmen, saw the Transvaal as a valuable market.

A similar struggle occurred over customs duties. A few months before the discovery of gold on the Witwatersrand, Kruger, desperate for funds, requested a share in the customs duties collected by the Cape for goods destined for the Transvaal, proposing the creation of a customs union. Though Rhodes urged the Cape government and parliament to respond positively, the Bond took a parochial view and refused to support Kruger's proposal. Once gold was discovered, the Bond altered course and began preaching the virtues of free trade in southern Africa, anxious to ensure the flow of Cape wine and brandy to the Transvaal market. The Cape government duly responded by despatching a delegation to Pretoria to discuss the possibility of a customs union. But Kruger, stung by the Cape's earlier rebuff, was no longer interested.

Distrustful of the Cape's intentions and its links to imperial Britain, Kruger instead sought to develop a republican axis in alliance with the Orange Free State, pointing to the need for 'closer union' against 'British South Africa'. Despatching delegations to Bloemfontein in 1887, he urged the Free State to disengage economically from the Cape and attach itself to the northern economic system of the Transvaal. When Free State politicians pointed out that they needed agreement with the Cape in order to get their share of customs duties collected in the Cape, Kruger responded, 'Let them keep their money, and wait for us. Cut yourself loose from the south. We cannot enter a customs union while we are dependent on their ports or they will dictate terms to us.' Kruger even offered the Free State a sum of £20,000 a year for ten years if they failed to secure a share in customs revenues. Although the Cape and the Free State eventually signed a customs agreement in 1889, Kruger was successful in drawing the Free State into a closer republican alliance. In March 1889, the Transvaal and the Free State concluded a defence pact: each Boer republic agreed to come to the aid of its neighbour in case of foreign attack.

Rebuffed by Kruger, Hofmeyr was more amenable to Rhodes' arguments about 'northern expansion' as the Cape's way forward. In September 1888, Rhodes advised: 'Let us leave the Free State and the Transvaal to their destiny. We must adopt the whole responsibility for the interior . . . [and] we must always remember that the gist of the South African question lies in the extension of the Cape Colony to the Zambesi.' Hofmeyr and Rhodes also shared common ground about the need for the Cape to remain within the British orbit. Reminiscing about Hofmeyr, Rhodes remarked:

He was anxious to maintain the [British] connection, not out of love for Great Britain, but because the independence of South Africa was at the mercy of whatever power had command of the sea. And . . . his hatred of the Germans amounted to a passion . . . Hofmeyr was chiefly interested in withstanding free trade and upholding protection on behalf of the [Cape] Dutch . . . I had a policy of my own . . . to keep open the road to the north, to secure British South Africa room for expansion.

When Queen Victoria celebrated her jubilee year in 1887, the Bond was profuse with expressions of loyalty. 'We assure you humbly and respectfully [of] our true loyalty to your throne, and we feel proud that in the great British Empire there are not more loyal subjects than those we represent.' In towns throughout the Colony, Cape Afrikaners made similar affirmations. That same year, Hofmeyr attended the first Colonial Conference in London as a member of the Cape delegation, speaking ardently in favour of strengthening the imperial connection.

Hofmeyr also saw a growing convergence of interests between Cape Afrikaner farmers and mine owners. They were, he said in the *Zuid Afrikaan* in 1888, both 'owners of land' needing labourers under proper supervision. 'Whereas until now the farmers' party in the Cape have cooperated more with the merchant class than with the mining interests in the diamond fields, it is very possible that a change will soon come, and this change is persistently aimed at by the most powerful representative of the mine owners [Rhodes].'

With Kruger continuing to block plans for a railway linking the Cape to the Transvaal through the Orange Free State and to thwart progress on a customs union, Hofmeyr and the Bond reluctantly abandoned their hopes for closer ties with the Transvaal and were drawn ever deeper into Rhodes' scheme for northern expansion. 'Under the British flag and with the help of British capital we are marching to the north,' declared the *Zuid Afrikaan* in January 1890. Kruger was furious with Hofmeyr for his willingness to collaborate with the British. 'You are a traitor,' he told Hofmeyr when they met in Pretoria in July 1890, 'a traitor to the Africander cause.'

When the Sprigg government fell in July 1890, Rhodes put himself forward for the post of prime minister. Asking for the Bond's endorsement at a meeting of Bond members of parliament on 16 July, he reminded them of all the support he had given them in parliament over the past eight years. They duly gave him their unanimous approval. At the age of thirty-seven, Rhodes was installed as prime minister. Describing his pact with Hofmeyr, Rhodes recalled: 'I . . . struck a bargain with him, by which I undertook to defend the protective system of [the] Cape Colony, and he pledged himself in the name of the Bond not to throw obstacles in the way of northern expansion.'

PART V

20

THE PLACE OF SLAUGHTER

The discovery of gold on the Witwatersrand produced a surge of speculation about the likelihood that even richer gold deposits would be found further north in Zambesia, the land of Ophir. Since Carl Mauch's explorations there in the 1860s, the legend had continued to grow. In 1871, after further travels in the region, Mauch suggested that impressive stone ruins he had encountered there known as Great Zimbabwe could once have been the capital of Ophir, built by Phoenicians; the central structure, he said, was probably a temple based on the design of a palace where the Queen of Sheba stayed when she visited King Solomon. In a book entitled *The Gold Fields of Southern Africa and How to Reach Them*, published in 1876, Richard Babb declared flatly: 'So the question of ancient Ophir is at last settled.' In 1881, a book written by a 30-year-old elephant hunter, Fred Selous, *A Hunter's Wanderings in Africa*, about his journeys through Matabeleland, stimulated widespread interest in the region. Rider Haggard used Selous as the model for his hero, Allan Quatermain, when writing his novel *King Solomon's Mines*. Published in 1885, *King Solomon's Mines* became a best-seller, giving the legend popular status. Both Rhodes and Kruger coveted this fabled land.

The gateway to Zambesia was controlled by the Ndebele king, Lobengula, a son of Mzilikazi. The Ndebele army, consisting of

15,000 men in 40 regiments based around Lobengula's capital of GuBulawayo – 'the place of slaughter' – was feared throughout the region; for years, it had raided neighbouring peoples – the Shona of Mashonaland, Tswana groups in northern Bechuanaland, and the Lozi, Ila and Tonga to the north of the Zambezi – exacting tribute from them.

Like Mzilikazi, Lobengula was vigilant about the entry of whites into his domain. Military posts were established along the frontier, where all travellers were stopped, interrogated and detained for a week or more until the king allowed them to proceed – in his own phrase, 'gave them the road'. A handful of missionaries were permitted to operate in Matabeleland. Lobengula tolerated their presence, as his father had done, recognising the advantage of being able to summon men who could read and write letters for him, but otherwise he gave them no encouragement.

White hunters too were allowed to enter for limited periods. Fred Selous was one of them. Having left his London home at the age of twenty in search of adventure, he arrived in Lobengula's capital in 1872. The king, a man of huge physique, with a fondness for meat and drink, was not impressed by his visitor. 'He asked me what I had come to do,' wrote Selous. 'I said I had come to hunt elephants, upon which he burst out laughing, and said, "Was it not steinbucks [a species of small antelope] that you came to hunt? Why, you're only a boy."' Lobengula made further disparaging remarks about Selous' youthful appearance and left.

But Selous persisted and again asked for permission. 'This time he asked me whether I had ever seen an elephant, and upon my saying no, answered, "Oh, they will soon drive you out of the country, but you may go and see what you can do!"' When Selous asked him where he might go, Lobengula replied impatiently, 'Oh, you may go wherever you like, you are only a boy.'

All visitors were made to feel they were in the country on sufferance, and were expected to pay for the privilege of entry by arriving with gifts for the king and his entourage – beads, blankets and brass wire. Lobengula acquired a particular liking for champagne. The royal store was soon replete with an immense collection of rifles, saddlery, furniture and household goods. In exchange for payments and bribes, Lobengula also allowed a few traders and hunters to settle permanently on the outskirts of his encampment at Bulawayo, but their presence was always dependent on the king's whim.

It was Kruger who first began to show an interest in Lobengula's kingdom. In 1882, as the Transvaal, newly liberated from British rule, sought to extend its borders to the east and to the west, the commandant-general Piet Joubert sent a letter to Lobengula, couched in effusive language, reminding him of a friendship treaty said to have been made in 1853 between Matabeleland and the Transvaal. Joubert expressed the Transvaal's ardent desire to live in amity and peace with its northern neighbour – a peace, he said, 'which is so strong that the vile evil-doers were never able to destroy it, and never shall be able to, as long as there shall be one Boer that lives, and Lobengula also lives'. Referring to the annexation of the Transvaal, Joubert warned of the English appetite for land. 'When an Englishman once has your property in his hand, then he is like a monkey that has its hands full of pumpkin seeds – if you don't beat him to death he will never let go.' He assured Lobengula that 'when the stink which the English brought is blown away altogether', he would ride up to Bulawayo to pay him a special visit to cement their long-standing friendship.

Joubert never made it to Bulawayo, but in 1887 Kruger resumed the initiative with a far more ambitious strategy, using the services of a Boer intermediary called Pieter Grobler. Grobler was a horse trader who had first tried his luck in Bechuanaland but, having fallen foul of the Ngwato chief, Kgama, had turned his attention to Matabeleland, making several trips to Bulawayo with horses and wagons for sale.

Grobler claimed to have gained great influence with Lobengula, and Kruger, believing him, personally drafted a seven-part agreement for Grobler to take to Lobengula. The agreement purported to bind the Transvaal and the Ndebele to 'perpetual peace and friendship'. It acknowledged Lobengula as an independent chief and declared him to be an 'ally' of the Transvaal. For his part, Lobengula was expected to assist the Transvaal with fighting forces whenever called upon to do so; to extradite offenders to the Transvaal; to permit Transvaalers holding passes from their government to hunt and trade in his country; and to accept a resident consul with powers to try offenders from the Transvaal.

Returning to Bulawayo in July 1887 with his brother Frederick, Grobler gave Lobengula £140 in cash, a rifle and some ammunition, and obtained what he claimed was the king's 'mark' of approval for the 'treaty', together with the signatures of four of his 'councillors'. No announcement was made about the Grobler 'treaty' for six months.

Other operators were meanwhile sniffing out the prospects. A party of German travellers appeared in the neighbourhood. The Portuguese, hitherto content with coastal trading stations, suddenly took an interest, claiming a large part of Matabeleland for themselves. A growing number of concession-hunters made their way to Bulawayo.

Among the first in the field was Frank Johnson, a young English adventurer who had arrived in Cape Town at the age of sixteen, enlisted in Colonel Warren's expeditionary force to Bechuanaland, then joined the Bechuanaland Border Police, a mounted unit set up by the British to control the Bechuanaland Protectorate. Finding police life tedious and hearing of gold finds to the north, Johnson left the police to organise support for a gold-prospecting expedition – the Northern Gold Fields Exploration Syndicate – winning the backing of twenty-two shareholders in the Cape, including four members of parliament, four bankers and the mayor of Cape Town.

In February 1887, he set out from Cape Town in possession of a letter from the syndicate to Lobengula asking his permission 'to search for gold, silver, or other minerals, as well as precious stones'. On the way to Matabeleland, he stopped at Mafeking, the headquarters of the Bechuanaland protectorate, to discuss the expedition with the administrator, Sir Sydney Shippard, Rhodes' old friend from Kimberley days. Shippard gave him a letter of introduction to Lobengula, recommending that he should be granted the concessions he sought. Further along the route, Johnson stopped at Shoshong, Kgama's capital, obtaining from him the sole right to prospect and work minerals in a 400-square-mile area. He eventually arrived in Bulawayo in May 1887 after a journey of 1,300 miles.

Johnson spent nearly three months at Bulawayo trying to coax Lobengula into giving him 'the road' to Mashonaland. Lobengula was suspicious of Johnson's intentions, interrogating him time and again. His councillors were even more hostile. 'I cannot understand this digging for gold,' Lobengula told Johnson. 'There is no place in my heart where you can dig for gold. But I will look for such a place. I am sorry you have come so far for nothing, but my head is troubled at present. Time is made for slaves; therefore there is no need for hurry.'

Johnson presented him with a range of presents: rifles, ammunition, tobacco, matches, knives, scissors, field-glasses, needles and thread, and a barrel organ. But Lobengula continued to prevaricate. A German prospecting party arriving after Johnson soon gave up in despair, but Johnson persevered. 'One needed the patience of a saint,' he wrote. Finally, on 12 July, he offered Lobengula £100 for permission to prospect and £200 a year while digging lasted. Lobengula replied: 'You are troublesome people, for when I say there is no gold in my country you do not believe me and insist on going on . . . You speak good words now, but after this there will be trouble.'

After further interminable discussions, Lobengula agreed to give Johnson 'the road'. Johnson travelled as far as the Mazoe Valley in Mashonaland where he came across plenty of evidence of alluvial deposits, but on his return to Bulawayo in November 1887, he found Lobengula in an angry mood. Johnson was accused of spying, murder and showing disrespect to the king. After agreeing to pay a fine of £100, ten blankets and ten tins of gunpowder, he was allowed to leave Matabeleland but travelled back to the Cape empty-handed.

British officials too began to cast their attention towards Matabeleland. In May 1887, Shippard wrote to Robinson, the high commissioner in Cape Town, pointing out the advantages of controlling Zambesia. 'The Power that can acquire that territory . . . will hold the key to the wealth and commerce of South and Central Africa,' he said. 'The whole would support itself, and thus hardly cost the British Treasury a penny.'

In June 1887, Robinson established a new post of deputy administrator for the Bechuanaland protectorate to assist Shippard, appointing John Moffat, a former missionary with first-hand experience of

Matabeleland. The son of Robert Moffat, John Moffat had helped set up the mission station at Inyati, forty miles north-east of Bulawayo, serving there from 1859 to 1865. He spoke Sindebele as well as Setswana and was trusted by Lobengula because of the family connection. But Moffat's missionary activity had not fared well. After thirty years of effort, the London Missionary Society in Matabeleland had won, at most, a dozen recruits. Moffat regarded Lobengula's Ndebele empire as a brutal tyranny, inflicting misery on 'myriads of other people' and standing in the way of Christian advancement. 'It will be a blessing to the world when they are broken up,' he remarked.

In December 1887, Shippard sent Moffat to Bulawayo to discuss a local border dispute between Bechuanaland and Matabeleland and to establish amicable ties. Moffat talked at length with Lobengula and found him anxious about the number of white suitors importuning him. 'I think he wants to be left alone,' Moffat reported to Shippard.

While Moffat was engaged on this mission, the British consul in Pretoria, Ralph Williams, who kept in close touch with both Robinson and Rhodes, discovered that Kruger was about to send a special envoy to Lobengula. While playing cricket one afternoon, he had been summoned from the pitch to an urgent meeting with a British merchant in his office. Telling Williams to look out of the window, the merchant said: 'Do you see that man out there loading his wagon? That man is . . . Grobler. He is starting tomorrow . . . to try and revive an old half-promise alleged by the Boers to have been made many years ago to General Joubert, to the effect that if any rights were in future granted to any white man over Matabele territory, they should be granted to the Boers and not to the English. If that mission succeeds there is an end of British expansion to the north.'

Alerted to the danger, Rhodes and Shippard hastened to Grahamstown to inform Robinson, who was on a ceremonial visit there. On the day after Christmas 1887, Robinson authorised Shippard to instruct Moffat to persuade Lobengula to sign a treaty acknowledging Britain's predominant influence in Zambesia. A messenger bearing these instructions reached Moffat at the end of January.

Moffat's negotiations with Lobengula were concluded with unusual speed. No other white man was trusted by Lobengula as much as Moffat. Lobengula denied the validity of the Grobler 'treaty' and thought that official British 'protection' – a treaty of friendship, as he saw it – provided a way of safeguarding his independence while fending off the predatory intentions of the Transvaal. Under the Moffat Treaty signed on 11 February 1887, Lobengula acknowledged Zambesia to be within Britain's sphere of interest, and agreed to refrain 'from entering into any correspondence or treaty with any foreign State or Power to sell, alienate, or cede, or permit or countenance any sale, alienation or cession of the whole or any part of the said Amandebele country . . . without the previous knowledge and sanction of Her Majesty's High Commissioner for South Africa'. Britain acknowledged Lobengula as ruler not only of the Ndebele but of the Shona.

Rhodes was delighted. 'I am very glad you were so successful with Lobengula,' he told Shippard. 'At any rate now no one else can step in.'

Grobler's appointment as Transvaal's consul to Lobengula's court was short-lived. After presenting his credentials to Lobengula in July 1888, he set out for Pretoria to collect his wife, taking a short cut across a disputed part of Kgama's territory, having failed to obtain permission in advance. Approaching the Limpopo River, he was stopped by Kgama's men on the British side of the river and mortally wounded in an exchange of fire. Kruger was convinced to the last that Rhodes was behind the killing. 'There is no doubt whatever,' he remarked in his memoirs, 'that this murder was due to the instigation of Cecil Rhodes and his clique.'

21

THE BALANCE OF AFRICA

With Zambesia secure as a British sphere of influence, Rhodes set out to gain a monopoly of its mineral wealth. Zambesia was where he hoped and expected to discover a 'second Rand', even more valuable than the Witwatersrand. During a visit to London in June 1888, arranged mainly to discuss his diamond ventures with Lord Rothschild, Rhodes met the Conservative colonial secretary, Lord Knutsford, and raised the possibility of forming a chartered company to handle Zambesia. In other areas of Africa, the British government had looked favourably on the formation of chartered companies as a way of extending Britain's writ without the expense of maintaining colonies or protectorates. In 1886, the Royal Niger Company had been granted a charter to act as an official commercial and administrative organisation in what was to become Nigeria. In 1888, the Imperial British East Africa Company had been awarded a similar charter. What was clear was that the British government had no appetite for establishing new protectorates like Basutoland and Bechuanaland that were costly to run and provided no revenue. Rhodes' difficulty was that he possessed no concession in Matabeleland, or elsewhere in Zambesia, on which to base his plan for a chartered company. Writing to Shippard about his discussions with the 'Home Government', Rhodes explained: 'They appeared favourable but unfortunately I had no concession to work on.' Nor was he the only one in the field. Lobengula was soon besieged by concession-hunters bearing gifts.

Among them were serious contenders. A London-based consortium, the 'Exploring Company', had already been formed for the purpose of exploring Zambesia. It was led by two entrepreneurs with powerful connections: one was Lord Gifford, a former British army officer who had won a Victoria Cross during the Ashanti war of 1873–4 and participated in the Zulu campaign; the other was George Cawston, a London financier. In April 1889, the Gifford–Cawston syndicate bought the concession that Frank Johnson had obtained from Kgama in Bechuanaland and then turned their attention to Matabeleland, appointing as their agent Edward Maund, a former British army officer. Maund had met Lobengula in Bulawayo in 1885 when he was sent on an official mission to explain the purpose of the new British protectorate over Bechuanaland to the king, and he claimed to have established a warm relationship with him. Maund was duly despatched to Bulawayo in July to obtain a concession.

Rhodes too had powerful allies, most notably the support of Hercules Robinson, the high commissioner in Cape Town. Along with Rhodes, Robinson had become a leading advocate of Cape colonialism, collaborating with him in the same cause. 'The true British policy for South Africa,' Robinson argued in 1889, 'seems to me to be what may be termed Colonialism, through Imperialism; in other words, colonial expansion through imperial aid.' Another British official in league with Rhodes was Shippard in Bechuanaland, who favoured annexation up to the Zambezi River. Rhodes, moreover, could count on the support of the Afrikaner Bond.

After returning to Cape Town in July 1888, Rhodes had a long private discussion with Robinson, outlining his plan for a chartered company, linked possibly to De Beers. Robinson immediately threw his weight behind the idea, reporting to Knutsford:

It appears to me that, looking to the reputed wealth of Matabeleland and its tributaries, the country is sure sooner or later to fall under the influence of some civilized power, and that a scheme such as that designed by Mr Rhodes might possibly provide for the security of Native rights and interests, as well as for the beneficial development of the resources of the waste lands by British Capital, without entailing on British taxpayers the burden which would be imposed on them by the annexation of the country, and its formation into a Crown Colony.

Mr Rhodes considers also, and I think with reason, that the extension of British interests in the interior of South Africa by a chartered company with Cape associations would be more in unison with the Africander sentiment than if the same result were attempted by the establishment of another inland Crown Colony.

Knutsford duly took the point, replying that no charter could be awarded to any enterprise that lacked Cape support.

Nothing could be accomplished, however, without a concession from Lobengula. Determined to overtake Maund's mission, Rhodes despatched a three-man team to Bulawayo, led by his trusted business partner, Charles Rudd. The two other members were both personal friends: Frank Thompson and Rochfort Maguire, an Oxford-educated lawyer who had served as a British official in Cape Town. They carried with them a letter of introduction, on official notepaper, to Lobengula from Robinson, referring to them as 'highly respected gentlemen who are visiting your country' – without a word of the purpose of their visit. In a long letter to Shippard written on 14 August, Rhodes told him:

Rudd is going up to look at the country and see what he can do . . . My only fear is that I shall be too late with Lo Bengula as, of course, if his whole country is given away to adventurers, it is no use my stepping in for my Company to assist in the govern-ment of a shell . . .

If we get Matabeleland we shall get the balance of Africa. I do not stop in my ideas at [the] Zambesi, and I am willing to work with you for it.

Rhodes wrote to Rothschild in a similar vein:

> I have always been afraid of the difficulty of dealing with the
> Matabele king. He is the only block to Central Africa as, once
> we have his territory, the rest is easy.

The Rudd party reached Bulawayo on 20 September, three weeks
ahead of Maund who had decided to delay his journey in
Bechuanaland. Rudd counted some thirty other concession-hunters
waiting around the king's encampment. As the king emerged from his
private quarters to meet the new arrivals, the Rudd party rose, took
off their hats and saluted him as 'Kumalo' in acknowledgement of his
status as a royal chief. Rudd then offered Lobengula a present of 100
gold sovereigns. 'The King,' he wrote in his diary, 'is just what I
expected to find him – a very fine man, only very fat, but with a
beautiful skin and well proportioned.' He was naked except for a skin
apron and a waxed head-ring. 'The King has a curious face; he looks
partly worried, partly good natured and partly cruel; he has a very
pleasant smile.'

Also staying in Bulawayo at the time was John Moffat, Shippard's
deputy, on hand to offer Lobengula discreet advice. Moffat suggested
to Lobengula that it would be advantageous for him to work with one
company rather than to disperse concessions among a number of
smaller entities, but advised him to make no decisions until Shippard
arrived on an official visit.

Lobengula, in any case, was in no hurry to make a decision. Not
only did he have to contend with a horde of concession-hunters but
with his councillors – *indunas* – hostile to the idea of allowing foreigners entry into Matabeleland. Young Ndebele warriors were keen
to 'make a breakfast' of all the whites in Matabeleland. Lobengula was
also unsure whether he could trust British officials. In conversation
with Charles Helm, a missionary from the London Missionary
Society, who acted as his interpreter, Lobengula remarked:

> The Boers are like the lizard, they dart about quickly, but the
> English proceed more cautiously. Did you ever see a chameleon

catch a fly? The chameleon gets behind the fly and remains motionless for some time, then he advances, very slowly and gently, first putting forward one leg and then the other. At last, when well within reach, he darts out his tongue and the fly disappears. England is the chameleon and I am that fly.

But Helm himself, given the task of explaining Rudd's business to Lobengula, was hardly neutral. According to Frank Thompson, he was working 'through thick and thin in our interests'.

For the concession-hunters, the waiting seemed interminable. 'Nobody can conceive the weariness of the ensuing days,' recalled Thompson. 'We were reduced to spending every day in our little camp, most of the time playing backgammon and reading. We did not dare to go far afield in case we might be called by Lobengula.'

Rhodes, meanwhile, bombarded Rudd with messages, warning him to keep an eye on Maund, suggesting that he 'buy him personally'. In any event, Rudd was told to stay in Bulawayo as long as necessary. 'You must not leave a vacuum,' Rhodes insisted. 'Nature abhors a vacuum and if we get anything we must always have someone resident or else they [other whites] will intrigue and upset us.'

Shippard eventually arrived in Bulawayo on 16 October, accompanied by a police escort and dressed in a tightly buttoned frock coat, patent leather boots and a white solar topee. He purported to be acting as an impartial official but used his position discreetly to advance Rhodes' cause. The Rudd party, he told Lobengula, represented a group with substantial resources, solid backing and the support of the Queen. 'Shippard and Moffat did all they could for us,' Maguire later confided to a friend.

Shippard had developed a particular aversion to the Ndebele and their plundering activities and he was already convinced about their ultimate fate. 'The accounts one hears of the wealth of Mashonaland if known and believed in England would bring such a rush to the country that its destiny would soon be settled whether the Matabele liked it or not,' he wrote to a member of his staff.

After leaving Lobengula's capital on 22 October, Shippard wrote in his official report: 'For my own part I can see no hope for this country save the purifying effects of war.' In a private letter to his assistant, Francis Newton, he was even more blunt: 'I must confess that it would offer me sincere and lasting satisfaction if I could see the Matabele ... cut down by our rifles and machine guns like a cornfield by a reaping machine ... The cup of their iniquities must surely be full or nearly full now.'

One week after Shippard's departure, and after a series of consultations with his indunas, Lobengula summoned Rudd, Thompson and Maguire to a meeting. 'We all went in and found the old king on a brandy case in a corner of the buck kraal [one of his private enclosures],' Rudd recorded in his diary. 'He said "Good morning" very good-temperedly but appeared much hustled and anxious.' For half an hour, Lobengula prevaricated, then told Helm to give him the document. 'The Concession was placed before him, and he took the pen in his hand to affix his mark, which was his signature,' recalled Thompson. 'As he did so, Maguire, in a half-drawling, yawning tone of voice, without the ghost of a smile said to me, "Thompson, this is the epoch of our lives."'

The concession that Lobengula signed on 30 October 1888 was highly controversial from the outset. He agreed, as 'King of Matabeleland, Mashonaland and certain adjoining territories', to assign to Rudd, Thompson and Maguire 'the complete and exclusive charge over all metals and minerals situated and contained in my kingdoms, principalities and dominions together with full power to do all things that they may deem necessary to win and procure the same and to hold, collect and enjoy the profits and revenues ... from the said metals and minerals'. Lobengula also gave Rudd and his partners authority to exclude all others seeking land, metals, minerals or mining rights from his territory.

In exchange, Rudd promised to pay Lobengula and his successors £100 every month and to provide 1,000 Martini-Henry breech-loading rifles, together with 100,000 rounds of ammunition. He also undertook to deliver an armed steamboat for use on the Zambezi River – an idea that came from Rhodes.

What was not included in the concession, according to Helm, was a promise made by Rudd and Thompson that no more than ten white men would be brought in to dig in his territory and that they would abide by the laws of Matabeleland. Lobengula was clearly under the impression that the document he had signed was limited in scope.

Moreover, though it may have pleased Lobengula to be described as the 'King of Matabeleland, Mashonaland and certain adjoining territories' and it certainly suited the interests of Rudd and company, Lobengula's rule extended effectively over no more than Matabeleland; Mashonaland and other areas were subject to intermittent military raids but not ruled by him.

A further flaw was that both Cape law and the terms of an international treaty prohibited the sale or gift of firearms to Africans living outside the Colony. Anyone who transported guns or ammunition across state boundaries could be fined or imprisoned. On that basis alone, the Rudd concession could be judged illegal. Yet it was the promise of guns more than any other factor, that persuaded Lobengula to sign the concession, believing that it would help protect his independence; without it, he had no reason to sign.

Rudd lost no time in rushing back to the Cape with his concession. The document was signed in Bulawayo at midday and by late afternoon he was on his way by mule cart, leaving Thompson and Maguire 'to hold the fort'. Rhodes was jubilant. 'Our concession is so gigantic,' he crowed, 'it is like giving a man the whole of Australia.' Robinson gave the Rudd concession his full support, recommending that it should be recognised by the British government. 'It appeared to me,' he recalled, 'although a monopoly of the kind was not free from objections, it was, on the whole, in the interests of the Matabele that they should have to deal with one set of substantial concessionaires, instead of . . . with a number of adventurers of different nationalities, who would have quarrelled among themselves and with the natives, and who would have been amenable to no practical control.'

Though the promise of arms to Lobengula was in flagrant breach of British policy, let alone Cape law, Robinson raised no objection. In a cable to Knutsford, he explained away the offer by implying that if Lobengula did not get arms from Britain, he would turn to rival states – the Transvaal – that would be only too eager to oblige in exchange for concessions.

In his memoirs, Graham Bower, Robinson's deputy in Cape Town, recorded: 'It was clearly illegal to deliver Martini-Henry rifles to a native chief. On the other hand unless the rifles were delivered the contract was not complete and the concession was invalid. Sir Sidney Shippard [in Bechuanaland] solved the problem by issuing a permit on his own authority.'

But there were soon signs of trouble. On learning that the concession had been obtained with the promise of guns, the Anglican Bishop of Bloemfontein, George Knight-Bruce, protested publicly. 'Such a piece of devilry and brutality as a consignment of rifles to the Matabele cannot be surpassed,' he declared. Rhodes acted quickly to 'square' him. 'Without telling you a long story,' Rhodes wrote to Rudd, 'I will simply say I believe [the bishop] will be our cordial supporter in future. I am sorry for his . . . speech . . . but he has repented.'

More serious ructions occurred in Bulawayo. Rival concession-hunters, aggrieved by what they had heard about the Rudd concession, warned Lobengula that he had, in effect, 'sold his country'. Alarmed by such talk, the king despatched two indunas to London to make enquiries. According to Moffat, Lobengula told the indunas, 'There are so many people who come here and tell me that they are sent by the Queen. Go and see if there is a Queen and ask her who is the one she has really sent.' He instructed them to deny that he had 'given away his country'. He also issued a statement sent to a Bechuanaland newspaper saying that in view of the controversy he had suspended the concession 'pending an investigation'.

Desperate to keep the concession alive, Rhodes organised delivery of the first consignment of arms and ammunition, relying on Shippard to clear it through Bechuanaland. Unless he could fulfil his side of the bargain, the concession was bound to expire. Rhodes entrusted the task to his old Kimberley friend Starr Jameson and another Kimberley doctor, Rutherfoord Harris. Both had been involved in the 'pink slip' scandal during the smallpox outbreak there. On their arrival in Bulawayo in February, Lobengula remained distrustful, but readily took his monthly stipend of £100. Jameson further earned Lobengula's gratitude by easing his gout with morphine. But Lobengula refused to accept the arms and they were left untouched in stacks at Thompson's camp. Jameson made a second delivery, but with the same result. The arms remained untouched for three years.

To bolster his position with the British government, Rhodes agreed to a Colonial Office suggestion to amalgamate his venture with the rival London consortium led by Gifford and Cawston. He also 'squared' a number of other claimants, paying out substantial sums. He then made plans to travel to London himself to persuade the British government to award him a charter. But the difficulties he faced were formidable.

The arrival of Lobengula's indunas – Babayane and Mtshete – in London in February 1889 became one of the events of the year. Accompanied by Edward Maund, they were taken to the ballet, to the London zoo, to the Bank of England, to Westminster Abbey and a military display at Aldershot. They were also granted an audience with Queen Victoria – the 'Great White Queen' – at Windsor where they delivered Lobengula's message. 'Lobengula desires . . . to ask [the Queen] to advise and help him, as he is much troubled by white men who come into his country and ask to dig for gold.'

There were many in London at the time who sympathised with Lobengula's plight. Rhodes' old adversary John Mackenzie was active in mobilising the missionary network to protest against the Rhodes group. 'They would "hammer" the natives, and rob them of their land and never recognize their right to own land, or to possess any civil right except to pay a hut-tax,' said Mackenzie. 'They would "level-down" the Cape Colony constitution to the condition of those [Boer] republics where a man, no matter how good he is, or how much he knows, or how much he has, in character, knowledge or property, can have no citizen rights, because he is a native African in his own country of Africa.'

A powerful lobby group – the South Africa Committee – argued vociferously in favour of imperial trusteeship in Africa. Its members included the Liberal politician Joseph Chamberlain and the editor of the *Pall Mall Gazette*, W. T. Stead. London businessmen resented the idea of a Cape monopoly getting preference. Within the Colonial Office, there were strong doubts about granting a royal charter for

Zambesia. 'This is a mere piece of financing,' wrote Edward Fairfield, an Africa expert. 'Something is to be got which will look well enough to invite fools to subscribe to. Such a Chartered Company would never really pay. It would simply sow the seeds of a heap of political trouble and then the promoters would shuffle out of it, and leave us to take up the work of preserving the peace, and settling the difficulties.'

Among those present in London who objected to the Rudd concession was Fred Selous. He had travelled there hoping to secure support for a prospecting expedition to Mashonaland. Having spent nearly twenty years in the region, he was regarded as its foremost expert. During his travels, Selous had developed a paternal liking for the Shona people and consequently an abiding dislike of Ndebele warriors who raided their territory. When the Anti-Slavery Society invited him to address a breakfast meeting 'in honour of the two Matabele envoys', Selous declined, describing the Ndebele as 'a people who, year after year, send out their armies of pitiless, bloodthirsty savages and slaughter men, women and children indiscriminately – except for those just the ages to be taken for slaves'.

Selous' objection to the Rudd concession, as he explained in the *Fortnightly Review*, was that although some Shona tribes adjacent to Matabeleland paid tribute to Lobengula, others were remote from Lobengula's influence. 'There are numerous tribes of Mashunas who are in no wise subject to Lobengula.' Rhodes' claims in Mashonaland, based on the Rudd concession, were therefore fraudulent; he had no legal rights there.

Shortly before the indunas returned to Matabeleland, the colonial secretary, Lord Knutsford, furnished them with a letter for Lobengula which appeared to be a lethal blow to Rhodes' prospects:

In the first place, the Queen wishes Lo Bengula to understand distinctly that Englishmen who have gone out to Matabeleland to ask leave to dig for stones have not gone with the Queen's authority, and that he should not believe any statements made by them or any of them to that effect. The Queen advises Lo Bengula not to grant hastily concessions of land, or leave to dig, but to consider all applications carefully. It is not wise to put too much power into the hands of the men who come first, and to exclude other deserving men.

Couching his remarks in a manner he thought might appeal to Lobengula, and made popular by Rider Haggard, he continued:

A King gives a stranger an ox, not his whole herd of cattle, otherwise what would other strangers arriving have to eat?

Arriving in London in March, Rhodes not only had to contend with this adverse tide of opinion, but deep suspicions about his own character. Little was known about Rhodes in London and what was known was largely unfavourable. In government circles he was regarded as a troublesome Cape nationalist who in the past had quarrelled with John Mackenzie, Livingstone's heir, and obstructed Colonel Warren during his Bechuanaland assignment. 'Rather a pro-Boer MP in South Africa, I fancy', remarked Lord Salisbury, the Conservative prime minister. Moreover, there was the matter of Rhodes' arms deal with Lobengula. Edward Fairfield's verdict on Rhodes was damning: 'In some aspects of his character, Mr Rhodes is apt not to be regarded as a serious person . . . he is grotesque, impulsive, schoolboyish, humorous and almost clownish.'

Rhodes' visit to Britain in the spring of 1889 thus turned into a tour de force of trying to overcome a host of obstacles. One by one, he picked off his opponents, offering some of them high positions or valuable share options in his new venture, bribing others with cash, stressing all the while the civilising mission that he intended to carry out in Zambesia. The editor W. T. Stead, once a staunch ally of Mackenzie, was one of the first to be 'converted'. Introduced by a mutual friend on 4 April 1889, he spent three hours with Rhodes and, after the offer of a gift of £2,000 he needed to settle a libel judgement and the promise of an additional £20,000 contribution to the *Pall Mall Gazette*, withdrew his reservations. 'Mr Rhodes is my man,' Stead wrote to his wife immediately afterwards. 'He is full of a far more gorgeous idea in connection with the paper than even I have had. I cannot tell you his scheme, because it is too secret. But it involves millions . . . His ideas are federation, expansion, and consolidation of the Empire . . . It seems all like a fairy dream.'

Other journalists whom Rhodes recruited to his cause included Flora Shaw, colonial correspondent of *The Times*; the Reverend John Verschoyle, deputy editor of the influential *Fortnightly Review*; and Sir Charles Dilke, a Radical MP who wrote on imperial matters for the *Review*.

Even more important was Rhodes' success in attracting members of the British establishment to join his venture, including those who had previously opposed him. The Duke of Abercorn, a wealthy landowner, accepted the post of chairman; and the Earl of Fife, soon to become the son-in-law of the Prince of Wales, accepted the post of vice-chairman. Neither of them had previously displayed any interest in Africa. Abercorn was preoccupied mainly with his estates in Ireland and Scotland. Fife had little experience of business. From Rhodes' point of view, they were ideal figureheads: neither had any taste for the drudgery of reading reports or overseeing company administration, leaving him free to run the venture in his own manner without interference.

Rhodes' most significant catch was Albert Grey, heir to the earldom of his uncle, a renowned former colonial secretary. Grey was a member of the South Africa Committee, well known as a champion of African rights, a close associate of Mackenzie, 'the Paladin of his generation', with a long record of conscientious public service. Grey justified his decision to become a director, telling Mackenzie that he would do more good from inside the company than remaining outside as a critic.

Other support came from Lord Rothschild, who was offered a tranche of shares for free. The secretary of the London Missionary Society, Wardlaw Thompson, was won over with promises of official backing in Matabeleland. From Cape Town, Robinson weighed in with dramatic advice in a letter that reached London in April. The only alternative to the proposed monopoly, he told the Colonial Office, was a free-for-all. 'Lo Bengula would be unable to govern or control such incomers except by a massacre; a British Protectorate would be ineffectual.' The choice then would be to let Matabeleland fall into the hands of the Transvaal or to annex it at great cost to the British taxpayer.

Rhodes also had the support of Irish members in the House of Commons. On a previous visit to London, he had agreed to pay the Irish nationalist leader Charles Parnell the sum of £5,000 in exchange for the backing of his bloc of eighty-five votes, with the promise of a second instalment of £5,000 at a later date.

To counter the onslaught from Mackenzie and the humanitarian lobby, the Rhodes group insisted that their consortium had been formed 'mainly in the interests of the natives and missionaries, to prevent unprincipled white men going in and ruining everyone'.

Despite his misgivings about Rhodes himself, Salisbury eventually concluded that Rhodes' venture offered the best prospect of extending British hegemony in southern Africa at no cost to the exchequer and would, at the same time, bring order to the fractious problem of the Matabeleland concessions. It could be used as a financially self-sufficient arm of imperial policy. There were additional advantages. When applying for a charter, the Rhodes consortium included a number of proposals that the British government welcomed: as well as developing mineral resources, it undertook to extend the railway and telegraph northwards through the isolated Bechuanaland protectorate; to encourage English immigration and colonisation in Africa; and to promote British trade and commerce in the hinterland. As a way of empire-building on the cheap, all this was difficult to fault.

While the charter was being drawn up, Lobengula sent the British government a letter which left no doubt about his attitude. Written on 23 April 1889, it arrived on 18 June. 'Some time ago a party of men came into my country, the principal one appearing to be a man called Rudd,' he wrote. 'They asked me for a place to dig, and said they would give me certain things for the right to do so . . . About three months afterwards I heard from other sources that I had given by that document the right to all minerals in my country . . . I will not recognise the paper as it contains neither my words nor the words of those who got it.'

When Rhodes was shown the letter, he replied that it was probably not genuine, but written by 'a certain section of the white inhabitants of Matabeleland' – in other words, rival concession-hunters. The British authorities made no further enquiries.

On 10 July 1889, the cabinet approved the granting of a charter to the Rhodes consortium. With nothing more to be accomplished, Rhodes set sail for Cape Town. 'My part is done,' Rhodes told Maund. 'The Charter is granted supporting Rudd Concession and granting us the interior. I am just waiting until I hear of its signature and to finish many small details . . . We have the whole thing recognised by the Queen and even if eventually we had any difficulty with king [Lobengula] the Home people would now always recognize us in possession of the minerals, they quite understand that savage potentates frequently repudiate.'

The mood in Bulawayo, meanwhile, had become ever more tense. The Queen's letter to Lobengula, deliberately delayed en route, served to intensify all his suspicions. In August he replied, thanking her and adding, 'The white people are troubling me much about gold. If the Queen hears that I have given away the whole country, it is not true.' The letter did not arrive in London until November.

As Rhodes' representative in Bulawayo, Frank Thompson was at serious risk. Time and again he had asked to be relieved, but Rhodes would not hear of it. Writing from the Westminster Palace Hotel before he left England, Rhodes urged: 'Stick to it. I trust you alone. Upon you depends the whole thing . . . I ask you is there a better chance in the world for you? Besides being one of the richest men in the Colony, you will have the kudos.'

Angry crowds of Ndebele began to gather in Bulawayo. 'Thousands came from all directions to ask the king if it were true that the white dog Thompson had bought the land,' Thompson recalled. 'Among the Matebili I was now the most notorious person in the country, and among a section of black and white schemers the most hated.'

In September, Thompson and Lotse Hlabangana, Lobengula's principal adviser, were hauled before a council meeting of three hundred indunas and faced a barrage of accusations of treachery and deception for ten hours, squatting on their haunches under a broiling sun. Lotse was condemned to death:

I saw the poor old fellow stand erect. He handed his snuff box to a man standing near. He was taken outside the council kraal, and on kneeling down he said, 'Do as you think fit with me. I am the king's chattel.' One blow from the executioner's stick sufficed.

The ostensible reason for Lotse's execution, wrote Thompson, was that he had advised the king to accept the rifles and sign the concession. 'But in reality he had been made the scapegoat to protect the king from the rising tide of suspicion among the Matebili that their king had traded away their rights in their land.' Scores of members of Lotse's family – men, women and children – were killed that night.

The next morning as he was preparing to ride to a nearby mission station, Thompson was given a warning by an African who followed him. 'Tomoson,' he called quietly, 'the king says the killing of yesterday is not yet over.' Thompson took off instantly on horseback, with no food or water, losing his hat in the scramble. When his horse collapsed, he continued on foot. On the third day, he was rescued by a trader. On reaching Mafeking, he telegraphed his wife, whom he had not seen for fifteen months, and sent a message to Rhodes, who was in Kimberley. He was, he said, 'surprised and disappointed' by Rhodes' reply. 'I want you to return because the king recognises you as the Concession', said Rhodes.

22

TO OPHIR DIRECT

The British South Africa Company, emanating from a flimsy agreement involving an illegal arms deal that had been obtained in dubious circumstances, and since repudiated repeatedly by its principal signatory, was formally granted a royal charter by Queen Victoria on 29 October 1889, with a remit similar to that of a government. Whereas Lobengula had granted Rudd a concession assigning to him no more than the right to mine metals and minerals, the royal charter empowered the BSA Company to build roads, railways and telegraphs; to establish and authorise banking; to award land grants; to negotiate treaties; to promulgate laws; to maintain a company police force; and to aid and promote immigration.

It was backed by substantial funds, with an initial capital of £700,000. Rhodes committed not only his own money to the venture but the support of De Beers and Gold Fields of South Africa. Other leading shareholders included Alfred Beit, Barney Barnato, Starr Jameson, Charles Rudd, Frank Thompson, Frank Johnson, Lord Rothschild and Sir Hercules Robinson. The shares were not opened to public subscription but offered at par to friends, associates and politicians who had been helpful. In South Africa, Rhodes used share offers to help overcome resistance within the Afrikaner Bond to his plan to build a railway northwards from

Kimberley, through Bechuanaland to Matabeleland — a basic requirement of the charter.

What no one outside a small Rhodes clique knew — not even the British government — was that the BSA Company did not actually own the Rudd concession, on which the whole structure had been built. It was still owned by the syndicate known as Central Search Association formed in London by Rhodes, Gifford and Cawston to amalgamate their interests. It had been leased by Central Search Association to the BSA Company on the condition that the Company bore all the costs of development, then passed half of its profits back to Central Search Association. As with the BSA Company, a number of useful individuals had been admitted to join in the spoils — Beit, Rudd and Rothschild were participants in Central Search Association from the start. In 1890, the Central Search Association, with a nominal capital of £121,000 was transformed into the United Concessions Company, with a nominal capital of £4 million and with the same set of shareholders. Although shares in the United Concessions Company sold at less than par, they still gave the company a market value of more than £1 million, all based on an original investment of 1,000 rifles — lying untouched — and £100 a month.

It was not until 1891 that the government discovered — to its shock — who owned the concession. A confidential memorandum on the origins of the BSA Company, submitted to the cabinet, concluded that the government had been deliberately misled. A senior official declared that if the facts had been known in 1889, 'the Charter would certainly have been refused'. Ministers declined to take any action, however, other than to insist that ownership of the Rudd concession be transferred to the BSA Company. The Central Search Association duly complied, exchanging its £4 million shares into £1 million in chartered shares, which were selling at a little above par at the time, and rose sharply shortly thereafter.

In view of the advice that Queen Victoria had given to Lobengula in her letter of March 1889, warning him 'not to grant hastily concessions' to passing Englishmen, the business of explaining why she had subsequently decided to grant a royal charter assigning vast powers to an English company without consulting him and in clear breach of the concession Lobengula had actually signed, proved awkward. A draft was written in the London office of the BSA Company and passed to the government for approval.

In the hope of demonstrating imperial splendour, the letter was conveyed to Bulawayo by a military mission consisting of five officers and men from the Royal Horse Guards. They arrived in Bulawayo in a gaudily painted four-wheeled coach adorned with the royal monogram and drawn by eight mules. Dressed in plumed helmets and glistening breastplates, they presented the letter to Lobengula on 29 January 1890.

Moffat was on hand to translate. Also present was Jameson whom Rhodes had chosen to replace Thompson. Thompson had made one last journey to Bulawayo, as Rhodes had requested, but wanted no further role there. The letter stated:

> Since the visit of Lo Bengula's Envoys, the Queen has made the fullest inquiries into the particular circumstances of Matabeleland, and understands the trouble caused to Lo Bengula by different parties of white men coming to his country to look for gold; but wherever gold is, or wherever it is reported to be, there it is impossible for him to exclude white men, and, therefore, the wisest and safest course for him to adopt, and that which will give least trouble to himself and his tribe, is to agree, not with one or two white men separately, but with one approved body of white men, who will consult Lo Bengula's wishes and arrange where white people are to dig, and who will be responsible to the Chief for any annoyance or trouble caused to himself or his people.

The Queen, said the letter, had therefore decided to approve the concession made by Lo Bengula to the representatives of Rhodes – Rudd, Thompson and Maguire. After careful enquiry, she was able to assure Lobengula of the reliability of these men: 'Some of the Queen's highest and most trusted subjects' were now associated with them.

They are men who will fulfil their undertakings and who may be
trusted to carry out the working for gold in the Chief's country
without molesting his people or in any way interfering with the
kraals, growers or cattle.

She announced the appointment of John Moffat as her representative
at Lobengula's court – a post paid for by Rhodes and described by
Moffat as 'a ghastly exile among unruly savages'.

Lobengula was not deceived by the honeyed words of the 'Great
White Queen'. After the guardsmen had left, he complained that
'the Queen's letter had been dictated by Rhodes and that she, the
Queen, must not write any more letters like that one to him again'.
He was later to accuse the Queen of speaking 'with two tongues'.

The duplicity, however, was far greater than he suspected. Even as
the Queen's letter was being read to him, endorsing the trustworthi-
ness of Rhodes, Rhodes in the Cape was planning for an armed
invasion across the Limpopo.

In December 1889, as Lobengula continued to prevaricate over giving
anyone 'the road', Rhodes initiated a scheme to remove him by force.
After a series of meetings at his cottage in Kimberley with Frank
Johnson and his associate Maurice Heany, Rhodes gave them a contract to recruit 500 white mercenaries to overthrow Lobengula on
behalf of the British South Africa Company. Under the terms of the
contract, signed on 7 December, Johnson's instructions were 'to carry
by sudden assaults all the principal strongholds of the Matabele nation
and generally to so break up the power of the Amandebele as to
render their raids on surrounding tribes impossible, to effect the
emancipation of all their slaves and further, to reduce the country to
such a condition as to enable the prospecting, mining and commercial
staff of the British South Africa Company to conduct their operations
in Matabeleland in peace and safety'. Rhodes agreed to bear all the
expense of raising and maintaining the mercenary force for a period of
six months 'or longer if required'. If the campaign was successful,
Johnson and Heany would receive £150,000 and 50,000 morgen of
land (about 100,000 acres).

For his part, Johnson proposed either to kill Lobengula or, prefer-ably, to take him hostage. In an extract from the manuscript of his autobiography *Great Days* – removed before its publication in 1940 – Johnson wrote: 'I had an open mind as to the procedure after secur-ing the King and his entourage. We might make a complete job of it by killing Lobengula and smashing each military kraal, before they had time to concentrate or organize. Or – and this I favoured most – I might dig myself in at Bulawayo with Lobengula and his entourage as hostages.'

Rhodes also invited Fred Selous to meet him in Kimberley. Selous had just returned to the Cape from an expedition to the Mazoe Valley in Mashonaland, travelling through Portuguese-controlled territory to get there. It was an area that he knew well. Since 1880 his despatches and maps had been published by the Royal Geographical Society in London. One of the landmarks he had identified was a hill near the source of the Mazoe River, which he named Mount Hampden. In 1884 he had written to the Royal Geographical Society describing the tract of highveld between the Hunyani and Mazoe rivers as the best-suited for European occupation in the whole of southern Africa. 'It is splendidly watered, droughts and famines are unknown, and nowhere do the natives get such abundant and diversified crops as here.' The local Shona population, he noted, was peaceable. 'They seem to have but little of the ferocity which usually forms so marked a feature in the character of uncivilized races, and in their inter-tribal quarrels blood is seldom shed.'

During his travels in 1889, Selous had obtained a mineral conces-sion in the Mazoe Valley from two headmen. In his report to the syndicate that backed his expedition, he wrote: 'The concession is perfectly square, fair and genuine, and nothing can upset it. The Matabele claim to the country is utterly preposterous.' He also encountered Portuguese activity in the area.

In discussing these matters with Rhodes in Kimberley in December, Selous made clear his intention to write articles in the British press confirming his opinion that a large part of Mashonaland – including the area for which he had the concession – was completely independent of Lobengula. Rhodes quickly set out to dissuade him. He later wrote to Abercorn in London: 'It took me a long time to show him that if he could prove Mashonaland to be independent of Lobengula it would not help the Mashonas but simply help the Portuguese to get the country.' What helped conclude the matter was a payment of £2,000 Rhodes made to Selous out of his private funds.

Rhodes then set out to recruit Selous for his own expedition. On learning of Rhodes' scheme to overthrow Lobengula by force, however, Selous immediately opposed it. It would result in disaster, he said, provoking retaliation against traders and missionaries in Matabeleland and causing uproar in England. All in all, Selous told Rhodes, 'This would be a bad beginning for the British South Africa Company'. Johnson continued to press for invasion, but Selous persuaded Rhodes to devise an alternative plan. He suggested that instead of heading for Bulawayo, his expedition should take a direct route to Mashonaland from the south, passing around the eastern fringes of Matabeleland through uncharted territory, avoiding Bulawayo altogether. And he identified Mount Hampden, near the source of the Mazoe River, as the most suitable destination.

The outcome was that, in Cape Town on 1 January 1890, Rhodes drew up a new contract with Johnson. The plan was for Johnson to recruit a corps of 120 'miners', rather than mercenaries, who would travel to Mashonaland accompanied by an armed police force. Selous was to act as guide to the expedition. The plan was approved by the new British high commissioner, Sir Henry Loch, at an official conference in Government House, Cape Town on 10 January. What was clearly intended, despite some of the language used, was that the expedition should become the first step in the occupation of Mashonaland.

The implications were quickly grasped in London by the Colonial Office official Edward Fairfield when he read a report of the conference. 'The cat is being now let out of Mr Rhodes's bag, and proves a very ferocious animal indeed.' Fairfield thought that the plan was bound to involve Britain in a war with Lobengula. 'The people in South Africa are getting out of hand,' he wrote. On 14 February, the colonial secretary, Knutsford, cabled Loch, making clear that the government could not 'sanction movement in force in Matabeleland or Mashonaland which is not specifically sanctioned by Lo Bengula'.

But Lobengula still refused to give his approval to any expedition. Impatient with the delay, Selous travelled to Bulawayo in March to talk to him, but made no headway. 'There is only one road to Mashonaland, and that goes through my country,' Lobengula said. Lobengula complained that he always had to deal with subordinates. 'Let Rhodes come, let Selous go for him tomorrow.'

Jameson tried next, reaching Bulawayo on 29 April on his fourth and last visit. In a long interview with the king the next day, Lobengula was told, for the first time, about the proposed expedition. Jameson recalled:

> He looked pretty grave and hummed a tune to himself during the recital, as much to say 'What damned impudence!' Then asked minutely after the police – what they were going to do, what we were going to do etc., etc.

Three days later, there was another interview. Jameson informed Lobengula he was going back to Rhodes to tell him that Lobengula had refused the road. Lobengula replied: 'No, I have not refused you the road, but let Rhodes come.' On that, they shook hands, and Jameson left at once for the south.

It was hardly the 'specific sanction' the British government wanted. What tipped the balance were reports from the Transvaal that Boer expeditions to Mashonaland were being organised by groups wanting to escape the influx of Englishmen into the republic following gold discoveries there. Lord Salisbury intervened to warn that 'It would be dangerous to withhold much longer from the High Commissioner authority to sanction the advance of the Company's armed police force into Mashonaland'.

By this time, Johnson had nearly completed the recruitment of volunteers – 'pioneers' as they were called – setting up a base camp for them, Camp Cecil, on the northern bank of the Limpopo in Bechuanaland. Each was provided with a uniform and weapon, paid seven shillings and sixpence a day, and promised fifteen mining claims and 1,500 morgen (about 3,000 acres) of land. Many were prospectors, drawn by stories that gold could be found in abundance, close to the surface, in Mashonaland, but there was a cross-section of other trades and skills. Rhodes insisted that Johnson find members of leading Cape families. When Johnson asked him why, Rhodes replied:

> Do you know what will happen to you? You will probably be massacred by the Matabele, or at least we shall one day hear that you have been surrounded and cut off! And who will rescue you, do you think? I will tell you – the Imperial Factor [the British government]. And who do you think will bring pressure to bear on the Imperial Factor and stir them to save you? *The influential fathers of your young men.*

On 27 June 1890, the pioneer column moved out of its base camp and headed eastwards for the Matabeleland border at Tuli. It consisted of 186 volunteers and 19 civilians, including two Anglican priests, a Jesuit father and Dr Starr Jameson, Rhodes' personal representative. The column was accompanied by a paramilitary police force of 500 men – the British South Africa Police – equipped with field guns, machine guns, and a searchlight with a portable steam dynamo borrowed from Her Majesty's naval station at Simonstown – 'to impress the superstitious Matabele'. Also in the column was an assortment of African scouts, drivers, artisans, cooks and labourers, numbering nearly a thousand.

Rhodes had arranged for a British major-general to give the column a ceremonial send-off:

LORD METHUEN: Gentlemen, have you got maps?
OFFICERS: Yes, sir.
LORD METHUEN: And pencils?
OFFICERS: Yes, sir
LORD METHUEN: Well, gentlemen, your destiny is Mount Hampden.

The British high commissioner, Loch, despatched a message to Lobengula giving assurances he knew to be false. 'I wish you to know,' he said, 'that these people come as your friends.' Lobengula was still not fooled. 'The Chief is troubled,' he replied. 'He is being eaten up by Mr Rhodes.' Lobengula also sent a message to the police camp at Motloutsi in Bechuanaland, that arrived on 30 June, asking: 'Why are so many warriors at Macloutsie? Has the king committed any fault, or have the white men lost anything that they are looking for?' Yet, mindful of the fate of the Zulu king, Cetshwayo, he held back from attacking the column, even though his own warrior regiments were thirsting for blood.

With Selous and a bevy of African scouts leading the way, the column crossed the Tuli river on 6 July, traversing the lowveld of the Limpopo valley, and climbed up into the open grasslands of Mashonaland, passing by the ruined city of Great Zimbabwe – the supposed capital of Ophir. Just to the north, they constructed a fort, naming it Fort Victoria. On 12 September, after a journey of 360 miles from the Tuli crossing point, the main party of settlers and police reached the vicinity of Mount Hampden, found the Makabusi River, and decided that they had attained their destination, naming it Fort Salisbury. At a ceremony the next day, Lieutenant Tyndale-Briscoe hoisted the Union flag up a crooked msasa pole; Canon Balfour offered a prayer; the police force fired a royal salute of twenty-one guns; and the pioneers gave three lusty cheers for the Queen.

23

KRUGER'S PROTECTORATE

The fate of Swaziland was next in line. Kruger coveted it for the ready access it would give him to the sea at Kosi Bay in Tongaland. Rhodes favoured giving it to the Transvaal in return for Kruger's agreement to forsake expansion to the north across the Limpopo, leaving the field there clear for the British South Africa Company. British officials in London were similarly inclined to offer up Swaziland as an appeasement to Kruger. In 1889, the colonial secretary, Lord Knutsford, wrote to the prime minister, Lord Salisbury:

> We should be much abused in this country if we let the Boers annex Matabeleland and Mashonaland, as they are rich territories and concessions by Lo Bengula are held by some influential people; but we shall have to face considerable danger of conflict with the Boers, if we bar them from extension to the North. I should be inclined to compromise with them, by letting it be known that if they come to terms with Umbandine [Mbandzeni, the king of Swaziland] we shall not prevent them from protecting or annexing that country.

Encircled by predators – the Boers, the Zulus and the Portuguese – Swaziland had managed to retain a semblance of independence while, all around, other African kingdoms had been struck down by the relentless advance of white rule. Under the terms of the Pretoria Convention of 1881 and the London Convention of 1884, Britain and the Transvaal were pledged to uphold Swaziland's independence. But the discovery of valuable gold deposits in the De Kaap valley close to the Swazi border in 1884 intensified the menace that Mbandzeni faced.

From an early stage in their encounters with white settlers, the Swazis had sought to collaborate with them rather than oppose them, forming alliances with Boer trekkers against their traditional rivals like the Pedi and the Zulu. The Swazis provided armies to support both the Boers and the British in their campaigns to crush Sekhukhune's Pedi state; they also helped the British defeat Cetshwayo's Zulu state. During the 1880s, however, the whites became increasingly acquisitive. First came Boer farmers seeking winter grazing concessions; then came white prospectors – mainly English-speaking – seeking mining concessions. By the end of 1886, the Swazi had lost most of their winter pasturage to Transvaal trek-boers; by the end of 1887, they had lost virtually all mineral rights. Mbandzeni next began to sell off other monopoly concessions.

As the scramble for concessions gathered momentum, Mbandzeni decided a white administrator was needed to control the concession business. He turned for help to the Shepstone family in Natal, appointing 'Offy' Shepstone, a son of Sir Theophilus, to the post of Resident Adviser and Agent to the Swazi King, believing that he could be trusted. Shepstone arrived at Mbandzeni's court at Embekelwini in 1887. He was given charge of all business transactions between the king and the whites, along with the revenue they gener-ated. He also set up a White Governing Committee to supervise the organisation of a police force and the courts, and the collection of non-concession revenues like licences and dues. But Shepstone turned out to be an unscrupulous and corrupt administrator who systemat-ically appropriated concession revenues for his personal use. He also began to deal in concessions himself, acquiring a railway concession for agents acting on behalf of the Transvaal.

Seeking to curb Shepstone's activities, Mbandzeni gave the White

Governing Committee greater powers. In 1888, the committee was granted a charter of administrative authority over all whites in Swaziland. But the result was wholesale plunder. Concessions of every conceivable description were wheedled out of the king, ranging from pawnbroking and patent medicines, to banking, customs and rights to the king's revenues. In failing health, Mbandzeni remarked:

> I have white men all round me. By force they have taken the countries of all my neighbours. If I do not give them rights, they will take them. Therefore I give them when they pay. Why should we not eat before we die?

The mayhem over concessions provided openings for both Kruger and the mining magnates of Kimberley and the Rand. As well as acquiring a railway concession, the Transvaal government bought telegraph and electricity concessions, aiming eventually to gain effective control over Swaziland and, with it, access to Kosi Bay. The mining magnates, for their part, saw lucrative opportunities in acting as intermediaries, buying and selling concessions offered to them.

In March 1889, Eckstein and Porges were approached by concessionaires selling various rights, including monopolies to operate a mint for fifty years and to issue licences and permits for any trade, business or profession for fifty years. They initially turned down the offers, considering the price too high. But within a few days, Eckstein was contacted by Kruger's business associate Hugo Nellmapius, acting, he said, on instructions from the Transvaal government. Nellmapius proposed that an Eckstein syndicate, including himself, should purchase the mint and licencing concessions for £50,000 and hold them on behalf of the government until it had succeeded in annexing Swaziland, at which point the syndicate would be reimbursed at a profit. As an additional incentive, Eckstein was offered access to government concessions in the Transvaal.

A deal was swiftly concluded. On 1 May 1889, under the guidance of officials from the White Governing Committee, Mbandzeni signed an agreement on concessions, accepting a payment of £100 per annum from Eckstein and Porges. In return, he undertook 'not to give up the independence of his country to any foreign power, excepting with the consent of the concessionaires and to resist conquest or annexation by any foreign power to whom the concessionaires, might object to the best of his ability and, if attacked or threatened, the concessionaires had the right to bring in such foreign powers as they might think fit for the protection of his kingdom'.

On 3 May, Kruger made an offer to the British government to relinquish all Transvaal's claims to the north in exchange for political rights in Swaziland and a road across Tongaland to Kosi Bay. He then concluded a private agreement with Eckstein which required his syndicate to cede their concession to the government, as and when instructed to do so, in exchange for a payment of £53,000, and in the meantime to promote the annexation of Swaziland by the Transvaal. In a letter accompanying the contract, Nellmapius told Eckstein: 'It is *quite impossible* that Swaziland should remain independent for another year . . . and immediately it loses its independence the Agreement comes into force and we get out money from one or other who gets possession of the country.' On 29 July, the White Governing Committee passed a resolution in favour of incorporating Swaziland into the Transvaal.

As Mbandzeni's authority waned, he ordered a wave of executions and killings of his opponents, throwing Swaziland into even deeper turmoil. By the time he died of jaundice in October 1889, his kingdom existed only in name. With some concessions sold several times over, he had 'conceded' more than the total area of his country.

The Transvaal and Britain both moved to fill the vacuum. Kruger laid claim to Swaziland, demanding sole control. The British sent an official, Sir Francis de Winton, for an on-the-spot investigation. De Winton concluded that much of the Transvaal's case was sound. But he recommended that in exchange for any official recognition of its rights to Swaziland, the Transvaal should be required to relinquish all claims to the north of the Limpopo, to accept free trade in Cape products and to allow the Cape to extend its railway to the Witwatersrand.

All these issues were discussed at a meeting between Kruger and the British high commissioner, Sir Henry Loch, held in March 1890 at Blignaut's Pont on the Vaal River; Rhodes attended the meeting as a representative of the British South Africa Company. Kruger proposed a deal whereby he withdrew Transvaal's rights to northern expansion in return for gaining Swaziland:

> Seeing the desire of Her Majesty's Government to have Matabeleland and Mashonaland, and also in view of the concession lately granted to the English by Lobengula, it appeared to me that an opportunity arose for encouraging the prosperity of South Africa – I supporting Her Majesty's Government upon my side, and Her Majesty's Government giving me rights I ask for in Swaziland, and a sea-border on the east.

Loch, however, refused to allow such a link between the future of Zambesia and of Swaziland. Zambesia, he said, was already within Britain's sphere of influence. After considerable argument, Kruger agreed to separate the two, and volunteered to support the British government efforts in Matabeleland. 'In case it should be necessary to resort to arms in Matabeleland, I could offer inducements to my burghers to go in and help Mr Rhodes if he wants them . . . Mr Rhodes must not think that my policy is to stand aside; it is to help him as much as I can.'

Turning to the issue of Swaziland's future, Loch insisted that instead of giving Kruger sole control there, Swaziland should come under joint administration. Kruger objected: 'How can two great farmers live together in the same house?' Loch was equally adamant over the arrangements allowing the Transvaal access to the sea. Britain, he said, was prepared to give Kruger a coastal port at Kosi Bay; it would permit a railway to be built there along a corridor traversing Swaziland and Tongaland; but it would not concede control of Swaziland and Tongaland to the Transvaal as Kruger wanted. Kruger retorted: 'How, if I cut my hand off and throw it away, can I still call it my hand?'

Towards the end of the day, Loch introduced a new issue. 'There is one point that I should have mentioned before,' he said. If the Transvaal government was given a seaport it would be on condition that it joined a customs union within three years. Kruger replied that he would be willing to join a customs union if he acquired a harbour on the coast, but he wanted more land on the coast than he was being offered.

Kruger left the meeting, saying that he needed to consult the Volksraad. When the Volksraad rejected the deal, Loch prevailed upon Jan Hofmeyr to negotiate with Kruger, using the threat of force as an additional spur.

The Convention that was eventually signed in August 1890 – without any consultation with the Swazis – placed Swaziland under joint control and authorised the Transvaal to acquire a three-mile-wide corridor to build a railway through Swaziland and Tongaland to Kosi Bay.

Kruger then used the Convention to tighten the Transvaal's grip over Swaziland. By 1892, the 'Joint-Government' was deemed a failure. A second Convention in 1893 gave effective control over the administration of Swaziland to the Transvaal. When Swazi elders were presented with the terms of the Convention, they refused to accept them, but were given short shrift.

In 1894, the British government retreated further. 'I am coming to the conclusion that we shall have to let the Boers go in,' the colonial secretary, Lord Ripon, wrote to the foreign secretary, Lord Kimberley, in September. 'I greatly dislike the measure – but the only practical alternative that I can see is to run [the] grave risk of war with the Boers which I regard as out of the question.'

Once more, the Swazis were given no hearing. On 10 December 1894, Britain agreed a third Convention consigning Swaziland into the hands of the Transvaal as a 'Protectorate'. According to Loch, this was 'the price which must be paid to avert war between the two white peoples of South Africa'.

The Swazis remembered this passage of their history as a time when 'the documents killed us'.

PART VI

24

GROOTE SCHUUR

In 1890, at the age of thirty-seven, Rhodes reached a pinnacle of wealth and power. As prime minister of the Cape Colony, he had command of an effective administration and the support of the Afrikaner Bond, the only organised political party in the country. As chairman of De Beers, he controlled a virtual monopoly of both diamond production and markets. As managing director of the British South Africa Company, he was empowered to act with 'absolute discretion' over a vast stretch of the African interior and allowed a private army – the British South Africa Police – to enforce his plans.

It was a dazzling feat of empire-building that won him many admirers. Rhodes regarded his achievements as evidence of his own unique genius. But, like other empire-builders, his success had depended on the work and talent of many key figures. His early business career had been held together by Charles Rudd; indeed, their partnership for several years was commonly known as Rudd and Rhodes, in that order. The mastermind behind the amalgamation of the diamond mines in Kimberley was not Rhodes but the self-effacing Alfred Beit – 'Little Alfred' – to whom he invariably turned for solutions. His drive to the north was facilitated by Hercules Robinson, a Cape imperialist who shared similar aims; it was Robinson's decisiveness that led to the Moffat Treaty, incorporating Matabeleland within Britain's sphere

of interest. His triumph in winning the support of the British establishment for a chartered company was due as much to the work of
Gifford and Cawston in London as to Rhodes' own efforts. Finally, he
managed to obtain a royal charter for his company only because it
suited the interests of Lord Salisbury; preoccupied with the need to
keep Britain ahead in the Scramble for Africa among European
powers, Salisbury saw a means to extend British influence on the
cheap, at no cost to the public exchequer.

In harnessing allies to his cause, Rhodes displayed remarkable
powers of persuasion. But what was equally influential was the
power of his money. Many hitched themselves to Rhodes' band-
wagon lured by the prospect of making their own fortunes. When
he encountered resistance or scepticism, Rhodes was adept at
providing incentives, bribes, share options, directorships and other
positions, convinced that every man had his price. Politicians,
journalists and churchmen in Britain and in southern Africa, even
those with distinguished records, had few qualms about signing up
as paid supporters for Rhodes' cause. The Anglican Bishop of
Bloemfontein, Dr Knight-Bruce, once so outspoken in his con-
demnation of Rhodes, was soon silenced by being offered the post
of first Bishop of Mashonaland. Earl Grey, the paladin of his generation, was similarly converted, reasoning to himself that he might be
able to do more good from within the British South Africa
Company than by remaining an outside critic.

In his memoirs, the Cape lawyer James Rose Innes gave a graphic
description of Rhodes at work, infecting the body politic, as he put it:

He offered to members of parliament, and other prominent persons the opportunity of subscribing at par for parcels of chartered
shares then standing at a considerable premium. It was delicately
put; the idea was to interest the selected recipients in northern
development. Of course the recipient paid for his shares, but
equally of course they were worth far more than he paid. In
effect it was a valuable gift, which could not, one would think,
be accepted without some impairment of independence. Yet
there were acceptances in unexpected quarters.

Rose Innes was one of the few who declined Rhodes' offer.

Lauded by the press, the Rhodes phenomenon caught the public imagination. With the Scramble for Africa reaching a climax, empire-builders in Africa were regarded as popular heroes. Rhodes was seen as upholding the tradition set by David Livingstone, General Gordon and, more recently, the Welsh-born journalist-explorer Henry Morton Stanley, blazing a trail that would bring civilisation to a benighted continent. Stanley's account of one of his epic journeys through the jungles of the Congo – *In Darkest Africa* – had just been published to widespread acclaim. Rhodes' plans to build railways and telegraphs into the interior and to develop mineral and agricultural resources were held up as examples of what needed to follow.

The Scramble for Africa added a sense of urgency, justifying the kind of decisive action that Rhodes was willing to take. In August 1888, an ardent young imperialist, Harry Johnston, after spending the weekend at Lord Salisbury's residence at Hatfield, wrote an article for the London *Times* advocating an end to Britain's 'magnificent inactivity' in colonising Africa. While conceding that other European powers had 'legitimate' interests in Africa – the French and the Italians in north Africa, for example – he argued that it was essential for the sake of British commerce that Britain should extend its control 'over a large part of Africa'. Picking up Edwin Arnold's original idea for a 'Cape-to-Cairo' policy, he urged the linking of Britain's possessions in southern Africa with its sphere in east Africa and the Egyptian Sudan 'by a continuous band of British dominion'.

Impressed by Johnston's zeal, Salisbury appointed him as consul in Portuguese East Africa (Mozambique). His remit was to secure for Britain territory in the interior which Salisbury was interested in acquiring by signing treaties with African chiefs before the Portuguese or the Germans or the Belgians got there. But, faced as ever with a tight-fisted Treasury, Salisbury was able to provide Johnston with only limited funds.

It was Rhodes who solved Johnston's predicament during his 1889 visit to London in pursuit of a royal charter. They met at the Marylebone apartment of John Verschoyle, deputy editor of the influential *Fortnightly Review*, and continued talking through the night at

Rhodes' suite at the Westminster Palace Hotel. Rhodes wrote Johnston a cheque for £2,000 for a treaty-making expedition and promised him more – £10,000 a year – for the occupation and administration of a swathe of territory in central Africa 'between the Zambesi and the White Nile'. And he took up the cause of a Cape-to-Cairo policy as his personal crusade.

Returning to London in 1891 with the occupation of Mashonaland under his belt, Rhodes was accorded star status, acclaimed a man of action with the Midas touch boldly leading the advance of civilisation. He was flooded with invitations from politicians, journalists and financiers, among them Salisbury and Gladstone. Queen Victoria invited him to dine at Windsor Castle. She asked him whether it was true that he was a woman-hater, to which Rhodes replied graciously: 'How could I possibly hate a sex to which Your Majesty belongs?'

Among the visitors who came to his suite at the Westminster Palace Hotel was the Irish nationalist leader, Charles Parnell, seeking the second instalment of £5,000 that Rhodes had promised him in return for political support. Rhodes sent his private secretary, Harry Currey, to Hoare's Bank to withdraw £5,000 in cash. Facing challenges to his leadership, Parnell often sought Rhodes' company. 'He used to call frequently about six in the evening and wait patiently in my room until Rhodes was disengaged,' recalled Currey:

> One evening he told Rhodes, 'I shall lose', and Rhodes asked 'Why do you say that?' Parnell replied, 'Because the priests are against me.' Rhodes, walking up and down the room, as he was wont, suddenly turned and asked, 'Can't we square the Pope?'

Rhodes also had a long conversation with the editor of the *Pall Mall Gazette*, W. T. Stead, spilling out his ideas for a union of the English-speaking world and indulging in other fantasies. Stead quotes him as saying, 'If there be a God, I think that what He would like me to do is to paint as much of the map of Africa British red as possible.'

Having moved his headquarters from Kimberley to Cape Town, Rhodes went in search of a residence that would provide him with a permanent home. For twenty years, he had been accustomed to living simply in spartan accommodation – tents, wagons, tin huts, boarding houses and hotel rooms – caring little for home comforts, frequently on the move. When he became prime minister, his Cape Town quarters were noisy rooms he shared with Captain Penfold, the harbour master, above a bank in Adderley Street, the main thoroughfare in Cape Town, which ran downhill from parliament to the harbour.

In early 1891, he took a lease on Groote Schuur, a residence that British governors had used as a summer retreat. It stood beneath Devil's Peak, the outlying shoulder of Table Mountain, a few miles from the eastern edge of Cape Town. The original building there had been constructed in the seventeenth century for use as a government granary – the Great Granary; but it had then been converted into a residence with Cape Dutch architectural features. Little remained of the early house; after a fire in 1866, the traditional thatched roof had been replaced by Welsh slates, but the site, with views stretching away to the mountains around Stellenbosch, was magnificent. Rhodes subsequently bought the property's freehold and then set about acquiring surrounding farms, assembling an estate of 1,500 acres of oak, pine and indigenous forest on the slopes of Devil's Peak.

Once he had moved in, Rhodes conceived the idea of rebuilding Groote Schuur in its original Cape Dutch style. By chance, at a dinner party, he encountered Herbert Baker, a young architect from England with an interest in colonial architecture, and asked him to take on the assignment. Rhodes gave Baker few instructions. 'I was surprised that such a man, the chairman of great business corporations, should give me no details or defined instructions of what he wanted,' wrote Baker in his memoir. 'He just gave me in few words his idea – his "thoughts" – and trusted me to do the rest.'

Rhodes' 'thoughts' said as much about his own character as his taste in architecture. 'The big and simple, barbaric, if you like'; 'nothing petty or finikin'; and 'I like teak and whitewash,' he told Baker. 'He abhorred the small and mean and any commercial things made with the machine and not with the hands and brain,' wrote Baker. He insisted on tearing out all deal joinery and replacing it with teak. 'I had also to replace all imported ironmongery, the things he hated, such as hinges and metalwork for doors and windows – even the screws in those places where they could be seen; and craftsmen had to be found and taught to hammer in iron or cast in brass and bronze, as in the golden days of the crafts before the hostile influences of machinery.'

Baker installed a new front to the house, added a long stoep at the back and a block for kitchens and staff, and constructed a new wing containing a ground-floor billiard room and a second-storey master bedroom above, with a large bay window facing Devil's Peak. He also restored a thatched roof. While the renovation was under way, Rhodes was content to sleep in a small room in an outbuilding that had once been part of slave quarters. The house's most distinctive feature was the stoep at the back, with a floor of black and white chequered marble and a view of Devil's Peak. Rhodes used it for many of his meetings and receptions. Inside the house, Baker created a spacious hall, framed by solid teak pillars and a massive fireplace.

When it came to furnishing the house, Rhodes took the opportunity during his London visit in 1891 to organise a delivery of modern furniture. Harry Currey was given the task of finding a suitable store and making a selection. Currey was directed to Maples in Tottenham Court Road but, overwhelmed by the range on offer, arranged for Maples to send round to Rhodes' hotel 'three of a kind' of everything that Rhodes required – chairs, rugs, wardrobes, salt cellars, table napkins. One of the hotel's main reception rooms was converted into a showroom and a convoy of vehicles arrived to deliver the furniture. Rhodes, however, had no interest in the matter and left Currey to make the choice. Groote Schuur was furnished 'from cellars to attic', according to Currey, 'in about quarter on an hour'.

Guided by Baker, Rhodes began to take an interest in traditional Cape furniture. When Baker showed him a plain wardrobe of stinkwood that he had found in a pawnbroker's shop in Cape Town, its colours of gold and brown darkened by age, Rhodes instantly wrote out a cheque for it. It marked the beginning of his collection of old colonial furniture. 'He had, I think, an inherently true, though perhaps crude and primitive, taste – a searching for the truth – and could quickly distinguish the good from the bad when both were put before him,' wrote Baker. 'But at first when acting on his own impulse and bad advice he made mistakes.'

The London furniture soon disappeared. As his enthusiasm for Cape items grew, Rhodes became a knowledgeable collector. He was particularly delighted to obtain chairs and benches made by Boer hunters on the frontier, with dates and initials inlaid in bone or ivory. He purchased Dutch glass and Chinese and Japanese porcelain imported by merchants from the Dutch East India Company. When no old furniture was available, Baker commissioned local craftsmen to produce replicas. In the hall, Rhodes displayed African shields and spears and hunting trophies. His library he filled with books, documents, journals, manuscripts and maps about the exploration and history of Africa. The centrepiece of his bathroom was an eight-foot-long bath hollowed out of a solid block of granite and transported forty-five miles from Paarl; shaped like a sarcophagus, it was decorated with lion-head spouts reminiscent of imperial Rome. On the stoep floor, he placed old kists, the ship chests of settlers, bound and studded with pierced and engraved brass locks, plates and hinges.

In the surrounding gardens, Rhodes demanded 'masses of colour'. At one end of the house there was a profusion of roses, 'bewildering to the eye'. A hollow within sight of the stoep was filled with a blue 'lake' of hydrangeas. Huge clumps of scarlet and orange cannas, bougainvilleas and fuchsias grew in semi-wildness. 'You can't overdo the massing of flower in a garden,' he said. 'In South Africa everything must be done in masses.' Herbert Baker observed: 'The activities of Rhodes in gardening and planting suffered often by the defects of his qualities, his "foible of size."' On the higher slopes of Devil's Peak, he established an enclosure for antelopes, zebra, eland, wildebeest, ostriches and other African wildlife. He also kept a few lions in cages, intending one day to build a grand edifice for them with portico and marble courts.

Rhodes used Groote Schuur not so much as a home as the headquarters of his business and political empire. His routine was to take early morning rides along the mountain slopes, sometimes with a friend or two, breaking prolonged silences with a flood of talk; he often sat brooding alone on a ledge above Groote Schuur where he could gaze at the Indian Ocean to the south and the Atlantic Ocean to the north. But otherwise Groote Schuur was a constant hive of activity. Rhodes was a generous host, keeping open house for a stream of friends, political colleagues, business associates and other visitors. His life at Groote Schuur revolved around a succession of luncheon and dinner parties. At receptions on the stoep, as many as fifty guests would attend.

'People of all conditions and degrees were welcome at his table,' wrote Baker, 'and he would with tact and sympathy put the uncouth, the unkempt and the unexpected at their ease.' He loved to talk his own 'shop' – about the Empire, or the north, or gold and diamonds; but had a horror of gossip and bawdy stories. 'His conversation would often seem to consist of simple enough platitudes: he reiterated them and hammered them, "rubbing them in like jewels", as has been said: but it was often to the boredom of the less imaginative and more habitual guests.' Baker observed that 'in some ways he retained some of the characteristics of a child'. He was shy of saying goodbye. When absorbed in talk, he would sit around the dinner table often up to ten o'clock, then suddenly break off and steal away to bed.

Among Rhodes' admirers at the time was the novelist Olive Schreiner. Her book *The Story of an African Farm*, a brilliant evocation of life in the Karoo, published in 1883, had been widely acclaimed. The daughter of a German missionary and an English mother, she was a woman of strong independent views, almost entirely self-taught, brought up in impoverished circumstances. Her father had been dismissed from the church and gone bankrupt. Much of her youth had been spent staying with other families in the Karoo, taking on domestic tasks and minding children. In December 1872, at the age of seventeen, she had arrived at New Rush in Kimberley to stay with a brother and sister, living, like Rhodes, in a tent and, like him, gazing down into the depths of the crater there, dreaming. She began her first novel, *Undine*, in Kimberley, depicting the mine not as a hell-hole of dust, toil and sweat, as indeed it was, but in a more romantic light, describing a night visit her heroine paid there.

> When the camp below was aglow with evening lights and the noise and stir in its tents and streets became louder and stronger, she rose and walked into the Kop in the bright moonlight. It was like entering the city of the dead in the land of the living, so quiet it was, so well did the high-piled gravel heaps keep out all sound of the seething noisy world around. Not a sound, not a movement. She walked to the edge of the reef and looked down into the crater. The thousand wires that crossed it, glistened in the moonlight, formed a weird, sheeny, mistlike veil over the black depths beneath. Very dark, very deep it lay all round the edge, but high towering into the bright moonlight rose the unworked centre. She crouched down at the foot of the staging and sat looking at it. In the magic of the moonlight it was a golden castle of the olden knightly days; you might swear as you gazed down on it, that you saw the shadows of its castellated battlements, and the endless turrets that overcrowned it; a giant castle, lulled to sleep and bound in silence for a thousand years by the word of some enchanter.

Schreiner stayed no more than ten months in Kimberley before resuming her peripatetic existence, taking up a string of posts as a governess in the Karoo. In 1881 she arrived in England, carrying the manuscripts of three books, and stayed for eight years, relishing intellectual life in London; but, suffering from chronic asthma and doomed love affairs, she returned to the Cape in November 1889, settling in the Karoo outpost of Matjesfontein, a railway halt on the line from Cape Town to Kimberley.

Even before she met Rhodes, she was entranced by him. She had heard reports about him from Stead and others in London, and on returning to the Cape expressed her hope of meeting him. Though living in Matjesfontein, she frequently visited Cape Town, becoming a star of high society there. In a letter to her friend Havelock Ellis, a London psychologist and writer, she complained of the uncultured nature of most of the white population in the Cape – 'Fancy a whole nation of lower middle-class Philistines, without an aristocracy of blood or intellect or of muscular labourers to save them!' – but added, 'There is one man I've heard of, Cecil Rhodes . . . whom I think I should like if I could meet him.' Shortly afterwards, in June 1890, she wrote to Ellis excitedly: 'I am going to meet Cecil Rhodes, the only great man and man of genius South Africa possesses.' She told Stead that she felt a 'curious and almost painfully intense interest' in 'the man and his career'.

Rhodes was similarly impressed by Schreiner and her writing. He had read *The Story of an African Farm* in 1887 and was moved by its passion, force and evocative descriptions of the vast spaces of the African interior. They struck up a warm friendship, often meeting at dinner parties and on the station platform at Matjesfontein when Rhodes would use his stopping-off point as an occasion to talk to her. After a dinner with him at Matjesfontein in November 1890, she wrote to Ellis relating how Rhodes reminded her of her character Waldo in *An African Farm*: 'the same, curious far-off look, combined with a huge, almost gross body'. She thought of him as a 'man of genius, as a sort of child', and felt curiously tender towards him. On another occasion she wrote that her feelings for Rhodes were different than those for any other person. 'It's not love, it's not admiration . . . it's not that I think of him as noble or good . . . it's the deliberate feeling, "That man belongs to me."' In December, they travelled together when Rhodes went to Bloemfontein to open a rail extension. 'He is even higher and nobler than I had expected,' she wrote afterwards, 'but our friends are so different [that] we could never become close friends. [Yet] he spoke to me more lovingly and sympathetically of *An African Farm* than anyone has ever done.'

At Groote Schuur, Rhodes often gave Schreiner precedence over other ladies. Her conversation there, recalled a visiting Irish politician, Swift MacNeil, was 'as perfect and as sparkling as that of her writings'. Others spoke of her 'vivid personality', her 'wonderful eyes', and her face 'alight with intellect and power'. Sir Henry Loch's young niece, Adela Villiers, who met her in 1890, described her as 'a symbol, a seer, a teacher with her intellect afire for all that was great and beautiful and her heart aflame with love and pity for those who were despised'.

The gossip in Cape Town was that they were destined to marry. Rhodes spent more time conversing and arguing with Schreiner than with any other woman in his life. Stead and others encouraged the idea of marriage. But Schreiner was well aware of Rhodes' general disdain for women. 'I do not wonder at [it],' she told Stead. 'If you had known Cape women you would not.' According to Jameson, one day while walking together on Table Mountain, Schreiner proposed to Rhodes, but Rhodes turned and fled.

In a remark to one of his aides, Philip Jourdan, Rhodes once explained: 'I know everybody asks why I do not marry. I cannot get married. I have too much work on my hands. I shall always be away from home, and I should not be able to do my duty as a husband towards his wife.'

In fact, Rhodes preferred the company of men almost exclusively and tended to feel uneasy in the presence of most women; indeed, he appeared to fear women. He surrounded himself with agreeable young men, acolytes, sometimes becoming emotionally attached to them, demanding in return unswerving loyalty, even devotion. They formed, said one of them, Gordon le Sueur, 'a sort of bodyguard'. Invariably, Rhodes was opposed to having married men in his personal entourage. According to Frank Johnson, he often used to say that no one could marry a wife and also keep secrets. 'You sleep with a woman and you talk in your sleep. A man may be perfectly honest, but he talks in his sleep.'

Marriage he regarded virtually as an act of betrayal. When his faithful secretary, Harry Currey, eventually plucked up the courage to tell Rhodes that he was engaged to be married, Rhodes threw a tantrum. Frank Johnson, who was visiting Groote Schuur at the time, recalled the incident.

Everyone knew that [Currey] was engaged – except Rhodes. Rhodes raved and stormed like a maniac. His falsetto voice rose to a screech as he kept on screaming: 'Leave my house! Leave my house!' No small schoolboy, or even schoolgirl, could have behaved more childishly than he did.

When Rhodes had calmed down, he tried inducements, as Currey recalled:

> He said that he would miss me very much, that we always got on 'exceedingly well' and that had I not proposed to get married we should doubtless have continued to live together until one or another of us dies . . . Then he talked a great deal about his income, both present and prospective, and what he intended doing with it.

On this occasion, Rhodes' money failed him.

25

A BILL FOR AFRICA

With so much power and money at his disposal Rhodes became increasingly arrogant and aggressive. He had grown accustomed to conducting business in a ruthless manner, cutting corners when it suited him, getting his way through bribes or bullying, and even being prepared to use force to implement his schemes, as in the case of his plot to overthrow Lobengula. Any checks on his designs enraged him. He regarded himself as virtually infallible, pouring scorn and abuse on anyone who opposed him. The London directors of the British South Africa Company soon discovered they had no means of controlling him. The Colonial Office came to regard him as reckless and untrustworthy. The British prime minister, Lord Salisbury, sought to restrain him, telling Abercorn in September 1890 that he had 'had enough of Rhodes'. But the genie was now out of the bottle.

His quest for territory was relentless. 'I would annex the planets if I could,' he once told Stead. He despatched agents to obtain 'treaties' from as many African chiefs as possible. 'Take all you can get and ask me afterwards,' he told one of his officers, Captain Melville Heyman. He acquired 'exclusive mineral rights' in Barotseland, north of the Zambezi, for a payment of £2,000. He obtained a treaty in Manicaland, 100 miles inland from the Indian Ocean coastline, conferring not only mineral rights but granting monopolies of public works, including railways, banking, coining money and the manufacture of arms and ammunition – all for an annual subsidy of £100.

He became as obsessed as Kruger with trying to gain access to the coast of Mozambique, plotting to snatch it from the Portuguese. 'They are a bad race,' said Rhodes in July 1890, 'and have had three hundred years on the coast and all they have done is to be a curse to any place they have occupied.' In December 1890, he ordered his paramilitary police to advance to Pungwe Bay and seize the settlement at Beira, but was told to withdraw by Loch. In May 1891, he made another attempt to occupy Beira but was thwarted by the arrival in the region of Loch's military adviser, Major Herbert Sapte, who instructed Rhodes' men to pull out. 'Why didn't you put Sapte in irons and say he was drunk?' Rhodes fulminated when he heard what had happened. He tried to negotiate the takeover of Gazaland and its coastal terrain, sending the Shangane chief an arms delivery in the hope of luring him away from the Portuguese, but was outmanoeuvred once again.

He made repeated efforts to acquire Delagoa Bay from the Portuguese. On his first visit to Pretoria as the Cape's prime minister in November 1890, he proposed acting in collusion with Kruger to get it:

RHODES: We must work together. I know that the Republic needs a sea-port. You must have Delagoa Bay.

KRUGER: How can we work together that way? The port belongs to the Portuguese, and they will never give it up.

RHODES: We must simply take it.

KRUGER: I can't take the property of other people . . . a curse rests upon ill-gotten goods.

In 1892, Rhodes launched a scheme for the Cape government to purchase Delagoa Bay. Making enquiries in London, he encountered no objections from British ministers. Lord Rothschild advised him that in view of Portugal's bankrupt state it might be possible for him to purchase not just Delagoa Bay but the whole of Portuguese East Africa, stretching for 1,300 miles along the coast. Negotiations with the Portuguese, however, eventually came to naught.

Rhodes' objective, as he explained to the Afrikaner Bond's annual conference in 1891, was a union of southern African states led by the Cape. 'The Cape should stretch from Cape Town to the Zambesi with one system of laws, one method of government and one people.'

On the domestic front, Rhodes and the Afrikaner Bond sought to overturn the established tradition of Cape liberalism with a series of measures restricting African rights. Rhodes regarded 'natives' as important only as an engine of labour. He frequently referred to them as 'lazy', as at best 'children', at worst 'barbarians', requiring discipline and instruction on 'the dignity of labour'. He disliked the political role they enjoyed under the Cape constitution, not only because of the threat their number posed to white domination, but because it conflicted with native policy in the Boer republics and Natal with which he hoped eventually to forge a union. He spoke of his own preference for the system in Natal where high property qualifications all but excluded Africans from obtaining the vote. A census in 1891, recording a white population of 376,000 and a black population of 1,150,000, highlighted the risk of continuing with the old liberal formula.

Rhodes made clear his intentions from the outset, supporting a parliamentary amendment to the Masters and Servants Act, proposed by a Bondsman, authorising magistrates to sentence Africans to flogging for trivial offences, such as disobedience to their employers. Opponents of the bill referred to it as 'Every Man Wallop His Own Nigger Bill' and succeeded in defeating it.

Rhodes and Hofmeyr launched into more serious business in 1891 proposing new restrictions on voting rights. Though no existing voters were to be disenfranchised, the qualifications needed to obtain a vote were raised to a higher level: the occupational threshold was increased from £25 to £75, and a literacy test was introduced. A petition of protest signed by 10,000 Coloureds and Asians was sent to the Queen, but the British government took no interest. In 1892, the Franchise and Ballot Act became law. The number of eligible black voters was halved: electoral registers showed a decrease of 3,350 Coloured voters and an increase of 4,500 whites.

Rhodes' agenda was interrupted briefly the following year by a corruption scandal. To the dismay of his more liberal colleagues, Rhodes in office continued to associate with 'a money-grubbing lot'. In April 1891, John Merriman, who agreed to serve as the government's treasurer, complained in a letter to a friend that, with few exceptions, 'all his familiars are self-seekers and stuff him with adulation for their own purposes'. Olive Schreiner urged Rhodes to break with the dubious characters who seemed perpetually to surround him, but Rhodes flew into a rage. '*Those* men my friends?' he retorted. 'They are not my *friends*! They are my tools, and when I have done with them I throw them away.'

Rhodes and Schreiner frequently quarrelled. 'As long as he and I talked of books and scenery we were very happy,' she wrote. But on political and social issues and 'the Native Question', they often ended 'by having a big fight, – and Rhodes getting very angry'. Nevertheless, even after the 'flogging' debate and Rhodes' success in restricting the African vote, they continued to meet on good terms. After an encounter at Matjesfontein in September 1892, Olive wrote to her brother, Will Schreiner, a Cambridge-educated lawyer who admired Rhodes, saying she found Rhodes 'great and sincere himself' with 'not a spot of hypocrisy'. When she had tried to argue with him, he had responded that his actions were 'all based on policy, all policy'. He never claimed he was acting out of principle. It was other men who made capital out of high principle and who became hypocrites when they played Rhodes' game. 'In a sense,' she wrote, 'Rhodes is the sincerest human being I know; he sees things direct without any veil. There is no man in the world to whom I could show myself so nakedly and who can at times show himself so nakedly to you.'

But the corruption scandal was too much for her and for Merriman. In November 1892, the *Cape Times* revealed that Rhodes' close associate James Sivewright, his commissioner for public works, whom he had recently put forward for a knighthood, had awarded a monopoly contract on the entire railways system for a period of eighteen years to a personal friend without taking any competitive bids or informing the government's law department. Sivewright was a Scottish engineer and speculator who had abused previous public works positions. As head of the Johannesburg Water Company, he had sold it water rights he had earlier acquired for himself for a huge profit. As manager of the Johannesburg Gas Company, he had accepted a large bribe in exchange for signing a contract. A Bondsman and confidant of Hofmeyr, he had joined Rhodes' cabinet in 1890 but alienated liberal members like Merriman by using underhand methods to try to reinstate a magistrate who had earlier been discharged for harshness and severity towards African offenders.

In September 1892, without advertising for tender, Sivewright gave James Logan, a former railway porter who had acquired a chain of stores along the Cape's main rail line, a monopoly of food and beverage sales on all Cape trains and in all stations. Disclosing the contract two months later, the *Cape Times* said it gave off a 'very ancient and fish-like smell'. Rhodes' attorney-general, James Rose Innes, recalled: 'Hardly believing the report, I sent down to the Railways Department and they sent me up a copy of the contract. Anything more improper, in my opinion, it would be difficult to conceive.'

Rhodes agreed to repudiate the contract, but showed considerable reluctance to dismiss Sivewright from his cabinet. When Rose Innes and Merriman threatened to resign, Rhodes still prevaricated. After much devious manoeuvring, Rhodes went to see the governor, offered his resignation, then accepted the governor's call to reconstitute a government. Rose Innes and Merriman were not included. Merriman was glad to be out of it: 'Now that the whole thing is over one feels a sense of relief at being free . . . also from [the] Rhodes-Hofmeyr way of doing business – the lobbying, the intrigue and utterly cynical disregard of anything approaching moral principle in the conduct of public affairs.'

As the liberals departed, Vere Stent, a correspondent for the *Cape Times*, commented: 'High honesty and a nice sense of honour, brilliant biting wit and moral courage, erudition and fearless criticism, [all] left Rhodes' cabinet, and the door was open for sycophancy, opportunism and time-serving.'

Olive Schreiner was shocked by the whole affair. 'I saw that he had deliberately *chosen* evil,' she wrote to her sister Ettie. 'The perception of what his character really was in its inmost depths was one of the most terrible revelations of my life.' She went on: 'Rhodes, with all his gifts of genius . . . and below the fascinating surface, the worms of falsehood and corruption creeping.'

In a final encounter, Rhodes and Sivewright met Schreiner at Matjesfontein. 'We had a talk,' she recalled, 'and my disappointment at Rhodes's action was so great that when both he and Sivewright came forward to shake hands, I turned on my heel and went home.' Rhodes later invited her to dinner at Groote Schuur, but she refused.

Freed from liberal constraints, Rhodes resumed his 'native' agenda, adding the portfolio of Minister of Native Affairs to his duties. The focus of his attention was a small district in the eastern Cape called Glen Grey, which Rhodes decided to use as a prototype for his policy for resolving 'the Native Question'. Occupied by some 8,000 Thembu families and a sprinkling of white settlers and missionaries, it was a fertile area but overcrowded and overgrazed. It presented in microcosm a range of all the unsolved problems of white expansion into African areas. Whites coveted land there for their own use; many black residents meanwhile were obliged to seek work outside the district to survive.

A government commission in 1893 recommended converting Glen Grey land from communal tenure to individual ownership, with safeguards to prevent wealthy whites getting their hands on new freeholds. It suggested that each black family should be allocated farms of fifty-five morgen, an area that would have enabled male holders to qualify for the vote and brought a potential 8,000 voters on to the electoral roll.

Rhodes fashioned these recommendations into a more desirable formula, presenting to parliament what he called 'a Native Bill for Africa'. He proposed four-morgen farms, owned on an individual basis by holders who would be prohibited from selling or subdividing them; the farms would pass intact to eldest sons; younger sons would effectively be required to seek work elsewhere in the Cape. A further 'stimulus to labour' would be provided by a labour tax of ten shillings a head; it would help combat 'loafing'. Africans would have to change their habits, said Rhodes. 'It must be brought home to them that in future nine-tenths of them will have to spend their lives in manual labour, and the sooner that is brought home to them the better.'

Rhodes promised to use revenues from the labour tax to pay for industrial schools where Africans would be taught trades and vocations. They would replace mission schools that were turning out a peculiar class of human being – 'the Kaffir parson', he said. 'Now the Kaffir parson is a most excellent type of individual but he belongs to a class that is overdone' – 'a dangerous class' that would develop into 'agitators against the government'.

To allay the fear that the Cape electorate would be swamped, Rhodes proposed a separate system of local government for Glen Grey. Though no existing voters would be disenfranchised, no other Africans there would be entitled to vote in Cape elections. The possession of land was specifically ruled out as a qualification for the parliamentary franchise. Instead Glen Grey would be run by its own local council funded by assessments on new property owners, relieving the Cape budget of the burden for local expenditure.

For their part, whites would be barred from buying land in Glen Grey. It was to serve purely as a 'native reserve', the first of many. 'My idea,' said Rhodes, 'is that the natives should be in native reserves, and not mixed up with whites at all.' He envisaged that the Glen Grey system would be extended until it covered all other similar areas in the colony. It could also be used, he said, as a template for other states in southern Africa.

Watching Rhodes explain his bill to parliament, a British journalist, George Green, noted the rapt attention he received, but found his style unappealing. Green wrote:

Being an irreverent newcomer who had not yet fallen under the spell of the magician, I was not very favourably impressed. My sense of propriety was startled by his careless, informal style of oratory. While the House listened breathlessly as to the voice of the Oracle, I . . . could but marvel at his bald diction and rough, unfinished sentences. At intervals he would jerk out a happy, illumining phrase or apt illustration; but the arrangement of the speech was distressingly faulty, and his occasional lapses into falsetto [and] . . . his flounderings rather resembled those of a schoolboy trying to repeat an imperfectly learned lesson.

Critics of the bill, including Merriman and Rose Innes, urged Rhodes to take more time to consider the implications of such far-reaching measures before asking for parliamentary approval. But Rhodes, impatient with parliamentary procedures, insisted on ramming through the bill in short order, sneering at those who stood in his way, repeatedly yelling 'obstruction' when challenged by the opposition. At the committee stage he flew into a rage at what he considered unnecessary delay and forced parliament into an all-night sitting. Rose Innes recalled that Rhodes 'for the first time had publicly displayed that dictatorial and impatient vein with which, in the near future, we were to become familiar'. When the bill was eventually passed in 1894, few changes had been made; only the labour tax proposals were dropped. At the end of the parliamentary session, the Kimberley *Advertiser* remarked: 'Parliament is utterly demoralized. Mr Rhodes's dictatorial demeanour, and even insulting methods, are in great measure responsible . . . Whatever Mr Rhodes may have done for his self-aggrandisement during the past 12 or 15 years, he has at least achieved a record for unparalleled selfish dominance, impatience and grasping.'

Rhodes also threw his weight behind a series of measures increasing social separation between whites and non-whites. Worried about the growing 'poor white' problem, Rhodes and Hofmeyr promoted a policy of segregated education, spending government funds to develop white public schools while leaving Coloured education to mission schools. Other discriminatory measures affected prisons, hospitals and juries. Rhodes also supported measures enabling all towns in the Cape to impose evening curfews on Africans, as Kimberley had already done. With the government taking the lead, the practice of segregation steadily spread. Railway officials ensured that first-class carriages were reserved for whites. The Young Men's Christian Association in Cape Town which had previously allowed Coloureds to sit at the back of their meetings, decided to exclude them, altogether. Sporting activities became increasingly segregated. In 1894,

Rhodes' paper, the *Cape Argus* declared itself opposed to mixed sport. 'The races are best socially apart, each good in their way, but a terribly bad mixture.'

Rhodes also turned his attention to the problem of Pondoland. It was the last of the independent chiefdoms on the east coast, lying between the Cape and Natal, with a history of internal strife and disorder. In 1893, the high commissioner, Loch, travelled there for talks with the Mpondo chief, Sigcawu, but was infuriated at being kept waiting for three days for an audience. Rhodes decided to take a personal interest. He described Pondoland as 'a barbarian power between two civilised powers' ruled by 'a drunken savage' that needed to be annexed. Accompanied by an escort of 100 men from the Cape Mounted Rifles, he set out for Pondoland in a coach drawn by eight cream-coloured horses to inform Sigcawu and his subordinate chiefs of their fate. They were to be ruled by proclamation from Cape Town, enforced by resident magistrates. Having annexed Pondoland, Rhodes then decided that Sigcawu was not being cooperative enough and issued a proclamation for his arrest and detention on the grounds of 'obstruction'; Sigcawu, he claimed, was a 'public danger'.

For once, Rhodes' increasingly arbitrary actions were held in check. When the matter was brought before the Supreme Court, the chief justice, Sir Henry de Villiers, gave a damning verdict. The government, he said, 'has arrested, condemned and sentenced an individual without the intervention of any tribunal, without alleging the necessity for such a proceeding, without first altering the general law to meet the case of that individual, and without giving him any opportunity of being heard in self-defence'. He continued: 'Sigcawu, it is true, is a native, but he is a British subject, and there are many Englishmen and others resident in the territories who . . . [if the government's case was upheld] would be liable to be deprived of their life and property as well as their liberty, otherwise than by the law of the land.'

Sigcawu was duly released.

In parliamentary elections in 1894, Rhodes and his Afrikaner Bond allies won a resounding victory, taking fifty-eight of seventy-six seats. Rhodes' triumph was due in part to his customary methods of distributing largesse, spending lavishly on behalf of candidates he favoured, defraying the campaign expenses of numerous other candidates, and buying the support of English-language newspapers.

But it was also due to the trust that many Afrikaners placed in Rhodes. He was assiduous in promoting Afrikaner interests, and became a tireless advocate for farmers, farming and agricultural development, setting up the first ministry for agriculture. He pressed Britain to give special preference to the Cape wine trade; promoted fruit exports; and encouraged modern methods of production and disease control. He introduced new American vinestock resistant to phylloxera, an insect infestation that was ravaging the country's vineyards; sponsored the importation of American ladybirds to control a pest that was laying waste to orange groves; and improved the breeding of horses, cattle and goats by importing Arab stallions, Angora goats and other foreign breeds. He pushed through government measures – unpopular at the time – making the dipping of sheep against scab disease compulsory, effectively saving the wool industry. No previous government had shown such initiative.

Rhodes was also careful to venerate Afrikaner culture and traditions. Herbert Baker, his architect, believed that Rhodes was 'impelled by a deeper feeling of sympathy for the history of the early settlers and of respect for their achievements in civilisation'. When Merriman suggested that he follow the fashion and build himself 'a fine Tudor house' in Cape Town, Rhodes had insisted on rebuilding and furnishing Groote Schuur in accordance with the original Cape Dutch design, and restoring its name. He also restored an old Dutch summer house – a *lusthuis* – on his estate and took care to protect the graveyards of three Dutch families which he found neglected there. He commissioned a statue of Jan van Riebeeck, the Dutch commander of the first white settlement at the Cape, to be placed at the foot of Adderley Street.

Afrikaners were also impressed that Rhodes kept an open house for them at Groote Schuur. He displayed none of the reserve and coldness for which the English were renowned, and was affably hospitable to all who came. When a deputation of two hundred backveld sheep farm-ers were due to call for luncheon to complain about compulsory dipping measures that Rhodes intended to impose, his trusted steward asked whether he should serve some of his less costly wines. Rhodes turned on him angrily, retorting, 'No, give them of my best.'

All this made his eventual betrayal of the Cape's Afrikaners even more striking.

26

NOT FOR POSTERITY

From their base at Fort Salisbury, Rhodes' pioneers scattered across Mashonaland in search of gold. They possessed only limited equipment – picks, shovels, pans and sieves – but their optimism remained high. One pioneer recorded: 'Such was the faith in the gold country that the officials thought that soon we would have several reefs eclipsing the Johannesburg main reef, and that the next season the country would be swarming with a population and we – equally sanguine – were scouring the country in search of these reefs.'

With similar expectations, scores of syndicates were formed to undertake mining operations in Mashonaland. Within three months of the arrival of the pioneer column in Fort Salisbury in September 1890, twenty-two syndicates were launched in Kimberley alone. By February 1891, some 7,000 claims had been marked off in Mashonaland. The same bout of gold fever affected investors in Britain, attracted by lavish advertisements about the potential of the Mashonaland goldfields. The journalist Edward Mathers added to the excitement with a book published in 1891 with the title: *Zambesia: England's El Dorado in Africa.*

The optimism of the pioneers, however, soon began to falter. They found plenty of evidence of old gold workings, but few signs of surface gold that they could exploit. The land of Ophir, it turned out, was no more than a myth. Torrential summer rains added to their woes. In December, the supply route from Kimberley, 800 miles away, was cut by flooded rivers and impassable wagon tracks, threatening starvation. Pioneers survived on maize and pumpkins traded with local Shona, but had few goods to offer in exchange. Their makeshift grass huts provided scant protection from the rain. Clothes and blankets were constantly sodden; footwear disintegrated. Malaria struck hard. The plight of Fort Salisbury was made worse by being sited close to a swamp. Newcomers trapped between swollen rivers succumbed to malaria and starvation. 'At the Lundi there were over forty graves,' wrote one traveller, 'and between that river and the Tokwe we counted forty more victims of fever and dysentery.' When supplies eventually got through, the price of goods was astronomical, provoking further disillusionment and anger.

Rhodes' British South Africa Company was itself in acute difficulty. By March 1891, most of the cash it had raised from the sale of shares – £600,000 – had been spent; expenses included £90,000 on the pioneer column; £200,000 on a paramilitary police force; £70,000 to 'square' rival concession-holders; and £50,000 on telegraph lines. Rhodes had hoped that syndicates would finance the development of mining, but many were no more than speculative ventures. Facing mounting criticism from his London directors, he was obliged to cut back expenditure; the police force was reduced first to one hundred men, then to forty.

Despite the absence of any significant gold finds, Rhodes continued to pump into the press rosy reports of the company's fortunes, desperate to keep the share price from collapse. The *Fortnightly Review* and the *Financial News* regularly published articles extolling the wealth of Mashonaland. Witnesses friendly to the company were cited favourably; adverse remarks were discounted.

Hoping for further favourable coverage, Rhodes encouraged Lord Randolph Churchill, an influential British politician, to visit Mashonaland. A former chancellor of the exchequer, Churchill had bought shares in the Chartered Company and was a friend of several of its London directors. Rhodes met him in March 1891 to discuss the idea. Churchill planned to write a series of articles for the *Daily*

Chronicle and Rhodes assumed he could be relied upon to promote the company's cause. His lavish expedition was financed by two exploring syndicates. It included a mining engineer, Henry Perkins, and a military surgeon.

A notably cantankerous figure, Churchill arrived in Cape Town in May 1891, and travelled first to Kimberley to inspect the diamond mines, descending deep underground. On being shown a parcel of diamonds, he remarked: 'All for the vanity of women!' To which a woman in his party retorted: 'And the depravity of man!' He proceeded next to Johannesburg and Pretoria, filling his reports to the *Daily Chronicle* with abusive remarks about the Transvaal Boers. 'I turned my back gladly on this people, hastening northwards to lands possessed I hope of equal wealth, brighter prospects, reserved for more worthy owners entitled to happier destinies.'

Churchill's caustic observations continued to figure prominently in his reports. The lowveld, he wrote, had fertile soils but suffered from two 'fatal disadvantages': malaria and horse-sickness. The highveld between Fort Victoria and Fort Charter he described as 'unsuitable and grievous either for man or domestic beast'; the climate was 'capricious and variable'; the soil was too sandy to cultivate. 'Where, then, I commenced to ask myself, is the much-talked-of fine country of the Mashona? Where is the promised land?'

Churchill arrived in Fort Salisbury in August and spent two months exploring the region. He was impressed by the bustle of the place. A settlement of 300 white residents, it had 'a thriving, rising, healthy appearance'. Walking around on the day after his arrival, he counted a hotel with clean napkins laid out on its tables; three auctioneers' offices; several stores; the hut of a surgeon–dentist, another of a chemist, a third of a solicitor – 'and last, but not least among the many signs of civilization, a tolerably smart perambulator'. He also noted that basic goods, like food and clothing, were 'costly in the extreme'. Bread, meat, butter and jam had risen 'to impossible prices'.

But what of gold discoveries? he asked. After making enquiries, he discovered there was scant information available in Fort Salisbury. 'In my opinion, at the present time all that can be said of Mashonaland from a mining point of view is that the odds are overwhelmingly against the making of a rapid or large fortune by any individual.'

In the weeks ahead, on their tour of mine sites, Churchill and his mining engineer, Henry Perkins, became increasingly convinced that there were no significant gold deposits to be found. The Mazoe Valley, regarded by Selous as one of the most promising areas, had proved disappointing.

> Although here and there were reefs of comparatively limited extent and depth, which might yield a small profit to the small individual miner, nothing had yet been discovered, nor did the general formation encourage much hope that there would be discovered in that particular district any reef of such extent, depth and quality as would justify the formation of a syndicate or company, and a large expenditure of capital to purchase and to work it.

Hartley Hills, another favoured spot, offered no better prospects. To emphasise the point Churchill wrote: 'What I have seen since I commenced my travels . . . has led me to the conclusion that no more unwise or unsafe speculation exists than the investment of money in exploration syndicates.' His overall conclusion was equally blunt: 'The truth has to be told,' he wrote. 'Mashonaland, so far as is presently known, and much is known, is neither Arcadia nor an El Dorado.'

A similar verdict was reached privately by Beit who was on tour in Mashonaland at the same time as Churchill. 'I think I will not undertake anything here,' Beit told a mining colleague. 'So far I have not seen anything that I think worth putting £100 into.'

Deciding that the company needed new management in Mashonaland, Rhodes took the fateful decision to appoint his friend Starr Jameson as administrator. Jameson's charm had won him many admirers, but he was an adventurer, an inveterate gambler who enjoyed taking risks and living by his wits; he possessed no administrative experience nor, as it turned out, any administrative ability. But Rhodes had complete confidence in him. 'Jameson,' he said in 1890, 'never makes a mistake.' He trusted Jameson as he did no other man. His instructions to him were simply: 'Your business is to administer the country as to which I have nothing to do but merely say "Yes" if you take the trouble to ask me.'

With Jameson installed in Fort Salisbury, Rhodes decided to take a look himself. Before leaving he wrote two long letters to Stead in London, wallowing in adolescent dreams of glory:

> I am off to Mashonaland . . . They are calling the new country Rhodesia, that is from the Transvaal to the southern end of [Lake] Tanganyika; the other name is Zambesia. I find I am human and should like to be living after death; still, perhaps, if that name is coupled with the object of England everywhere, and united, the name may convey the discovery of an idea which ultimately led to the cessation of all wars and one language throughout the world, the patent being the gradual absorption of wealth and human minds of the higher order to the object . . . The only thing feasible to carry this idea out is a secret [society] gradually absorbing the wealth of the world to be devoted to such an object.

Rather than travel along the Selous road to Fort Salisbury, Rhodes decided to test the eastern route from the Portuguese settlement at Beira on Pungwe Bay, taking with him two companions, Frank Johnson and David de Waal, a Cape parliamentarian, and a manservant. He was in an agitated state of mind, livid about the reports that Churchill had sent to the *Daily Chronicle*.

The journey made him even more bad-tempered. He was infuriated when a Portuguese official demanded to inspect his luggage. 'I'll take their [expletive] country from them!' Rhodes screamed repeatedly, according to Johnson. After a journey of sixty miles in a flat-bottomed boat up the Pungwe River, they reached a Portuguese military outpost where a track that Johnson had previously carved out of the bush led up the escarpment to the highveld of Manicaland. Once more, Rhodes lost his temper over delays in unloading horses. Johnson's track then turned out to be far rougher than he had claimed beforehand. One cart and its entire load were lost in a marsh; another had to be repeatedly unpacked at difficult stretches and was eventually abandoned.

Reaching the Amatonga forest, Rhodes became visibly angry when Johnson decided to light fires around their camp to keep marauding lions at bay. Johnson reminded him that a correspondent from *The Times* had recently been eaten in the neighbourhood; only his booted feet had been found. 'I will not be frightened,' said Rhodes. During the night, Rhodes left their tent and moved beyond the ring of fires, when a lion roared nearby. 'Almost immediately I saw the strange spectacle of the Prime Minister of the Cape dashing back towards our tent,' Johnson recalled, 'with the trousers of his pyjamas . . . hanging down well below his knees.'

After an arduous climb up the escarpment, Rhodes' party reached the eastern frontier of Chartered territory, where Jameson was waiting with a mule cart to take them to Fort Salisbury. Johnson described their arrival in October 1891:

As we got nearer to the capital, Rhodes became more and more excited. He was just like a schoolboy in his spirits, and was obviously delighted at being in his own country.

At last we reached the last ridge in our long journey. I turned to Rhodes saying: 'Now you'll see Salisbury in a few minutes.' Then the 'town' lay before his eyes. I could see he was very disappointed. He had pictured some magnificent city, but in its place there appeared a few corrugated iron shacks and some wattle-and-daub huts. We crossed the Makabusi stream and made our way to Jameson's huts. As we travelled along, Rhodes kept on asking, 'What building is this?' 'What building is that?' He made no comment, but I could see he felt depressed on his first arrival. It was only when I pointed out to him the foundations of the Jewish Synagogue that he became cheerful once more and quite excited.

'My country's all right,' he kept on exclaiming. 'If the Jews come, my country's all right.'

The mood of the settlers, however, was distinctly hostile. Rhodes was presented with a long list of grievances: the high cost of food; the shortage of labour; punitive company taxes; the fact that there was no gold bonanza. When Rhodes tried to win them over by praising the great work they were doing for the Empire and for posterity, a Scottish settler retorted: 'I'll have ye know, Mr Rhodes, that we didna come here for posterity.' Another disgruntled settler, when asked what he thought of the country, replied: 'Well, if you want my opinion, it's a bloody fyasco.'

The position of the British South Africa Company had meanwhile grown even more precarious. Churchill's reports in the *Daily Chroniclec* caused a slide in the company's share price, halving its value. A London director told Rhodes that a plan to raise a £200,000 loan to keep the company solvent had been made impossible and he urged Rhodes to travel to London to 'smash Randolph with the public'. Directors in London even discussed a scheme to rig the market to boost the share price.

A new predator had also appeared on the scene. In April 1891, a German concession-hunter, Edouard Lippert, announced that he had obtained from Lobengula a concession giving him exclusive rights to grant lands, establish banks and conduct trade in the territory of the chartered company, thus trumping the Rudd concession which related only to mineral rights. Lobengula had apparently consented to the concession on the assumption that Lippert was an enemy of the British South Africa Company and would help him undermine it. Rhodes' first reaction to the Lippert concession was to denounce it as fraudulent and to enlist the support of Loch, the high commissioner, in blocking it. Loch duly issued a proclamation declaring that all concessions not sanctioned by his office were invalid and he banned Lippert and his agent Edward Renny-Tailyour from entering Matabeleland. But Beit urged a more cautious approach, warning that English courts might uphold Lippert's concession; he recommended negotiation instead.

The outcome was a contract that was kept secret from Lobengula. In exchange for handing Rhodes the Lippert concession, Rhodes agreed to give Lippert £50,000 worth of shares, £5,000 in cash and the right to select an area of seventy-five square miles in Matabeleland with all land and mineral rights there. To complete the deal, Lippert first needed to renegotiate his concession with Lobengula to put it on a firmer legal basis, while leaving Lobengula under the impression that he remained an enemy of Rhodes and implacably opposed to his designs. This piece of deception was approved by Loch who wrote a letter to Lobengula explaining in plausible terms why he had decided to lift the ban on Lippert and Renny-Tailyour from entering Matabeleland. Loch further assisted the plot by ordering John Moffat, the Queen's representative in Bulawayo, to cooperate. In a letter to Moffat in September 1891, Loch instructed: 'Your attitude towards Messrs. Lippert and Renny-Tailyour should not change too abruptly, though if consulted by the King you might profess indifference on the subject.' Moffat found the matter repugnant. 'I feel bound to tell you,' he wrote to Rhodes in October, 'I look on the whole plan as detestable, whether viewed in the light of policy or morality.' He nevertheless agreed to cooperate.

In Moffat's presence, Lobengula in November 1891 granted Lippert the sole right for a hundred years to lay out, grant or lease farms and townships and to levy rents in the territories of the chartered company's operations. Loch swiftly approved the concession; so did the Colonial Office in London. Rhodes now held rights not only to minerals but to land, opening up a vast new area for exploitation and profit.

Nearly thirty years later, the judicial committee of the Privy Council ruled the whole transaction illegal. The concession, it found, had merely made Lippert the agent in land transactions; it had given him no right to use the land or to take its usufruct. Indeed, under customary law, Lobengula had no authority to make any award of Ndebele land, let alone Shona land. But by then, Lobengula was long since dead; and both the Ndebele and the Shona had been stripped of much of their land.

Given a free rein by Rhodes to run Mashonaland as he saw fit, Jameson distributed land on a wholesale basis to syndicates and speculators on promises that they would plough in investment. By 1893, more than two million acres had been designated as white farmland, although few farms were developed. Even church organisations were involved in the scramble. A young assistant working for the Anglican

Bishop of Mashonaland, Knight-Bruce, was soon exhausted by his constant demands for more farms. 'The one thing I strongly object to,' he wrote to his parents in 1892, 'is to go looking for more farms, which I hear . . . is the Bishop's great idea. He already has more than 40!! All over 3,000 acres!'

One consequence was to fuel the grievances of the Shona population. Oblivious of the danger, Jameson turned his attention to Matabeleland.

27

THE LOOT COMMITTEE

At the second annual meeting of the British South Africa Company in November 1892, Rhodes told shareholders:

> We are on the most friendly terms with Lobengula. The latter receives a globular sum of £100 a month in sovereigns, and he looks forward with great satisfaction to the day of the month when he will receive them. I have not the least fear of any trouble with Lobengula.

Yet Rhodes regarded war with Matabeleland as inevitable. An independent military power, it remained not only a potential threat to the company's control of Mashonaland; it stood in the way of Rhodes' plan for a federation of British territories in southern Africa – the Cape Colony, Natal, the Bechuanaland Crown Colony, the Bechuanaland Protectorate, Mashonaland and Manicaland.

What was uncertain was the timing of the war. At the beginning of 1893, Rhodes assumed that it was some years away. The company remained in a parlous state; its capital was all but exhausted; its bankers had refused to honour any more cheques without a guarantee; no significant revenue was likely for several years ahead; the share price continued to fall. Another heavy rainy season had disrupted communication.

But local factors produced a momentum of their own towards war. Once it was realised that Mashonaland was not going to deliver a gold bonanza, white settlers looked covetously at Matabeleland, believing it offered better prospects. So did Jameson. When Jameson was faced with the choice in 1893 between war and peace, he chose war.

Well aware of the danger that the advancing tide of white rule posed to his kingdom, Lobengula strove to avoid incidents that would give the company's agents an excuse to intervene. But his regiments were restless. In 1891, a regimental commander told Lobengula that he should 'think well over the whites' invasion into his country and . . . allow them to go and exterminate the whites'. Lobengula replied that 'he would never attack the whites, for see what over took Cetewayo'. Three months later, Moffat reported encountering a detachment of Ndebele warriors who had 'behaved with the greatest insolence to me personally, shaking their clubs and cursing me'. To keep the regiments occupied, Lobengula authorised a number of raids, in the traditional manner. In November 1891, he sent an impi to chastise the Shona chief Lomagunda for his refusal to recognise Ndebele supremacy or to pay tribute; Lomagunda and three of his indunas were killed. When Jameson told Lobengula that in such circumstances the 'proper course' for him to take would be to ask the company to intervene, Lobengula retorted: 'I sent a lot of my men to go and tell Lomagunda to ask you and the white people why you were there and what you were doing. He sent word back to me that he refused to deliver my message and that he was not my dog or slave. That is why I sent some men in to go and kill him. Lomagunda belongs to me. Does the country belong to Lomagunda?' Lobengula was careful, however, to instruct his soldiers to avoid any contact with whites.

In June 1893, Lobengula sent a warrior group to the Fort Victoria area to punish a Shona chief, Bere, for allowing his people to steal Lobengula's cattle, warning the police commander at Fort Victoria, Captain Charles Lendy, in advance of his intentions:

Sir – an impi is at present leaving this neighbourhood for the purpose of punishing some of Lo Bengula's people who have lately raided some of his own cattle. The impi in its progress will probably come across some white men, who are asked to understand that it has nothing whatever to do with them. They are likewise asked not to oppose the impi in its progress. Also, if the people who have committed the offence have taken refuge among the white men they are asked to give them up for punishment.

Lobengula sent similar messages to Jameson in Fort Salisbury and to Moffat in Bechuanaland, but none of his warnings arrived before the impi attacked.

Although whites in Fort Victoria were left untouched, Lobengula's impi laid waste to Shona villages in the area, slaughtering several hundred people and seizing cattle. Several Shona were killed in the settlement itself. An Ndebele commander who arrived at Fort Victoria with Lobengula's letter demanded that all the Shona men, women and children seeking refuge there should be handed over to him, but Lendy refused.

At his headquarters at Fort Salisbury, Jameson was at first inclined to treat the incident lightly. He told Rhodes in Cape Town that the whites were in no danger; he told Lobengula to keep his impis out of Mashonaland and to return stolen cattle; he cautioned Lendy that 'from a financial point of view' war 'would throw the country back till God knows when'. Rhodes, however, was more concerned. The Ndebele raids, he said, not only called into question the company's authority over the Shona and its ability to protect them but disrupted the labour supply to mining and agriculture. When a mass meeting of white settlers in Fort Salisbury demanded company action, Jameson changed his tune. After travelling to Fort Victoria, Jameson reported to Rhodes on 17 July:

The labour question is the serious one. There is no danger to the whites but unless some shooting is done I think it will be difficult to get labour even after they have all gone. There have been so many cases of Mashona labourers killed even in the presence of white masters that the natives will not have confidence in the protection of the whites, unless we actually drive the Matabele out.

Rhodes replied, 'If you do strike, strike hard.'

Jameson summoned Lobengula's commanders to a meeting at Fort Victoria to give them an ultimatum to withdraw. One of the witnesses of the meeting on 18 July was Hans Sauer, who had just arrived in Fort Victoria on a prospecting expedition. The commanders, Sauer recorded, listened intently to what Jameson had to say; then the senior induna among them rose to reply. They were acting on the orders of the king, he said. Mashonaland was still a province of the Ndebele kingdom. Lobengula had never ceded any governing rights to the company, only the right to dig for gold and other minerals. He was entitled to assert his overlordship of the Ndebele nation, as he had done in the past. 'To those of us who were acquainted with the conditions under which the Chartered Company had been permitted to enter Mashonaland,' wrote Sauer, 'the reply of the old Matabele induna was conclusive. The old man had correctly stated the facts, and from the legal point of view there was no answer to him.'

Jameson, however, had no time for such arguments. The Ndebele impis, he said, must depart for 'the border' within an hour or they would be driven out by force. Two hours after the meeting ended, Jameson sent out Captain Lendy and a posse of forty armed white volunteers, mostly Boer transport riders, to find the Ndebele with instructions that 'if they resist, shoot them'. A few miles outside Fort Victoria, Lendy encountered a group of Ndebele. Obeying Lobengula's command to avoid conflict with whites, they offered no resistance. Lendy nevertheless ordered his men to fire. About ten were killed. Lendy claimed the number was about thirty.

On their return to Fort Victoria, Lendy's men, carrying shields and spears as mementoes of their victory, were given a rousing welcome. One of the troopers exulted that the encounter had been 'as good as partridge shooting'; and said that 'fox-hunting couldn't hold a candle to it'.

Jubilant at how easily a group of white volunteers had defeated Ndebele warriors, Jameson impulsively decided that a war of conquest of Matabeleland might be feasible. He asked Hans Sauer to consult Boers in the Fort Victoria settlement, knowing their long experience of fighting African wars, about the number of men they thought would be needed. Sauer returned to say that a mounted force of 800 to 1,000 men would suffice. Jameson at once said: 'I'll do it'.

That evening, Jameson sat in the telegraph office in Fort Victoria determined to convince Rhodes and Loch in Cape Town of the merits of going to war. 'We have the excuse for a row over murdered women and children now and the getting of Matabeleland open would give us a tremendous lift in shares and everything else. The cost of the campaign could be kept to a minimum by paying volunteers in land, gold and loot [cattle].'

Rhodes replied: 'Read Luke xiv 31.' Jameson recalled:

I asked for a Bible and looked up the passage and read: 'Or what king going to make war against another king, sitteth not down first, and consulteth whether he be able with ten thousand to meet him with twenty thousand?' Of course, I understood at once what the message meant. The Matabele had an army of many thousands. I had nine hundred settlers available for action. Could I, after careful consideration, venture to face such unequal odds?

I decided at once in the affirmative, and immediately tele-graphed back to Mr Rhodes at Cape Town. 'All right. Have read Luke fourteen thirty-one.'

Losing no time, Jameson headed back to Fort Salisbury to organise his campaign. He prevailed upon Rhodes to sell £50,000 worth of shares to finance the war – 'You have got to get the money. By this time tomorrow night you have got to tell me that you have got the money.' He then ordered the purchase of a thousand horses from the Transvaal and the Cape Colony and issued contracts to volunteers promising them 3,000 morgen (6,350 acres) of land 'in any part of Matabeleland', twenty gold claims and 'loot'. Jameson and Rhodes also worked hard to convince the press that the need for war had been forced on the company by the Ndebele themselves.

In Bulawayo, Lobengula reacted angrily to the news that his men had been gunned down by Lendy's posse without provocation. 'I thought you had come to dig gold,' he told a company official on 27 July, 'but it seemed to me that you have come not only to dig the gold but to rob me of my people and country as well.' He fired off protests to Queen Victoria, to Loch and to Moffat. But he also made clear repeatedly that he wanted to avoid conflict.

It was to no avail. By early October, Jameson had assembled a force of 650 volunteers and 900 Shona auxiliaries and was ready for action. To fortify the case for war, he continued to paint Lobengula as the aggressor, sending out false reports of Ndebele manoeuvres, claiming at one time that an impi of 7,000 warriors had passed north-east of Fort Victoria. Lobengula's denials were ignored. 'Every day I hear from you reports which are nothing but lies,' he cabled to Loch on 12 October. 'I am tired hearing nothing but lies. What Impi of mine have your people seen and where do they come from? I know nothing of them.'

The Matabeleland missionary Charles Helm expressed his distaste in a letter to a friend on 9 October: 'As you know it is my opinion that we shall never do much good in Matabeleland until the Matabeles have had a lesson. And their treatment of the Mashona and other tribes deserve punishment. But I wish we entered on a war with clean hands.'

The war was soon over. As Jameson's army advanced into Matabeleland, Lobengula unpacked his Rudd Concession rifles, but they were of little assistance. Armed with machine guns and artillery, the whites mowed down Ndebele defenders in their hundreds. Facing defeat, Lobengula ordered the destruction of his capital and fled northwards. When an advance column reached Bulawayo on 4 November, they found only a smoking ruin and two white traders playing poker on the roof of a store, left unmolested on Lobengula's orders.

Pursued by company troops, Lobengula made a last, desperate attempt to get away. Addressing a council of his indunas at a camp on the Shangani River, he told them: 'The white men will never cease following us while we have gold in our possession, for gold is what the white men prize above all things. Collect now all my gold . . . and carry it to the white men. Tell them they have beaten my regiments, killed my people, burnt my kraals, captured my cattle, and that I want peace.'

Lobengula's gold was said to amount to a thousand sovereigns. Two messengers were entrusted to deliver it, along with a message conceding defeat. Approaching the main body of troops, the messengers came across two white stragglers. They handed them the gold and the message and left with assurances that they would be passed on to the right quarters. But neither the gold nor the message was delivered. Lobengula died a few weeks later after drinking poison.

Rhodes arrived in Bulawayo in December and authorised Jameson to hand out cattle, land and mining concessions to the volunteers. A 'Loot Committee' was established to manage the distribution of Ndebele cattle. Virtually all the highveld for sixty miles around Bulawayo, the very heart of Ndebele territory, was pegged out as white farmland. The Ndebele themselves were assigned two 'native reserves' in outlying areas.

Several of Rhodes' officials managed to accumulate massive landholdings in Matabeleland and Mashonaland. Major Sir John Willoughby, who had been seconded from the Royal Horse Guards to act as chief staff officer to the pioneer column, acquired 600,000 acres on condition that he raised £50,000 for the development of his property; he failed to raise the money but retained possession of the land. Rhodes' surveyor-general, on taking up his post, was 'awarded' 640,000 acres.

A senior British official, William Milton, who was subsequently required to sort out the land mess in Matabeleland and Mashonaland, declared in horror: 'Jameson has given nearly the whole country away to Willoughbys, Whites and others of that class so that there is absolutely no land left which is of any value for the settlement of Immigrants.' Jameson, he suggested, 'must have been off his head.'

As with Mashonaland, Jameson was oblivious of the danger he was creating.

In 1894, the British government recognised the British South Africa Company's jurisdiction over Matabeleland and left Rhodes to rule there as he saw fit. And in 1895 the company adopted the name of Rhodesia in place of Zambesia to describe its territories there. 'Well, you know,' Rhodes told a friend, 'to have a bit of country named after one is one of the things a man might be proud of.'

At a banquet in Cape Town to celebrate his victory over the Ndebele, Rhodes told an enthusiastic audience that he had pursued expansion for the benefit of the Cape Colony, which he hoped would provide the nucleus of a united South Africa. In a long conversation he had with Queen Victoria in December 1894, he dwelt on the same theme. When she opened the conversation by asking him politely, 'What are you engaged on at present, Mr Rhodes?' he replied, 'I am doing my best to enlarge Your Majesty's dominions.' Since they had last met, he said, he had added 12,000 square miles of territory. But there was more to be done. He expressed his belief that the Transvaal – 'which we ought never to have given up' – would ultimately return to the Empire, an idea the queen found gratifying.

Two other bits of Rhodes' African jigsaw now became the focus of his attention: the Bechuanaland Crown Colony and the Bechuanaland Protectorate. The future of the Crown Colony in the southern half of Bechuanaland was settled with little difficulty. When it was established by Britain in 1885, its likely destination had always been annexation to the Cape. The British government was only too keen to be relieved of the expense of administering it. During discussions in London in December 1894, Rhodes urged that it be handed over to the Cape within a year.

Two southern Tswana leaders, Montshiwa, the Rolong chief, and Mankurwane, the Tlhaping chief, raised objections, but their views were ignored. In 1895 Rhodes rammed through legislation in the Cape parliament, incorporating the Colony as part of the northern Cape.

Rhodes' attempt to take over the Bechuanaland Protectorate, however, encountered stronger resistance. He approached the task in the same impatient manner he had used with the Crown Colony, writing to the new colonial secretary, Joseph Chamberlain, in June 1895: 'I am anxious to take over the Bechuanaland Protectorate at once. It will save you £80,000 a year and if you give it me I promise to build the Railway from Mafeking to Bulawayo in four years and to begin the Railway a month after the transfer.' Seeing no need for haste, Chamberlain replied smoothly: 'As far as I understand your main lines of policy I believe that I am in general agreement with you, and if we differ on points of detail I hope that as sensible men of business we shall be able to give and take, and so come to an understanding.'

In July, Rhodes sent his confidential agent, Dr Rutherfoord Harris, to London to pursue the matter. A series of meetings followed in August between Chamberlain, Colonial Office officials and representatives from the British South Africa Company. The company proposed that it should acquire a strip of land along which to build its railway and a 400-square-mile block of land around Gaberones for settlement; it further asked for permission to station its police force at Gaberones to protect against possible Tswana disturbances; and it wanted these arrangement to be carried out with the least possible delay.

While these negotiations were under way, three Tswana chiefs – Kgama, Sebele and Bathoen – arrived in London to make clear to the Colonial Office their vehement opposition to any plan to hand over the Bechuanaland Protectorate to the company. Mindful of the experience of Matabeleland, they expressed fears that they would lose their land under company rule as the Ndebele had done:

> You can see now that what they really want is not to govern us nicely but to take our land to sell it that they may see gain. And we ask you to protect us . . . The Company have conquered the Matabele, and taken the land of the people they conquered. We know that custom: but we have not yet heard that it is the custom of any people to take the best lands of their friends. In Bathoen's country [around Gaberones] they seek a large piece of land, and in that land Bathoen's people have gardens and cattle posts. In Kgama's country they seek nearly all the best parts . . . Where will our cattle stay if the waters are thus taken from us? They will die. The Company wants to impoverish us so that hunger may drive us to become the white man's servants who dig in his mines and gather his wealth.

Their case won widespread sympathy. The Colonial Office was flooded with resolutions and petitions from church and welfare organisations.

The outcome in November 1895 was seen as a compromise. Chamberlain agreed to continue with imperial protection for the lands of the Tswana chiefs, but allowed the company to obtain control of the balance of the Protectorate – about 100,000 square miles of territory, including a strip of land along the eastern border with the Transvaal.

Rhodes was furious at being forced to compromise, inundating Harris with telegrams: 'It is humiliating to be utterly beaten by three niggers. They think more of one native at home, than the whole of South Africa . . .'; 'settlement is a scandal'; 'I do object to being beaten by three canting natives.' In a letter to the Duke of Fife in December, Rhodes expressed his disgust:

> A large country as big as the British Isles will now be definitely beaconed and dedicated to these people. It will be very difficult in future to alter these reserves. Who are these people? They are only sixty thousand in number and the worst specimens of humanity – certainly in Africa – and perhaps in the whole world. It means trouble in the future. And why was this done? Simply to please the temperance and missionary section of the English people.

Nevertheless, Rhodes had gained one vital immediate objective. For months he had been engaged in a conspiracy to overthrow Kruger's government in the Transvaal. Chamberlain and senior Colonial Office officials had known of his intentions since August. Now, with the British government's approval, he had secured a territorial base on the Transvaal border, only 170 miles from Johannesburg, from which he could launch an armed invasion.

PART VII

28

A TALE OF TWO TOWNS

The Transvaal's new wealth from gold transformed Pretoria from a village into a town. Grand public buildings sprang up around Church Square; electric light and telephone systems were installed. Ralph Williams contrasted the character of Pretoria when he first arrived there as British consul in 1887 with the changes that occurred within the space of a few years. Government buildings then, he said, were 'homely to a degree':

> The Old Executive Council Office, the workroom of a govern-ment strong enough to defy the power of England, was a dirty, tumble-down place, containing a rough deal table and eight or ten common chairs.

His encounters there were similarly basic:

> Whenever I had need to put any matters officially forward I was asked to attend the council. At the head of the table sat the State Secretary [Dr Willem Leyds], with on one side of him the famous General Joubert, the Commandant General, and on the other the Vice-President, General Smit, our conqueror at Majuba Hill. The other members sat around the table. The

President sat in an easy chair away from the table, smoking continually an old Dutch pipe, and opposite him was another easy
chair in which I sat. There was no spittoon in the room, though
there was sad necessity for it, and it was the invariable habit of Mr
Kruger to put his leg under the table near the State Secretary's
chair and drag out the waste-paper basket to serve as a spittoon
for himself (and for me had I needed it) during the interview. He
used it copiously, and I was constrained to draw in my legs lest he
should exceed its limits and trench within my domain.

Flush with gold revenues, Kruger ordered the construction of an
opulent new building for government offices and for parliament on
the west side of Church Square. Laying the foundation stone in May
1889, he remarked: 'Who would have believed five years ago that such
a building was possible?' Designed in the Italian Renaissance style by
the government architect, Sytze Wierda, the Raadzaal cost £155,000.
Kruger took a lively interest in all its details. On the ground floor, he
was provided with two offices to the left of the main entrance. On top
of the central tower stood a female statue. Some said it was an alle-
gorical figure representing Freedom or Liberty; others that it
represented Minerva, the Roman goddess of war. When Kruger was
shown the statue before it was put in place, he was said to have
objected to it being bare-headed. 'A lady can't stand up there in
public with nothing on her head. She must have a hat.' Accordingly,
a helmet was fashioned and fixed on with rivets around the brim. The
building was completed in 1891. An 1893 guidebook, Brown's *South
Africa, A Practical and Complete Guide for the Use of Tourists, Sportsmen,
Invalids and Settlers*, described it as 'one of the handsomest and probably the costliest pile in South Africa'. Kruger enjoyed the routine of
the daily ride to his office in a state carriage accompanied by mounted
troopers; he also awarded himself a huge salary increase, raising it
from £3,000 a year to £8,000. Yet despite the new buildings and the
occasional pomp, Pretoria retained the ambience of a sleepy village,
where Afrikaner traditions of church and family life were closely
observed.
    Thirty miles to the south, amid a landscape of mining headgear, ore

dumps and battery stamps, stood Johannesburg, an overgrown mining camp, brash and bustling, renowned for drunkenness, debauchery and gambling. On windy days, clouds of yellow dust from the ore dumps swirled through the streets. On the northern outskirts, over the crest of the ridge, wealthy whites lived in luxury houses, with views stretching away to the Magaliesberg hills, protected from the noise and dust of the mine workings by northerly winds which blew it all south-wards. But most white miners and other employees lived in boarding houses in working-class districts close to the mines, frequenting the bars and brothels set up there. Two-thirds of the uitlander population consisted of single men. Black mine workers were confined to com-pounds, as in Kimberley.

During the boom years of 1888 and 1889, scores of prostitutes arrived from the Cape Colony and Natal. More came when the rail link to the Cape was completed in 1892. With the opening of the rail-way from the port of Lourenço Marques on Delagoa Bay in 1894, there was an influx of prostitutes from Europe and New York City. A survey in 1895 counted ninety-seven brothels of various nationalities, including thirty-six French, twenty German and five Russian; the brothels in one part of Johannesburg were so numerous that it became known as 'Frenchfontein'.

A correspondent for the London *Times*, Flora Shaw, visiting Johannesburg in 1892, said she was repelled by its brash character. 'It is hideous and detestable, luxury without order, sensual enjoyment without art, riches without refinement, display without dignity. Everything in fact which is most foreign to the principles alike of morality and taste by which decent life has been guided in every state of civilisation.' Olive Schreiner, who went to live in Johannesburg with her husband, described it in 1898 as a 'great, fiendish, hell of a city which for glitter and gold, and wickedness, carriages and palaces and brothels and gambling halls, beat creation'.

Kruger found it difficult to come to terms with this industrial monster in his backyard and the godless uitlander community that lived there; *Duivelstad* – Devil's Town – he called it. Rhodes, initially, expressed some sympathy for Kruger's predicament, telling the Cape parliament in July 1888:

I regard him as one of the most remarkable men in South Africa, who has been singularly unfortunate. When I remember that Paul Kruger had not a sixpence in his Treasury when his object was to extend his country over the whole of the northern interior, when I see him sitting in Pretoria with Bechuanaland gone, and other lands around him gone from his grasp, and last of all, when he, with his whole idea of a pastoral Republic, finds that idea vanishing, and that he is likely to have to deal with a hundred thousand diggers, who must be entirely out of sympathy and touch with him, I pity the man.

Kruger also resented the way in which foreign mining magnates – the Randlords, as they were dubbed by the British press – made fortunes on the Witwatersrand and then took their money abroad to indulge in luxury lifestyles in Britain. Beit bought himself a house on London's Park Lane and a Georgian mansion with a 700-acre estate in Hertfordshire; Wernher lived at Bath House, Piccadilly, filling it with treasures from around the world; Barnato bought a site on Park Lane for £70,000 and built a new house there, spending recklessly on horses, West End shows and lavish parties; and J. B. Robinson took up residence in Dudley House, a stately mansion on Park Lane, spending his money on assembling a fabulous art collection.

Kruger's encounters with the uitlander community became increasingly abrasive. Fearing that the sheer weight of their numbers would swamp the Boer population, he resisted demands to accord them political rights. 'I will make no difference in my treatment of old or new burghers – except one or two points, namely in regard to voting and representation in the Volksraad,' he said. Even at a local level, Johannesburg was not allowed its own municipality but was run by a sanitary board with limited powers. Despite the preponderance of English-speakers on the Witwatersrand, the only official language remained Dutch; the only medium of instruction allowed in state-supported schools was Dutch. 'Every attempt to expand education in English will help towards the destruction of the *landstaal*,' declared Kruger.

During the slump in 1890, when many uitlanders were thrown out of work and lost their savings through speculation in gold shares, their mood was particularly truculent. Passing through Johannesburg in March, on his way to Blignaut's Pont to meet Loch, Kruger addressed a mass meeting at the Wanderers' Club pavilion where he was greeted by loud grumbling, interjections, and the strains of 'Rule Britannia' and 'God Save the Queen'. Later in the day, an angry crowd gathered outside the magistrate's house where he was staying, wrecked the garden railings and part of the garden wall, then moved on to the post office and tore down the Vierkleur flag and trampled on it. When Loch asked him what had happened, Kruger replied:

> Sir Henry, those people remind me of a baboon I once had, which was so fond of me that he would not let anyone touch me. But one day we were sitting round the fire, and unfortunately the beast's tail got caught in the flames. He now flew at me furiously, thinking that I was the cause of the accident. The Johannesburgers are just like that. They have burnt their fingers in speculations and now they want to revenge themselves on Paul Kruger.

In 1891 Kruger endeavoured to meet the uitlander demand for political representation by establishing a second volksraad while simultaneously tightening the qualification for the franchise. The original qualification that uitlanders needed for the franchise was one year's residence. Then, in 1882, to counteract the influx of new immigrants to the Lydenburg goldfields, Kruger raised the qualification to five years' residence and payment of a £25 fee for naturalisation. His new scheme raised the residence qualification for the full franchise from five years to fourteen years and introduced a further hurdle by limiting the vote to uitlanders over the age of forty. To compensate for these restrictions, uitlanders were given the right to take up Transvaal citizenship after only two years' residence for a reduced fee of £5 and to vote in elections for a second volksraad. The second volksraad, however, had limited functions; it was also subject to veto by the first volksraad where the old burghers remained in control.

Kruger explained his views in simple terms to a Johannesburg audience in 1892:

> Imagine that a man has given his blood and his being for a farm, and says to someone else – you can come and live on my farm as a squatter [*bijwoner*] and make a profit from it. But if this *bijwoner* now starts to declare that he has the same rights to the farm as the owner, then, if this matter were brought before a court, the verdict could never be given in favour of the *bijwoner* . . . Now this farm is all that we have left of what our forefathers inherited. The stranger comes here to make his profit, and would it be right to hand over to him the voortrekkers' rights of ownership?

He then added:

> When in the course of time they [the strangers] have shown themselves to be true burghers, then their franchise can be enlarged . . . The old burghers must first know whether the newcomer was to be trusted.

Kruger's two-class system of 'old burghers' and 'new burghers' – of first and second-class citizenship – won little support among uitlanders. They were taxed but still left without adequate representation.

Kruger also faced a growing band of Boer critics, disaffected with his style of leadership. Now in his sixties, he became increasingly dictatorial, resentful of opposition, prone to monumental rages and obstructive of change, still believing himself to be divinely inspired. His speeches were more than ever like sermons, long, rambling and repetitive, with endless references to God and the Bible. His eyesight and hearing were both impaired. He caused outrage by interfering in the judicial process. When his friend Nellmapius was charged with embezzlement, found guilty by a jury and sentenced to eighteen months' imprisonment with hard labour, Kruger arranged for the executive council to grant him a pardon. When the chief justice, John Kotzé, a Cape-educated lawyer, pointed out that the executive council had acted illegally, Kruger retorted that Nellmapius would be pardoned whatever the decision of the courts. Nellmapius' conviction was subsequently quashed.

There was also mounting criticism of Kruger's concession policy and the corruption it spawned. Introduced in the 1880s as a way of promoting industrial development in a near-bankrupt state, it had become a central part of Kruger's method of government. He awarded monopoly concessions to favoured individuals and companies to establish not only factories but a whole range of public utilities: a state bank; water, gas and electricity supplies; municipal services in Pretoria, Johannesburg and other towns; tramways; road repairs; and markets. The benefits, Kruger argued, included a substantial income for the state as well as the provision of local goods and services to the public. His critics pointed to the high prices that resulted from monopoly control and from the tariff barriers needed to protect monopolies. The system, moreover, was used by many concession-hunters not to build factories or provide services but for speculative purposes: once in possession of a concession, they hoped to sell it for profit.

With so many concessions available, the concession business was soon mired in corruption. Some episodes became notorious. In 1889, the executive council granted a concession to supply Johannesburg with water to Frikke Eloff, the president's private secretary and son-in-law, without consulting the Volksraad. According to an opposition newspaper, *Land en Volk*, Eloff was able to make £20,000 out of the deal 'without so much as digging a spadeful of earth'. In 1892, a young French speculator, Baron Eugène Oppenheim, gained a concession to build a railway spur to the Selati goldfields; according to his own account, he spent some £30,000 on 'travelling expenses' and payments 'to different members of the Executive Council and Volksraad and their relatives and friends as the price for granting the concession'. Kruger's response, when presented with the evidence, was that he saw no harm in anyone receiving a present as long as it did not amount to bribery.

The most controversial concession concerned dynamite. In 1887, in a deal in which Kruger participated, the German concession-hunter Edouard Lippert, formerly of Kimberley, gained the exclusive right to manufacture dynamite, gunpowder, explosives and ammunition for a term of sixteen years. A factory to manufacture dynamite was to be erected within a year. Lippert was permitted to import all raw materials and machinery free of duty, but not dynamite itself. Once the factory output was able to meet local demands, no further imports of dynamite would be allowed. This deal was approved by the Volksraad in 1888.

Lippert sold the concession to a French consortium based in Paris which appointed a Dutch businessman, Lambertus Vorstman, as managing director of its Transvaal subsidiary – *Zuid Afrikaansche Maatschappij voor Ontplofbare Stoffen Beperkt* (The South African Explosives Company) – and Lippert as its chief salesman at a commission of 12.5 per cent. A rival Anglo-German consortium, the Nobel Trust, was meanwhile allowed to continue importing dynamite for a period of two years until the local product was available. The French factory began production in January 1889 and in due course the government cancelled all import permits for dynamite.

It soon became evident, however, that the French consortium was importing not raw materials for manufacturing dynamite but dynamite itself – all duty-free. Kruger rushed to the defence of the French consortium. But the British government now entered the fray complaining that while French dynamite was being imported duty-free into the Transvaal, English-manufactured dynamite was excluded, in contravention of trade agreements.

A government commission concluded in 1892 that Lippert and the French consortium had indeed been importing dynamite and avoiding payment of customs duties, in clear breach of their concession. In the Volksraad, there was uproar. 'Rarely has such a scene taken place in a free Republic as occurred during the eleven o'clock adjournment of the Volksraad last Saturday morning,' reported *Land en Volk*:

On the motion of Jan Meyer a Committee of the Volksraad was then set up. The whole Volksraad then decided to go and test the material to see if it was explosive. Between 10.30 and 11 the President got hold of Jan Meyer, and quite audible to the Press Gallery – indeed in the street – shouted at him that it was grossly unfair to make such a test. He and everyone else knew well enough that it was explosive. The only question was, was it dynamite? Jan Meyer was weak enough to give way, and the tests thus took place only in the presence of the State Mining Engineer, the Minister of Mines, the Manager of the Dynamite Factory and the scientific experts. The stuff that Mr Lippert alleged was not dynamite exploded with terrific force, throwing great masses of rock into the air.

In the acrimonious debate in the Volksraad that followed, when members insisted that the concession be cancelled, Kruger pleaded for a compromise. To cancel the contract, he declared, would be an act against the government not against the company. 'It would destroy the credit of the State completely and bring rejoicing to our enemies.' He suggested that the government should take over the factory then hand back management to Lippert.

Under the headline 'Gigantic Fraud', *Land en Volk* fumed in July 1892:

> We cannot credit the President's behaviour. We understand his reluctance to expose the rottenness of his concession-politics, but to suggest to the Volksraad that the State buy the factory and appoint a fraudulent company as officials is too much! We expect but little of the Volksraad; but will the People allow this? . . . Lippert is having coffee with the President every morning.

In August 1892, the government decided to cancel the dynamite concession and to allow English, French and German firms to import dynamite. The eventual outcome in 1893 was that the government itself took over the dynamite monopoly and then signed a contract with the old South African Explosives Company to act as agents for the manufacture and sale of dynamite for a period of fifteen years. Shares in the company were awarded to both the French consortium and the Nobel consortium – and to Lippert. Lippert was also allowed a royalty of 8 shillings per case of dynamite. The effect was to place ownership of the dynamite industry in foreign hands; nearly all profits went overseas; the government received only 5 shillings per case as its share of the profit compared to the 40 shillings per case profit made by foreign investors – a rate of about 100 per cent. A Volksraad commission subsequently concluded that as a result of this arrangement the cost of dynamite was at least 40 shillings per case higher than it need have been.

So noticeable was the miasma of corruption in Pretoria that critics began to refer to the existence of a 'third volksraad', the collection of businessmen, politicians and officials willing to trade favours for payment. The opposition newspaper, *Land en Volk*, frequently cited examples of bribery and corruption. In 1891, it accused Kruger of trying to divert the railway line from Pretoria to Delagoa Bay over the farms of his relatives and friends, namely Eloff and Nellmapius. 'The friends of the President are becoming rich while the burghers sweat.' Even the pro-government *Pretoria Press* admitted that there was 'widespread corruption in the civil service' and bemoaned the way in which senior officials cared more for their own enrichment than for the interests of the state while petty officials routinely expected bribes for small favours. In 1892, it was discovered that government officials, with the connivance of the executive council, had been buying up scores of valuable stands in Johannesburg without advertising them for sale, putting them up for auction and then selling them, often the next day, at huge profit; the minister of mines and his son were among the beneficiaries. Kruger endeavoured to defend these transactions: 'The government had felt it better to save the costs of advertising in all the local newspapers, which came to more than the stands brought in, by selling the stands by public auction without advertisement.'

Adding to the problem of corruption was the government's lax financial management. Though government revenues rose from an average of £188,000 between 1883 and 1890 to £4.2 million in 1895, no adequate controls were put in place. Kruger was accustomed to signing order-forms from the treasury without proper checks. No inspectorate was established until 1896. When a Volksraad committee investigated treasury disbursement in 1898, it discovered that in the previous sixteen years sums 'advanced' to officials without a proper account being kept amounted to almost £2.4 million.

Another bone of contention was Kruger's policy of relying on

Hollanders he recruited from Europe to fill key positions in the civil service and the railways management. The prominent role played by Kruger's state secretary, Dr Willem Leyds, aroused particular dislike. 'It is doubtful whether either he or his wife made a single Boer or Afrikaner friend,' wrote the historian Johannes Marais.

The groundswell of criticism of Kruger's government led eventually to the emergence of an opposition movement led by General Piet Joubert, the commandant-general. Standing against Kruger in the 1893 presidential election, Joubert quickly gathered the support of a group of Boer politicians demanding reform – 'Progressives', as they were known. The election was fought with unprecedented hostility. Rival newspapers hurled furious insults at the candidates and at each other. Kruger was accused of corruption, nepotism and mismanagement and criticised for his bad temper, his autocratic ways and his love of Hollanders. Joubert was portrayed as a weak and vacillating lackey of the uitlanders.

Kruger won the election, but only by a narrow margin; he gained 7,854 votes to Joubert's 7,009. Much of the electorate judged that his old-fashioned style of leadership was ill-suited to tackling the pressing issues that the Transvaal faced, in particular the growing impact of the uitlander population.

Addressing a large crowd in Church Square from the balcony of the new Government Building to mark the inauguration of his third term as president in May 1893, Kruger assured newly naturalised citizens that they were entitled to all the privileges granted by law. But he also felt the need to warn them that 'Nobody can serve two masters.'

29

THE RANDLORDS

With the advent of deep-level mining on the Witwatersrand, the Randlords began to reorganise their interests to cope with the new demands of the gold industry. At the forefront of the changes were Alfred Beit and the Corner House. Beit had been an early convert to the idea of deep-level mining propounded by the American mining engineers employed by Wernher, Beit & Co – Joseph Curtis, Henry Perkins, Hennen Jennings and Hamilton Smith. Beit's partner, Julius Wernher, was more sceptical. The costs of deep-level mining – of sinking shafts to a depth of 1,000 feet or more – were huge, with no guarantee of success. To spread the risk, Beit decided to invite the Rothschilds in London and in Paris, and other business associates to participate in a new mining vehicle.

The outcome was a company called Rand Mines that was floated in February 1893, with a nominal capital of £400,000 in £1 shares. The firm of H. Eckstein & Co contributed 1,300 claims to the new company as well as the controlling interests in five existing companies; the partners in Eckstein, including Beit and Wernher in London and Phillips and Taylor in Johannesburg, were compensated with 200,000 shares in Rand Mines. Rothschilds picked up 60,000 shares. Other associates allowed in 'on the ground floor' were the American mining engineers and members of the diamond marketing syndicate that

Wernher had founded in London. Beit also used the distribution of shares to cement working alliances with other Randlords and with potential allies. The Transvaal's state secretary, Willem Leyds, the chief justice, John Kotzé, and the editor of the Johannesburg *Star*, Francis Dormer, were each offered 200 shares at par. Bought for £1 each, the shares would be worth a small fortune if the theories about the scope of deep-level mining proved accurate. Within five years of flotation, they were priced at £45 apiece.

Among the chief beneficiaries was Rhodes. Rhodes had hitherto regarded the Witwatersrand as a sideshow to his Zambesia venture. But once it was clear that Zambesia was not the Eldorado he had been expecting, he pressed Beit for a foothold in Rand Mines. 'I shall make some arrangements with Rhodes and Rudd,' Beit wrote in July 1892, 'so as to make their interests fall in line with ours. I think it would be wise to do so. Rhodes's brains are not to be despised and if we had interests apart from theirs there would always be friction . . .' Beit duly offered Rhodes' company, Gold Fields, an allocation of 30,000 shares in Rand Mines at par, helping to save Gold Fields from oblivion and allowing Rhodes back in as a serious player on the Witwatersrand.

A late-comer to the deep-level business, Rhodes moved vigorously to consolidate his position, merging Gold Fields with three other companies to form Consolidated Gold Fields of South Africa with a capital of £1.25 million. The new company soon prospered. Its assets included 1.2 million shares in existing or prospective deep-level mines; 50,000 shares in undeveloped outcrop properties; 25,000 shares in De Beers; 47,000 shares in the British South Africa Company; and 87,000 shares in other Rhodesian businesses. It showed a profit of £207,000 in 1893, nearly £309,000 in 1894, and £2.1 million in 1895 – a larger return than had ever been shown in one year by a limited liability company registered in London. Dividends paid to shareholders amounted to 10 per cent in 1893, 15 per cent in 1894, and 125 per cent in 1895.

Rhodes also acquired the services of John Hays Hammond, an ebullient American mining engineer of world reputation, giving him free rein to develop his gold interests. They met to discuss terms at Groote Schuur in 1894. Hammond wrote in his auto-biography:

> I told him frankly that I had a very poor opinion of his proper-ties but I felt that, with his backing, I could acquire some other mining interests to level up his investments. Rhodes picked up a scrap of paper only a few inches long and wrote on it: 'Mr Hammond is authorised to make any purchases for going ahead and has full authority, provided he informs me of it and gets no protest.' In this brief manner I was made chief consulting engineer of the Consolidated Gold Fields of South Africa, and soon afterwards of the British South Africa Company . . . On the sole strength of this little scrap of paper I spent many hundred thousands pounds.

Rhodes agreed to pay Hammond a salary of £12,000 a year, making him the highest-paid individual in southern Africa. A deep-level enthusiast, Hammond went on to acquire a string of Rand properties that proved highly productive, establishing Gold Fields as a major mining enterprise and providing Rhodes with another fortune.

Despite the huge profits they were beginning to make, the Randlords constantly grumbled about the difficulties the industry faced. Whereas the price of diamonds was variable and had fluctuated wildly in the two decades before De Beers established its monopoly, the price of gold was fixed by international agreement at 85 shillings per fine ounce. The only way for the Randlords to win bigger prof-its was to cut costs. Yet the problems of cost-cutting proved intractable. Skilled white miners commanded premium salaries. A shortage of black labour meant higher wages were needed to attract workers. With the expansion of deep-level mining, the high price of dynamite, fixed by Kruger's monopoly concession, became an increas-ingly prominent grievance. There was similar resentment over Kruger's refusal to join a customs union with the Cape and Natal, which resulted in imports for the mining industry being subjected to duties at Cape ports or at the Natal port of Durban as well as the duties imposed by the Transvaal; foodstuffs and beverages were also taxed. High railway charges on the three lines running into Johannesburg – from the Cape, Durban and Lourenço Marques – provided another source of grievance; with a monopoly of all railway traffic linking the Transvaal to the sea, the Netherlands South African Railway Company was able to levy exorbitant charges on coal, imported mining machinery and foodstuffs.

Mining companies also became increasingly worried by the effects of the liquor monopoly used to supply African workers with cheap drink. According to the Chamber of Mines:

> In very many cases the liquor supplied to the natives is of the vilest quality, quickly inflaming those who take it to madness, and causing the faction fights which sometimes have fatal results, and always lead to the, at any rate, temporary disablement of some of the combatants, and the damaging of property. Accidents, too, are often attributable to the effects of drink, and altogether . . . a large percentage of the deaths among the natives here is directly due to drink. In its bearing on the labour question, drink also plays an important part. The shortness in supply, as compared with the demand for labour, has been accentuated by it. Where possible more natives are kept in compounds than are actually required for the work to be done, to make allowance for those disabled by drink.

Along with grievances over monopolies, the scale of government corruption was another aggravating factor. 'The Industry is blackmailed in every possible way,' complained Jim Taylor, Wernher, Beit's resident representative in Pretoria. 'Every department has to be bribed to enable the merest trifle becoming accomplished.'

Two other disputes caused further acrimony. In 1894, a struggle broke out between Kruger and the Randlords over the underground rights to 'bewaarplaatsen' – the areas set aside by mining companies for dumping crushed residue and for water storage. The mining companies held the surface rights and, once they realised that payable reefs existed under the bewaarplaatsen, they claimed the underground rights. Their claim was supported by members of the Second Volksraad. But

Kruger insisted that the underground rights belonged not to the surface-holders but to the state – a useful source of patronage. Large sums were used to influence the outcome. Lionel Phillips, the president of the Chamber of Mines and a member of Wernher, Beit & Co, wrote to Beit in London: 'The Bewaarplaatsen question will, I think, be settled in our favour, but at a cost of £25,000, and then only because Christiaan Joubert [the minister of mines] has stuck to us like a leech.' Kruger prevailed upon the First Volksraad to overrule the Second Volksraad but the Second Volksraad retaliated by passing a motion condemning the actions of the minister of mines and his officials. The Dutch-language newspaper *Volkstem* joined the attack. 'Our State needs a Minister of Mines who not only *is* honest and clean, but who is *known* to be so.' In the end, the matter was shelved, but it added to the pile of grievances.

A similar struggle occurred over the cyanide patent for winning gold from ore. Kruger wanted a state cyanide monopoly to control it, with a favoured company acting as the government's agent. Phillips wrote to Beit: 'The cyanide monopoly . . . suddenly comes up again and is in a rather dangerous state. Fortunately Dr Leyds and Esselen [the state attorney] are dead against it and we may baulk it this year . . . next year however it will come up again [in the Volksraad] even if we succeed in postponing it. The other side is spending lots of money in bribes and we shall probably have to spend more next year than this to oppose it.' On this occasion, Phillips succeeded in 'baulking' the monopoly.

The uitlander community, meanwhile, had become increasingly vociferous about their own grievances over political rights. By 1895, the white population of Johannesburg had reached about 50,000; most of them came from Britain and the Cape Colony; only 6,000 were Transvaalers, mainly impoverished Boers. No accurate survey of the overall white population of the Transvaal had ever been conducted, but even Kruger was prepared to accept that uitlanders by then outnumbered Boers.

The first organised uitlander opposition to Kruger came in 1892 when a 'Transvaal National Union' was launched 'to obtain by all constitutional means equal rights for all citizens of this republic, and . . . the redress of all grievances'. Its leader, Charles Leonard, a prominent Johannesburg solicitor, explained the need for such an organisation to a public meeting in August 1892:

> Who made the Transvaal? We came here and found the original burghers settled upon farms; they had no market; no means; their only means of living was to contract their wants . . . Who enabled them to live, who made markets for them? We! Yet we are told that we are mere birds of passage, and that, because they were here before us, we have no rights. We send our best men to Pretoria and let them plead their best – only to be snubbed. Memorials are sent to the Volksraad, and referred to a committee, and thereafter they are never heard of again. Unless we rise as one man and tell our feelings we shall never be understood and listened to.

But Kruger would not be budged. Petitions that the national union sent to Pretoria in 1893 received scant attention; a petition with 13,000 signatures in 1894 was no more successful; another petition sent in August 1895 was said to have been signed by 35,000 people, though some signatories were clearly bogus. Opposition members in the Volksraad were sympathetic to their cause. Lukas Meyer proposed that uitlanders resident in the Transvaal for five years who had reached the age of thirty-one and possessed a property qualification should be enfranchised. But after a long and heated debate, the proposal was rejected.

Leading uitlanders and newspapers such as the Johannesburg *Star* became increasingly abusive. Uitlander numbers were exaggerated to bolster their case; many claimed that 'nine-tenths of the population' were denied the vote. A British visitor to the Witwatersrand, James Bryce, noted in 1895: 'Hearing nothing but English spoken, seeing nothing all round them that was not far more English than Dutch . . . it was natural that the bulk of the Uitlanders should deem themselves to be in a country which had become virtually English, and should see something unreasonable and even grotesque in the control of a small body of persons whom they deemed in every way their inferiors.' In

Cape Town, Rhodes threw his weight behind the uitlander cause. 'The Transvaal and President Kruger will have to consider whether a system should continue which refuses nine-tenths of the population under it the franchise.'

Another dispute over citizenship flared up when Kruger ordered a white mobilisation to deal with a dissident African chief, Lebogo, in the Zoutpansberg; British residents – twenty-three in all – as well as Hollanders and Germans were included. When five conscripts refused to obey the order, they were arrested. Their case went to the Supreme Court where Chief Justice Kotzé decided in favour of the state. The men were put under armed escort and sent to the Zoutpansberg. Leonard's national union jumped in to protest, appealing for British intervention. The British government duly instructed Sir Henry Loch, the high commissioner, to visit Pretoria to sort out the dispute.

The farce that ensued was long remembered by both sides, but by Kruger with particular bitterness. As Loch's train drew in to the new Pretoria station, a huge pro-British crowd was there to greet him with renditions of 'God Save the Queen' and 'Rule Britannia', much to Kruger's obvious displeasure. As Kruger and Loch sat side by side in the carriage taking them to the Transvaal Hotel where Loch was staying, an Englishman carrying a Union flag leapt up on to the coachman's seat. The flag draped itself around Kruger's shoulders and though he struck at it repeatedly with his stick, he was unable to free himself from it. On their arrival at the Transvaal Hotel, there were further demonstrations of British loyalty. The incident was swiftly brought up in the Volksraad where it was deemed to be an open insult to the president. Kruger himself remarked: 'I have not for a moment believed that decent Englishmen were involved. But, I am afraid, this is only oil on the fire, and that bitter feelings between the old and new section of the population are aggravated.'

As a fervent imperialist, Loch saw the matter differently. He believed that uitlander discontent could be used as a means for Britain to reoccupy the Transvaal. While he was in Pretoria, deputations arrived from Johannesburg urging him to intervene, telling him that Britain would be assured of a warm welcome from 10,000 able-bodied men if it decided to act. As a result of these discussions, Loch became convinced that an uitlander uprising was inevitable at some stage. In a secret despatch to the Colonial Office in July he spoke of the need 'to force matters with a high hand on the ground', warning 'that the Uitlanders were bound to win in the struggle with the Boers, and that if they won without British help, they would probably maintain the independence of the Republic and pursue a policy hostile to federation'. He proposed that he should be authorised to deploy the Bechuanaland Protectorate police to support the uitlanders in the event of an uprising, prior to the intervention of British garrisons stationed in the Cape and Natal, and suggested that the railhead at Mafeking on the Transvaal border would provide a suitable base for launching an invasion.

A senior Colonial Office official, Sir Robert Meade, described Loch's proposal as 'extremely dangerous'. It would simply encourage the uitlanders 'to make excessive demands and the Boers will understand that we deliberately mean to force things to an issue and bloodshed will be the inevitable result'. Meade concluded: 'Every nerve should be strained to prevent such a disgrace as another S. African war.' The colonial secretary, Lord Ripon, concurred. In trying to obtain the Transvaal by force, he pointed out, Britain might lose all of southern Africa. Loch was subsequently rebuked for his 'extraordinary injudicious manner in coquetting with the would be Rebels' and recalled from his post. But his scheme for external armed intervention in support of an uitlander uprising impressed Rhodes.

Adding to this pot-pourri of disputes and grievances was an even more potent factor. To counteract British pressure on the Transvaal, Kruger decided to cultivate links with Germany, rattling not only Rhodes in the Cape but British politicians in London. 'If one nation [Britain] tries to kick us, the other [Germany] will try to stop it,' Kruger explained in 1894. He encouraged German investment and German immigration. At a banquet to mark Kaiser Wilhelm's birthday in 1895, Kruger spoke of cementing his ties with Germany. He referred warmly to the visit he had made to Germany in 1884 and to the cordial reception the Kaiser's father had given him; even though the Transvaal was then only 'a small child', the Kaiser had treated him as 'head of an important, independent State'. The time would come, he said, 'when our friendship will be closer than ever'.

> As for my German subjects, I have found them ever loyal, and willing to obey the laws of the land. I have had many difficulties with the Natives in this Republic, and I must say that, though Her Majesty's subjects behave well and are loyal to the State, in times of trouble they turn to Great Britain and declare that they are the subjects of Her Majesty. The Germans, in this State, will not behave in a similar manner. Joyfully and willingly they obey the laws of the land and are not involved in the incitement of Transvaalers against these laws.

With the support of Germany and revenue gushing from the gold mines, Kruger was now in a position to establish the Transvaal as the dominant state in southern Africa, thus challenging British hegemony in the region and thwarting Rhodes' plan for a confederation of British-ruled states. Rhodes decided the time had come to remove him.

The consequences were disastrous.

30

THE RHODES CONSPIRACY

The conspiracy was hatched at Groote Schuur. In June 1895, Rhodes invited Beit there to discuss his plan for a coup d'état in the Transvaal. Rhodes needed the support of Beit and the Corner House to help finance and organise an uprising in Johannesburg. Beit had hitherto kept his distance from Rhodes' political schemes, but, along with Jameson, he remained one of Rhodes' most devoted followers.

Beit was once asked by a colleague, Percy FitzPatrick, about how he dealt with Rhodes' increasingly rude and overbearing manner. 'You must have found him difficult at times?' Fitzpatrick suggested:

> Beit snapped back instantly. 'Not at all; never! It is true,' he added, 'that you have to know him, but when you know him he is perfectly splendid. Some people take offence at his manner. Sometimes he is rude and sounds dictatorial, but that only means he is very much in earnest and convinced and hates to waste time. He does not suffer fools gladly; but then one cannot do that and do the enormous work he's got on hand. But in all the big things he is wonderful, and he is one of the most generous and kind-hearted of men. I have found him the best in the

world to work with, and I think he is satisfied too. We get along splendidly.'

On this occasion, however, Beit had deep misgivings about the project. Nevertheless, he agreed to help Rhodes finance the purchase of arms and equipment.

The circle of conspirators slowly widened. Rhodes invited Lionel Phillips, the chairman of Rand Mines and president of the Chamber of Mines, and Charles Leonard, chairman of the national union, to Groote Schuur to seek their involvement. He appointed his brother, Colonel Frank Rhodes, a former cavalry officer, as manager of Gold Fields in Johannesburg, intending he should act as military director of the operation. His consulting engineer, John Hays Hammond, joined the conspiracy. Rhodes also arranged for his old friend Sir Hercules Robinson to be reappointed British high commissioner in Cape Town, knowing his help would be needed.

Rhodes assumed that, given the extent of uitlander grievances, an uprising in Johannesburg was bound to happen at some stage – talk of it was commonplace. His idea of helping to organise an uprising took root during a journey of inspection that Rhodes, Jameson and Hammond made of Matabeleland and Mashonaland in September 1894 to ascertain the real mineral potential of the area. Hammond's conclusion, like that of previous experts, was that although mineral deposits were rich in places, they were too limited to offer much of a bonanza; certainly, there was no second Rand to be found. The total gold produced in Mashonaland over four years was no more than 4,400 ounces – less than the Witwatersrand was then producing per day. Hammond emphasised that the Rand was likely to be unique; the gold there would last for decades. As well as enriching the mining companies, it would fortify the Boer state. During the long rides and evenings spent around the camp-fire, the conversation often dwelt less on the prospects of Matabeleland and Mashonaland than on the future of the Witwatersrand and the grievances of the uitlanders. 'Unless a radical change is made,' Hammond predicted, 'there will be a rising of the people of Johannesburg.' Jameson visited Johannesburg in October 1894 and again in March 1895 reaching the same verdict. The plan that Rhodes and Jameson devised was to support an uprising in Johannesburg with an armed invasion from the Bechuanaland Protectorate, led by Jameson and using Rhodes' private army, the BSA Company's paramilitary police, as a fighting force.

The journalist Francis Dormer met Rhodes in his office in July 1895 and endeavoured to persuade him to adopt a more conciliatory approach to the Transvaal issue. A former editor of the Johannesburg *Star*, he was no admirer of Kruger but argued for a political solution. 'I am all for tackling Mr Kruger,' he told Rhodes, 'but I am not for tackling the Transvaal.' There was a strong Progressive party in the Volksraad, said Dormer. 'If we go the right way about the business, some man of liberal tendencies will become President at the next election. Then we shall get all that is necessary in the way of reforms.' Rhodes, however, was not prepared to listen to any of this:

'But I don't want your reforms, or rather your reformed Republic,' was his quick response. 'The ideal system is that of a British colony . . . I also do not like the idea of British subjects becoming burghers, and that is why I prefer that burghers should become British subjects . . .'

Rhodes, Dormer recorded, 'seems to think far more of giving Kruger a fall than dealing with these difficulties in the manner of a prudent statesman'.

Dormer described how much Rhodes had changed since their first encounter in Cape Town fifteen years before:

He is peremptory where he used to be open to reason, impatient where he was formerly content to accommodate his pace to that of the most halting and hesitating Boer, and he has clearly become possessed of the idea that, if there are some whom money cannot 'square', there are none who are able to withstand its might when brought to bear upon them by a genius such as his.

At the end of their meeting, Rhodes suggested to Dormer that on his return to Johannesburg he should get in touch with Jameson, who was there 'prospecting' on behalf of Gold Fields. Dormer duly met Jameson at the Rand Club.

> Jameson was even less convincing than Rhodes [wrote Dormer] . . . Jameson appears to think the place is 'seething with rebellion' and 'ripe for anything'. Boer fighting qualities are 'the biggest bubble of the century.' They are less to be dreaded than even those of Lo Bengula. Prick the bubble once and it's all over!
>
> I tried hard to persuade the dear doctor that he had made a wrong diagnosis. There was discontent, to be sure, but not discontent of the kind or degree that would induce prosperous men to take their lives in their hands and engage in mortal combat with their oppressors. It was ridiculous to dream of a revolution while a 'boom' was in full swing, and every man an actual or potential millionaire . . .
>
> 'You underrate the patriotism of the Boer, and you overrate the discontent of the uitlanders [Dormer told Jameson]. Revolutions are not affected by the kind of men you have taken into your counsels . . . So my advice to you is to leave it alone.'

Rhodes and Jameson were now involved in several monumental miscalculations. One was that, having captured Matabeleland, the overthrow of Kruger's regime would be similarly straightforward; another, that the uitlander population was ready and willing to participate actively in an uprising; and a third, that white settlers in Rhodesia would be safe from African revolt once the company police had been withdrawn to take part in a Transvaal coup.

Nothing, however, was to deflect Rhodes from his objective, so accustomed was he to getting his own way. He put increasing pressure on the new colonial secretary, Joseph Chamberlain, to agree to the rapid transfer of the Bechuanaland Protectorate into the hands of the BSA Company, sending his confidential agent, Dr Rutherfoord Harris, to London in July to argue the case. Rhodes needed a military base on the Bechuanaland border if the coup was to succeed. The

Bechuanaland border was only 170 miles from Johannesburg, a ride of three or four days. The alternative of a base on the Rhodesian border 400 miles distant was too far away for a filibustering expedition. 'The Protectorate is essential,' Rhodes wrote to Beit in London in August. 'I assure you if we have the Protectorate I do not feel one atom of doubt as to matter. As a last resort, if everything else fails go yourself and see Chamberlain. You are more convincing than most people and show him the whole position of England in the South depends on it and that next year may be too late.' He added: 'I am told Chamberlain is a strong man and a far seeing man and we can give Africa to England if he will only take one step.'

A prosperous businessman, once a radical member of Gladstone's cabinet, Chamberlain had moved across the political spectrum becoming an ardent imperialist in Lord Salisbury's Conservative–Unionist coalition government. He was commonly known as 'Pushful Joe'. Like Rhodes, he regarded the British 'race' to be the greatest of all governing races, but he favoured imperial control rather than colonial control. Imperial federation, he argued, was essential both to maintain Britain's role as a world power and to ensure its economic prosperity. 'Is there a man in his senses,' he asked the London Chamber of Commerce in 1888, 'who believes that the crowded population of these islands could exist for a single day if it were cut adrift from the great dependencies which now look to us for protection and which are the natural market for our trade?' The development of imperial trade became one of his growing preoccupations. He regarded the Transvaal both as an anomaly and as a possible threat to British supremacy, an independent state within Britain's sphere of interest willing to embrace Germany; with its gold reserves and German support, it had the potential to become the leading state in southern Africa. In 1895, nearly sixty years old, after spending ten years in the political wilderness, Chamberlain was impatient to make his mark.

Chamberlain's initial response at the first of a series of meetings with Harris, Earl Grey and other associates of Rhodes that began on 1 August was to insist on a proper consideration of all the issues, including the rights of Tswana chiefs. Chamberlain's attitude, Harris subsequently reported to Rhodes, was 'without compromise and decisive'. However, when Harris mentioned Rhodes' plan for extending the Bechuanaland railway to Bulawayo, Chamberlain became more amenable and suggested the idea of handing over a 'strip of land' in Bechuanaland for railway construction, in advance of a more general decision. At this point, Harris, according to his own testimony, made a 'guarded allusion' to Rhodes' real motive for wanting to take control of the Protectorate with some degree of urgency: 'the desirability of there being a police force near the border at Gaberones', to render assistance 'in the event of a rising in Johannesburg'. Chamberlain, according to Harris, at once demurred at this turn of conversation. 'I stopped him at once,' Chamberlain claimed. 'I said: "I do not want to hear any confidential information; I am here in an official capacity. I can only hear information of which I can make official use."' Earl Grey then intervened, took Harris out of the room and returned alone to discuss the matter with Chamberlain.

Grey subsequently described details of this encounter in a letter he sent to Chamberlain on 10 December 1896. 'I told you privately that the . . . rising of the Uitlanders to secure for themselves the common rights of free men would shortly take place, and that being so it was desirable that an armed force should be stationed on the Transvaal border available for use if required.' In a cable that Harris and Grey sent to Rhodes on 2 August, the day after the meeting with Chamberlain, they gave a similar version of events:

> We decided therefore to inform Secretary of State for Colonies guardedly reason why we wish to have base at Gaberones and advisable our presence in Protectorate. Secretary of State for Colonies heartily in sympathy with C. J. Rhodes's policy but he would not on this ground alter decision with regard to Protectorate, but offered as alternate [sic] to justify residence B.S.A.Co in Protectorate to consider favourable at once application for large land grant [in] Protectorate in exchange for Railway extension north.

Another of Rhodes' associates, James Maguire, a BSA Company director, met Chamberlain on 13 August and gained the same impression that he favoured the plot. Harris cabled to Rhodes on 13 August: 'Chamberlain will do anything to assist except hand over the administration Protectorate provided he officially does not know anything of your plan. He does consider Rhodes's ingenuity resource can overcome any difficulty caused by refusal Protectorate now.'

Chamberlain subsequently tried to deny any prior knowledge of the plot. But his friend Earl Grey was adamant about it. In a record of an interview with Grey, the historian Basil Williams wrote in his notebook: 'Grey said Chamberlain certainly knew about the force intended to go into TV [Transvaal]. Grey said that for the honour of England it should not come out, just as it was not blurted out by any of the people at the time. The great difficulty was R. Harris – it took a lot of trouble to try and silence him.'

Harris and Grey went to see Chamberlain again on 20 August, after which Chamberlain sent a cable to Robinson in Cape Town instructing him to obtain from the Tswana chief Bathoen a grant of land in the Gaberones area for the use of the BSA Company – the area that Rhodes had in mind as his military base for the invasion of the Transvaal. To Rhodes' fury, Bathoen refused to cooperate. Rhodes thus turned to two other Tswana chiefs, persuading them to place their forty square miles of territory around Pitsani Potlugo, north of Mafeking, under the company's jurisdiction. On 18 October, with Chamberlain's consent, Robinson issued a proclamation handing over this strip of territory to the company. On the same day, he appointed Jameson 'resident commissioner' there. Immediately afterwards, detachments of company police began to move from Bulawayo to Pitsani. The pretext was that they were needed to protect the construction of a new railway from dissident natives. But there was no railway construction for them to protect.

While these machinations were under way, a tariff war broke out between the Transvaal and the Cape over railway charges to Johannesburg. For several years, until the completion of the Delagoa

Bay line and the Durban line, the Cape line had held a monopoly on rail traffic to Johannesburg; in 1895, its share of traffic was still 85 per cent, but steadily declining. To boost its share, the Cape government started undercutting the other two lines. The Transvaal retaliated, trebling its rates on the 51-mile section of the line between the Vaal River and Johannesburg. To sidestep these charges, the Cape government arranged for freight to be offloaded at the Vaal River border and transported to Johannesburg at competitive rates by ox-wagon. On 1 October, Kruger struck back by closing the drifts or fords across the Vaal River to ox-wagon traffic. The Cape government appealed to Chamberlain. Chamberlain gave Kruger an ultimatum to withdraw his proclamation and ordered British troops on their way to India to divert to the Cape. On 7 November, Kruger backed down and let wagons across the Vaal. The 'Drifts crisis', as it was called, added to the pile of grievances held by both sides and heightened tensions all round. It also provided Rhodes with further justification for pressing ahead with his plot.

In Johannesburg, the main topic of conversation centred on when the 'revolution' would come. 'Little else was talked of,' wrote James Bryce, 'not in dark corners, but at the club where everybody lunches, and between the acts at the play.' Most people believed that an insurrection was imminent.

Yet despite all the talk of grievances and the constant attacks the Johannesburg press made on Kruger's government, there appeared to be little popular enthusiasm for an uprising. 'The inhabitants of Johannesburg are not a seditious, rebellious, quarrelsome set of men,' reported the London *Times* correspondent, Captain Francis Younghusband, in December. 'They are money-makers. Rebellion and money-making do not go together.' The ordinary miners, business employees and clerks were all enjoying high wages; while willing to agitate for reform, they had no appetite for an uprising. 'They none of them want to see the British flag hoisted here,' reported Younghusband. 'They none of them want to see the present Republic done away with. There is not a sign among the Uitlanders of the Transvaal of any agitation in that direction. There is no wish to turn out the Boers.' In a letter to Beit and Wernher in London, Lionel

Phillips remarked candidly: 'As to the franchise, I do not think many people care a fig about it.'

The Randlords themselves had divided views. Barney Barnato had always tried to remain on friendly terms with Kruger, happy to gossip with him on the front veranda at his home when visiting Pretoria. J. B. Robinson thought that the agitation against Kruger was factitious, that uitlander grievances were exaggerated and that any attempt at a coup was doomed to failure. The German entre-preneurs Adolf Goerz, George Albu and Sigismund Neumann were also hostile.

Nor did the conspirators have any coherent view of what ulti-mately they wanted to achieve. To attract support for the conspiracy, Rhodes gave different explanations of his objectives to different people. During November, Rhodes discussed his intentions with two key Johannesburg figures, Charles Leonard, the leader of the national union, and Lionel Phillips, president of the Chamber of Mines, who had travelled to Cape Town to ascertain his precise aims. What Leonard favoured was a 'reformed republic'. He wanted assurances from Rhodes that the Union flag would not be used as the symbol of the uprising and that the Transvaal would not be forced into a federation. Rhodes appeared to agree. According to Leonard:

> We read to him the draft of our declaration of rights. He was leaning against the mantel-piece smoking a cigarette, and when it came to that part of the document in which we refer to Free Trade in South African products, he turned round suddenly and said: 'That is what I want. That is all I ask of you. The rest will come in time. We must have a beginning, and that will be the beginning. If you people get your rights, the Customs Union, Railway Convention and other things will all come in time.'

But Rhodes had no interest in a reformed republic. Nor had Chamberlain. When Chamberlain wanted reassurance that Rhodes was 'working for the British Flag', Harris in London was quick to stress this was the case. To make sure, Harris cabled Rhodes: 'We have stated positive that results of Dr Jameson's plans include British flag. Is this correct?' Rhodes replied: 'I of course would not risk everything as I am doing except for British flag.' He remarked afterwards: 'You might be sure that I was not going to risk my position to change President Kruger for President J. B. Robinson.' Yet Rhodes was equally determined to ensure that the Transvaal did not fall under imperial control. What he really wanted was his own South African empire under the banner of a British flag.

As well as drawing in conspirators, Rhodes confided in Sir Hercules Robinson and in the imperial secretary, Sir Graham Bower, needing their assistance, but swearing them to secrecy. A group of Johannesburg capitalists, he told them in October, had decided to support an uitlander rising. Rhodes claimed that Chamberlain knew of the plan and supported it. Robinson, looking forward at the age of seventy-one to a trouble-free tour of duty and suffering from dropsy and a heart condition, was alarmed by what he heard. 'He has taken it rather badly,' Rhodes told Bower. When Bower subsequently broached the subject with Robinson, Robinson stopped him, saying, 'The less you and I have to do with these damned conspiracies of Rhodes and Chamberlain the better.'

Chamberlain himself was keen to discover more of what was going on and wrote a private letter to Robinson in October asking him about the likelihood of a revolt in Johannesburg 'with or without assistance from outside' and what might follow.

After consulting Rhodes and Bower, Robinson replied saying that he considered an outbreak of hostilities inevitable 'sooner or later'. He expected that, following an uprising, a provisional government would be proclaimed in Johannesburg. As high commissioner, Robinson would insist that both parties should submit to his arbitration. He would leave at once for Pretoria and order the election of a constituent assembly. The electorate would consist of every white male in the Transvaal, leading to an 'English' victory at the polls. Most Englishmen, he added, would prefer to live within 'an Anglicized and liberalized Republic'.

Chamberlain telegraphed back:

Agree generally with your idea in private letter of Nov. 4th . . .
I take for granted that no movement will take place unless success is certain, a fiasco would be most disastrous.

He also made it clear that the outcome he wanted was the establishment of a British colony not a liberalised republic. Chamberlain feared
that 'An entirely independent Republic, governed by or for the capitalists of the Rand, would be very much worse for British interests in
the Transvaal itself and for British influence in South Africa'.

By December, preparations for a coup were well advanced.
Chamberlain, Robinson and Bower were all aware of what was
planned. Rhodes had also managed to secure the support of the
London *Times*. Both the manager of *The Times*, Moberley Bell, and its
colonial correspondent, Flora Shaw, had long been admirers of
Rhodes and were eager accomplices, acting as a secret link between
Rhodes and Chamberlain and ready to orchestrate a press and propaganda campaign on Rhodes' behalf. Shaw was mesmerised by
Rhodes. 'I have met now most of the English public men of my day,
but the impression conveyed to me by Mr Rhodes is one of unselfishness of aim greater and more complete than I have ever recognised
before,' she told her friend Captain Frederick Lugard in November
1895. 'He appears to me to seek nothing for himself. He cares neither
for money, nor place, nor power, except in so far as they are a necessity for the accomplishment of the national idea for which he lives.'
Keen to ensure success, she cabled to Rhodes on 10 December: 'Can
you advise when you will commence the plans, we wish to send at
earliest opportunity sealed instructions representative London Times
European capitals. It is most important using their influence in your
favour.'

Throughout December, the conspiracy gathered momentum at
Groote Schuur. At Rhodes' insistence, Beit joined him from London.
Harris also returned from London. Staying as a house guest at Groote
Schuur at the time was Hans Sauer, now a resident of Matabeleland,
who was recuperating from illness. He noticed the comings and
goings but was not privy to the plot. Not once over a period of four
weeks did Rhodes make any mention to him of the Transvaal issue:

I usually had tea with Rhodes on the back veranda of his house, and almost always Sir Graham Bower – the Imperial Secretary at the Cape – used to turn up just as we were finishing this pleasant repast. On Bower's arrival, he and Rhodes would stroll off into the beautiful little valley or Dene where the blue hydrangeas grew, and I used to watch them absorbed in deep and earnest conversation . . .

In the evenings after dinner we usually retired to the billiard-room to smoke, drink our coffee, and play pyramids. Usually, in the middle of our game, Dr Rutherfoord Harris would turn up, having driven out from Cape Town in a Cape cart, which always waited to take him back at some late hour of the night. Immediately on Harris's arrival, he, Rhodes and Beit would vanish upstairs to Rhodes's private rooms, as we saw no more of them for the rest of the evening. I did notice once or twice that all three of them looked very preoccupied . . .

Even at that stage, the plot had begun to unravel.

31

JAMESON'S RAID

Jameson took to the task of organising a coup with schoolboy enthusiasm. Though a rank amateur in military matters, he was supremely
confident of his own abilities. In a conversation with Hans Sauer in
Bulawayo in October 1895, he expressed contempt for the fighting
spirit of the Boer population. 'I could drive them out of the Transvaal
with five hundred men armed with sjamboks [rawhide whips],' he
boasted. A short, balding figure, insignificant in appearance, Jameson
hardly looked the part of a revolutionary leader. He walked with a
slight stoop, rode slackly and tended to lounge about with his hands in
his pockets. But his energy and love of adventure carried him head-
long into the fray.

The plan, on paper, was relatively straightforward. Jameson
intended to raise a force of 1,500 men and equip it with Maxim
guns, field artillery and spare rifles, ready to invade the Transvaal from
base camps in Bechuanaland on a date pre-arranged with conspirators
in Johannesburg. The Johannesburg conspirators – Reformers, as they
called themselves – would meanwhile recruit an army of 7,500 volunteers and prepare for an insurrection. The volunteers would be
armed with rifles and Maxim guns purchased in Britain by Harris 'for
Rhodesia', shipped to the Cape, transferred to De Beers premises in

Kimberley and then smuggled into Johannesburg in oil drums and stored on mining company premises there. With 9,000 men under their command, the conspirators expected to overwhelm any Boer resistance with ease. Once in control of Johannesburg, they would declare a provisional government and despatch a force to seize the government's arsenal in Pretoria. The British high commissioner would then intervene. A new era would begin.

To disguise their intentions, the conspirators devised a series of codewords for use in telegraphic communications. Their insurrection was referred to as 'the races' or 'the polo tournament' or 'the flotation'; Jameson was 'the veterinary surgeon' or 'the contractor'; the conspirators were 'the subscribers'; the British high commissioner was 'the chairman'; Jameson's commissariat, set up to procure horses, mules, wagons and large quantities of food and forage, was 'the Rand Produce and Trading Syndicate'.

As the central figure in the drama, Jameson was constantly on the move. On 1 November, he inspected and approved a site for the main base camp at Pitsani. Police volunteers arrived from Matabeleland and Mashonaland. With Chamberlain's approval, members of the Bechuanaland Border Police were allowed to transfer to the BSA Company police. In Cape Town, Jameson recruited about 100 men from the Duke of Edinburgh's Own Volunteer Rifles, a Cape Town regiment.

On 19 November he arrived in Johannesburg for a meeting with the principal Johannesburg conspirators: Charles Leonard, Lionel Phillips, John Hays Hammond and Frank Rhodes. They set a provisional date for the insurrection: 28 December, shortly after Johannesburg's annual Christmas horse races; and agreed that Jameson's force would cross the border two days in advance. With no military experience and no knowledge of the terrain, Jameson assumed that two days would be sufficient for his heavily armed force, dragging cannon and machine guns, to cover the 170 miles from Pitsani.

Jameson also induced the conspirators to sign a letter inviting him to come to the aid of the people of Johannesburg. Jameson said he needed the letter to avoid entering the Transvaal 'like a brigand' and to enable him to justify his actions with the BSA Company if the need arose. The letter predicted an imminent conflict:

> The position of matters in this State has become so critical that we are assured that at no distant period there will be conflict between the Government and the Uitlanders . . .
>
> Thousands of unarmed men, women and children of our race will be at the mercy of well-armed Boers, while property of enormous value will be in great peril . . .
>
> It is under these circumstances that we call upon you to come to our aid, should a disturbance arise here . . .
>
> The circumstances are so extreme that we cannot but believe that you and the men under you will not fail to come to the rescue of people who will be so situated . . .

The letter was drafted by Charles Leonard and signed by all four conspirators; a fifth conspirator, George Farrar, a mining entrepreneur, added his signature subsequently. The letter was left undated; it was agreed that a suitable date should be filled in later. Worried that the letter might fall into the wrong hands, the conspirators stressed to Jameson that the letter was intended only for his personal use and that it was not to be acted upon without their specific approval. The following day, sensing a potential disaster, Leonard tried to get Jameson to give the letter back. 'Awfully sorry, old man,' replied Jameson, 'but it has gone down to Cape Town by the last train.'

Later that day, opening the new Chamber of Mines building, Lionel Phillips publicly declared the mining companies' support for the reform movement:

> All we want in this country is purity of administration and an equitable share and voice in its affairs. I hope that wiser counsels may prevail and that the Government of this country may be induced to see that the present policy will not do. Nothing is further from my heart than a desire to see an upheaval which would be disastrous from every point of view and which would probably end in the most humble of endings – in bloodshed.

But I should say this, that it is a mistake to imagine that this much maligned community, which consists of a majority of men born of free men, will consent indefinitely to remain subordinate to the minority in this country . . .

Yet there was a noticeably amateurish character about the whole operation. When Jameson turned up for a rendezvous at Frank Rhodes' house to discuss conspiracy business, he discovered that his host, a renowned ladies' man, had preferred a different assignment. 'Dear Jimjams,' wrote Colonel Rhodes in a note, 'sorry I can't see you this afternoon, have an appointment to teach Mrs X the bike.' The *Times* correspondent, Younghusband, later remarked: 'The great mistake made was trying to run races with cart-horses.'

Jameson's confidence, however, remained unshaken. When Fred Hamilton, the editor of *The Star*, lunched with Jameson and Colonel Rhodes in Johannesburg in November, he expressed the view that they would face tough opposition. 'I shall get through as easily as a knife cuts butter,' retorted Jameson. 'You do not know the Maxim gun. I have seen it work. I shall draw a zone of lead a mile each side of my column and no Boer will be able to live in it.'

From Johannesburg, Jameson travelled to Cape Town to discuss final arrangements with Rhodes. Other conspirators joined them on 24 November for a summit meeting at Groote Schuur: Leonard, Phillips, Hammond and Frank Rhodes. Jameson ensured that Robinson was kept informed: 'The night before I left for Mafeking,' Jameson subsequently confided to a friend, 'I went to see him. I was his doctor, and therefore private interviews were very easy to arrange on the score of his health. On that last occasion we went over the ground of our joint action again.'

But in the first week of December, the ardour of the Reformers cooled rapidly. Talk of an uprising had been easy. Some Reformers had hoped that mere talk would induce Kruger to implement the reforms they wanted. But preparing for an uprising brought home the magnitude of what they had set in motion. There was no sign of any popular support for such an action. Observing the notable lack of enthusiasm, Colonel Rhodes cabled Jameson on 7 December to tell him that 'The polo tournament here is postponed for one week, as it would clash with race week'. In exasperation, Jameson replied: 'Surely in your estimation do you consider races is of the utmost importance compared to immense risks of discovery daily expected . . .? Let J. H. Hammond inform weak partners. More delay, more danger.' But in Cape Town, Rhodes had no alternative but to agree to postpone the revolution until after New Year's Day.

No sooner had Rhodes dealt with that issue than further complications arose. In London, Flora Shaw discovered that Kruger's state secretary, Willem Leyds, had arrived in London en route to Paris, the Hague and Berlin and suspected that he intended to stir up a 'stop Rhodes' campaign in the chancelleries of Europe. In a cable to Rhodes on 12 December, Moberley Bell, the *Times* manager, urged swift action. 'Delay dangerous sympathy now complete but will depend very much upon action before the European powers given time to enter protest which as European situation considered serious might paralyse Government.' Five days later, after Shaw had interviewed Leyds, Bell reinforced the warning. Chamberlain, he said in a cable on 17 December, would be prepared to shrug off European protests provided swift action was taken. 'Chamberlain sound in case of interference European powers but have special reason to believe wishes you must do it immediately.'

At this crucial juncture, another issue erupted. On 17 December, President Cleveland of the United States threatened Britain with war over a long-standing boundary dispute between Venezuela and British Guiana. Chamberlain took the view that if there was to be an uprising in Johannesburg, it needed to occur as soon as possible, before European opposition became too strong and before Britain was more deeply involved in an American imbroglio over Venezuela. 'The longer it is delayed the more chance there is of foreign intervention,' he told Sir Robert Meade, the permanent secretary at the Colonial Office. 'It seems to me that either it should come *at once* or be postponed for a year or two at least. Can we ensure this?' Chamberlain asked Edward Fairfield, the Colonial Office expert on southern Africa, to contact Rhodes' associate in London, Rochfort Maguire, 'to make the situation clear'. Fairfield asked Maguire whether it was possible to defer the uprising for a year, but Maguire, wanting to see action, replied that it was now too late. Fairfield therefore, passing on Chamberlain's views, told him that 'the sooner it came off the better'. As a result of this meeting, Maguire and Lord Grey cabled Rhodes on 20 December urging him to 'hurry up' on account of the approaching trouble with Venezuela. On the basis of this telegram Beit cabled Phillips in Johannesburg: 'Our foreign supporters urge immediate flotation.'

But many of the Reformers had become disenchanted with the whole project. There was growing distrust of Rhodes' intentions. The dispute over whether the revolution was to be carried out under a British flag or under the Vierkleur, which Rhodes had endeavoured to settle in November, broke out anew. Leonard and Phillips together with Hammond and other Americans wanted a reformed republic; Hammond went so far as to warn that he would shoot anyone who raised any flag other than the Vierkleur. 'We won't stand for having a British flag hoisted over Johannesburg,' Hammond told a meeting of American miners. 'All we want is justice from Kruger and his grafters. You can rely on me that I'll shoot any man who hoists any flag but the Boer flag.'

To clarify the issue, the Reformers asked the *Times* correspondent, Francis Younghusband, to travel to Cape Town to see Rhodes. Younghusband arrived at Groote Schuur on Sunday, 22 December, as Rhodes was entertaining a host of guests on the back veranda. As they strolled among the blooming hydrangeas, Younghusband told Rhodes that there was no enthusiasm for an uprising in Johannesburg and strong opposition to the Union flag; and he advised him to postpone the whole idea. Rhodes was furious:

> RHODES: Is there no one in Johannesburg who will risk being shot and will lead the malcontents?
> YOUNGHUSBAND: There is no one willing to do this.
> RHODES: Then won't you do it? Do you mind being shot?
> YOUNGHUSBAND: I have no interest in the proposed revolution and would not dream of leading it.

After much heated discussion, Rhodes decided: 'If they won't go . . . they won't. I shall wire Jameson to keep quiet.'

Rhodes received similar advice from another visitor to Groote Schuur that day, Sir Graham Bower, the imperial secretary. Bower had become increasingly convinced that the revolution was petering out and was doomed to fail, with potentially disastrous consequences. His efforts to get Rhodes to abandon the project had hitherto met only with growing irritation, but he decided that one more attempt was worth the while. Rhodes agreed that the Reformers were growing cold and spoke of them contemptuously: 'You know the sort they are, there is no fight in them,' he said. Why then, asked Bower, put so much at risk? According to Bower, Rhodes replied:

> The Johannesburg people are bound to get their rights. With Joubert and Kotzé [Transvaal moderates] they will be over-whelmingly strong. The result will be a cosmopolitan republic more dangerous to England than Kruger. I prefer Kruger to a Johannesburg financier or speculator. Either may call Germany and Germany will come fast enough . . .
>
> If the Johannesburgers succeed without me, it is all up with a South African union. Now I fear those fellows may have a rev-olution and a successful revolution in spite of me. They will gravitate to Europe and away from South Africa. We shall have J. B. Robinson or Barney Barnato or Ed. Lippert or Albu, or someone else blackmailing us all, or putting us up for auction in Europe. If I assume control, I can steer them into a South African union . . . They can keep their flag, if I get the thing.

Their encounter became increasingly acrimonious. Rhodes accused Bower of being disloyal to Chamberlain who wanted him to 'hurry up':

> I resented this [wrote Bower] and said: 'What I allege is that you are mad to risk yourself in a matter which will ruin you and the country if you don't look out. If the Dutch find you hurrying up the reformers what will they think of you?' He again accused me

of disloyalty to Chamberlain. I gave him my opinion, and when I left he asked me not to speak to him again. I left saying I had certainly no desire to speak to him again, or to associate with a madman.

Instead of postponing the plot, Rhodes decided to heed Chamberlain's call for haste. On Monday, 23 December, he cabled to Jameson stating that the rising would take place on the date originally fixed – 28 December. 'Company will be floated next Saturday.' Nothing henceforth – neither cables nor messengers – was to deflect Jameson from launching his escapade.

In Johannesburg, however, the Reformers had now lost all confidence in the plot. As rumours of rebellion spread, several members of the stock exchange, led by George Albu, called a meeting where they denounced the plan as 'foolish', accused uitlander leaders of 'arrogance' and pledged their support for Kruger's government. The Mercantile Association, a business organisation, declared it would take no part in the revolt.

Early on Christmas Day, George Farrar went round to Leonard's house to voice his concerns: 'I hear if Jameson comes in he is going to hoist the Union Jack. I have induced every man who has joined me and who is helping me in this business to go in on the basis that we want a reformed republic.' And he warned Leonard: 'This is Boer country; it would be absolutely morally wrong to do anything else and I will not go a yard further in this business unless that basis is maintained.' Leonard heard much the same view that day from an American, Captain Thomas Mein at the Rand Club. 'If this is a case of England gobbling this country up,' said Mein, 'I am not in it.'

Later on Christmas Day, the Reformers decided to postpone action, saying they needed further confirmation from Rhodes that no British flag would be raised. Charles Leonard was sent to Groote Schuur to insist on the matter. Frank Rhodes cabled his brother telling him that Leonard was on his way to Cape Town for further discussions and that the rising had to be postponed until matters were resolved. Jameson's brother Sam was given the task of telling Jameson in Pitsani. 'Absolutely necessary to postpone flotation,' he cabled from

Johannesburg. 'You must not move until you have received instruction to.' Harris in Cape Town reinforced the message in his own cable: 'So you must not move until you hear from us again. Too awful! Very sorry.'

The vacillation of the Johannesburg conspirators enraged Jameson. There was no need for delay, he replied on 27 December. The pledge on the flag they wanted from Rhodes had already been given. Squads had already been sent out for 'distant wire cutting' of telephone lines, 'therefore let J. H. Hammond telegraph instantly all right'. Jameson also sent messages to Harris in Cape Town complaining of the cowardice of the Johannesburg conspirators and insisting that he keep to the original timetable. '. . . expect to receive a telegram from you nine tomorrow morning Saturday 28th authorizing movement . . . we must carry into effect original plans.' And he threatened to use the 'women and children' letter he had obtained from the Reformers. 'They [the Reformers] will then have two days for flotation. If they do not, we will make our own flotation with help of letter which I will publish.'

Back came further demands for Jameson to stay his hand. 'Expert reports decidedly adverse,' Hammond retorted. 'I absolutely condemn further developments at present.' Jameson was told that two special envoys from Johannesburg were on their way to explain the position. Phillips told Beit in Cape Town that if an immediate rising was insisted upon it would end in 'complete failure'. But Rhodes himself made no effort to send Jameson his own instruction.

As dawn broke on Saturday, 28 December, Charles Leonard reached Cape Town, accompanied by Fred Hamilton, editor of the Johannesburg *Star*. They quickly made their way to Groote Schuur to explain to Rhodes that Johannesburg was not ready; there were too few supporters and not enough weapons; six months' more time was needed. Rhodes appeared agreeable. He would telegraph at once, he said, halting Jameson. According to Leonard, Rhodes said: 'I will keep Jameson six months or nine months or longer on the border as a moral support to you. We will get these arms in to put you on a more level basis with the Boers.' He told them to 'await development of events'.

Later in the day, Rhodes asked Bower to meet him at Groote Schuur. Bower found him on the old tennis court. 'You will be glad to hear,' said Rhodes, 'that the revolution has fizzled out like a damp squib. You can tell the Governor. He will be glad to hear it.'

Acting on behalf of Rhodes, Harris sent Jameson several cables on 28 December. 'It is all right if you will only wait.' All foreign friends were 'dead against' a flotation. 'We cannot have fiasco.' 'Public will not subscribe one penny towards it even with you as director.' But still there was no direct message from Rhodes himself. Jameson's reply to Harris was adamant. 'Unless I hear definitely to the contrary shall leave tomorrow evening.' The telegram was sent to the offices of the Chartered Company, but by the time it reached Cape Town, the building had closed and it remained undelivered in the Cape Town telegraph office overnight.

On Sunday morning, 29 December 1895, Jameson sent a second telegram to Cape Town. 'Shall leave tonight for the Transvaal.' Both telegrams were picked up by Harris' confidential secretary at 11 a.m. and taken to Groote Schuur. Rhodes deliberated for several hours before deciding to reply. He subsequently claimed to have told Jameson: 'On no account must you move, I most strongly object to such a course.' But his telegram was never sent because by then the lines had closed.

After spending a comfortable Christmas Day at Highbury, on the outskirts of Birmingham, Chamberlain thought it advisable to inform the prime minister, Lord Salisbury, of the coup that was about to occur. His latest information was that it would take place on the following Saturday.

> My dear Salisbury,
>   I have received private information that a rising in Johannesburg is imminent and will probably take place in the course of the next few days . . .
>   If the rising is successful it ought to turn to our advantage.

The following day, however, Chamberlain received the disconcerting news that the Reformers had decided to postpone their uprising. Even more disturbing was a letter from Fairfield warning him of a conversation he had had with Bouchier Hawksley, Rhodes' solicitor in London. 'He seemed to think that Rhodes (whom he does not much like) might be driven into an attitude of frenzy and unreason, and order Jameson to "go in" from Gaberones with the Company's police and manipulate a revolution.'

Scenting danger to his own position, Chamberlain sent a confidential telegram to Robinson on 29 December:

> There seems to be a fiasco at Johannesburg owing probably to Rhodes having misjudged the balance of opinion there.
>
> It has been suggested, although I do not think it probable, that he and Jameson might endeavour to force matters at Johannesburg to a head by Jameson or someone else in the service of the Company advancing from the Bechuanaland Protectorate with police.
>
> In view of Articles nos. 22 and 8 of the Charter I could not remain passive were this to be done. Therefore, if necessary, but not otherwise, remind Rhodes of these Articles, and intimate to him that, in your opinion, he would not have my support, and point out the consequences which would follow to his schemes were I to repudiate the action.

In Pretoria, Kruger watched the hubbub in Johannesburg with grim patience. The conspirators had long since lost the element of surprise. Pretoria, as much as Johannesburg, was awash with rumours. James Bryce recorded: 'The visitor had hardly installed himself in an hotel in Pretoria before people began to tell him that an insurrection was imminent, that arms were being imported, that Maxim guns were hidden, and would be shown to him if he cared to see them, an invitation which he did not feel called on to accept.' In response to the clamour in Johannesburg, Kruger promised minor reforms. But otherwise he was prepared to wait. 'If I want to kill a tortoise,' he told burghers, 'I wait until he sticks his head out.'

In Pitsani, as he prepared to depart, Jameson was brimming with confidence. Although he had managed to raise a force of only 500 men, he still expected to slice his way through to Johannesburg within three days. When the two special envoys arrived via separate routes bringing letters instructing him to postpone the mission, he shrugged them off with a laugh. Addressing a parade of his men on Sunday afternoon, before crossing the border that night, he read out to them parts of the bogus letter he had obtained from the Reformers:

> . . . thousands of unarmed men, women and children at the mercy of Boers . . .

The men gave him a hearty cheer. 'We would have followed the Doctor to hell,' said one afterwards.

32

MISSING TELEGRAMS

A few hours after Jameson's filibusters had left Pitsani, Sir Graham Bower was about to go to bed when Rhodes' butler arrived on horseback to tell him that Rhodes was anxious to speak to him at once. Bower went round to Groote Schuur, a mile distant, and found Rhodes in his bedroom in an agitated state of mind. After spending a relaxed evening with guests, Rhodes had begun to panic. Holding Jameson's last telegram in his hand, his face ashen, he told Bower that Jameson had invaded the Transvaal, though he had sent word to try to stop him. 'It may yet come all right,' he said. Sitting on the bed, he was clearly distressed, full of self-pity. 'I know I must go,' he said. 'I will resign tomorrow. But I know what this means. It means war. I am a ruined man. But there must be no recrimination. I will take the blame.'

Bower was staggered by the news, but, with the telegraph office closed, considered there was nothing more to be done immediately and left at midnight. At 5 a.m. on Monday, 30 December, he sent his gardener to deliver a note for Robinson:

My dear Sir Hercules,

I hope you will come to Town early. There is, I fear, bad news from Jameson. He seems to have disobeyed Rhodes, and to have taken the bit between his teeth.

When Robinson arrived at his office at 10 a.m., having taken his usual train, Bower told him of his conversation with Rhodes. 'But, good God,' expostulated Robinson, 'he has not gone in without a rising? If so, you never told me.' Bower replied: 'Certainly not. I had never dreamt of Jameson doing such a thing.' Bower suggested sending a telegram to Frank Newton, the resident commissioner in Bechuanaland, instructing him to order Jameson to return. Robinson hesitated: 'Perhaps Chamberlain has sent him in. He is such an extraordinary fellow, it is possible he may support Jameson.' Bower disagreed and the telegram to Newton was sent.

Later in the day, having received Chamberlain's telegram sent on Sunday, Robinson wrote an official letter to Rhodes repudiating Jameson's action and warning him that it would probably lead to the cancellation of his Charter. When the Transvaal government asked Robinson for information about an incursion from Bechuanaland, Robinson made clear he had repudiated the action and ordered the filibusters to return.

Rhodes meanwhile remained holed up at Groote Schuur, planning his next moves. He made no attempt to send a message recalling Jameson, as Robinson had done; or to repudiate the invasion; or to resign as prime minister. Believing that Jameson would still get through to Johannesburg, he decided to whip up public support in England by making use of Jameson's bogus 'women and children' letter of invitation. In a confidential message to his London agents, he sought to portray Jameson as a valiant hero riding to their rescue.

Dr Jameson moved to assist English in Johannesburg because he received strong letter begging Dr Jameson to come signed by leading inhabitants. This letter will be telegraphed to you verbatim tomorrow. Meanwhile do not refer press. We are confident of success. Johannesburg united and strong on our side.

The bogus letter was duly sent to *The Times*, with a few extra touches to make it more convincing, for publication on 1 January 1896.

Rhodes also sent an angry message to Flora Shaw telling her to give

Chamberlain his response to the telegram he had sent threatening to cancel the Charter:

> Inform Chamberlain that I shall get through all right if he supports me, but he must not send cable like he sent the High Commissioner in South Africa. Today the crux is, I will win and South Africa will belong to England.

On Monday evening, the Cape's attorney-general, Will Schreiner, Olive's younger brother, called by to ask whether the news about Jameson was true, unaware of Rhodes' involvement in the plot:

> The moment I saw him I saw a man I had never seen before. His appearance was utterly dejected and different. Before I could say a word he said: 'Yes, yes, it is true. Old Jameson has upset my apple-cart. It is all true . . .' Whatever the reason may have been, when I spoke to him he was broken down . . . He could not have acted that part . . .

> SCHREINER: Why do you not stop him? Although he has ridden in, you can still stop him?
> RHODES: Poor old Jameson. Twenty years we have been friends and now he goes in and ruins me. I cannot hinder him. I cannot go in and destroy him.

The impression Rhodes gave Schreiner was that his inertia was due to the shock of a friend's betrayal and the obligations of friendship he still felt, but it was more a stratagem to give Jameson time to reach Johannesburg.

Among the Cape's Afrikaner politicians, there was rising fury at the news. 'If Rhodes is behind this, he is no more a friend of mine,' said Jan Hofmeyr, and he sent Kruger a telegram expressing solidarity:

> I hope your burghers will acquit themselves like heroes against Jameson's filibusters.

On Tuesday, 31 December, Hofmeyr went to see Robinson to insist that the British government issue a public proclamation disavowing Jameson and making clear that 'the criminal law . . . will be enforced to the utmost against him'. Robinson hesitated, uncertain whether he could do so without Chamberlain's authority. 'But I am afraid Pushful Joe is in it,' Robinson told Hofmeyr. In the end he gave his assent to a proclamation, forbidding British subjects to support Jameson.

On learning about the proclamation, Rhodes dashed to Government House to plead for delay. 'It's making an outlaw of the Doctor,' he complained to Robinson. In Hofmeyr's presence, Rhodes told Bower that he had offered his resignation to the cabinet. 'Mere resignation is not enough,' Hofmeyr retorted. 'You must issue a manifesto repudiating Jameson, suspending him as Administrator of Rhodesia, and declaring that the law will be set in force against him.' 'Well, you see,' Rhodes replied, 'Jameson has been such an old friend, of course I cannot do it.'

Still believing he could retrieve the situation, Rhodes tried to persuade Robinson to travel to Johannesburg and establish his authority there, as the original plan envisaged. In a final cable to Flora Shaw on 31 December – intending to shift some of the blame for failure – Rhodes wrote:

> Unless you can make Chamberlain instruct the High Commissioner to proceed at once to Johannesburg the whole position is lost. High Commissioner would receive splendid reception and still turn position to England's advantage.

When the editor of *The Star*, Fred Hamilton, called at Groote Schuur, Rhodes talked of a plan to travel to Pretoria himself:

RHODES: I'll go to Pretoria to see Kruger.
HAMILTON: He'll hang you.
RHODES: Hang me? They can't hang me. I'm a Privy Councillor. There are only 200 of us in the British Empire.

Rhodes then dropped the idea of tackling Kruger in favour of turning the heat on Chamberlain:

> RHODES: Well, anyhow, I have got Chamberlain by the short hairs . . .
> HAMILTON: Then he really is in it, Mr Rhodes?
> RHODES: In it? Up to the neck.

In London, Chamberlain was busy covering his tracks. On learning that Jameson had crossed the border, he had at first feared political ruin. But he soon took the initiative. At midnight on 30 December he sent a cable to Robinson, instructing him to 'Leave no stone unturned to prevent mischief.' On 31 December, he told Rhodes and the London directors of the BSA Company that the invasion was 'an act of war' that might cost them their Charter. And he wrote to Salisbury telling him of the approaching storm:

> I am sorry to say the Transvaal business has entered on a more acute stage. Having failed to get up a revolution in Johannesburg Rhodes . . . has apparently sent in Dr Jameson who has crossed the border of the Transvaal with 800 armed police. This is a flagrant piece of filibustering for which there is no justification that I can see in the present state of things in the Transvaal. If it were supported by us it would justify the accusation of Germany and other powers that having first attempted to get up a revolution in a friendly State and having failed, we had then assented to an act of aggression and without any grievance of our own, had poured in British troops. It is worth noting that I have no confidence that the force now sent, with its allies in Johannesburg, is strong enough to beat the Boers — and if not we should expect that conflict would be the beginning of a race war in South Africa . . .

In an attempt to mollify Kruger, Chamberlain sent him a direct cable:

> Regret to hear of Jameson's action. Sir Hercules Robinson has

sent messengers to call him back. Can I cooperate with you further in this emergency in endeavouring to bring about a peaceful arrangement which is essential to all interests in South Africa, and which would be promoted by the concessions that I am assured you are ready to make?

The first that Kruger knew about Jameson's raid was when General Joubert, the commandant-general, walked in to a meeting of the executive council in Pretoria on Monday, 30 December, waving a telegram from Zeerust, a village near the border with Bechuanaland, warning of troop movements at the nearby settlement at Malmani. Despite weeks of preparation, Jameson's men had failed to cut the telegraph line between Zeerust and Pretoria. The telegram had been sent by an official from Malmani relating how, at 5 a.m. that morning, 800 troops from the Chartered Company, armed with Maxim guns, had passed through Malmani heading in the direction of Johannesburg. Joubert ordered an immediate mobilisation. Within hours, hundreds of armed burghers were on their way to intercept the raiders.

In Johannesburg, news that Jameson had crossed the border reached the conspirators on Monday afternoon. 'The contractor has started on the earthworks with seven hundred boys; hope to reach terminus on Wednesday.' The conspirators were furious that Jameson had forced on them the prospect of a revolt, defying all the messages they had sent him insisting on postponement. The danger to their position became all the more evident when they learned that Kruger had called out the commandos.

In haste, they assembled an emergency directorate of sixty-four uitlanders – mine-owners, solicitors, doctors, engineers and company directors – naming it the Reform Committee. Many joined knowing little or nothing of the conspiracy under way. In charge was an inner group consisting of Lionel Phillips, representatives from the Gold Fields, Wernher, Beit and Farrar companies, and Percy FitzPatrick, a Cape-born adventurer. As headquarters, they used the Gold Fields building. Representatives of other companies – Barnato, Albu and J. B. Robinson – refused to participate.

The Reform Committee effectively took over the governance of Johannesburg, declaring their aim to be to preserve order and defend the town. They called on residents to commit no hostile act against the government and disavowed 'any knowledge of, or sympathy with' the armed incursion from Bechuanaland. To emphasise their loyalty to the Transvaal, members ostentatiously hoisted a Vierkleur flag above the Gold Fields building. But the Reform Committee also gave their support to a manifesto published by Leonard's national union on 27 December demanding political rights. And they authorised the distribution of arms. While anxious to avoid fighting, they hoped to use the turn of events to extract maximum concessions from Kruger.

Johannesburg's white population was at first stunned by the news of Jameson's invasion. The *Star* published a special edition telling residents he had crossed the border: 'Forces Making for Johannesburg. Conflict Lamentably Imminent'. 'I well remember the looks of utter dumbfoundedness with which the news was received,' wrote the *Times* correspondent, Francis Younghusband. 'It simply took men's breath away: the audacity of the move, and the awful consequences which it might involve.' Hundreds decided to flee by train.

But as the Reform Committee took control, a sense of purpose, even excitement, spread. Volunteers drilled in the squares. Trenches were dug. Ambulance and nursing units were formed. Three Maxim guns were brought out and exhibited at the Rand Club. A mounted corps – Bettingham's Horse – appeared.

Yet, like members of the Reform Committee, residents were keen to avoid a fight. In his report to *The Times* on Tuesday, Younghusband wrote: 'The news of the advance of an armed party from Bechuanaland is not very favourably received. There is no general wish in the community to resort to arms except in defence, and equally little wish to destroy the independence of the Republic.'

Kruger, too, wanted to avoid a fight over Johannesburg. He was unsure how well armed the population was. On instructions from Pretoria, the police in Johannesburg withdrew to barracks. Key government officials in Johannesburg were told to act as a 'Peace Committee' in discussions with the rebels; envoys were sent from

Pretoria. 'While I am beating out the fire at the frontier,' Kruger told them, 'on no account let it burst out in Johannesburg.'

The Reform Committee, in turn, decided to send a deputation to Pretoria, becoming increasingly confident that Jameson's force would soon arrive and enable them to dictate terms. Leading the deputation, Phillips told Kruger's officials: 'We come with the rifle in one hand and friendship in the other.' When asked how the government could be sure that the Reform Committee represented the Johannesburg population since the identity of its members was not known in Pretoria, the deputation, with astonishing naïveté, telegraphed for a full list of members and handed it to Kruger's officials. That list was the only evidence the government obtained on which to order the subsequent arrest of the whole Reform Committee. Assured that the government had no intention of attacking them, the rebel deputation returned to Johannesburg in high spirits.

Having defused the threat of outright rebellion in Johannesburg, Kruger still had to deal with Jameson's advancing filibusters.

From Malmani, Jameson's column rode eastwards towards Krugersdorp, a village twenty miles from Johannesburg, but soon discovered they had lost the advantage of surprise. After only a few hours along the route, they were shadowed by small groups of armed Boers. On Monday evening, while stopping for rest and refreshment, Jameson received a message from the local Boer commandant telling him to go back. Jameson replied: 'I intend proceeding with my original plans' and cited the bogus 'letter of invitation' as justification. His force, he said, had 'no hostile intentions against the people of the Transvaal', but they had come 'in reply to the invitation from the principal residents of the Rand to assist them in their demand for justice and the ordinary rights of every citizen of a civilized state'.

Early on Tuesday morning, a messenger from Newton, the British resident commissioner in Mafeking, arrived just as the column was saddling up, having ridden through the night. He brought a sealed package with orders from Robinson instructing Jameson to go back. Jameson did not bother to reply.

On Wednesday morning, another messenger arrived, sent by the British Agent in Pretoria, Sir Jacobus de Wet, giving Jameson the same orders:

> Her Majesty's Government entirely disapprove your conduct in invading Transvaal with armed force; your action has been repudiated. You are ordered to retire at once from the country and will be held personally responsible for the consequences of your unauthorized and most improper proceeding.

Again Jameson ignored the orders. He had advanced 150 miles into the Transvaal and was now only a few miles from Krugersdorp. Though his men were tired and hungry, he was confident he could make it to Johannesburg. Apart from light skirmishing, the Boer groups trailing him had shown no inclination to engage his column.

In Krugersdorp, however, Boer commanders had assembled a force of 500 men to defend the village and held commanding positions on a ridge three miles outside it. Jameson's military commander, Sir John Willoughby, wanted to avoid Krugersdorp; but Jameson insisted on heading there, expecting to find supplies and reinforcements from Johannesburg awaiting him. After shelling Boer positions, Willoughby ordered a frontal attack. As an advance party made their way up the ridge, they were cut down by Boer fire; about thirty men fell dead or wounded, another thirty who sought shelter were captured; the rest retreated.

Forced to skirt around Krugersdorp, harassed by Boer riflemen, Jameson's raiders found themselves on 2 January 1896 surrounded near a hill called Doornkop. Exhausted, and with casualties mounting, they put up a brief fight, then decided to surrender, hoisting a white apron belonging to a domestic worker on a nearby property. They looked, said a Boer commandant, Piet Cronjé (of 1881 fame), dirty and miserable. Some stood around weeping. Jameson, he said, 'trembled like a reed'. On Joubert's orders, the wounded were taken to hospital in Krugersdorp. Jameson and some 400 other raiders were carted off to prison in Pretoria.

★

It was left to Sir Hercules Robinson to sort out the mess as best he could. From the time he had first learned of Rhodes' conspiracy, he had tried to distance himself from it. 'The whole scheme is I believe sheer piracy,' he told Bower in November. Now, suffering from heart trouble, his legs swollen with dropsy, he was required to deal with the consequences. On the night of 2 January, he climbed on board a train leaving Cape Town for Pretoria to try to reach a deal with Kruger and avoid the possibility of war. Bower accompanied him, equally worried. 'During the month of January 1896,' he recalled, 'the issues of peace and war were trembling in the balance. I could not say from day to day, or from hour to hour, which way the balance would turn.'

The crisis was indeed becoming ever more complex. In London, Chamberlain had ordered two British regiments to call at the Cape in case of an uprising in Johannesburg. In Cape Town, Hofmeyr was convinced of a British plot against the Transvaal; he told Chamberlain that Rhodes' BSA Company was 'a source of danger to the public peace of South Africa' and demanded a full enquiry. Bower feared that Chamberlain would rather go to war than face an enquiry that would expose his involvement in Rhodes' conspiracy. In Pretoria, Kruger's commanders, having defeated Jameson, were keen to march on Johannesburg to deal with the rebels. British public opinion, meanwhile, as a result of the publication in *The Times* of the 'women and children' letter, had swung in Jameson's favour. Chamberlain found that his decision to repudiate publicly the invasion was unpopular. In its leader on 2 January, *The Times* added further pressure. By repudiating Jameson, said *The Times*, Chamberlain had 'saved' the Boer government; he was therefore morally responsible for transforming it.

On 3 January, while Robinson was on the train to Pretoria, another factor exploded on to the stage: Germany. The Germans had become increasingly annoyed about British agitation against Kruger. On 24 December, the German consul in Pretoria had reported to Berlin that 'the British party' in Johannesburg was thought to be 'preparing trouble in the next few days'. On 28 December, the British ambassador in Berlin was told that the German government could not accept 'any change in the status quo [in the Transvaal] in the direction sought by Cecil Rhodes'. Chamberlain denied that he planned any change. But Jameson's invasion from British Bechuanaland seemed to confirm German suspicions of British meddling and inflamed German public opinion. Kruger made it clear that he looked to Germany for support. Once Jameson was defeated, the Kaiser decided to send a telegram of congratulation to Kruger. It was published on 3 January:

> I express to you my sincere congratulations that without calling on the aid of friendly Powers you and your people, by your own energy against the armed bands which have broken into your country as disturbers of the peace, have succeeded in re-establishing peace, and defending the independence of the country against attacks from without.

In Britain, there was uproar. The press was outraged at both what they took to be a German challenge to British supremacy in southern Africa, and by the Kaiser's remark implying that if Kruger had needed help Germany would have given it. The folly of Jameson's Raid was soon forgotten. What mattered now was the menace of German aggression.

Queen Victoria, the Kaiser's grandmother, was quick to rebuke him:

> I cannot refrain from expressing my deep regret at the telegram you sent President Kruger. It is considered very unfriendly towards this country, which I feel it is not intended to be, and has, I grieve to say, made a most unfortunate impression.

Kaiser Wilhelm was equally quick with a barbed response:

> Most Beloved Grandmamma,
>   Never was the Telegram intended as a step against England or your Government. [I thought the raiders were] a mixed mob of gold-diggers . . . the scum of all nations, never suspecting that there were real Englishmen or Officers among them . . . I was

standing up for law, order and obedience to a Sovereign whom I revere and adore.

Taking advantage of the popular mood, Chamberlain saw an opportunity to shake a fist at Germany and to flex his muscles with Kruger. 'I think what is called an "Act of Vigour" is required to soothe the wounded vanity of the nation,' he wrote to Lord Salisbury on 4 January, adding: 'It does not matter which of our numerous foes we defy, but we ought to defy someone.' He ordered ostentatious naval preparations. Two days later, he sent Kruger a vivid warning: 'The President would find that the little finger of Germany is thicker than England's loins.'

In conversation with the Kaiser three years later, Rhodes remarked: 'You see, I was a naughty boy, and you tried to whip me. Now my people were quite ready to whip me for being a naughty boy, but directly *you* did it, they said, "No, if this is anybody's business, it is *ours.*" The result was that Your Majesty got yourself very much disliked by the English people, and I never got whipped at all!'

By the time that Robinson's train steamed into Pretoria station on Saturday night, the complexities of his 'peace-making' mission were thus considerably greater than they had been when he left Cape Town. His dropsy, meanwhile, had become so acute that he was obliged to lie on a couch during the course of his negotiations. His task was made all the more difficult by a stream of telegrams from Chamberlain insisting on the terms he wanted from Kruger. 'It will be your duty to use firm language.' Siding outright with the uitlanders, Chamberlain demanded the redress of all their grievances: the franchise after five years' residence; English-medium schools; full municipal powers for Johannesburg; tax cuts; and acceptance of the Reform Committee's manifesto. The Transvaal government, said Chamberlain, was to be reminded that 'the danger from which they have escaped' might recur if they were obdurate.

But, as Robinson fully recognised, Kruger, with the lives of Jameson and other prisoners in his hands and 8,000 Boer fighters at his disposal, held all the trump cards. Yet Kruger too had his difficulties. His burghers clamoured for the execution of the ringleaders. Kruger, however, saw an advantage in being magnanimous. 'What do the lives of these people matter to us?' he asked a council meeting on 6 January. 'The future does. Thousands of Englishmen live in our country, and no matter how just the sentence, how well deserved the death-penalty, the seven or nine executed will be so many martyrs and will make the schism between burghers and Englishmen unbridgeable.' What he proposed instead was to hand over the raiders to Britain to punish. If they were not punished, the Transvaal would still gain, for then Britain would be seen as the protector of criminals. As for the Reformers, the Transvaal government would deal with them separately.

In negotiations with Robinson, Kruger refused to discuss what might happen to the raiders. What he wanted, he told Robinson, was the unconditional surrender of Johannesburg within twenty-four hours. When Robinson tried to raise the issue of uitlander grievances, Kruger cut him short. Grievances would be considered only after surrender, he said. Seeing no worthwhile alternative, Robinson advised the Reform Committee to surrender unconditionally, warning that if they refused, they would 'forfeit all claim to sympathy from Her Majesty's Government' and jeopardise the lives of Jameson and other prisoners. When Chamberlain telegraphed that he was thinking of 'immediately sending large forces . . . to the Cape to provide for all eventualities', Robinson told him curtly to 'leave the matter in my hands'.

In Johannesburg, following the capture of Jameson, the mood resembled a mixture of 'Armageddon and a psychopathic ward', according to John Hays Hammond. Recriminations flew thick and fast. 'Tonight', Percy FitzPatrick wrote to his wife on 3 January, 'we are all hooted and howled at by the crowd because they say we have deserted Jameson. We have done nothing of the sort but he has failed to reach [us] and, as far as we can learn has had to surrender to the Boers. It is the blackest and most cruel game of treachery every played. Chamberlain sold Jameson and the High Commissioner or Rhodes sold us both.' Yet the conspirators had little appetite for trying to hold out. On receiving Robinson's cable, they replied that they would lay down their arms and 'place themselves and their interests unreservedly in the hands of Your Excellency'.

On 9 January, Kruger promised a pardon to all those who surrendered their arms, other than the leading conspirators, and
simultaneously ordered the arrest of the sixty-four members of the
Reform Committee whose names he had been given by their own
deputation. Despite all that had happened, he said, he hoped that
Johannesburg's residents would make it possible for him to 'forgive
and forget'.

Facing ruin, Rhodes remained holed up at Groote Schuur, roaming
the mountain slopes during the day, pacing up and down in his
bedroom at night. His conspiracy to overthrow Kruger had ended in
fiasco. It had cost him his position as prime minister and placed all
his business interests in jeopardy. The charter of the British South
Africa Company was under threat; De Beers was implicated in gun-
running; Gold Fields had been used as the headquarters of the failed
Johannesburg uprising. His fellow conspirators – including Jameson
and his own brother Frank – faced long terms of imprisonment.
Rhodes himself was liable to prosecution under the Foreign
Enlistment Act, which made it an offence for anyone to prepare an
expedition on British soil against a friendly state. His political ambitions in the Cape were in tatters. Hofmeyr and the Cape Afrikaners
were bitter at his betrayal. 'I could explain better if you had ever
been a married man,' Hofmeyr told Rhodes.

> You were never married. I have not yet forgotten the relation
> of perfect trust and intimacy which a man has with his wife.
> We have often disagreed, you and I, but I would no more have
> thought of distrusting you than a man and his wife think of dis-
> trusting each other in any joint undertaking. So it was until
> now; and now you have let me go on being apparently intimate
> while you knew that this was preparing and said nothing.

Amid the wreckage, Rhodes resolved to ensure he kept the Charter,
knowing he had enough evidence of Chamberlain's complicity in the
conspiracy to blackmail him. Rhodes was aware that a number of
telegrams implicating Chamberlain were held by company officials. In

all, his London solicitor, Bouchier Hawksley, assembled a dossier of fifty-nine telegrams. On 15 January, Rhodes set sail for England ready to confront Chamberlain. 'I am going home to face the unctuous rectitude of my countrymen,' he told a public meeting in Cape Town, with obvious disdain. Arriving in London on 3 February, he discussed tactics with Hawksley. The following day, Hawksley met Fairfield to let him know of the telegrams in his possession implicating Chamberlain. When Chamberlain asked to be shown the telegrams, Hawksley declined. 'I think perhaps enough has been done, and we may leave matters at this point. Mr C [Chamberlain] knows what I know and can shape his course with this knowledge.' He added smoothly: 'As I hope I made clear to you there is not the slightest intention to make any use whatever of confidential documents.'

When Rhodes met Chamberlain on 6 February, not a word was mentioned about the telegrams. After a two-hour discussion, Rhodes left with Chamberlain's assurance that, as far as he was concerned, the Charter was safe. The blackmail was mutual. While Rhodes used his possession of the cables to prevent Chamberlain from abrogating the Charter, Chamberlain used his power to withdraw the Charter to prevent Rhodes from publishing the cables.

The fate of the conspirators unfolded in the following months. Three weeks after his capture, Jameson was released from prison to stand trial in Britain. In England he had become a music-hall hero. In January, *The Times* published a ballad by Alfred Austin, the Poet Laureate, to commemorate his valiant dash for Johannesburg:

> When men of our own blood pray us
> To ride to their kinsfolk's aid,
> Not Heaven itself shall stay us
> From the rescue they call a raid . . .
>
> There are girls in the gold-reef city,
> There are mothers and children too,
> And they cry: 'Hurry up! For pity!'
> So what can a brave man do.

Jameson was charged under the Foreign Enlistment Act with preparing 'a military expedition' against 'a friendly state'. While he was awaiting trial, Chamberlain paid him a secret visit in prison, presumably to ensure that he remained discreet when giving evidence. Jameson was sentenced to fifteen months' imprisonment, but, after falling ill, served only four months.

The Johannesburg conspirators fared less well. Jameson's raiders had been foolish enough to carry with them a host of incriminating documents, including telegrams, code books and a copy of the infamous letter of invitation. In view of the weight of evidence against them, their lawyers advised them to plead guilty to charges of treason. Four of the signatories of the 'women and children' letter – Lionel Phillips, Frank Rhodes, John Hays Hammond and George Farrar – were sentenced to death for treason; the fifth signatory, Charles Leonard, never returned from Cape Town and fled to England. Percy FitzPatrick, the secretary of the Reform Committee, was also sentenced to death. Other Reformers were sentenced to two years' imprisonment and a fine of £2,000 each.

The death sentences were commuted the next day. After a deluge of petitions, Kruger further reduced the sentences – 'magnanimity by inches', it was called – and finally opted for fines. Rhodes and Beit between them spent £200,000 settling the fines. Rhodes subsequently admitted that the Raid had cost Beit and himself £400,000 each.

In the wake of the trial, the Transvaal government published a 'green' book of all the evidence in its possession. Rhodes and Jameson were exposed as the main culprits behind the conspiracy, but there were also hints about British government complicity. In July, the Cape parliament published its own report on the Raid in a 'blue' book, adding further information. It described Rhodes, Beit, Jameson and Harris as 'the promoters and moving spirits' behind the plot and judged that the whole Johannesburg movement had been 'largely financed and engineered from outside'. It laid the heaviest blame on Rhodes. It was Rhodes, said the report, who 'directed and controlled the combination' that had made the Raid possible.

In London, Parliament set up a committee of inquiry into the

Raid that was little more than a sham. Chamberlain himself sat on the committee carefully steering it away from dangerous territory. He denied any involvement: 'I never had any knowledge, or, until I think it was the day before the actual raid took place, the slightest suspicion, of anything in the nature of a hostile or armed invasion of the Transvaal.' Other witnesses – Rhodes, Jameson, Willoughby, Beit, Phillips, Leonard, Hawksley and Shaw – were similarly evasive. 'Dr Jameson went in without my authority,' said Rhodes. Committee members appeared reluctant to probe too far, fearful of what they might find. In its conclusions, the committee gave Rhodes a slap on the wrist: he had been guilty, it said, of 'grave breaches of duty to those to whom he owed allegiance'. Chamberlain was exonerated. 'Neither the Secretary of State for the Colonies nor any of the officials at the Colonial Office received any information which made them or should have made them or any of them, aware of the plot during its development.' Critics of the committee were scornful. Lord Rosebery, leader of the opposition, remarked: 'I have never read a document at once so shameful and so absurd.'

Chamberlain compounded the sense of outrage about the whole affair by loudly praising Rhodes. 'There has been nothing proved – and in my opinion there exists nothing – which affects Mr Rhodes's personal position as a man of honour.' When a move was made to deprive Rhodes of his membership of the Privy Council, Chamberlain rallied to his defence: Rhodes had been honoured, he said, 'for invaluable services nothing can dim'.

Thus, the Rhodes conspiracy ended as it had begun: in collusion, lies and deceit.

But there were lasting repercussions. Cape Afrikaners never forgave Rhodes for his treachery. The working alliance between Afrikaners and English that had prevailed for decades was irretrievably damaged. Faced with yet another example of British aggression, Afrikaners across southern Africa – in the Cape, the Transvaal and the Orange Free State – rallied behind Kruger. Out of the ashes of the Rhodes conspiracy came a resurgence of Afrikaner nationalism, rekindled with new intensity.

In London, meanwhile, Chamberlain brooded over the unfinished business of the plot. In a 'statement of policy' he sent to Fairfield in April 1896, he argued that previous generosity to the Boers was a piece of Christian chivalry that had brought no benefit. He described Kruger as 'an ignorant, dirty, cunning and obstinate man who has known how to feather his own nest and to enrich all his family and dependants'. He was mindful, he said, of the consequences of war:

> I shall never go into such a war with a light heart, and at the present time we have no reason – either of right or of interest – which would justify the enterprise.
>
> If we ever were forced into it against our will I should try to seize and defend the gold-bearing districts. This is the key of S. Africa . . .
>
> I do not believe that there will be war – but Kruger will not be wise if he dismisses that possibility altogether from his calculations . . .

What he wanted, he claimed, was 'a fair settlement' between Boers and uitlanders in the Transvaal.

> We shall not do it, I admit, by a policy of empty menace or arbitrary impatience – neither, I think, shall we succeed if we underestimate our reserve force and allow Kruger to have it all his own way.

Speaking in the House of Commons in May 1896, Chamberlain was more explicit about the repercussions of war.

> A war in South Africa would be one of the most serious wars that could possibly be waged. It would be in the nature of a Civil War. It would be a long war, a bitter war and a costly war . . . it would leave behind it the embers of a strife which I believe generations would hardly be long enough to extinguish . . . to go to war with President Kruger, to force upon him reforms in the

internal affairs of his state, with which [we] have repudiated all rights of interference – that would have been a course of action as immoral as it would have been unwise.

Yet Chamberlain himself was to preside over just such a war.

In Matabeleland and Mashonaland, meanwhile, Rhodes had left white settlers exposed to the danger of African revolt.

33

BY RIGHT OF CONQUEST

When white residents of the new town of Bulawayo heard in October 1895 that virtually the entire white police force was to be sent to Bechuanaland, they drew up a letter of protest. A three-man delegation delivered it to Jameson, the administrator of Matabeleland, in his office in Bulawayo, and demanded to know whether it was true that the police were being withdrawn as part of a plan to invade the Transvaal. Jameson denied it, saying that they had been assigned to Bechuanaland to deal with a dissident African chief. Their absence would be only temporary. Furthermore, he said, he had made all the necessary arrangements for calling out volunteers in the unlikely event of any trouble with the Ndebele population, and he had also ensured that there was an ample supply of arms and ammunition for everyone. Two months later, when Jameson launched his invasion, Matabeleland was left with only forty-eight white policemen; in the whole of Rhodesia, there were no more than sixty-three.

Once it became known that Jameson's police force had been defeated in the Transvaal by the Boers and locked up in Pretoria prison, the Ndebele seized the opportunity to revolt. Deprived of most of their cattle and much of their best land, subjected to forced labour and harsh treatment, they were seething with discontent. Drought, locusts and rinderpest, a cattle disease, added to their grievances. Despite the demise of Lobengula in 1893, their old regimental system had remained largely intact; their arms had been hidden, not surrendered. Members of Lobengula's family and senior indunas were still at large. Among those who joined the revolt was Babayane, the Ndebele envoy who had met Queen Victoria at Windsor Castle.

The whites were taken completely by surprise. The renowned hunter Fred Selous, who had returned to Matabeleland to manage Willoughby's 200,000-acre estate at Essexvale, close to the Matopo Hills, recalled that he had been closely questioned by a prominent Ndebele leader, Mlugulu, about the arrest of Jameson and the fate of the police, but did not consider it a cause for suspicion at the time. The Ndebele, he wrote, were 'as quiet and submissive in their demeanour towards Europeans as they ever had been since the war, and there was absolutely no evidence of any secret arming amongst them'. The veteran missionary Charles Helm also believed that there was no prospect of trouble from the Ndebele. 'They acknowledge themselves to be a conquered people,' he said. A month before the revolt, Weston Jarvis, a former Tory member of parliament, who had arrived in Matabeleland to inspect Willoughby's properties, wrote to his mother: 'There is a rumour of a possible rising among some of the tribes in the Matoppo Hills but that was of course all moonshine . . . This is *grand* country, exceeding my most sanguine expectations. It is undoubtedly *very* rich and fertile. The natives are happy, comfortable and prosperous and the future must be magnificent.'

The revolt began in March 1896 with attacks on whites at isolated farms, mining camps and trading stores in outlying districts. Whole families perished. In all, about 200 whites died in the onslaught. Within a week, no whites were left alive in outlying districts. Those managing to escape fled to the main settlements of Bulawayo and Gwelo, raising the alarm. In Bulawayo, there was a brief moment of panic as crowds besieged the government's armoury, clamouring for weapons. 'Men fought their way up to the source of supply, clambering on to each other's shoulders, grabbing and snatching the coveted weapons . . . until the last of the supply had been given out,' wrote one eyewitness.

By attacking outlying districts first instead of the main settlements, the Ndebele rebels lost the advantage of surprise and enabled the whites to throw up hasty defences. 'If two thousand of them, or even a smaller number, had made a night attack upon the town [of Bulawayo] before the laager had been formed,' said Selous, 'I think it more than probable that the entire white population would have been massacred.' At great personal risk, volunteers went out in search of survivors. They returned with tales of terrible scenes, of men, women and children hacked to death and mutilated, 'vowing a pitiless vengeance against the whole Matabele race'.

Reinforcements were sent from the Cape and from Natal – colonial volunteers from Kimberley; imperial troops from Natal; and African units from the Cape – 'Cape Boys'. Rhodes arrived at the Gwelo laager from Fort Salisbury with a detachment of 150 Mashonaland volunteers. At Chamberlain's insistence, all were placed under the command of imperial officers, though the British South Africa Company was obliged to pay for the full cost of the campaign.

After conferring on himself the rank of colonel, Rhodes joined the campaign, riding into combat wearing white flannel trousers and armed only with a riding crop. 'He is very like Napoleon,' Weston Jarvis wrote to his mother. 'He quite thinks that he was not intended to be killed by a damned nigger . . .' Rhodes was as keen on vengeance as most whites. His aide, Gordon Le Sueur, recalled a conversation between Rhodes and an officer who had just returned from an engagement:

On Rhodes asking how many [enemy] were killed [the officer] replied, 'Very few as the natives threw down their arms, went on their knees, and begged for mercy.' 'Well,' said Rhodes, 'you should not spare them. You should kill all you can, as it serves as a lesson to them when they talk things over at their fires at night.'

Other eyewitnesses described how after an engagement Rhodes would arrive on the scene to count the number of corpses. Weston Jarvis wrote of how he and Rhodes accompanied a patrol which had burned down villages and crops and captured cattle and women. 'I have been out with Rhodes looting corn all morning and he is now keen to be off again.' In Olive Schreiner's contemporary novel *Trooper Peter Halket of Mashonaland*, Rhodes is the undisguised villain of the story.

By June, Ndebele forces north of Bulawayo were falling back to defensive positions in the Mambo Hills, harassed at every turn by mounted patrols. Rhodes was confident that the revolt was nearly defeated. 'I see daylight', he told Lord Grey, the new administrator appointed in place of Jameson. Grey was less optimistic. 'Until we catch them and thoroughly convince them that this country is to be the country of the white, and not the black, man we must go on ham-mering and hunting them.'

But just when it seemed that the tide had turned in Matabeleland, the Shona joined the revolt. Once again, the whites were taken by surprise. Believing the Shona to be a docile people, only too grateful for having been liberated from Ndebele raids, white residents of Mashonaland had willingly despatched 150 of their fighting men to help in Matabeleland without any qualms about their own safety. Yet Shona resentment about white rule – over hut taxes, harsh treatment and the loss of land – had been mounting with similar intensity. Taking advantage of the Ndebele uprising, the Shona turned on the whites with greater ferocity than any resistance they had previously shown against the Ndebele. Within a week of the beginning of the Shona revolt in June 1896, more than 100 men, women and children were murdered in outlying districts of Mashonaland. Survivors strug-gled to reach Fort Salisbury and four other settlements. In all, during the course of the 1896 revolts, white casualties amounted to 372 killed and 129 wounded – about 10 per cent of the entire white pop-ulation.

The impact on the fortunes of the BSA Company was severe. Critics accused the company of gross mismanagement. Evidence of war atrocities began to filter through. Even worse, the cost of two simultaneous campaigns threatened to drive the company into bank-ruptcy.

In Matabeleland, the campaign had reached deadlock. The main Ndebele stronghold in the Matopo Hills, a region of huge granite boulders, deep clefts, caves and tangled bush stretching for 1,500 square miles south of Bulawayo, seemed impregnable. A major assault in the Matopos on 20 July ended in little else but high casualties. Another assault on 5 August was no more effective and nearly culminated in disaster. Over camp dinners at General Frederick Carrington's base camp in the Matopos, Rhodes started to calculate aloud how long it would be, given such a high casualty rate, for Carrington's force to be exterminated. 'As may be imagined,' wrote his friend Hans Sauer, 'these calculations were not appreciated by the military gentlemen.'

The deadlock convinced Carrington that only with massive rein-forcements would he be able to take the Matopos. He proposed a new campaign, starting in the dry season of 1897, with 2,500 more white troops, one or two thousand carriers, engineers for blasting opera-tions, mountain guns and a string of forts. Carrington was bent on military victory whatever the cost.

For Rhodes, this meant financial ruin. In secret, he set up his own peace initiative, recruiting a handful of trusted individuals, including Hans Sauer and Johann Colenbrander, a former chief native commissioner. A captured royal widow, Nyamabezana, was sent back into the hills with a white flag and simple instructions: if the rebel leaders were interested in peace, they were to show the white flag. Risking their own lives, two Mfengu scouts – Jan Grootboom and James Makhunga – spent a week in the hills making preliminary contact. On 21 August, after telling Carrington of his plan at the last minute, Rhodes set out for an 'indaba' in the hills. He was accompanied by three whites – Sauer, Colenbrander and Vere Stent, a correspondent for the *Cape Times* – and Grootboom and Makhunga:

It was a lovely winter's day [wrote Stent], the sun just beginning to western; comfortably hot; the grasses, bronze and golden, swaying in the slight wind; the hills ahead of us blurred in the quivering mirage of early afternoon. We talked very little. Must I confess it? – we were all a little nervous.

Sauer reminded Rhodes of the fate of Piet Retief, the Boer leader killed on the orders of the Zulu king, Dingane, after he and his followers entered the royal enclosure unarmed.

At the appointed rendezvous, a small clearing in the hills, the party dismounted and tied their horses. Escape was now impossible. With Rhodes leading the way, they sat down on an old ant heap, watched from the hills by a mass of Ndebele warriors. From a distance, a group of about forty indunas approached, escorted by Makhunga, bearing the white flag on a stick. Among them were Babayane and Mlugulu.

Prompted by Colenbrander, Rhodes gave them a greeting of peace in Sindebele: '*Amehlo Amhlophe*'– 'the eyes are white'. A chorus of '*Amehlo Amhlophe*' came in reply. When they were all seated, the old chief Somabhulana, at Rhodes' request, rose to explain their grievances.

After a long recital of Ndebele history, Somabhulana spoke of the white war of conquest of Matabeleland:

> You came, you conquered. The strongest takes the land. We accepted your rule. We lived under you. But not as dogs! If we are to be dogs it is better to be dead. You can never make the Amandebele dogs. You may wipe them out . . . but the Children of the Stars can never be dogs.

There was an angry murmur, a restless stirring, among the group of indunas. 'The moment was inflammable,' wrote Stent. 'The least indiscretion might precipitate a massacre.' Rhodes calmly asked Somabhulana to continue. 'By whom and how were they made dogs?'

Somabhulana referred to the arbitrary rule of white officials, citing as an example how he himself had been humiliated by the chief magistrate in Bulawayo. He spoke of the 'brutality' of the native police and an incident in which tax-collectors had shot dead four women in cold blood for refusing to disclose the whereabouts of cattle. Rhodes promised reform and assured Somabhulana that the indunas would face no reprisals or punishment.

It was late in the afternoon. Somabhulana stood up, signifying that the indaba was concluded. 'Is it peace or war?' Rhodes asked. An intense silence followed. 'It is peace,' replied Somabhulana and lifted a stick and placed it on the ground before him. 'Here is my rifle. I lay it down at your feet.'

Rhodes spent the following eight weeks camping in the Matopos, meeting Ndebele delegations, trying to reassure them that their demands would be met. Some of the encounters were tense occasions, as Stent recorded:

> A young chief who might best be described as insolent to the elders of his own tribe and particularly so to the white men put in a pertinent question. 'Where are we to live when it is over?' he said. 'The white man claims all the land.' Rhodes replied at once, 'We will give you settlements. We will set apart locations for you; we will give you land.' The young chief shouted angrily, 'You will give us land in our own country! That's good of you!'

Rhodes then objected to talking to the young chief while he still had his rifle in his hand. The young chief said: 'You will have to talk to me with my rifle in my hand. I find if I talk with my rifle in my hand the white man pays more attention to what I say. Once I put my rifle down I am nothing. I am just a dog to be kicked.'

After further protracted meetings, the terms of a peace deal were agreed in October. Much to the fury of white residents and many imperial officials, the leaders of the revolt went unpunished; and indunas who proved their loyalty were given appointments and salaries.

Thus Rhodes saved his company. The Ndebele, however, still lost most of their land. Despite promises he had made about restoring land to the Ndebele, the whites had no intention of giving it up. Two-thirds of the Ndebele people returning home found themselves living on 'white' land.

In Mashonaland, there was no peace treaty. Shona rebels were hunted down and blasted from caves until the last pocket of resistance had been eliminated. As the British government subsequently acknowledged, Rhodesia was established by right of conquest.

PART VIII

34

THE RICHEST SPOT ON EARTH

A new British high commissioner arrived in Cape Town in May 1897. Sir Alfred Milner was an imperial zealot, obsessed by the need to bolster the realms of empire and appointed by Chamberlain to ensure that British supremacy was upheld in southern Africa, whatever the cost. Like Chamberlain, he believed that the British 'race' was the greatest of all governing races. In a statement which he called his 'Credo', he wrote: 'I am a British (indeed primarily an English) Nationalist. If I am also an Imperialist, it is because the destiny of the English race, owing to its insular position and long supremacy at sea, has been to strike fresh roots in distant parts of the world. My patriotism knows no geographical but only racial limits. I am an Imperialist and not a Little Englander, because I am a British Race Patriot.' Milner took up the cause of imperialism as a personal crusade, describing it as 'a great movement of the human spirit' with 'all the depth and comprehensiveness of a religious faith'. In a farewell speech in London marking his departure for Cape Town, he spoke of himself as 'a civilian soldier of Empire', committed to working for its advancement with his 'whole heart and with a single mind'.

A repressed and rigid man, impatient of opposition and of conflicting views, Milner possessed a formidable intellect but a narrow mindset. 'There is one question upon which I have never been able to see the other side,' he told the distinguished gathering assembled at the Café Monico to bid him farewell, 'and that is precisely the question of closer union. My mind is not so constructed that I am capable of understanding the arguments of those who question its desirability or its possibility.'

Born in Germany in 1854, the son of an improvident half-German medical student and an English mother, he had been acclaimed a brilliant student at Oxford, winning a string of academic prizes. After trying his hand as a political journalist for two years and standing unsuccessfully for parliament, he had opted for officialdom, serving as under-secretary at the Egyptian ministry of finance, then as chairman of the Board of Inland Revenue; he was adept at writing reports and found it easier to communicate with people on paper rather than in person.

Both Milner and Chamberlain regarded southern Africa as being 'the weakest link in the Imperial chain'. They considered the rise of the Transvaal as a wealthy, independent state, producing nearly one quarter of the world's gold supply, to be a threat not only to Britain's hold on southern Africa but to its standing as a global power. What Milner and Chamberlain feared was that, because of its economic strength, the Transvaal would absorb other territories in the region – the Cape Colony, Natal and the Orange Free State – and lead them into an independent union, a 'United States of South Africa', outside the realms of the British empire.

This fear was set out vividly in a Colonial Office memorandum on imperial prospects in southern Africa, written in 1896 in the wake of the Jameson Raid, by Chamberlain's under-secretary, Lord Selborne. The key to the future, said Selborne, was the Transvaal. 'It is the richest spot on earth.' Its white population was fast expanding, out-stripping other areas of southern Africa. 'It is going to be the natural capital state and centre of South African commercial, social and polit-ical life':

The Transvaal will be the market for South Africa: the market for the manufactures of Cape Colony and Natal; the market for the agricultural products of those Colonies and Rhodesia. The commercial interest of the closest connexion with the Transvaal will outweigh all other considerations. These British Colonies will sue for closer commercial union. The Transvaal will reply that so long as these Colonies remain British they will not grant it; that they have no intention of becoming British, but that if these Colonies will unite with them in forming a United Republic of South Africa they will welcome them with open arms.

Selborne envisaged two possible outcomes:

1. If we can succeed in uniting all South Africa into a Confederacy on the model of the Dominion of Canada and under the British Flag, the probability is that that confederacy will not become a United States of South Africa.
2. If South Africa remains as now a congeries of separate States, partly British Colonies and partly Republics, it will inevitably amalgamate itself into a United States of South Africa.

Chamberlain and Milner were agreed that the ultimate objective of British policy in southern Africa should be to steer the Transvaal into an imperial dominion before the Transvaal became too strong to resist the pressure. The longer that the Transvaal survived as an independent state, the more likely it was to succeed as emerging as the dominant power in southern Africa. If Britain failed to retain its hold on southern Africa, then its prestige, trade and defence interests would be irreparably damaged. Thus southern Africa, as Chamberlain and Milner saw it, was a test case about the future of the empire.

Both were ready to risk a Boer war in pursuit of establishing a British dominion. When Lord Salisbury, the prime minister, expressed his misgivings about the possibility of war in a letter to Chamberlain in April 1897, Chamberlain replied:

There are two possibilities to guard against. The first is a war with the Transvaal which might be . . . unpopular in England and which might easily strain our relations with Germany.

The other is the loss of confidence of the British in South
Africa which would certainly lead to a republic – the elimination
of the Imperial factor. Of the two this is the greatest evil, yet
there is undoubtedly a strong party anxious to bring it about.

In view of the rumpus over the Jameson Raid, however, Chamberlain
and Milner decided that what was needed was 'a waiting game'. They
hoped that Boer opposition to Kruger's rule might do the job of
removing Kruger for them, opening the way to reform and moves
towards a federal dominion. The British government, in any case, had
other foreign preoccupations at the time, such as the Sudan. 'I
decided,' said Chamberlain, 'that our policy for the present was to let
the Boers "stew in their own juice", fight out their internal quarrels
and not be able to raise prejudice and confuse the issues by pointing
to external interference as the danger to be faced. The decision may
be right or wrong, but I intend that it shall have a fair trial.'

As a middle-aged bachelor fond of intellectual pursuits, long accustomed to the delights of London society, but with no interest in
outdoor activity, Milner soon found much to dislike about life in the
Cape. In letters to friends back home, he complained of the boredom
and the 'most uncongenial people' whom he encountered daily.
'Socially it is the most detestable life you can imagine.' He was disdainful of the Cape's political elite, preferring to keep his distance
from them. 'My only personal interest is in my English friends and my
only amusement hearing from them,' he wrote.
    Cape politicians similarly found little to like about Milner. John
Merriman regretted that Milner had been 'trained in the school of
newspapers and books rather than that of men' – which had made
him a 'poor nervous ignorant fellow, utterly out of sympathy with
South Africa'. Recalling his first impression of Milner at a ceremony
at Government House in the heart of Cape Town, James Rose Innes
wrote: 'In appearance a scholar rather than a man of action, but with
an air of grave assurance which indicated fixity of purpose, a man
more apt to give than to take advice . . . As we walked down
Parliament Street after the ceremony Merriman broke out: "Mark my

words, we shall have a rough-and-tumble with that fellow.'" The veteran Afrikaner politician Jan Hofmeyr was even more pessimistic. According to his biographer, 'Hofmeyr saw after a few interviews with him that war must come.'

Indeed, Milner looked on Cape Afrikaners – nearly two thirds of the white population – as a potential enemy, part of the rising realm of Afrikanerdom that needed to be crushed. 'Half of the white people in this Colony, indeed I fear more than half, while owing a formal allegiance to Britain, are at heart fellow-citizens with the Free Staters and Transvaalers,' he wrote to a friend in August 1897:

> As long as there is no friction between Great Britain and the Republics, they don't mind being British subjects, in fact, being comfortable and lazy, they don't desire a change. But the moment Great Britain and either of the Republics are at log-gerheads, they side openly and vehemently with the latter. Of course, the remedy may be found in time in an English party in the Transvaal getting the franchise and counterbalancing on that side the influence of the Colonial Dutch on this. But the Boer oligarchy of the Transvaal is going to die hard. And it is not going to precipitate its own demise by provoking us too much.

In Pretoria, Kruger watched Britain's manoeuvres with profound suspicion. The Jameson Raid had opened a chasm of distrust of British intentions. Kruger was convinced that Chamberlain was as culpable for the attempt to overthrow him as Rhodes, yet, despite all the evidence against them, Chamberlain had remained in office and Rhodes had been let off with nothing more than a slap on the wrist. The uitlander population meanwhile remained a potential fifth column for Britain to use. Kruger assumed therefore that further attempts would be made against him.

Determined to bolster the Transvaal's defences, he ordered a vast array of modern military equipment from Germany and France – field guns, siege guns, Maxim guns, howitzers and modern rifles. Between 1896 and 1899, more than one third of the Transvaal's annual revenues were allocated to defence expenditure. Instead of burghers being required to provide their own arms and ammunition, they were now equipped by the government with the latest Mausers and Martini-Henry rifles. Fortresses were constructed in Pretoria and Johannesburg.

Kruger also drew closer to the Orange Free State. By the 1890s, the Free State had emerged as a 'model republic'. Visiting it in 1895, James Bryce, a British constitutional expert, described it as 'an ideal commonwealth . . . the kind of commonwealth which the fond fancy of the philosophers of the last century painted'. Following the opening of the first railway from the Cape in 1890, modern buildings had sprung up in Bloemfontein: a new parliament, new schools, a hospital, a club. While Bloemfontein remained essentially a small town, with a white population numbering only 2,500, it possessed a cosmopolitan atmosphere, with its own orchestra, church and choral societies, language study circles, Shakespeare readings, dances and amateur theatricals, parks and public gardens. Visitors from Europe were given a warm welcome. Although only Dutch was permitted in the Volksraad, English was commonly spoken in town and business life.

A presidential election in 1895 had brought to office Marthinus Steyn, a 38-year-old lawyer, the first Free State-born burgher to become president. After studying law in London, he had been appointed a judge in Bloemfontein. He was married to the daughter of a Scottish parson. The London press described Steyn as 'a man of high culture and sterling character, possessed of a balanced judgement and dignified personal appearance'.

In March 1897, Kruger travelled to Bloemfontein to discuss with Steyn the prospects for a closer union between the Transvaal and the Free State. They renewed a defence treaty, first agreed in 1889, pledging mutual support 'when the independence of one of the two States may be threatened or attacked', and added a new clause proclaiming the goal of a federal union between them. Steyn declared himself to be 'strongly in favour' of a closer union. 'We have the same people, the same history, the same language, and the same form of government'.

Kruger also endeavoured to get on better terms with the Rand mining companies, assisting them with new pass laws and labour recruitment measures to facilitate a plentiful supply of cheap immigrant labour from Portuguese East Africa (Mozambique). He also set up an Industrial Commission to 'institute a thorough and searching inquiry into the alleged grievances of the Mining Industry'.

However, when the commission pointed out the adverse effect of Kruger's policy of monopoly concessions, notably the damaging impact of the dynamite concession, Kruger refused to take action, precipitating another round of grumbling among the mining magnates.

Nor was he willing to countenance any reform of the franchise system. On a visit to Pretoria in March 1897, during an attempt to mediate in a dispute between Kruger and the Transvaal's chief justice, the Cape's chief justice, Sir Henry de Villiers, broached the subject of franchise reform:

DE VILLIERS: Would not the removal of the Uitlanders' grievances have given you a contented population?

KRUGER: The discontented people will not be satisfied until they have my country. If I give them the franchise they may ask the Chartered people [i.e. Rhodes] to rule over them. Their other grievances we are quite ready to redress, if there are any . . . Don't be under the delusion that any concessions that I can make will ever satisfy the enemies of my country.

DE VILLIERS: President, you have to satisfy not the enemies but the friends of your country. It is your real friends who would advise you to meet the demands of the new population. Many of them would, perhaps, abuse the franchise; but a majority would be grateful for it and use it for the advantage of the country . . . If redress is not granted, the danger will always exist that it may be sought elsewhere. I know the main difficulties under which you labour, and I have never wished to add to them by publicly abusing you and the Republic, but if any private advice of mine is of any value, I trust you will accept it in the spirit in which it has been given.

KRUGER: I know that you are not one of our enemies. Your mediation shows that you mean it well with us. But I am responsible for the independence of the State, and must take care that it is not lost.

In this stubborn frame of mind, Kruger stood for election for a fourth term as president. At the age of seventy-three, much of his old vigour had gone: the great shoulders sagged; the bags under his eyes were more pronounced than ever; he had become increasingly deaf; he suffered from a painful eye affliction – ingrowing eyelashes; and his mood was often irritable. But no Transvaaler doubted his commitment to the cause of independence.

Two other candidates stood for election: Piet Joubert, the commandant-general, and Schalk Burger, a reformist politician. Campaigning on a platform of modernisation and a modest extension of the franchise, Burger received considerable financial support from the mining industry. His mining friends did not expect Burger to win but hoped he would emerge as the leader of an opposition strong enough to force Kruger to agree to reform. To enhance Burger's chances, they tried to induce Joubert to withdraw, but to no avail. The Johannesburg *Star* openly supported Burger, but probably not to his advantage. In a letter to Julius Wernher, Percy FitzPatrick, one of Wernher, Beit's representatives in Johannesburg, warned:

> You can be sure of this: if there be any sign of movement or restlessness on the part of the Uitlanders, or a disposition on England's part to meddle, there will be only one man in the hunt. Kruger is hunting about for evidence to show that Rhodes or Chamberlain or Johannesburg is at the bottom of opposition to him. His organ, the *Volkstem*, has gone to the length of stating that we have put up £50,000 to secure Burger's election. He will go *any* length.

The election result, announced in February 1898, was a triumph for Kruger. Kruger won 12,764 votes; Burger, 3,716, and Joubert, 1,943. Not only in the rural areas, but in the towns – Johannesburg as well as Pretoria – Kruger was returned by large majorities.

For Milner, the election result was a turning point. After playing a 'waiting game' for nine months, hoping for evidence that an effective opposition to Kruger might emerge, he found himself having to deal with a 'despotic oligarchy' more deeply entrenched than before, and as recalcitrant as ever. His patience running out, Milner wrote a private letter to Chamberlain:

> There is no way out of the political trouble of S. Africa except reform in the Transvaal or war. And at present the chances of reform in the Transvaal are worse than ever. The Boers quarrel bitterly amongst themselves, but it is about jobs and contracts, not politics! In their determination to keep all power in their own hands and to use it with a total disregard of the interests of the unenfranchised, as well as their own hatred and suspicion of Great Britain, the vast majority of them are firmly united . . . Kruger has returned to power, more autocratic and more reactionary than ever . . . He has strengthened his hold on the Orange Free State and the Colonial Afrikanders [of the Cape Colony] continue to do obeisance to him . . .
>
> *Looking at the question from a purely S. African point of view*, I should be inclined to work up to a crisis, not indeed by looking about for causes of complaint or making a fuss about trifles, but by steadily and inflexibly pressing for the redress of substantial wrongs and injustices. It would not be difficult thus to work up an extremely strong *cumulative* case.

What Milner wanted was a more 'active' British policy towards Kruger, backed up by the threat of force. In the past – as during the 'drifts crisis' in 1895 – Kruger had shown a tendency to 'climb down' when threatened by force. Milner believed he might react in a similar manner now. But if he did not, Milner was quite prepared to follow the threat of force by recommending war, confident that it would be a short affair before Britain won.

Milner shared his views in a long private conversation with Percy FitzPatrick, who made contact with him during a holiday trip to Cape Town in February 1898. FitzPatrick had been disbarred from political activity in the Transvaal for three years for his part as secretary of the Reform Committee at the time of the Jameson Raid; his employers, Wernher, Beit & Co., had also warned him to steer clear of political activity and to stick to business matters. But FitzPatrick had an appetite for political intrigue and was keen to learn of Milner's views, making extensive notes of their conversation. According to FitzPatrick, Milner remarked at one point: 'There is only one possible settlement – war! It has got to come . . . The difficulty is in the occasion and not in the job itself, that is very easily done and I think nothing of the bogies and difficulties of settling South Africa afterwards. You will find a very different tone and temper when the centre of unrest is dealt with.'

Milner also went on the offensive against what he viewed as the 'disloyalty' of certain sections of the Cape Afrikaner population. After the governor of Natal, Henry Binns, sent a telegram to Kruger congratulating him on his election victory, Milner reprimanded him, propounding his own views:

> There has got to be a separation of the sheep from the goats in this sub-continent, by which I don't mean the English and the Dutch, but those who disapprove and are not afraid to show their disapproval of the present dishonest despotism in Pretoria, and those who either admire or truckle to it. There has been a great deal too much secret truckling and the time has come when we should, I think, quietly but firmly force the wobblers to show their colours and not expect us to recognize them as loyal citizens of a free British Community, as long as they give any countenance to men who trample on freedom and on everything British in a neighbouring state.

Two weeks later, opening a new railway branch line in Graaff Reinet, a predominantly Afrikaner town, Milner made clear his views in public for the first time in a speech exuding menace. His target was 'extremist' members of the Afrikaner Bond, who, he said, whilst enjoying the advantages of British citizenship were 'for ever adulating the Transvaal while casting suspicion on the actions and intentions of Her Majesty's Government'. The effect of this had been 'to encourage the Transvaal oligarchy in the present policy till it becomes intolerable and ends in war'. It was not the aggressiveness of Britain that had caused 'the spirit of unrest in South Africa', but the 'unprogressiveness, I will not say retrogressiveness, of the Government of the Transvaal'. What Cape Afrikaners needed to do was to encourage the Transvaal government to reform. 'That is the direction in which a peaceful way out of these inveterate troubles, which have now plagued this country for more than thirty years, is to be found.'

By casting aspersions on their loyalty, Milner outraged many Cape Afrikaners, moderates as well as 'extremists', and gave encouragement to the growing 'jingo' movement among English-speaking nationalists in the Cape Colony. Milner openly admitted, when forwarding his speech to the Colonial Office, that one of his intentions had been to give 'the British section of the community . . . something to cheer about'.

But there were more sinister implications contained within his speech. For by publicly raising the possibility of a war with the Transvaal, Milner was in effect challenging whites to choose which side they wanted to join in what he evidently believed was a forthcoming struggle between Boers and British for supremacy, thus intensifying all the mistrust between them that had arisen from the Jameson Raid. Milner henceforth was regarded by many Afrikaners as 'commander-in-chief' of the 'pro-British' party.

In London, Chamberlain and Selborne sought to damp down Milner's reckless talk of war. 'We must endure a great deal rather than provoke a conflict,' Chamberlain told Milner. 'A war with the Transvaal would certainly arouse antagonism in Cape Colony and leave behind it the most serious difficulties in the way of South African union.' Above all, 'A war with the Transvaal, unless upon the utmost and clearest provocation, would be extremely unpopular in this country'. He warned Milner that other difficulties that the British government currently faced – with France, Russia and Germany – were of a far more serious nature.

Selborne responded at some length, taking a similarly cautious approach:

Peace is undoubtedly the first interest to South Africa, but not peace at any price. Our object is the future combination of

South Africa under the aegis of the Union Jack, and I think we all feel that, if by the evolution of events this combination can be achieved without a rupture, or war, of any sort between the two white races in South Africa, it will have a more durable and valuable result than it would have if the same result were achieved by means of war.

Selborne explained the conditions 'under which we must manoeuvre' if war were to come:

It must command the practically unanimous consent of the British in South Africa – it must conquer the moral assent of as large a proportion as possible of our own Dutch in South Africa, and the action must be endorsed by the practically unanimous assent of public opinion at home.

Milner was thus required to bide his time.

You may rely on me not to do anything to render the situation more acute [he replied]. It is exceedingly difficult in view of the aggressive and insolent temper of the Transvaal to pass the time without a quarrel and yet without too conspicuously eating humble pie. Still, I hope we may manage, by a judicious combination of caution and bluff, to worry on without discredit until we are in a better position to 'round' upon them.

Yet, in further correspondence with Selborne, he again revealed his frustration, speaking of the inevitability of a clash:

Two wholly antagonistic systems – a medieval race oligarchy, and a modern industrial state, recognizing no difference of status between various white races – cannot permanently live side by side in what is after all *one country*.

He was similarly blunt in a letter to a friend on 20 April. 'If it had not been for all our troubles elsewhere, I should not have striven, as I did, for a peaceful issue. The Boer Govt. is too great a curse to all S. Africa to be allowed to exist, if we were not too busy to afford a considerable war, wh[ich] alone can pull it down.'

Until Milner's speech at Graaff Reinet in March 1898, few people outside the Colonial Office knew of his agenda. Afterwards, Kruger realised he had a warmonger on his hands.

35

NEMESIS

Despite his downfall as prime minister, Rhodes continued to haunt the political arena. His critics in the Cape had hoped that henceforth he might focus his energies on the distant reaches of Rhodesia. 'They have devised all sorts of retreats for me . . .' he said, 'a hermit's cell on the Zambesi.' But Rhodes still hankered after power in the Cape, ever confident of his ability to manipulate men and events there. 'I was told that my public life was at an end,' he said in a speech in Port Elizabeth in December 1896, 'but the first thing I told them was that it was only beginning.'

Having forfeited the support of the Afrikaner community Rhodes, with characteristic opportunism, sought to establish himself as the champion of English nationalists to provide him with another political base. In the aftermath of the Jameson Raid, as the two communities divided, a new pro-imperial movement gathered pace in the Cape. Formed as the South African League in May 1896, it aimed to strengthen British interests and supremacy in southern Africa and campaigned for a federation under the British flag. The League took root not only in the Cape but developed branches in Natal and the Transvaal, and was supported by a London-based affiliate, the South African Association.

In the Cape, the League's main objective was to create a 'British party' capable of challenging the Afrikaner Bond. In the Transvaal it proclaimed loyalty to the British Crown and aimed openly to unite the Transvaal in 'a federation of the States of South Africa under the British flag'. Whereas uitlander reformists in the old national union had previously looked to Kruger's government to redress their grievances, the League appealed directly for support from the British government. British officials, in turn, sought to use the League to advance British interests in the Transvaal but often found the more raucous jingoists among them difficult to restrain. 'In dealing with the South African League, I am placed in a very delicate position,' the British Agent in Pretoria, Conyngham Greene, wrote to Milner:

> The League is . . . the only body in Johannesburg that has a spark of real Imperial feeling, or a particle of any higher ambition than the worship of mammon . . . It therefore, in a certain sense, deserves sympathy, and looks to me for encouragement. On the other hand . . . it requires careful and constant watching. Up till now I have managed to keep some sort of control over the Executive, notwithstanding that they are, of course, being continually pressed by the mass of the League to resort to more vigorous action.

Taking advantage of the rising tide of jingoism, Rhodes plunged back into the hurly-burly of Cape politics, offering his services as leader of a parliamentary opposition group known as the Progressives.

'You want *me*. You can't do without me,' Rhodes said in an interview with the *Cape Times* on 9 March 1898. 'The feeling of the people – you may think it egoism, but these are the facts – is that somebody is wanted to fight a certain thing for them, and there is nobody else able and willing to fight it.' Addressing a meeting in Good Hope Hall in Cape Town on 12 March, he told the crowd: 'The best service I can render to the country is to return here and assist you in your big aims of closer union.'

Along with his change of allegiance, Rhodes adapted his policies to suit a different clientele. Whereas once he had favoured the interests of Afrikaner farmers, he now championed the interests of urban voters. He lent support to proposals for a radical redistribution of parliamentary seats to remove the rural weighting that benefited the Afrikaner Bond. With similar expediency, he tailored his slogan of 'equal rights for every white man south of the Zambesi', designed to promote the uitlander cause, to 'equal rights for every *civilised* man south of the Zambesi', hoping to attract the Coloured vote. Asked to explain himself further, he defined a civilised man as someone 'who has sufficient education to write his name – has some property or works'. His attacks on his former friends in the Afrikaner Bond became increasingly vindictive. He accused Hofmeyr of exercising 'terrorism' over Afrikaner farmers in the Cape and claimed that the Bond was bent on 'oligarchical domination'.

Campaigning in the 1898 general election six months later, Rhodes set out to regain power as prime minister, distributing vast sums to ensure a favourable result. On one occasion, he instructed his banker to pay £11,000 to a parliamentary colleague; on another occasion, a further £10,000. He spent lavishly, not only on financing the campaigns of his allies but on attempts to engineer the defeat of particular rivals like the liberal John Merriman. His former friend Olive Schreiner remarked: 'He has chosen . . . not only the worst men as his instruments, but to act on men always through the lowest side of their nature, to lead them through narrow self-interest instead of animating them with large enthusiasms.'

Indeed, Rhodes' own speeches consisted of little more than boasts of his past accomplishments and personal attacks on his political opponents. Still smarting from humiliation over the Jameson Raid, he accused Hofmeyr and the Afrikaner Bond of supporting 'everything rotten at Pretoria' and of 'simply spreading hatred as hard as they can spread it'. In fighting against the Bond, Rhodes maintained, he was attacking 'Krugerism'. Without providing any evidence he claimed that the Bond was in receipt of secret funds from the Transvaal government.

Standing against Rhodes was his former attorney-general, William Schreiner, Olive's brother. Schreiner launched the South Africa Party on a moderate platform, advocating friendly relations with neighbouring states including the Transvaal. Writing to Chamberlain,

Milner acknowledged that Schreiner was not hostile either to the British empire or to British interests. What Schreiner was opposed to, said Milner, was 'the personal domination of Mr Rhodes, to "the Chartered clique" and their corrupt methods of government, "the influence of Mammon in politics"'.

The 1898 election campaign was the most bitterly contested, corrupt and corrosive the Cape had ever known. When the results were declared in September, Schreiner's South Africa Party emerged with a majority of one and he went on to form a new government with the support of the Afrikaner Bond. It was an outcome that Milner found unsatisfactory. For while Schreiner declared himself to be 'a loyal colonist' owing allegiance to Queen Victoria, he also made it clear he was determined to 'respect and maintain the right of the free republics to work out their own destiny' and would oppose any move by Britain to go to war against them.

While enjoying his status as hero of the jingo crowd, Rhodes found little that appealed to him about the role of leader of the opposition, despite encouragement from Milner. Milner's first impressions of Rhodes were not favourable:

> He is too self-willed, too violent, too sanguine, and always in too great a hurry. He is just the same man as he always was, undaunted and unbroken by his former failure, but also untaught by it . . . Men are ruled by their foibles, and Rhodes's foible is *size*.

When Rhodes tried to manoeuvre himself into office after narrowly losing the 1898 election, Milner complained that it was 'just the Raid over again'. 'I mean,' he wrote, 'it is the same attempt to gain prematurely by violent and unscrupulous means what you could get honestly and without violence, if you would only *wait and work for it*.' Nevertheless, Rhodes and Milner managed to establish a cordial relationship, both of them wedded to the cause of empire.

In parliament, however, Rhodes found himself constantly taunted by critics of the Raid. 'You deceived the Dutch people,' a government minister, Jacobus Sauer, jeered. 'You deceived others who trusted you, with whom you had supped.'

He was, moreover, increasingly preoccupied with his deteriorating health. A series of accidents had taken its toll. A riding accident on the Cape flats in 1891 had left him unconscious for a whole day, with a broken collar-bone. The following year, when his cart overturned on a mountain road, he was tossed out and badly bruised. In 1894, riding near Kokstad, he had another 'nasty fall'. In 1895, he endured a long bout of influenza, combined with malaria. The cardiovascular disease that eventually killed him also began to have an effect. He sometimes had difficulty in breathing. An 1896 photograph showed him with blotchy skin. After years of heavy eating, drinking and smoking, he had become a portly, ponderous figure. Visitors referred to his 'enormous bulk'. From the mid-1890s, though still in his forties, he appeared to age rapidly.

Rhodes was often troubled by premonitions of an early death. It prompted him to write a series of wills with grandiose notions intended to ensure his personal immortality. In his first will, drawn up in 1877 while he was a student at Oxford, he instructed his executors to establish a secret society with the aim of extending British rule throughout the world, restoring Anglo-Saxon unity and creating 'a power so great as to render wars impossible'. His next four wills – in 1882, 1888, 1891 and 1892 – followed much the same theme; in a covering letter to his 1888 will, he suggested to Lord Rothschild that he should use the constitution of the Jesuits as a template for a secret society, inserting 'English Empire' in place of 'Roman Catholic Religion'.

In 1899, at the age of forty-five, sensing he had not long to live, he drew up his seventh and final will, refining his previous 'great idea' into something more practical. He made bequests to members of his family and to his Oxford college, Oriel; and he directed that Groote Schuur should be used as the official residence for future prime ministers of a federal South Africa. But his main 'great idea' focused on the education of young colonists. He gave instructions for scholarships to be awarded to suitable colonial candidates to study at Oxford, stipulating the qualifications they needed. In the first place, only men were eligible. Discussing other necessary qualifications with W. T. Stead in London, Rhodes envisaged a points system:

> You know I am all against letting the scholarships merely to people who swot over books, who have spent all their time over Latin and Greek. But you must allow for that element which I call 'smug', and which means scholarship. That is to stand for four-tenths. Then there is 'brutality' which stands for two-tenths. Then there is tact and leadership, again two-tenths, and then there is 'unctuous rectitude', two-tenths. That makes up the whole. You see how it works.

In the terminology he finally used, Rhodes instructed points to be awarded for: literary and scholastic attainments; success in 'manly outdoor sports'; 'qualities of manhood', including devotion to duty, protection of the weak, and unselfishness; and 'moral force of character'. He listed fifteen colonies from which sixty scholars from the British Empire were to be drawn; and he added a further ninety-six scholarships for students from the United States. After meeting Kaiser Wilhelm in 1899, Rhodes allocated fifteen scholarships to German students.

Despite his ailments, Rhodes threw himself energetically into an array of projects ranging from railway and telegraph schemes to afforestation and irrigation projects. He devoted much effort to establishing fruit farms, instructing a young English horticulturalist, Harry Pickstone, to buy up the 'whole Drakenstein Valley' in the western Cape. Aghast, Pickstone replied that it would cost 'a million'. He was nevertheless told to proceed and went on to acquire twenty-nine properties. Rhodes also set aside part of his Cape Town estate for the site of a university. He rebuilt Groote Schuur after it was badly damaged by fire. He also built a Cape Dutch cottage in the grounds of Groote Schuur – the Woolsack – for the use of poets and artists, hoping they would be inspired by the grandeur of their surroundings. Rudyard Kipling, the laureate of empire, made it his home for several months each year, writing some of his *Just So Stories* there – 'How the Leopard Got its Spots' and 'The Elephant's

Child'. It was on an expedition Rhodes arranged for him that Kipling came across 'the great grey-green, greasy Limpopo River, all set about with fever-trees' which he subsequently used as a location to explain how the elephant acquired its trunk.

Having spent a lifetime avoiding entanglements with women, Rhodes was caught up in 1899 in a fateful encounter. Princess Catherine Radziwill was a vivacious, witty and talented socialite, fluent in five languages, a familiar figure at one time in the salons of Berlin and St Petersburg. She was also a fabricator and fantasist, addicted to political intrigue and gossip. The daughter of a Polish count, she had married a Polish prince at the age of fifteen and produced five children, but, estranged from her husband, she had since chosen the life of a journalist, working in Paris and London, where she was introduced to W. T. Stead, Rhodes' friend and admirer.

Though he had difficulty in recalling the occasion, Rhodes had first met Princess Radziwill at a dinner party at the London home of Moberley Bell, manager of *The Times*, in 1896. Three years later, when Rhodes was making another visit to London, she wrote to him, purportedly to ask for his advice on investment. Rhodes replied, in rather abrupt terms, that he considered it dangerous to advise friends on money matters but nevertheless suggested she might like to subscribe to Mashonaland Railway debentures.

Radziwill then arranged to book a passage to Cape Town in July on the same ship taking Rhodes back home, contriving on the first night to sit at his table in the dining salon and taking her place there for the rest of the eighteen-day journey. Rhodes at first found her an engaging companion. At the age of forty-one, slim and elegant, her early beauty had begun to fade, but she remained highly attractive. 'She was a bright and versatile conversationalist,' recalled Philip Jourdan, his secretary. 'She appeared to know everyone, and kept us all amused during the whole voyage.' But Jourdan also remembered an incident that left Rhodes with an 'absolutely abject look of helplessness on his face'. While sitting beside Rhodes on the main deck, the Princess suddenly fell into his lap in an apparent faint. From then on, according to Jourdan, Rhodes steered clear of the main deck as much as he could.

In Cape Town, she stayed at the fashionable, newly opened Mount Nelson Hotel, running up huge bills. Having acquired a standing invitation to dine at Groote Schuur, she became a regular guest, insinuating herself into Rhodes' ménage and dropping hints that Rhodes intended to marry her. Rhodes soon found her company tiresome and tried to avoid her, telling his friend James McDonald one morning: 'On no account leave me alone with her. Never mind what she may say to you or how she may look at you. You must put up with it.'

But Princess Radziwill was not so easily spurned. And Rhodes came to rue the day he had allowed her to infiltrate into his private world.

36

THE GREAT GAME

Following his election victory in 1898, Kruger sought to give his administration a more modern character, appointing two Afrikaners from outside the Transvaal to key positions. To replace Leyds as state secretary, he chose Frank Reitz, a Cape-born, British-trained barrister, who had served first as chief justice of the Orange Free State then as its president for six years. His sister Fanny was married to the politician William Schreiner, shortly to become prime minister of the Cape Colony. Like Kruger, Reitz had fathered a large family: seven sons and one daughter by his first wife and six sons and one daughter by his second. He was also as committed as Kruger to protecting republican independence.

Kruger's other appointment was more remarkable. As state attorney, he chose Jan Smuts, a 28-year-old lawyer who had graduated from Cambridge University with a string of prizes and a double first in law. Born on a farm in the wheat-growing area of Malmesbury in the western Cape, Smuts had once admired Rhodes, when he was prime minister, for his efforts to promote a concord between the Boers and the British in the Cape Colony, but like many other Cape Afrikaners, he had been disillusioned by the Jameson Raid. It had served, he said, as an 'electric shock' to Afrikanerdom. In 1897, he set up a law practice in Johannesburg, concentrating on professional work but keeping a close watch on political developments.

Like Reitz, Smuts was a committed republican. Republicanism, he said in an article in 1897, was a grand cause around the world. 'Nowhere in the world has it such a chance as in South Africa . . . its day is coming and may be nearer than many think . . . The old ship of state is at last leaving her moorings, but it is the wind of republicanism and not of imperialism that is speeding her along.' The trend of events favoured the republican cause.

> Already the political centre of gravity in South Africa has followed the commercial centre of gravity and shifted from Cape Town to the republican capital. The Colonies will gradually have to accustom their pride and readjust their economic and political relations so as to fall in with the new disposal of political forces in South Africa . . . The Dutch and even the English in the Colonies will come to look more and more to the Transvaal for material help and support. The Union Jack – which has been in South Africa, not a symbol of peace and goodwill, but of blood, force and aggression – will more and more be relegated to that limbo of innocuous fads in which 'imperial federation' and similar entities and nonentities flourish.

He warned Britain against adopting a policy based on the use of force and intimidation. 'The British Empire cannot be kept together by force and armaments.' The 'vigorous' policy Britain was pursuing was already having the effect of drawing the two republics of the Transvaal and the Orange Free State closer together against 'a common danger', propelling them 'on the road to a greater federal republic'. Moreover, it was affecting the attitude of the wider Afrikaner community. Afrikaner loyalty to Britain was fragile. It owed nothing to 'a bloodrelationship nor to long political habits of thought and life nor to an overwhelming feeling of gratitude'. It rested on a conviction about British rule being fair and just and a force for good that could easily 'decay and shrivel up'. Any shift in British policy 'intended to substitute for local self-government in South Africa an increased exercise of imperial authority from Downing Street is bound to miscarry fatally'. By promoting 'war policies' and 'Jingoistic movements', Britain would merely stiffen Afrikaner resistance:

> It is simply the law of action and reaction: but who knows whether such insignificant Jingoistic matches, primarily intended to inflame Jingo-minds, may not set fire to the Imperial stack in South Africa? . . . To my mind, the die is already cast in the [Cape] Colony; the Dutch are absolutely committed to the support of the [Transvaal] Republic . . . and should an ambitious Colonial Minister choose to bring his 'vigorous' policy into operation in South Africa the entire South Africa will be speedily involved in a final conflagration.

Chamberlain, with his 'vigorous' policy, he argued, was 'a more serious obstruction to progress than any other force in South Africa'. He dismissed as bogus Chamberlain's claim that Britain had the right to exercise 'suzerainty' over the Transvaal by virtue of the 1884 London Convention; it had no basis in international law, he said. As for the grievances of the uitlanders, some were legitimate, but most were exaggerated. 'I think that if the franchise were offered them tomorrow not ten per cent would accept it.' But in any case, there could be no redress of grievances so long as Chamberlain was 'flaunting war in the face of republican South Africa'.

To enable Smuts to serve as state attorney, Kruger enrolled him as a 'second-class' burgher. Smuts soon found himself amidst a swirl of intrigue and complained of being surrounded 'by political and official enemies, by liquor syndicates, scheming concessionaires and powerful evildoers in high places'. But he quickly made his mark, tackling corruption and malpractice in the police force and racketeering in liquor sales, prostitution and counterfeit money. It was, he said, like 'clearing out the Augean Stable'. He became an indispensable member of Kruger's team, responsible for drafting virtually all new legislation as well as providing legal advice.

Smuts also had to contend with the growing groundswell of uitlander agitation against Kruger's regime. The agitation was led by members of the South African League, aided and abetted by British officials in Cape Town and Pretoria who used it as a means of trying to bring about British intervention in the internal affairs of the Transvaal.

In December 1898, the death of a British uitlander, Tom Edgar, at the hands of the Transvaal police provided the trigger for mass uitlander protest. A boilermaker from Lancashire, Edgar had been making his way home in Johannesburg on the Sunday before Christmas when he was involved in a drunken brawl and knocked a man unconscious. Under the impression the man was dead, neighbours summoned the police. Four Boer policemen arrived outside Edgar's house and called on him to open the door. When he failed to respond, one of them, Barend Jones, forced entry without a warrant. When Edgar attacked him with an iron-shod stick, Jones shot him dead. By Johannesburg standards, this was a routine incident.

Jones was promptly arrested and charged with murder. The public prosecutor, however, reduced the charge to culpable homicide and released Jones on bail. Members of the South African League immediately began organising a public protest. When a British official in Pretoria, Edmund Fraser, issued his own protest, Smuts agreed to order the re-arrest of Jones and reinstate the charge of murder.

The South African League, however, was determined to carry on with the protest. It placed notices in the local press and distributed leaflets calling on British subjects to assemble in front of the British consulate to sign a petition to Queen Victoria. It then sent the text of the petition for publication in advance to the local press and to newspapers in Britain. On Christmas Eve, a crowd of some 5,000 uitlanders gathered outside the consulate to demonstrate their support. The petition was read out from the consulate balcony by a League official and handed to the British vice-consul who undertook to deliver it to 'the proper quarters'.

The thrust of the petition was that for years British subjects on the Rand had suffered 'innumerable acts of petty tyranny at the hands of the police', yet had no recourse to an independent judiciary; nor did they have a voice in the government. They therefore sought 'the extension of Your Majesty's protection to the lives, liberties, and property of your loyal subjects here, and such other steps as may be necessary to terminate the existing intolerable state of affairs'.

The Transvaal authorities reacted by arresting two League officials for helping to organise an unauthorised public meeting, prompting further protests – in the Cape as well as Johannesburg. A huge meeting in Johannesburg on 14 January 1899 ended in clashes between British uitlanders and Boer hecklers. The League subsequently accused the Transvaal government of instigating the disorder.

Because Milner was on leave in England at the time, the matter was handled by the acting high commissioner, General Sir William Butler, the commander of British forces in southern Africa. Unlike Milner, Butler had no liking for the jingo crowd. He regarded the uitlanders as troublemakers and the South African League as 'an agency of disquiet'. In his autobiography, he claimed that Johannesburg's residents were 'probably the most corrupt, immoral and untruthful assemblage of human beings in the world' and quoted a remark made by Merriman describing Johannesburg as 'Monte Carlo superimposed on Sodom and Gomorrah'. The Edgar furore, he told Chamberlain, was a 'prepared business', worked up by the League to try to draw the British government into confrontation with Kruger. He resented the way the League had used the press to try to stir up a crisis with the intention of 'forcing our hands by newspaper publicity'. What was needed was not 'a surgical operation' but an effort at compromise and conciliation. Accordingly, he refused to forward the petition to London.

Uitlander grievances over the Edgar affair were inflamed again when the charge against Jones was reduced once more to manslaughter. At his trial, a 25-year-old judge, whose father was a member of Kruger's executive council, made a long rambling summary of the case during which he commended the police for doing their duty 'under difficult circumstances' and virtually directed the jury to acquit him. Jones was duly acquitted.

Milner spent much of his ten weeks' leave in England, lobbying for a more 'vigorous' policy towards the Transvaal. He wanted, he said, to interview '*all* the leading politicians and pressmen . . . and to stamp on rose-coloured illusions about S. Africa'. 'You may think me a bore,' he told Lord Rosebery, a Liberal Imperialist, 'but I should like to tell you some things about that little corner of the imperial chess-board I am especially concerned with.' Milner dwelt on the dangers of 'Krugerism', emphasising that time was running out. He also met several of the Randlords, including Alfred Beit and Julius Wernher, and sought to enlist their support. To Milner, it was all part of 'winning the great game between ourselves and the Transvaal for the mastery in South Africa'.

At the Colonial Office, however, Milner found Chamberlain and his officials still committed to a 'no-war' policy. The aim of the government, he was told, was 'to keep the peace with Kruger unless he were very outrageous'. In a candid letter to a member of his staff in Cape Town, Milner wrote:

> Joe [Chamberlain] may be led but he can't be driven. I go on pegging mail after mail, month after month, and I think it tells; but if I were *once* to make him think that I am trying to rush him, he would see me to the devil and we might as well all shut up. I put everything in the way most likely to get him to take our view of *himself*. Whether he takes it, or rather when he takes it, depends on the amount of external pressure and excitement corresponding to our prodding of him from within. If only the Uitlanders stand firm on the formula 'no rest without reform' and can stand on it not 6 days, but 6 weeks, or six months, we shall do the trick yet my boy. And by the soul of St. Jingo they get a fair bucking up from us all one way or another.

Not only was Chamberlain reluctant to be bounced into a more aggressive stance, but Milner detected no public appetite for confrontation with Kruger. By the time he left England, he had decided different tactics were needed. There was no point in trying to 'force' his views upon others, he told Selborne on his departure in January

1899. He would have to rely instead on his own actions and prepare the public for a gradual 'awakening' of the threat Kruger posed.

> If I can advance matters by my own actions, as I still hope I may be able to do, I believe that I shall have support when the time comes. And if I can't get things 'forrader' locally, I should not get support whatever I said. I quite realise that public opinion is dormant on the subject, though it would take, I believe, but little to wake it up in a fashion that would astonish us all. My great fear is lest the waking up should come suddenly, perhaps irrationally, over some 'incident', which may turn out more or less hollow, instead of gradually in support of policy, carry conviction to all but the absolutely biased.

Nevertheless, Milner left England on 28 January 'well pleased with the result' of his visit. Furthermore, on the international stage, by the end of 1898 Britain's room for manoeuvre had improved considerably. Many of the constraints that had previously preoccupied Chamberlain had been resolved. General Kitchener had completed his conquest of the Sudan. The French had been faced down at Fashoda – and Germany had agreed to stop meddling in the Transvaal. Following a rapprochement with Britain, Germany not only advised Kruger to implement reforms, it warned him against risking war with Britain and made it clear that, if war came, Germany would not interfere. Kruger was thus left without a European ally.

Amidst rising tension, Smuts sought to keep up a reform agenda. He struck up an amiable relationship with Percy FitzPatrick, Wernher, Beit's representative, discussing with him ways in which the mining industry and the Transvaal government might resolve their differences. By 1899, as a result of amalgamations, the shape of the mining industry had changed significantly. Whereas in 1888, there had been forty-four separate mining companies, there were now only nine major finance houses controlling 114 out of the 124 Main Reef outcrop and deep-level companies. Although the nine had many common interests, they had differing views about the merits of political involvement. Since the Jameson Raid, Rhodes' firm, Consolidated Gold Fields, had been determined to avoid political entanglements and sought a cordial relationship with Kruger's government. A Gold Fields employee who became prominently active in the South African League was sacked. Its London-based chairman, David Harris, told Chamberlain in November 1898: 'I may say that we are by no means ill disposed towards Kruger. We wish he could establish an honest executive . . . but we don't think . . . that we are working under a crushing tyranny.' Wernher, Beit & Co., the premier mining house, was inclined to play a more active role. Percy FitzPatrick, in particular, believed initially that much could be gained. In a despatch to Beit, he described Smuts as 'very fair, when he has the facts, very willing and very bright, but he has a heartbreaking task'.

Smuts and FitzPatrick soon encountered stumbling blocks, however. FitzPatrick, a colonial maverick with his own political agenda, was intent on linking the mining industry's complaints to a wider political settlement and wanted the British government to be involved. Smuts, while recognising the need to resolve the *bewaarplaatsen* issue and end the dynamite monopoly, dismissed any notion of British involvement in the Transvaal's affairs as 'inconsistent with the dignity of an independent state'.

FitzPatrick, according to his own account, was exasperated by Smuts' apparent reluctance to see 'the desperate seriousness of the position', and 'let himself go'.

'Do you realize what it's leading to,' he demanded, 'and what must inevitably happen if we don't make a supreme effort to get a settlement; do you realize that it means war?'

'Yes, I realize it, I think the position is very threatening,' replied Smuts and walked towards FitzPatrick, making a wide sweep of his arms and bringing his hands together. 'I seem to see two great thunderclouds approaching, and when they meet there will come the crash.'

'And do you know what such a war means?' FitzPatrick continued. 'It will extend from the Zambesi to the ocean. It will divide the races and the States; it will split us from one end to the other; communities divided, families divided, father against son, brother against brother; God alone knows where the thing will end. It will mean utter ruin to South Africa; and you will risk all this for a little thing which is only vanity. Inconsistent with your dignity, that's all it is!'

'I know what it means,' Smuts replied calmly.

Smuts' calmness goaded Fitzpatrick further. 'Your dignity! Your independence! Good God, you know England, you were educated in England: you know what the Empire means; in six months you will have no dignity left; you will have no independence; no State; nothing! What kind of madness is this!!'

'Yes, I know England; better than perhaps you think,' said Smuts. 'Not in six months, my friend, not in six years; you may take the cities and the mines, for we would not meet you there, but for six or seven years we shall be able to hold out in the mountains, and long before that there will be a change of opinion in England. Other things will crop up, they will become tired and lose interest.'

While these private exchanges were under way, Kruger made clear that his own views about the dynamite monopoly remained unchanged: it represented a cornerstone of the Transvaal's independence, he said. Instead of reform, he proposed to ask the Volksraad to extend the monopoly for a further fifteen years.

When Milner learned of the matter, he saw an opportunity of working it up 'into a general row'. Hitherto, he had regarded the dynamite issue as 'a capitalists' issue, pure and simple', best left alone. Now he recommended to Chamberlain that it could be used as a 'peg to hang our remonstrance on'. Chamberlain duly authorised a despatch to Pretoria arguing that the dynamite monopoly was in breach of the London Convention. He also suggested to a British official in Pretoria, Edmund Fraser, that he should let mining companies know that the British government was taking up the dynamite issue and encourage them to do the same. Accordingly, at its annual general meeting in February, the Chamber of Mines passed a resolution condemning the dynamite monopoly, together with Kruger's plan to extend its term. Representatives of the major mining companies put forward their own proposal to Kruger's government to buy out the dynamite monopoly for £600,000. Kruger rejected both the British protest and the buy-out offer but countered with a hint that there might be room for negotiations between the government and the mining companies.

Authorised by Kruger, Smuts and Reitz opened confidential talks in March with the mining companies proposing a general settlement that came to be known as the 'Great Deal'. The aim, the mining companies were told, was to find a way to reach 'peace' between the government and 'the whole uitlander population'. The mining industry was asked: to acquiesce in the continuation of the dynamite monopoly; to discourage press agitation against the government; and to dissociate itself from the South African League. In return, the government was prepared to settle the *bewaarplaatsen* issue on terms favourable to the mining industry; to appoint a qualified financial adviser to oversee the financial administration of the state, including taxation; and to support changes to the franchise law.

In a series of public speeches, Kruger conceded that changes were needed to accommodate 'aliens' and 'strangers'. He proposed that the period of time required before newcomers could gain full burgher rights should be reduced from fourteen years' residence to nine. But he also dwelt at length on the question of loyalty. The distinction he wished to draw, he said, was not between nationalities but between those who were loyal to the state and those who were not:

> We don't allow bigamy in this country. When I speak of bigamy, I refer to the Government of this country and the Government of England and other countries. If you want to live here, first divorce your other wife – then you can marry us. This is naturalisation. No man can serve two masters, and if he has two wives he will love one and despise the other. Therefore, if a man wants to make this country his home, let him first become naturalised. If he doesn't, let him remain a stranger. He will still be treated with all hospitality – provided he obeys the law – protected, helped to make money, to live comfortably, and to come and go as he pleased.

The Great Deal proposals received a mixed reception. There was a gulf of distrust separating the two sides. Percy FitzPatrick, who became a central figure in the negotiations, regarded the proposals as a device to entrench the dynamite monopoly in exchange for relatively minor concessions, and an attempt to divide the uitlander community by winning over the mining magnates while isolating the South African League. Though FitzPatrick believed that Smuts' efforts were genuine, he doubted Kruger's good faith and was convinced that the Volksraad would never accept the proposals. He fully expected the negotiations to fail. Nevertheless, he considered they were worth pursuing 'in order to secure for future use a number of witnesses and plenty of evidence to demonstrate that the Govt. admit impossibility of position and propose radical change'. FitzPatrick's primary objective was to draw the British government into any final settlement. Without the threat of British intervention, he believed, Kruger would never agree to reform. In London, both Wernher and Beit took a similarly sceptical view of Kruger's intentions. But Consolidated Gold Fields was more positive. When presented with the terms of the deal, David Harris said he was inclined to accept it.

Chamberlain's response was also positive. 'Whether this offer is genuine or not I regard it as the most important move made since the Raid. It should certainly be treated as serious.' He was, however, dismissive of the terms of the deal. When Harris told him on 14 March that he was prepared to accept the deal unless he objected, Chamberlain's reply was blunt: 'I said that Her Majesty's Government would not interfere but that public opinion would probably say that the Financiers had sold their cause and their compatriots – and sold them cheap and would not in the long run get even the price they had accepted. It was however their business not ours . . .'

In Cape Town, Milner too feared the possibility of a 'sell-out'. He instructed Conyngham Greene to keep in close touch with the uitlanders:

> If they ask for our advice, we ought not to refuse to give it. The more they rely on us the better, as, while they look to us, they will neither do anything rash, nor come to terms with the

[Transvaal] Government behind our backs which, if we *disinterest ourselves*, is always a danger.

On 16 March, mining magnates and their representatives met in London to sort out a common position. Alfred Beit attended on behalf of Wernher, Beit & Co. J. B. Robinson was there, along with George Farrar and three representatives from Gold Fields. In the detailed response the mining companies subsequently gave the government, they expressed their total opposition to the granting of monopolies and concessions, but added that, in order to reach a general settlement, they might be willing to make 'a great monetary sacrifice' over the dynamite concession, which burdened them with an unnecessary extra cost of £600,000 per annum, provided that it was agreed that the concession was not extended beyond its current contract and that the price would be lowered. They also tied themselves firmly to uitlander demands over the franchise. Though only a small minority of uitlanders were thought to be willing to exchange their existing citizenship for that of the Transvaal, the magnates declared that the franchise was 'the vital point upon which a permanent and peaceful settlement must hinge'. An accompanying memorandum proposed a five years' retrospective franchise for the uitlanders and a redistribution of seats in the Volksraad. It was said to represent the views of 'a very large and influential section' of the uitlander community. However, the mining companies pointed out that they were not qualified to speak on behalf of the uitlander community. The uitlanders themselves needed to be consulted.

FitzPatrick added his own flourish. Addressing a group of twenty-four prominent Rand leaders at the Rand Club in Johannesburg, he emphasised that the mining industry had no intention of coming to a settlement on its own account at the expense of the rest of the uitlander population, and further stressed the need for the British government to be involved – 'by hook or by crook'. But he also expressed his doubts about the whole exercise, describing it as 'a spoof' designed to sow dissension among uitlanders. He finished on a belligerent note: the surge of industrialisation and immigration in the Transvaal, he said, would eventually overwhelm Kruger and his burghers. 'It means the absolute wiping out of these people. We have got to win and we will win as sure as God is above us.'

Chamberlain's attitude too became increasingly aggressive. In a speech to the House of Commons on 20 March, he claimed that in the past Kruger 'had kept no promise with regard to the uitlanders and redressed no grievance'. His current promises of reform were 'entirely illusory'. In what was a clear invitation to the uitlander community to respond, he explained that the British government had not so far attempted to intervene on their behalf because they had not yet asked the government to do so. He therefore did not feel 'at the moment that any case has arisen which would justify me in taking the very strong action'.

The uitlanders wasted no time. Orchestrated by the British Agent in Pretoria, Conyngham Greene, the South African League produced a second petition to the Queen, supported by 21,684 signatures, listing their grievances and complaining that Kruger's government had failed to implement its promises of reform:

> Your Majesty's subjects [said the petition] are still deprived of all political rights, they are denied any voice in the government . . . Maladministration and peculation of public monies go hand in hand, without any vigorous measures being adopted to put a stop to the scandal. The education of Uitlander children is made subject to impossible conditions. The police afford no adequate protection to the lives and property of the inhabitants of Johannesburg; they are rather a source of danger to the peace and safety of the Uitlander population.

The petition was delivered to Conyngham Greene in Pretoria on 24 March, reached Milner in Cape Town on 27 March and was forwarded to the British government on 28 March. Details were published in the Johannesburg *Star* and the London *Times*.

Coming at the same time as the mining companies' stand in defence of uitlander rights, the petition provided Chamberlain with the excuse he needed to intervene. He was, however, in two minds as to how to respond. 'If we ignore altogether the prayer of the petitioners,' he said in a memorandum to the cabinet, 'it is certain that British influence will be severely shaken. If we send an ultimatum to Kruger, it is possible, and in my opinion probable, that we shall get an offensive reply, and we shall then have to go to war, or to accept a humiliating check.'

Working in tandem, Milner and FitzPatrick decided on their own course of action. Now that Chamberlain had been given an opportunity to intervene in the Transvaal, neither saw any merit in continuing with the Great Deal negotiations. At the behest of the Transvaal government, the negotiations had been conducted in strict secrecy. At a meeting in Cape Town on 31 March, Milner urged FitzPatrick to find a way of getting details of the negotiations, including the government's offer and the mining companies' reply, into the open. Publication in the press might wreck the negotiations, but it would reveal that the mining companies were united behind the uitlander cause.

Reluctant to expose himself to the danger of leaking the documents, FitzPatrick arranged for a journalist to bribe a Transvaal government official to obtain copies, providing him with the necessary funds. 'You do the work, but there's no reason why you should pay the expenses when it's our cause too.' The documents were published in the London *Times* on 3 April, and three days later in the *Cape Times* and in other local newspapers.

Smuts and Reitz were furious at this betrayal of trust. 'Our earnest attempt to promote a lasting reconciliation has been a disastrous failure,' wrote Smuts. 'Conditions are worse here today than they have been for fifteen years – thanks to our efforts.'

Well pleased with the result, Milner prepared for the next phase of his plan of action: a press campaign. As a former journalist, he had a clear understanding of how the press could be used to manipulate public opinion. In Cape Town, he was in regular contact with the editor of *The Cape Times*, Edmund Garrett, an English journalist of similar mind. During his recent visit to London he had played an influential role in recruiting William Monypenny of *The Times* as the new editor of *The Star*, the leading English-language newspaper on the Rand; it was owned by the Argus group belonging to Wernher,

Beit & Co. Arriving in Johannesburg in March, Monypenny performed a dual role, acting as a correspondent for the London *Times* as well as editing *The Star*. Milner gained another ally in March with the launch of a new uitlander newspaper, *The Transvaal Leader*, also financed by Wernher, Beit & Co. Milner praised Wernher and Beit for their commitment to the uitlander cause, describing them as 'a new and astonishing kind of millionaire: men with some higher conception then the piling up of money'.

As well as using the press in southern Africa, Milner carried his press campaign to England. Outlining his plan to FitzPatrick, he asked for FitzPatrick's help, explaining that he himself could not risk direct involvement. 'The biggest real danger I have is that Chamberlain might get the idea I want to rush him.' If that happened, 'the whole business would be dashed and done for'. Chamberlain, he said, would 'see me damned before he moved a finger'. He therefore looked to FitzPatrick 'to do the press' and 'get before the House [of Commons] and the public the mass of damning evidence that was in the petitions . . . You must *not* allow the petitions to fizzle.'

As well as his covert manipulation of the press, Milner kept up a stream of instructions and advice to British officials in the field and to the Colonial Office in London. In a despatch to Conyngham Greene in Pretoria on 15 April, he wrote:

> The great point seems to be (1) to keep the future course of negotiations public and (2) to force the [Transvaal] Govt. into some definite position – yes or no – about the franchise . . . The other thing is to get the Uitlanders – as they cannot have a mass meeting – to express in any way they can – by a series of smaller meetings along the Rand, if they can be organized – their approval of the scheme of reforms outlined in the memorandum. This would have a double effect. It would, so to speak, *canonize* that scheme as the Uitlanders' recognized programme, their Petition of Rights – at present it is merely the opinion of a few individuals and it would keep up English interest and *rub the real issue well into the public mind*.

In a despatch to Chamberlain on 5 April, he urged him to put the franchise issue at the centre of his strategy. 'Political reform goes to the root of individual grievances,' he wrote, 'and moreover it may become, if it is not today, a splendid battle cry, exciting sympathy throughout the Empire and even in some foreign countries.' Writing to Selborne on the following day, he suggested the government should publish a 'Blue Book' setting out in detail the background to the uit-lander crisis so that it could 'get rubbed into the public mind' – 'I wish to goodness some of my vitriol could get in too. But I am afraid to put too much vitriol into public despatches lest they should ever see the light of day.'

To Milner's delight, Chamberlain eventually decided to compile a 'Blue Book' and asked Milner for a contribution. Milner let fly with relish:

> The spectacle of thousands of British subjects kept permanently in the position of helots [the slaves of ancient Greece] . . . calling vainly to Her Majesty's Government for redress, does steadily undermine the influence and reputation of Great Britain and the respect for the British Government within the Queen's dominions.

He claimed that the pro-Boer press openly preached 'the doctrine of a Republic embracing all South Africa' and supported it by 'menacing references to the armaments of the Transvaal, its alliance with the Orange Free State, and the active sympathy which in case of war it would receive from a section of Her Majesty's subjects':

> I regret to say that this doctrine, supported as it is by a ceaseless stream of malignant lies about the intentions of the British Government, is producing a great effect upon a large number of our Dutch fellow colonists . . . I can see nothing which will put a stop to this mischievous propaganda but some striking proof of the intention of Her Majesty's Government not to be ousted from its position in South Africa. And the best proof alike of its power and its justice would be to obtain for the Uitlanders in the

Transvaal a fair share in the Government of the country which owes everything to their exertions.

The case for intervention, he concluded, was overwhelming.

In a further despatch to Chamberlain, sent on the eve of a cabinet meeting in May, Milner spoke of meetings of working men and ordinary uitlanders taking place up and down the Rand at which the franchise was being demanded after five years' residence. 'We should be making a serious, and perhaps irretrievable mistake, if we did not take the present opportunity of defiantly ranging ourselves on the side of the Uitlander Reformers in their struggle with the Transvaal Government.'

Milner said he realised that by intervening on behalf of the uitlanders, the British government risked war. 'The Boers will yield to nothing less than the fear of war, perhaps not even to that. But then this is a risk which, with the present rotten government in the Transvaal, we are running all the time . . . If we succeed we shall get rid of this nightmare for ever.'

When the British cabinet met on 9 May, with the words of Milner's 'helot' despatch ringing in their ears, they decided unanimously on intervention on the side of the uitlanders. In a letter to Queen Victoria, Lord Salisbury explained: 'We cannot abandon them without grave injustice – without endangering Your Majesty's authority in the whole of South Africa.'

Thus the grievances of the uitlanders became fatefully entwined with the question of preserving British supremacy in southern Africa. For Milner, it was a triumph that he hoped would hasten 'the great day of reckoning'.

37

THE DRUMBEAT FOR WAR

As talk of the possibility of war swirled around southern Africa, a group of Cape intermediaries strove assiduously to ward off the prospect. In April, the Cape's chief justice, Sir Henry de Villiers, travelled to Pretoria hoping to persuade Kruger to grant reforms and to broach the idea of a face-to-face meeting with Milner. The Cape's prime minister, William Schreiner, held talks with Milner, offering his good offices, and wrote to Smuts, making clear his support for franchise reform. The Afrikaner Bond leader, Jan Hofmeyr, urged Milner to meet Kruger on neutral ground in Bloemfontein. In May, De Villiers returned from Pretoria, reporting that Smuts and Reitz were willing 'to work for a liberal franchise' and were in favour of a summit meeting. In Bloemfontein, President Steyn duly offered to host the meeting.

Milner described the plan for a meeting as 'a good stroke of business on the part of the enemy'. It had already produced one effect, he said, 'that of mollifying the British press a bit and relaxing for the moment, unfortunately as I think, the *screw* upon the enemy'. He expected little to come of it. 'If I do go,' he told Conyngham Greene, 'it will be simply because the home Government do not wish to be accused of having refused any chance of arranging matters.' He was quick to make clear the demands he would make at the meeting: full

enfranchisement of the uitlanders after five years' residence; modification of the oath of allegiance; and at least seven seats at once for the
Rand in the Volksraad. He was confident that this time the British
government would intervene 'if Kruger does not grant large reforms'.
In a letter to the governor of Natal on 8 May, he remarked: 'Perhaps
it would be best if Kruger hardened his heart and the smash came.'
Britain, he said, should be prepared to fight rather than accept 'a piffling measure' of reform.

> The great thing now, in this intervening breathing space before
> the bomb bursts, is for us to stiffen the wobblers. I know per
> fectly well that as soon as it becomes evident that H.M.G. means
> business, we shall have the usual outcry . . . that there is nothing
> to fight about, that a race war would be too awful, etc. It is
> under cover of these bogeys that Kruger and Co. have kept up
> their game so long. *Once you convince the wobblers* . . . that the
> British Government is *resolute*, the whole force of the peace-at-
> any price party will be directed to getting the Transvaal to give
> in. Sir H. de Villiers is decidedly on that tack already, and with
> a little more pushing, Schreiner will follow suit.

In London, Chamberlain welcomed the idea of a meeting. It was
important, he said, to explore this option 'before exerting pressure in
any other way'. He told Milner: 'In view of the momentous consequences of an actual breach with the Transvaal, public opinion will
expect us to make every effort to avoid it.' He regretted, however, that
it would mean postponing publication of the Blue Book.

In Pretoria, Kruger was pessimistic about the outcome. According
to Smuts, 'The President thinks, so far as I can gauge his feeling, that
war is unavoidable or will soon become so – not because there is any
cause, but because the enemy is brazen enough not to wait for a
cause.'

Smuts himself was becoming increasingly belligerent. In a letter to
Hofmeyr on 10 May, he wrote:

> If England should venture into the ring without a formally good

excuse, her cause in South Africa would be finished. And then the sooner the better; as we for our part are quite prepared to meet her. Our people throughout South Africa must be baptized with the baptism of blood and fire before they can be admitted among the other great peoples of the world. Of the outcome I have no doubt. Either we shall be exterminated or we shall fight our way out; and when I think of the great fighting qualities that our people possess, I cannot see why we should be exterminated.

Hofmeyr was unimpressed by such bravado. 'Cherish no illusions about the Colony,' he replied on 15 May, 'you must not expect that Colonial Afrikaners will rush *en masse* to arms if hostilities break out – especially as most of them know nothing about the bearing of arms.'

The train carrying Kruger and his entourage steamed into Bloemfontein on 30 May 1899. During the journey across the winter landscape of the Orange Free State, Kruger had remained unusually taciturn. His oculist, Dr Guillaume Heymans, noticed that his eyes were noticeably swollen. Officials in the welcoming party on the platform at Bloemfontein commented on how much he had aged.

On their way from the railway station, Kruger cupped his ear to listen to Steyn's candid advice. 'Much will depend on your attitude,' Steyn told him. 'You *must* make concessions on the franchise issue, Your Honour. Franchise after a residence of fourteen years is in conflict with the first principles of a republican and democratic government. The Free State expects you to concede, and will give you full support should you do so. Should you not give in on this issue, you will lose all sympathy and all your friends.'

Kruger replied that he had come to resolve all the troubles he faced with Britain. 'I am prepared to do anything,' he replied, 'but they must not touch my independence. They must be reasonable in their demands as I have my people and my Volksraad to reckon with.'

Milner's train arrived later in the day. He stepped down briskly, an elegant figure dressed in a morning suit and grey top hat, outwardly polite and affable, but in reality, an imperial predator. In a letter to his wife, Smuts remarked: 'Milner is as sweet as honey,' but added, 'there is something in his very intelligent eyes that tells me that he is a very dangerous man' – 'more dangerous than Rhodes . . . a second Bartle Frere'.

The proceedings opened the next day in an oak-panelled chamber next to the railway station. At Milner's insistence, only he and Kruger were involved in the discussions. When Chamberlain suggested that Schreiner should be included – 'He wants peace and will try for a settlement' – Milner blocked the idea. He also refused to allow either Hofmeyr or Steyn to play a role. Everything was confined to a series of straight exchanges between Milner and Kruger. A venerated Free State politician, Abraham Fischer, sat between them, acting as interpreter. No agenda was agreed in advance.

Kruger wanted the discussions to cover a range of disputes. Milner's intention was to focus on a single issue: the franchise. Milner had no particular interest in the welfare of the uitlander population. Indeed, he was often disparaging about the merits of democracy. But he saw the franchise issue as the means to 'break the mould' of Transvaal politics, to wrest the Transvaal from Boer control. What he wanted was 'immediate and substantial' representation for the uitlanders. If Kruger rejected what appeared to be a reasonable demand, then the franchise issue could be used as a suitable *casus belli*.

From the outset, Milner took the initiative. The main cause of tension between Britain and the Transvaal, he said, was the Transvaal's refusal to grant adequate voting rights to uitlanders. If that issue could be settled, then it would bring about 'a better state of feeling all round' and enable other issues to be resolved. 'I do not want to swamp the old population,' he said, 'but it is perfectly possible to give the new population an immediate voice in the legislation, and yet to leave the old burghers in such a position that they cannot possibly be swamped.' He proposed that the full franchise should be given immediately to every foreigner who had been resident in the Transvaal for five years and that seven new constituencies should be established to accord them representation in the Volksraad.

Kruger replied that Milner's proposal would mean, in effect, handing over his country to foreigners. 'Our enfranchised burghers are probably about 30,000, and the newcomers may be from 60,000 to

70,000 and if we give them the franchise tomorrow we may as well give up the Republic.' It would be 'worse than annexation', he said, 'and the burghers would not agree to it'. He wanted to know what concessions he might gain in return that might help him appease his burghers. 'I must tell them that something has been given to me, if I give in to something.' But Milner dismissed this as a 'sort of Kaffir bargain'.

On the third day of their discussions, Kruger presented Milner with a 'complete Reform Bill', worked out in detail. Milner reported to London that he must have had it 'in his pocket all the time'. It provided for a sliding scale varying from two to seven years' residence for citizens applying for the full franchise. Uitlanders who had settled in the Transvaal before 1890 could obtain the franchise after two years; settlers of two or more years' standing after five; the rest, after seven years. Kruger also offered to create five new seats in the Volksraad for gold-mining districts.

Milner admitted in private that the deal on offer was a 'great advance'. Abraham Fischer commented that Kruger had conceded far more than anyone had expected. The gap between Kruger's proposals and Milner's demands was now relatively narrow: seven years for the franchise instead of five; five seats in the Volksraad against seven. But the offer nevertheless failed to meet Milner's objective of achieving an 'immediate' enfranchisement of a substantial number of uitlanders and Milner had no intention of negotiating over the matter. What he wanted was Kruger's capitulation. He raised a host of objections.

On Sunday, 4 June, Milner cabled to Chamberlain warning that although he had been 'studiously conciliatory', the conference seemed likely to fail. Chamberlain was swift to reply: 'I hope you will not break off hastily. Boers do not understand quick decisions but prefer to waste a lot of time over a bargain without coming to terms. I am by no means convinced that the President . . . has made his last offer, and you should be very patient and admit a good deal of haggling before you finally abandon the game.'

But Chamberlain's telegram arrived too late to prevent Milner from terminating the proceedings. Though Kruger was willing to continue discussions, Milner regarded them as a waste of time. 'My principal aim at the Conference,' he explained later to Chamberlain, 'was not to fight out the various points of difference between the Governments, but, by arriving at a settlement on the Uitlander question, which went to the root of many of those differences, to pave the way for the settlement of all.' But the only settlement Milner had in mind was a victory for British supremacy. As Kruger kept repeating in his last encounter with Milner on 5 June: 'It is our country you want.'

Even before the failure of the Bloemfontein conference, Milner was preparing for the next phase of his campaign. What was required, he told Selborne a fortnight before the conference opened, was a diplomatic offensive backed up by a show of military force. One week later, explaining in more detail what he had in mind, he proposed that an 'overwhelming' force – 10,000 men or more – should be sent out at once to Natal and that Laing's Nek on the Transvaal frontier should be occupied to frustrate a Boer attack. The defence of Kimberley and Ladysmith also needed to be organised. With this forward position assured, he wrote, 'we should have a means of pressure which would be irresistible':

> My view is that (1) absolute downright determination plus a large temporary increase of force will ensure a climb down. It is 20 to 1. And (2) that, if it didn't, and there was a fight, it would be better to fight now than 5 or 10 years hence when the Transvaal, unless the Uitlanders can be taken in, in considerable numbers, will be stronger and more hostile than ever.

Unless the right military precautions were taken '*before* the crash', the British might find themselves involved in 'not only a biggish war, but much civil dissension afterwards'.

Milner also began to agitate for the removal of General Butler as commander of British forces, describing him as 'a violent Krugerite'. 'He does not and cannot sympathise with my policy,' said Milner, and he had failed to realise 'the intense gravity of the situation'. For his part, Butler told the War Office in London that he believed that 'war would be the greatest calamity that ever occurred in South Africa'. He was soon obliged to resign.

Adding to the gathering storm, Chamberlain went ahead with publication of his Blue Book, detailing in 243 pages 'the complaints of British subjects' in the Transvaal and incorporating Milner's 'helot' despatch. Smuts was infuriated by Milner's overt hostility towards the Transvaal: 'The situation is being forced from the outside in order by an armed conflict to forestall or defeat the work of time,' he wrote in a letter to John Merriman. 'I have great hope that within a few years all just causes of complaint will have disappeared altogether and it fills me with savage indignation to think that the work of those who are spending their . . . lifeblood for South Africa is to be undone in a moment by academic nobodies who fancy themselves great imperial statesmen.'

With the help of intermediaries from the Cape and the Orange Free State – Hofmeyr, Schreiner, Steyn and Fischer – Smuts sought to persuade Kruger and his executive council that further concessions on the franchise would have to be made to secure a settlement. The outcome was that in July the Volksraad accepted a new franchise law similar to the 'Reform Bill' that Kruger had presented to Milner in Bloemfontein, but with some additional concessions. It provided for a seven-year retrospective franchise and six uitlander seats.

Schreiner, on behalf of the Cape government, declared the new franchise arrangement to be 'adequate, satisfactory, and such as should secure a peaceful settlement'. Chamberlain, too, was impressed, telling both Milner and the London *Times* on 18 July that he now saw an end to the crisis.

If Kruger has really given seven years' retrospective franchise [he told Milner] . . . I congratulate you on a great victory . . . No one would dream of fighting over two years in a qualification period. We ought to accept this as a basis for settlement and make the most of it. Kruger, we should assume, has conceded in principle what we asked for, viz. immediate substantial representation.

Milner was aghast at such euphoria. 'Very bad day indeed,' he wrote in his diary. 'Telegram from S of S [Secretary of State] this morning showing great change for worse in attitude of Government.' He regarded the new franchise arrangements as a sham designed to 'bamboozle' the British public. It was full of 'traps' and 'pitfalls'. Kruger's government, he insisted, could not be trusted. It would never agree to make changes that would put at risk Afrikaner control:

> No scheme adopted by [Transvaal] Government of its own accord will be calculated to carry out object we have in view [he told Chamberlain]. By one means or another administration will retain power to obstruct enfranchisement of obnoxious Uitlanders, whilst facilitating admission of its own friends or enfranchising them, though without regular qualification, under special cause. Arrangements as to new seats, as to registration, as to method of presidential election, all leave room for any amount of juggling to make measure a sham.

He suggested that a joint commission of inquiry should be set up to examine the franchise issue.

In London, Selborne was equally alarmed by Chamberlain's apparent readiness to settle for the new franchise and moved smartly to steer him towards Milner's position. 'There was a movement in a certain impulsive quarter to assume, even to pretend, that we had now secured all we wanted,' Selborne told Milner. 'We got over that and back on the old right tack in 24 hours.'

In the House of Commons on 20 July, Chamberlain was duly far more cautious about the merits of the new franchise law, pointing out some of the 'pitfalls' that Milner had identified. Encouraged by Milner, Chamberlain also began to widen the scope of British demands. Milner argued that Kruger's manoeuvres over the franchise issue were tantamount to a challenge to British supremacy. What was at stake was not just the question of the franchise but the wider issue of British supremacy. 'Franchise and every other question have merged in one big issue: is British paramountcy to be vindicated or let slide?' he asked. In a telegram to Chamberlain on the eve of a parliamentary debate on

South Africa on 28 July, Milner said he hoped that the debate would 'bring out wider aspects of questions which have been lost sight of in the long wrangle over details of franchise Bill. It is practical assertion of British supremacy in forcing [the Transvaal] to move in direction of equal rights and genuine self-government which is real issue.'

In his address to the House of Commons, Chamberlain accordingly raised the stakes, making clear that the fundamental aim of Britain's policy in southern Africa was to enforce its supremacy. 'A race antagonism' between Boers and British had developed in the Transvaal, he said. It had spread into neighbouring states, threatening the peace and prosperity of the region and endangering 'our position as the paramount power in South Africa'. The problem was discussed sometimes as if it were a question of petty reform – 'a matter of two years' difference in the qualification for the franchise'. But it was nothing of the kind. 'It is the power and authority of the British Empire. It is the position of Great Britain in South Africa. It is the question of our predominance and how it is to be interpreted, and it is the question of peace throughout the whole of South Africa.' Although the Transvaal's new franchise law was generally considered to be a great advance, it needed to be carefully examined by a joint inquiry, he said. He acknowledged that this meant Britain intervening in the internal affairs of the Transvaal but claimed it had the right to do so both because of its obligation to protect British subjects and because of its position 'as suzerain Power'. In a comment to Lord Selborne, Lord Salisbury, the prime minister, put the issue more succinctly: 'The real point to be made to South Africa is that we, not the Dutch, are Boss.'

From many quarters, Kruger was urged to accept the British demand for a joint inquiry. Both the Dutch and German governments warned Pretoria against rejection. A rejection was likely to precipitate a British ultimatum and a resort to war. Kruger's Cape friends – Hofmeyr, Schreiner and De Villiers – all pleaded with him to avoid war at all costs, even if it meant compromising Transvaal's independence.

I know the strong views which you hold as to your duty to preserve the independence of your Republic [wrote De Villiers], but a patriot should also be prudent and he should even be prepared to surrender part of his independence if by that means alone he can prevent the loss of the whole . . .

The question no longer is: 'What right has the British Government to make its demands?' but 'What concessions on your part will preserve the peace?' Whether a war should become a war of races or not, it can only end in a destruction of your Republic. The issue of war or peace is in your hands . . .

Kruger's reply was adamant:

I am sworn to uphold the independence of my country, and I have the very best reason for believing that Chamberlain and Milner are determined to rob me of that independence. Can you give me the assurance that if I consider all their demands, others will not be sprung upon me which no self-respecting President could for a moment entertain? If we are to lose our independence, let it be taken from us by force, but do not ask me to be a consenting party. I am sorry that you think war can end only in the destruction of the Republic, but do you not believe that there is a power above greater than that of England which will see that right and justice will prevail?

In a cable to President Steyn, he said it was 'impossible' for him to comply with the request for a joint inquiry. 'It would be equivalent to a destruction of our independence.' Steyn concurred, but urged Kruger to make an additional concession on the franchise – a five-years' retrospective franchise, along the lines demanded by Milner at Bloemfontein.

Just when a collision seemed inevitable, Kruger offered a package of measures that went even further than Milner's demands at Bloemfontein: a five years' retrospective franchise and a total of ten seats for mining areas – one quarter of the total seats in the Volksraad. There were, however, two conditions: Britain would have to agree to drop its claim to suzerainty and to refrain from further interference in the Transvaal's internal affairs.

Milner dismissed the offer as merely another 'manoeuvre', an 'unsatisfactory compromise' that would result in 'nothing but confusion'. It showed, he said, 'their absolute determination not to admit our claim to have a voice in their affairs as the Paramount Power in South Africa'. He told Chamberlain: 'They will collapse if we don't weaken, or rather if we go on steadily turning the screw.' Further turns of the screw would bring the required result. If they did not, then force should be used. The prospect of war did not daunt him. He assumed it would be a short affair, culminating in the removal of Kruger's government within a matter of months.

Chamberlain's reaction was initially more favourable. Kruger's proposals, he said, appeared to promise 'a complete climb down'. He told Salisbury: 'I really am sanguine that the crisis is over.' On further consideration, however, prompted by Milner, Chamberlain began to have doubts. He foresaw difficulties in getting Kruger to adhere to commitments over the franchise that he had made only under duress. 'If there is a climb down,' Milner warned, 'it will almost exceed the wit of man to prevent their cheating us.'

In this final tussle, what was really at stake, as both sides well knew, was not the issue of the franchise. The franchise was little more than a device to terminate Boer control. As Milner put it in a letter to a government official on 7 August: 'They want to squeeze the new-comers into the existing mould. I want them to burst it.' The British were using the franchise as a pretext to advance the case for British intervention. In his analysis of the crisis, made the day before war finally broke out, the Liberal opposition leader, Henry Campbell-Bannerman, observed:

> If you ask me my own opinion, I hold this 'franchise' movement as the biggest hypocrisy in the whole fraud. It was designed in order that:
> a) Kruger, seeing the real drift of it, might refuse it, and supply a direct ground of quarrel;
> b) If he accepted it, it would mean that not being able to get in by the front door they would get the area gate opened and get possession in this way of the country;

c) The innocent Briton would be gulled by the flavour of legality and of civilised progress in the word 'franchise' . . . the Outlander does not care about it and would not use it if he might.

The franchise issue, then, was a means to a larger end: to establish British supremacy. The conditions that Kruger set out in his offer directly challenged the notion of British supremacy. Chamberlain believed that the threat of war and war preparations might be sufficient to force Kruger into a final capitulation. But if Kruger refused to acknowledge British supremacy, then Chamberlain was prepared to resort to war.

In an official government minute written on 26 August, Chamberlain expressed his impatience:

It is clear that we cannot go on negotiating for ever and we must try to bring matters to a head. The next step in military preparations is so important and so costly that I hesitate to incur the expense . . . so long as there seems a fair chance of a satisfactory settlement. But I dread above all the continued whittling away of differences until we have no *casus belli* left, although the Boers may claim a partial diplomatic victory and be as disagreeable and intractable in the future as in the past.

At a rally in Birmingham two days later, he aimed to stir up public opinion:

Mr Kruger procrastinates in his replies. He dribbles out reforms like water from a squeezed sponge and either accompanies his offers with conditions which he knows to be impossible or he refuses to allow us to make a satisfactory investigation of the nature and the character of those reforms . . . The sands are running down in the glass.

What was needed, he said, was to establish 'once and for all' who was the 'paramount power in South Africa'.

On August 28, the British government sent a Formal Note to the Transvaal accepting the franchise concessions but refusing to abandon its claims to suzerainty or the right to intervene in the Transvaal's affairs. Smuts gave his verdict in a memorandum on 4 September:

> If at Bloemfontein last June there was still a hope of a peaceful solution, honourable to both sides, the last months have taught us that this hope is idle . . . the enemy is determined that this country shall either be conquered or be brought by diplomatic means to the position practically of a British colony.

He was now convinced that war was inevitable. It was, he wrote, bound to be a long and bloody war. 'South Africa is on the eve of a terrible blood bath, from which our people will emerge either as an exhausted remnant, wood-cutters and water-carriers for a hated race, or as victors, founders of a United South Africa, of one of the great empires [*rijken*] of the world . . . an Afrikaner republic . . . stretching from Table Bay to the Zambesi.'

38

ULTIMATUMS

Despite all the talk of war, the British government dithered over preparing for one. Ministers were worried about the lack of popular support for military action. 'The state of public opinion in this country is so strongly against going to war, that it is not possible for the Government to go to that length upon the present issue respecting the franchise,' Sir Edward Grey told Milner in July 1899. 'War, in the absence of provocation, is not practicable.' Selborne gave Milner a similar warning. 'Public opinion insists on our using great patience and endeavouring to avert war.'

Ministers were also reluctant to approve any expenditure on military preparations that might prove unnecessary. Most believed that Kruger would 'bluff up to the cannon's mouth and then capitulate' rather than contest the might of the greatest empire in the world. When the War Office requested funds for military preparations in August, Lord Salisbury remarked: 'The wiser plan is not to incur any serious expenditure until it is quite clear that we *are* going to war.' Moreover, it was thought that war preparations might themselves jeopardise the chance of a peaceful settlement and provoke Kruger into making a pre-emptive strike.

There was also considerable unease at Milner's appetite for confrontation. His inflammatory language; his lack of flexibility; his relentless demands for action; his manipulation of the press; the abrupt manner in which he broke up the Bloemfontein conference; all had aroused deep concern that he was committed to 'working up a crisis'. Officials at the Colonial Office complained that Milner was becoming 'too excited and impatient', in danger of being 'carried away' into siding with the extremist camp that wanted to avenge Majuba and re-annex the Transvaal. Opposition politicians accused Milner of attempting to 'bully the Transvaal government'. A growing section of the Liberal Party talked of 'Milner's war'.

Salisbury himself wanted to move at a slower pace. 'There is no need to hurry,' he said after the failure of the Bloemfontein conference. 'Anything approaching an ultimatum should be delayed as long as possible.' As the momentum towards war increased, he rued the fact that Milner had been allowed such a loose rein. Writing to the Secretary of State for War, Lord Lansdowne, on 30 August, Salisbury grumbled:

> His view is too heated, if you consider the intrinsic significance and importance of the things which are in controversy. But it recks little to think of that now. What he has done cannot be effaced. We have to act upon a moral field prepared for us by him and his jingo supporters. And therefore I see before us the necessity for considerable military effort − and all for people whom we despise, and for territory which will bring no profit and no power to England.

While ministers dithered, Britain's military commanders fretted at the lack of decision-making, fearing that they would be landed with a war for which no adequate preparations had been made. Three days after the failure of the Bloemfontein conference in June, the army chief, Field Marshal Lord Wolseley, recommended mobilising an army corps and a cavalry division − some 35,000 men − for manoeuvres on Salisbury Plain as a 'demonstration' to overawe Kruger and induce him to submit to British demands. In July, he urged the despatch of 10,000 troops to double the size of existing garrisons in the Cape and Natal as 'an open demonstration of a warlike policy'. But Lansdowne rejected both proposals.

Wolseley judged that in the event of a war with the Transvaal some 50,000 troops would be needed in addition to the existing garrisons. In August, the War Office calculated that to equip, mobilise and position an army corps of 50,000 men in the Cape would take four months, but that the time-lag could be reduced to three months provided that orders for a million pounds' worth of mules, carts and clothing were placed immediately. But Salisbury, Lansdowne and Chamberlain decided against 'the expenditure of a million which we cannot recover if we do not go to war'. The most that ministers were prepared to countenance in August was the despatch of 2,000 men to shore up Natal's defences.

Amid the wrangling, however, there was general agreement that if war came, it would be a 'small' war, of short duration. Wolseley reckoned it would last for three to four months. An assessment by the War Office Intelligence Department dismissed the Boers as a serious military adversary. It predicted that the Orange Free State would join the Transvaal in a war against Britain, but maintained that, although on paper the two republics could commandeer citizen forces totalling 54,000 men, they would be no match for a professionally trained British army. The only threat that the Cape and Natal would face was from 'raiding parties'. British forces would meanwhile sweep across the highveld, overwhelming Boer resistance. 'It appears certain that, after [one] serious defeat, they would be too deficient in discipline and organization to make any further real stand.' The British also assumed that they would be able to control the timing of the war, that it would only start when they were ready and that therefore there was no cause for undue haste.

At a cabinet meeting on 8 September, Chamberlain pressed the case for sending a force of 10,000 men as reinforcements. In a memorandum he prepared for the meeting, he insisted that after three months of negotiating in an attempt to reach an 'amicable' settlement over uitlander grievances, the time had now come 'to bring matters to a head' and formulate demands for a final settlement. The example of the Transvaal 'flouting, and flouting successfully, British control and interference' was affecting the whole of southern Africa. Afrikaners, he claimed, were bent on ousting British influence from the region

and establishing their own 'United States of South Africa'. It was
now up to the British government to decide 'whether the supremacy
which we have claimed so long and so seldom exerted is to be finally
established or for ever abandoned'. What was at stake was not only the
reputation of Britain in southern Africa but its standing throughout
the world.

The cabinet sanctioned the despatch of reinforcements and authorised the army to set up an expeditionary force, but held back from
sending an ultimatum to Kruger until the reinforcements had arrived.
Salisbury was still determined not to be rushed, hoping that Kruger in
the meantime might capitulate. Only gradually during the course of
September was an army corps for southern Africa mobilised. In a note
to an intelligence officer, Wolseley fulminated over the dilly-dallying
of the politicians:

> We have lost two months through the absolute folly of our
> Cabinet & the incapacity of its members to take in the require-
> ments & the difficulties of war . . . It is no wonder we never
> achieve much in war & have to struggle through obstacles cre-
> ated by the folly & war ignorance of civilian ministers & War
> Office clerks.

In Pretoria, the effect of Britain's war preparations, far from intim-
idating Kruger's government, was to make it all the more
determined to resist. 'The only thing that can bring an end to the
situation is a definite answer that will show the British Government
that we will not go further upon being threatened,' said Smuts.
'They must then make peace or war.' Kruger was convinced that
nothing would satisfy Chamberlain except total surrender. The
Transvaal government accused Britain of acting in bad faith and
withdrew its conditional offer of a five-year franchise. 'With God
before our eyes,' Kruger told Hofmeyr, 'we feel that we cannot go
further without endangering if not totally destroying our independence.'

In Johannesburg, the momentum towards war aroused increasing
alarm. The gold industry was booming. Gold output in 1899 was

double that of 1895, making the Transvaal the world's leading producer. In July, output reached record levels, valued at £1.7 million for the month. Whatever complaints the mining companies raised against Kruger's government, they enjoyed substantial profits and a relatively benign regime. Investment in the Rand gold mines by 1899 had reached about £75 million; about two-thirds of it was British. The president of the Chamber of Mines, Georges Rouliot, a senior partner in Wernher, Beit & Co., believed that war would have disastrous consequences. The mining companies faced not only disruption but possible closure and the risk of long-term damage through flooding and sabotage. Already, the business sector was faltering; trade was at a standstill; uitlanders were being thrown out of work.

In August, an exodus set in. Trains to the Cape Colony and Natal were packed with immigrant miners, shopkeepers, artisans, prostitutes and pimps. In September, panic took hold; passengers stood in open cattle-trucks to get away. In all, an estimated 100,000 whites fled the Transvaal. Tens of thousands of black workers were sent home. By the end of September, two-thirds of businesses in Johannesburg and most mines on the Witwatersrand had shut down. An eerie calm descended over the town.

In London, after further prevarication, the cabinet decided on 29 September to press ahead with preparations for mobilising an expeditionary army and to draw up an ultimatum to be delivered to Pretoria after the arrival of reinforcements in southern Africa. Considerable effort was put into producing the draft of an ultimatum. Milner's advice, after he heard that Kruger was planning to issue an ultimatum of his own, was to postpone the whole matter. In a cable to Chamberlain on 29 September, he remarked:

Personally I am still of opinion not to hurry in settling ultimatum, as events of next few days may supply us with a better one than anybody can compose. Ultimatum has always been great difficulty, as unless we widen issue, there is not sufficient cause for war, and if we do so, we are abused for shifting our ground and extending our demands.

The following day, he pointed out another reason for withholding the ultimatum:

> It will be great moral advantage to us, especially here, that conflict should be brought about by attack on us without the excuse which the ultimatum would give them.

Chamberlain agreed that 'the technical *casus belli* is a very weak one'. But he doubted that the Boers would stage a pre-emptive strike and put themselves in the role of aggressor. Nor did he fear a British reverse if they did. 'When all the reinforcements are landed, my own feeling is that we shall be quite a match for the Boers even without the army corps.' His main concern, he told Milner, was that a deal to avoid war might be cobbled together at the last minute.

> What I fear is some suggestion of compromise from them which will be totally inadequate to provide a permanent settlement but will nevertheless strengthen the hands of the Opposition at home and make many foolish people inclined to give more time and to patch up some sort of hollow agreement.

In an exchange over the draft ultimatum, the chancellor of the exchequer, Sir Michael Hicks Beach, wanted clarification over the objective. Provided that a political settlement was reached 'with the equality of the white races as its basis', then he saw no harm in maintaining the 'present independence' of the Transvaal. 'I see no reason for proposing anything now which could be taken as a revocation of independence. We can never govern from Downing Street any part of South Africa in which the whites are strong enough to defend themselves against the natives: so that equality of white races in the Transvaal would really secure all we can desire, viz. British supremacy.'

Chamberlain concurred: 'I agree we do not want . . . to make ourselves responsible for the Government of the Transvaal. It must be a Republic or a self-governing Colony – under the British flag in either case.'

While these discussions were under way, Kruger mobilised his commandos, anxious to take advantage of the delays in British troop movements. 'The Lord will protect us,' Kruger told the Volksraad. 'The Lord orders the flights of bullets. The Lord gave us the triumph of the War of Independence and the capture of Jameson. The Lord will also protect you now, even if thousands of bullets fly about you.'

The Orange Free State followed suit on 2 October. Even though the risks of defeat were high, when members of the Free State Volksraad met in secret to decide whether to stand together with the Transvaal, their view was unanimous, as Abraham Fischer recorded: 'There was no bounce or *grootpraat* [boasting] but quiet determination, and the spontaneous and unmistakable enthusiasm with which the members burst out into the Volkslied [the national anthem] was something to remember. They were all most cheerful learning that the best had been done to avert war and that they were unjustly being dragged into it.'

In a letter to Hofmeyr, Fischer explained:

> Every reasonable concession has been granted and the British Government's requests complied with, and the only result of every concession has been trickery and increased demands. Further compliance would, I feel sure, only be an inducement for, and lead to further dishonourable and insulting treatment of [the Transvaal] . . . We have honestly done our best, and can do no more: if we are to lose our independence — since that is palpably what is demanded — leave us, at all events, the consolation that we did not sacrifice it dishonourably.

On 9 October, the Transvaal presented its own ultimatum, demanding the withdrawal of British troops from its borders and the recall of all reinforcements. Unless the British government complied within forty-eight hours, the Transvaal would 'with great regret be compelled to regard the action as a formal declaration of war'. Awakened on the morning of 10 October, Chamberlain read the ultimatum with a sense of relief. 'They have done it!' he exclaimed. Lord Salisbury was similarly jubilant. The Boers, he said, had 'liberated us from the necessity of explaining to the people of England why we are at war'. Lansdowne remarked: 'My soldiers are in ecstasies.' London newspapers predicted a short war – 'a tea-time war'. It would all be over by Christmas.

PART IX

39

THE FORTUNES OF WAR

In high spirits, Boer commandos assembled along the borders of Natal in early October, 1899, ready to strike deep into British territory. 'There was not a man who did not believe that we were heading straight for the coast,' wrote Deneys Reitz, the 17-year-old son of Frank Reitz, who signed up with the Pretoria commando. Addressing a huge parade of mounted riflemen on 10 October at his headquarters at Sandspruit, ten miles from the border, Piet Joubert, the 68-year-old commandant-general, told them of the ultimatum that had been sent to the British. 'The excitement that followed was immense,' wrote Reitz. 'The great throng stood in its stirrups and shouted itself hoarse.' In the early hours of 12 October, after war had been officially declared, the commandos moved out on the road towards Laing's Nek and Majuba Hill, where British forces had been humiliated eighteen years before. 'As far as the eye could see the plain was alive with horsemen, guns and cattle, all steadily going forward to the frontier,' wrote Reitz.

The invasion of Natal formed a central part of the Boers' war strategy. Based on a plan drawn up by Smuts in September, the aim was to use overwhelming numbers of men to punch through the lightly defended north-western districts of Natal, capturing the line of rail all the way to the port of Durban and thwarting the landing of Britain's

expeditionary army. Some 21,000 men – 15,000 from the Transvaal
and 6,000 from the Free State – were committed to the Natal offensive. Simultaneous offensives were launched into the northern Cape,
cutting off the railway linking the Cape to Rhodesia and isolating the
towns of Mafeking and Kimberley. By seizing control of the main rail
network, the Boers intended to block the advance of British troops
heading for the Transvaal. Early victories, Smuts believed, would dis-
hearten the British and induce them to negotiate a settlement, just as
they had done after General Colley's defeat at Majuba Hill in 1881.
Military success would also encourage Cape Afrikaners to rally to the
republican cause. Moreover, it would result in 'an immediate shaking
of the British Empire' that Britain's rivals – Germany, France and
Russia – would hasten to exploit.

As well as the military campaign, Smuts placed great store on the
use of propaganda, hoping to stir up both Boer outrage in the colonies
and international opinion against Britain. He compiled a 100-page
tract entitled *Een Eeuw Van Onrecht* – A Century of Wrong – portraying British rule since 1806 as a bloodstained tyranny. Written in
High Dutch and translated into English by Smuts' wife Isie, the tract
pinned the blame for the present crisis on a conspiracy between mine-
owning capitalists and the British government to seize the riches of
the Transvaal, a conspiracy that had first surfaced during the Jameson
Raid. The Jameson Raid, according to Smuts, was 'the real declaration of war in the great Anglo–Boer conflict'.

> If it is ordained that we, insignificant as we are, should be the first
> among all peoples to begin the struggle against the new-world
> tyranny of Capitalism, then we are ready to do so, even if that
> tyranny is reinforced by the power of Jingoism.

He concluded with the slogan: 'Africa for the Africander'.

As the Boers struck deep into British territory, Britain's main expeditionary army was still being assembled in England. After months of
wrangling, the order for mobilisation, calling out the reserves, had not
been issued until 7 October. It was only at the last minute, once

Kruger had issued his ultimatum, that public opinion rallied behind the war effort. 'You cannot realise the enormous difficulty we have had with public opinion at home,' Selborne wrote to Milner. As a result of the press campaign conducted by Milner and Chamberlain, the public was eventually persuaded that war was necessary to liberate the maltreated English-speaking population of the Transvaal from Kruger's repressive regime. Appeals went out for funds to support soldiers' dependants and for gifts of clothing, tobacco, cigarettes and 'delicacies' for the men. The most potent appeal of all was made by Rudyard Kipling:

> When you've shouted 'Rule Britannia', when you've
>   sung 'God Save the Queen',
> When you're finished killing Kruger with your mouth,
> Will you kindly drop a shilling in my little tambourine
> For a gentleman in Khaki ordered South?
> He's an absent-minded beggar, and his weaknesses are
>   great –
> But we and Paul must take him as we find him –
> He's out on active service, wiping something off a slate –
> And he's left a lot of little things behind him! . . .

It was not until 20 October that the first infantry transports sailed for Table Bay. By 31 October, some 27,000 men, 3,600 horses and 42 artillery guns were on the high seas. The last transport ship sailed on 15 November, bringing the expeditionary army to 47,000 men. But by then, British forces on the ground were in retreat.

Within two weeks of crossing the border into Natal, Boer commandos had routed a brigade of British troops at Dundee, driven British forces in northwestern Natal back to Ladysmith, the third largest town in the colony, and taken prisoner more than a thousand British soldiers. By the end of October they had encircled Ladysmith, cutting the railway line to the capital, Pietermaritzburg, and trapping 12,000 troops there, the largest British force in Natal. Only 3,000 British troops were left to defend the whole of the south of Natal.

Moving further southwards, a Boer group of 2,000 men crossed the Tugela River on 14 November, heading along the line of rail towards Pietermaritzburg. The next day, a commando led by Louis Botha, a 38-year-old farmer and politician, ambushed an armoured train near Chievely. Among the sixty prisoners captured was Winston Churchill, then a correspondent for the *Morning Post*. As the son of Randolph Churchill, he was a prize captive. Brought before Smuts for interrogation, he appeared 'dishevelled and most indignant', Smuts recalled, claiming immunity as a non-combatant. Smuts pointed out that he had been carrying a pistol when captured and sent him off to a detention camp in Pretoria. Boer patrols, meanwhile, rode further south.

To the west, a Boer army commanded by Piet Cronjé, veteran of the 1881 war and the Jameson Raid, encircled Mafeking, ten miles from the Transvaal border, calling for its surrender. A dusty outpost of some 1,500 whites, with 5,000 Africans living in the adjacent settlement of Mafikeng, Mafeking was held by a British garrison of 750 colonial troops and mounted police. The garrison commander, Colonel Robert Baden-Powell, was a resourceful 43-year-old officer with a passion for scouting and an eye for self-promotion, who had been sent there with secret instructions to raid the Transvaal in the event of war but found himself instead under siege. Baden-Powell not only refused to surrender, but decided to arm Africans to help defend the town. Cronjé was outraged: 'an enormous act of wickedness', he told Baden-Powell. 'I would ask you to pause and even at this eleventh hour, reconsider the matter, and even if it cost you the loss of Mafeking, to disarm your blacks and thereby act the part of a white man in a white man's war.' To show what was in store for the British unless they surrendered, Cronjé ordered an artillery bombardment. But Baden-Powell was unimpressed. After the first day's shelling, he sent out a message by runner saying: 'October 21st. All well. Four hours' bombardment. One dog killed.' His stiff-upper-lip manner made him an instant hero in England. Mafeking fortuitously possessed substantial supplies. But the garrison's isolated position nevertheless made it vulnerable.

The day after Mafeking's siege began, Kimberley came under threat

from Free State forces. It stood not only as a symbol of British industrial might, but possessed workshops and supplies useful for the Boer
war effort. Another prize was Cecil Rhodes, who arrived there by
train on 10 October, a day before the Boer ultimatum was due to
expire. Fearing that his presence would encourage attack, the mayor
of Kimberley had urged him to stay away, but Rhodes saw a heroic
role for himself, defending the front line of empire. He set up headquarters in the Sanatorium, a double-storeyed, red-brick hotel
recently refurbished by De Beers as a health resort. No sooner had he
arrived than he sought to wrest control of the town's defences from
the garrison commander, Colonel Robert Kekewich, causing rows
and disruption. He also bombarded highly placed contacts like Milner
with messages pleading for the immediate despatch of relief forces –
'otherwise a terrible disaster'. On 5 November, he cabled Milner: 'If
you do not advance at once from Orange River you will lose
Kimberley.'

For Milner, the news went from bad to worse. Not only were
three strategic towns in British territory under siege – Ladysmith,
Mafeking and Kimberley – but on 1 November, Free State commandos crossed the Orange River, overrunning frontier districts of the
Cape Colony and recruiting rebel Afrikaners as they went. A string of
frontier towns and villages fell into Boer hands. What Milner now
began to fear was the possibility of a wider Boer uprising all over the
colony. In his diary, he wrote on 4 November: 'The blackest of black
days . . . everything going wrong.' To Chamberlain, he cabled on 9
November: 'I write this quaking, for one fears every hour for
Kimberley.'

But just when Milner was giving way to despair, the first British
troopship steamed into Table Bay. The arrival of the expeditionary
army, led by General Sir Redvers Buller, seemed certain to turn the
war in Britain's favour. It was, however, to lead to yet more disasters.

Although he had been given overall command of the army corps,
General Buller decided to take personal charge of the Natal campaign,
leaving the Cape's troublespots in the hands of other generals. Natal
was an area with which he was familiar. During the Zulu war in

1879, he had won a Victoria Cross for rescuing wounded British soldiers. A tall, burly figure, with a florid complexion, multiple chins and a walrus moustache, sixty years old, he looked the epitome of a British bulldog commander, stolid and resilient. Taking half of the army corps with him, Buller established a huge forward base at Frere, a railway halt south of the Tugela River, some twenty-five miles from Ladysmith. The force he commanded included 14,000 infantry, 2,700 mounted men and 44 field guns. His aim was to punch his way across the Tugela and relieve Ladysmith. The river crossing was expected to be a 'walk-over'.

For several weeks, however, the Boer commander at Tugela, Louis Botha, had been preparing for a British assault, anticipating they would attempt to cross the river at Colenso on the line of rail. A network of trenches had been dug over a stretch of nine miles running along the hills overlooking the river, keeping the Boer defenders protected and hidden from view.

Buller's plan of attack was spectacularly inept. On 13 December he launched two days of artillery bombardment, expecting Boer resistance to crumble, then sent infantry battalions across exposed ground in broad daylight with orders to cross the river. Buller's forces were cut to pieces in a storm of rifle-fire; more than a thousand men were killed or wounded. At eight o'clock in the morning, Buller decided to withdraw; ten field guns had to be abandoned. Newspapers spoke of 'another Majuba'. Despondent at the outcome, Buller sent a heliograph message to the British commander in Ladysmith, General George White, warning that it would take at least another month for him to break through Boer defences and suggesting that if the town proved unable to hold out that long, the garrison should destroy its ammunition and seek 'the best terms you can'.

In the space of a week – 'Black Week', as it became known – Britain's army corps suffered two other reverses. Advancing northwards along the line of rail to relieve Kimberley, General Methuen's force of 8,000 infantry crossed the Orange River on 20 November, fought past Boer resistance at Belmont, Graspan and Modder River and then, bolstered by reinforcements, prepared to challenge Koos de la Rey's stronghold in the Magersfontein hills that barred its way to

Kimberley, sixteen miles beyond. Methuen opened his attack with an artillery bombardment, expecting the Boers to retreat, but the Boers were already dispersed in different positions. When Methuen ordered his Highland Brigade to advance after a night march, they ran into withering fire from Boer fighters concealed in a line of trenches at the foot of Magersfontein Kop. With casualties of nearly a thousand men, Methuen was forced to retreat back to the Modder River.

Further south in the Cape Colony, General Gatacre set out to dislodge invading Boer commandos who had occupied a key railway junction at Stormberg. Without making any preliminary reconnaissance, he ordered his 3,000 troops to embark on a night march over rough and broken countryside before launching a dawn assault. In muddle and confusion, Gatacre's force lost its way and he was forced to retreat, leaving behind 600 men to be taken prisoner.

Far from winning the war by Christmas, Britain's army corps, including several elite units, had been subjected to one humiliating defeat after another. The level of casualties was shattering: seven hundred killed in action or dead of wounds; three thousand wounded, and two thousand taken prisoner; and three strategic towns still under siege, facing disease and starvation. And all at the hands of a group of peasant farmers dressed in civilian clothes – 'stock-breeders of the lowest kind', according to the *Economist* – whom the British had confidently predicted would pack up and go home after firing a few shots. The only light relief came when Winston Churchill managed to escape from his detention camp in Pretoria, crossed the border into Portuguese territory on a train, hidden in wool bales, and turned up on the Natal war front in time for Christmas.

Stung by accusations that the war had been mismanaged, the British government ordered a change of command and appointed as commander-in-chief Field Marshal Frederick Roberts – 'Lord Bobs' – a diminutive, 67-year-old war hero, blind in one eye; but it was decided to leave Buller in charge of the Natal army. Two more divisions – the last readily available – were despatched from England. The government also realised that it had been trying to fight the wrong kind of war, relying too much on slow-moving infantry battalions to deal with mounted Boer riflemen using highly mobile tactics; British mobility needed to match Boer mobility. Britain called for civilian volunteers to join a new 'Imperial Yeomanry'. Some 20,000 men from the 'hunting and shooting' fraternity signed up, including thirty-four members of parliament and peers. The City of London paid for one thousand volunteers. Further reinforcements came from other parts of the empire – from Canada, Australia and New Zealand. By January 1900, the total number of troops Britain had shipped to South Africa had reached 110,000. Additional support was provided by uitlander refugees and colonial volunteers formed into two mounted corps of their own – the Imperial Light Horse and the South African Light Horse – financed in part by Wernher, Beit & Co.

Even members of the Indian community in Natal – originally immigrants employed as indentured labourers to work on sugar plantations – volunteered to serve as stretcher-bearers. Their organiser was a 28-year-old lawyer, Mohandas Gandhi, who had arrived from India in 1893, spending a year in Pretoria before settling in Durban. Gandhi expressed sympathy for the Boer cause but considered he was bound by loyalty to Britain. 'I felt that, if I demanded rights as a British citizen, it was also my duty, as such, to participate in the defence of the British Empire.' The Natal authorities at first turned down Gandhi's offer. But after Black Week, their attitude changed. Gandhi's ambulance corps of 'free' Indians and indentured labourers recruited 1,100 volunteers.

Just as the British won support from the empire, so Boer ranks were bolstered by foreign volunteers. Some 2,000 uitlanders – Germans, French, Dutch, Irish, Irish-Americans, Russians, Scandinavians, even some English – joined the Boer cause. Another 2,000 foreign volunteers arrived from abroad. A retired French army colonel, Count de Villebois-Mareuil, enlisted, hoping to capture Cecil Rhodes. 'History will add a fresh flower to the glory of France,' he wrote in his diary. 'To take Kimberley and see the face of the Napoleon of the Cape.' He rose to the rank of *Vecht-generaal* – combat general – but was killed in action in April 1900. In all, the Boer allies were able to raise armed forces totalling more than 70,000 men. In addition, about 10,000 Africans served as auxiliaries to Boer commandos – retainers, porters, gun-bearers and labourers – many of them conscripted under duress.

Yet early Boer advantages were soon frittered away by poor strategy. By committing such a large proportion of their forces to the siege of three towns, Boer generals lost the opportunity to drive deeper into Natal and the Cape Colony when both areas were highly vulnerable to mobile attack. As their forward thrusts began to ebb, they turned to a more defensive stance, preparing for a much tougher British assault. By December, the Boer offensive had reached its limits. Unlike 1881, there had been no crushing blow to induce the British to negotiate.

40

MARCHING TO PRETORIA

When Lord Roberts landed at Cape Town on 10 January 1900, he received some unwelcome news. Despite repeated instructions he had sent to Buller to remain on the defensive, Buller, hoping to redeem his battered reputation, had decided to try to cross the Tugela River once more and lift the siege of Ladysmith. Yet another British disaster was in the making.

The crossing point that Buller chose was a drift eighteen miles upstream from Colenso. The massive force that he assembled – 24,000 infantry, 2,500 mounted troops, eight field batteries, ten naval guns and vast amounts of supplies – took more than a week to deploy. Heavy rains had left rivers in flood and roads waterlogged. A correspondent for the *Manchester Guardian*, John Atkins, described how Buller's army waded, 'sliding, sucking, pumping, gurgling through the mud', with men, animals and wagons strung out for miles. Forewarned of the attack, Louis Botha had ample time to prepare his defences, bringing reinforcements from Colenso and deploying his artillery in advantageous positions.

Buller's main force crossed the Tugela River on 20 January in good order, gained a foothold on the northern bank and then tried to advance between two summits, Spion Kop and Twin Peaks, hoping to reach the open plain beyond leading to Ladysmith. After two rebuffs,

Buller authorised General Sir Charles Warren's division to make an assault on Spion Kop – Lookout Hill – the highest peak in the area rising more than 1,500 feet above the Tugela, believing it would give him a commanding field of fire.

A night assault was made on 24 January. Only a light Boer picket had been posted to defend Spion Kop. Clambering up the steep, rock-strewn slope, Warren's men soon put the picket to flight and in the dark started digging defence works. As the ground was rocky, the main trench they managed to gouge out was no more than a broad, shallow ditch, running for some 200 yards. When the morning mist lifted, they discovered they had won only part of the summit. Their position, moreover, was exposed both to Boer artillery fire from surrounding hills and to Boer fighters creeping up the slopes below them, unsighted, determined to recapture the hill. Among them was Deneys Reitz:

> Many of our men dropped, but already the foremost were within a few yards of the rocky edge which marked the crest, and the [British] soldiers were rising from behind their cover to meet the final rush. For a moment or two there was confused hand to hand fighting, then the combatants surged over the rim of the plateau.

With no adequate cover, British ranks were ripped apart by Boer artillery fire. The main trench was soon filled with bodies, two or three deep. In the British command, there was muddle and confusion. Reinforcements were sent up, but counter-attacks and diversions on Boer positions elsewhere to relieve the pressure on Spion Kop were delayed or called back. Watching the carnage unfold through a telescope from Buller's headquarters on a hill south of the Tugela River, John Atkins wrote: 'I shall always have it in memory – that acre of massacre, that complete shambles.'

Some soldiers surrendered to the Boers; others fought on, while the vast bulk of Buller's army stood idle. In the late afternoon, Winston Churchill climbed up the narrow track to the summit, passing streams of wounded men:

Men were staggering along alone, or supported by comrades, or crawling on hands and knees, or carried on stretchers. Corpses lay here and there . . . The splinters and fragments of shell had torn and mutilated in the most ghastly manner. I passed about two hundred while I was climbing up. There was, moreover, a small but steady leakage of unwounded men of all corps. Some of these cursed and swore. Others were utterly exhausted and fell on the hillside in stupor.

During the night, the British retreated in disarray, having lost 1,100 men, killed, wounded and captured. The Boers too suffered heavy casualties – more than 300 men – and abandoned their forward positions:

We were hungry, thirsty and tired [wrote Reitz], around us were the dead men covered with swarms of flies attracted by the smell of blood. We did not know the cruel losses that the English were suffering and we believed that they were easily holding their own, so discouragement spread as the shadows lengthened. Batches of men left the line . . .

The Boers were on the brink of retreating altogether when a few scouts climbed up to the summit at dawn and found it deserted.

Rather than hold on to a bridgehead across the Tugela, Buller withdrew his entire army to the south bank and began to prepare for yet another assault. But his third attempt was no more successful. Crossing the river by pontoon downstream from Spion Kop on 5 February, Buller's 20,000-strong army greatly outnumbered the Boer commandos ranged against it around Vaalkranz and Doornkop, but Buller dithered, countermanded his own orders and, after incurring 400 casualties, decided to retreat across the Tugela once more. Two months after setting up his headquarters at Frere, Buller was still no further forward. In England, he became known derisively as the 'Ferryman of the Tugela'.

While Buller set about planning a fourth assault across the Tugela, three hundred miles to the west Lord Roberts marshalled a 'grand

army' of 60,000 men south of the Modder River. Roberts' original
plan had been to make a direct thrust at Bloemfontein, forcing its
capitulation, before turning to sort out other difficulties like the siege
of Kimberley. Though Kimberley had been under siege for nearly four
months, it was in no danger of imminent collapse. Its population of
50,000 civilians – 13,000 whites, 30,000 Africans and 7,000
Coloureds – had grown accustomed to the hazards of being shelled
almost daily by artillery; most of the Boer bombardment was ineffect-
ive. While many blacks were close to starvation, whites had survived
the ordeal with relative ease.

Roberts had been obliged, however, to amend his plan to deal
with agitation by Rhodes insisting that the relief of Kimberley should
take priority. Rhodes was openly contemptuous of the British military
for their endless delays in lifting the siege. His running feud with the
garrison commander, Colonel Kekewich, had become increasingly
fractious. He constantly sought to undermine Kekewich's authority,
obstructing his orders and setting up his own communication system
with the outside world to make his views known.

What brought matters to a head was a panic that set in when the
Boers began pounding the town on 7 February with a devastating
new weapon: a six-inch 'Long Tom' Creusot gun. It was more accurate than anything they had hitherto used at Kimberley.

Twenty-two shells fell that day; thirty the following day; seventy-
four the day after. Calling at Kekewich's headquarters near the
Kimberley Club on 9 February, Rhodes threatened to organise a
public meeting to protest against the delays in rescue, hinting at the
possibility of surrender. When Kekewich responded by banning the
holding of a meeting, Rhodes became abusive, telling Kekewich he
would go ahead despite the ban unless Kekewich disclosed within
forty-eight hours 'full and definite' information about Roberts' plan
to advance. 'Before Kimberley surrenders,' Rhodes shouted, 'I will
take good care that the English people shall know what I think of all
this.'

The following day, Rhodes' newspaper, the *Diamond Fields
Advertiser*, carried an editorial entitled 'Why Kimberley Cannot Wait'
which heaped scorn on the British military.

How utterly the public and the authorities have failed to grasp the claim which Kimberley, by the heroic exertions of her citizens, has established upon the British Empire is only too apparent . . . [from] the utter indifference with which our fate appears to be regarded by the military hierarchy . . . We have stood a siege which is rapidly approaching the duration of the siege of Paris . . . They shout to us 'Have patience' . . . Is it unreasonable, when our women and children are being slaughtered, and our buildings fired, to expect something better than that a large British Army should remain inactive in the presence of eight or ten thousand peasant soldiers?

Outraged by the paper's breach of censorship rules, Kekewich ordered the arrest of the editor, only to be told that Rhodes had hidden him down a mine.

Rhodes followed up his newspaper attack by convening a meeting of twelve of Kimberley's leading citizens. He then took a statement they produced to Kekewich, demanding that it should be transmitted immediately to Roberts. The statement was a long one, listing the suffering that Kimberley's residents had endured while British troops had been camped for more than two months 'within twenty miles'. Residents wanted to know, said the statement, 'whether there is any intention on your part to make an immediate effort for our relief'.

Kekewich pointed out that signallers were working under great pressure and could not send the full statement for some time, but he offered to send an abbreviated version. At this, Rhodes flew into a rage, hurling insults and making a lunge at Kekewich. 'I know what damned rot your signallers are wasting their time in signalling,' he shouted. 'You low, damned, mean cur, Kekewich, you deny me at your peril.'

On receiving the abbreviated version, Roberts responded with two messages. One authorised Kekewich to arrest anyone, no matter how illustrious, if they presented a danger to security. The other urged Kekewich to try to mollify Rhodes and his colleagues, to stress 'as strongly as you possibly can disastrous and humiliating effect of surrendering after so prolonged and glorious defence'. In a cable marked 'secret', he told Kekewich that only a few more days would pass before Kimberley was relieved. 'We commence active operations tomorrow.' Shown the cable, Rhodes took it to read aloud to passers-by from the steps of the Kimberley Club.

Keeping himself at the centre of the drama, Rhodes made arrange-ments to use the diamond mines as shelter against the Long Tom. During a respite from the shelling on Sunday, 11 February, while frantic efforts were made to build sandbagged shelters on the surface, Rhodes posted notices in prominent parts of the town, telling resi-dents:

> I recommend women and children who desire complete shelter to proceed to Kimberley and De Beers shafts. They will be low-ered at once in the mines from 8 o'clock throughout the night. Lamps and guides will be provided.

Residents assumed that Rhodes had definite information about a worse bombardment to come. In renewed panic, hundreds of women and children fled to the mine shafts, huddling together three hundred feet below the surface.

Four days later, a British cavalry division led by General John French charged through Boer lines and ended the 124-day siege. Rhodes, relishing the limelight, greeted French and his accompanying press contingent with a champagne reception. British newspapers were exuberant. 'Kimberley is won,' exulted the London *Daily Mail*, 'Mr Cecil Rhodes is free, the De Beers shareholders are all full of themselves, and the beginning of the war is at an end.'

On the Tugela front, Buller resumed his offensive on 14 February, this time concentrating his army – 25,000 strong – on a six-mile arc of ter-ritory downstream from Colenso. The Boers threw in reinforcements but could only muster 5,000 men to oppose him. Demoralised after losing possession of key hill positions, Boer fighters began to drift away, making for home. Botha tried in vain to stop them and in despair telegraphed Kruger suggesting that the Tugela and the siege of

Ladysmith should be abandoned. Kruger replied with a stern rallying call, quoting at length from the Bible.

> The moment you cease to hold firm and fight in the name of the Lord, then you have unbelief in you; and the moment unbelief is present cowardice follows and the moment you turn your backs on the enemy then there remains no place for us to seek refuge, for in that case we have ceased to trust in the Lord. No, no, my brethren; let it not be so . . . Has not the Lord hitherto given us double proof that He stands on our side? Wherever our burghers have stood fast, however hard the task, the Lord has beaten back the enemy with a small number of our burghers.

Botha fought on for ten more days. But by 27 February, Buller was firmly in control of the Tugela heights, the Boers were in retreat and the way to Ladysmith was open. Mounted troops entered Ladysmith on 28 February, ending 188 days of siege. 'I thank God we have kept the flag flying,' General White told a cheering crowd. Enjoying his victory, Buller organised a formal entry into the town three days later. In a Special Army Order, he claimed that the campaign to relieve Ladysmith had been a 'glorious page' in the history of the British empire. The cost of the 'glorious page' had been more than 5,000 British casualties.

Having secured Kimberley, Roberts' 'steamroller' army advanced into the Orange Free State, eastwards along the Modder River, heading for Bloemfontein with overwhelming numerical superiority. After bombarding Boer positions at Paardeburg for ten days, the British forced General Piet Cronjé's surrender on 27 February, capturing 4,000 Boer combatants. As Boer morale crumbled, Kruger rushed to the Modder River front to rally burghers to the cause. But he had barely arrived at General Christiaan de Wet's camp near Poplar Grove on 7 March when British shells began falling nearby. De Wet bundled Kruger back into his Cape cart and sent him off with an armed escort. Rather than make a stand at Poplar Grove, the last strongpoint before

Bloemfontein, fifty miles to the east, De Wet fought a rearguard action, then escaped with 6,000 men.

As the British approached Bloemfontein, Boer resistance melted away. Thousands of burghers fled northwards. President Steyn left on 12 March on one of the last trains to get away before the British cut the line. On 13 March, Roberts' army entered Bloemfontein without firing a shot. Cheered on by English residents, Roberts rode at the head of a triumphal procession to Steyn's Presidency and watched as the Union flag was hoisted aloft in the garden.

Roberts endeavoured to put the Boer population at their ease by allowing most Boer officials to remain in their posts and inviting them to banquets and parties. He launched a new bilingual daily newspaper called *The Friend*, telling British war correspondents to produce it in their spare time. Among those whom he recruited to the task was Rudyard Kipling who arrived from Cape Town at Roberts' behest shortly after Bloemfontein had been captured. Printed on the presses of an anti-British newspaper that the British had banned, *The Friend* contained proclamations and a large number of old advertisements. Kipling recalled: 'We used all the old stereos [stereotype plates], advertising long-since-exhausted comestibles, coal and groceries (face powder, I think, was the only surviving commodity in the Bloemfontein shops).'

The impact of British occupation was nevertheless devastating. Bloemfontein, a town with a total population of 4,000, was suddenly inundated with 50,000 troops in need of shelter, supplies and sanitation. The Raadzaal, schools, clubhouses and private residences were commandeered for British use. An outbreak of typhoid among British troops brought further crisis. Hundreds of soldiers were struck down and left lying packed together on the ground in filthy conditions with no adequate care or medical attention. By early April, nearly a thousand soldiers had died; by the end of April, two thousand had died.

Two weeks after the British took control at Bloemfontein, Lord Milner arrived to inspect his new domain. His journey from Cape Town had given him little cause for comfort. In a letter to Lady Edward Cecil, he described the north-east of the Cape as 'reeking with treason'. Nor did he have much faith in the army. 'The more I see of the Army,' he wrote, 'the more unhappy I feel about it.' To cheer him up, members of staff at *The Friend* held a banquet in his honour at the Railway Bureau in the very room where Milner had met Kruger nine months before. Kipling rose to propose a toast to Kruger, a man, he said, to whom they owed so much – 'who has taught the British Empire its responsibilities, and the rest of the world its power, who has filled the seas with the transports and the earth with the tramp of armed men . . .'

On 3 May, Roberts led his army out of Bloemfontein and headed northwards along the line of rail, confident of bringing the war to a swift conclusion. 'We are marching to Pretoria' became a popular imperial song. At his disposal Roberts had a total of 170,000 troops, with more reinforcements still due. The Boers' fighting forces consisted of no more than 30,000 men scattered over a wide area. To the east, Buller's army crawled northwards through Natal, on a direct route to the Transvaal through Laing's Nek. To the west, a flying column left Kimberley heading for Mafeking.

The relief of Mafeking by now had become a matter of urgency. Food supplies were nearly exhausted. Through strict rationing, Colonel Baden-Powell had managed to keep going for six months of siege but warned Roberts that the town could not hold out much longer. The white population, given superior rations, had survived in relative comfort, but hundreds of blacks had died of starvation. Baden-Powell tried to shore up morale by organising sports events and amateur theatricals, often playing a leading role himself. 'What a wonderful man our Colonel is,' wrote his chief clerk, 'he can sing, recite, mimic, in fact do almost anything under the sun.' Baden-Powell had also successfully improvised a series of defences, fortifying the town with trenches, shelters and makeshift artillery. But boredom and frustration had sapped morale. Nobody much liked horse-meat. 'Heard from three sources,' Baden-Powell wrote in his diary on 18 March, 'that the townspeople are expressing themselves tired of the siege and of me etc. They say . . . that I am asking for reinforcements not to be sent in order that I may gain Kudos afterwards . . .'

The plight of Mafeking gripped the imagination of the British public. It stood as a symbol of seemingly heroic resistance, a dusty outpost in the African wilderness bravely defying bombardment and bullets for the sake of the empire. In April, Queen Victoria sent Baden-Powell a message expressing her admiration for 'the patient and resolute defence' of Mafeking 'under your ever resourceful command'.

When the relief column from Kimberley finally broke through to Mafeking on 17 May after 217 days of siege, Britain celebrated in an orgy of nationalist fervour; crowds erupted on to the streets, cheering, dancing, waving flags and banners and singing patriotic songs. A new verb was added to the English language – to maffick – meaning, according to the Oxford English Dictionary, to exult riotously.

Ten days later, Roberts' grand army crossed the Vaal River into the Transvaal, only forty miles south of Johannesburg. By arrangement with Boer commanders, he paused on the outskirts of Johannesburg to allow Boer forces to withdraw unhindered, then entered the town on 31 May, raising the Union flag in the main square.

The British made plain that their intention now was to turn both the Orange Free State and the Transvaal into British territories. Despite Salisbury's previous protestations that 'We want no gold, we want no territory', on 28 May Britain formally annexed the Orange Free State, renaming it the Orange River Colony. The Transvaal was destined for the same fate.

As Boer forces retreated on all fronts, Kruger's inner circle decided that rather than make a stand at Pretoria with the inevitable result of defeat, they would abandon the capital, relocate the government in the eastern Transvaal and take the war into the veld. A special train was prepared for Kruger's escape; it included a sleeping car, a dining car, a conference car, a communications room, an office, a bathroom and kitchen. On his last day in Pretoria – 29 May – Kruger's house on Church Street was full of relatives and friends come to bid him goodbye. His wife, Gezina, was too infirm to accompany him, so she too had to say farewell. After conducting family prayers in the sitting room, Kruger took his wife's hand and led her into their bedroom. Nobody spoke or moved. Outside the carriage horses snorted. Then the old couple reappeared. Kruger pressed her against him, then released her, looking at her intently, silently. Then he turned and walked out to the carriage. They were never to meet again.

On the streets of Pretoria, as the British approached, there was confusion and looting. The main road from Johannesburg was crowded with retreating burghers, wagons and herds of cattle. With a cry of 'Huis-toe' – 'off-home' – thousands abandoned the fight. Meeting at the telegraph offices on 1 June, the Transvaal's generals, including Botha, debated whether to surrender. Only 7,000 burghers could be mustered. The cause seemed hopeless. 'I shall never forget the bitter humiliation and despondency of that awful moment when the stoutest hearts and strongest wills in the Transvaal army were, albeit but for a moment, to sink beneath the tide of our misfortune,' wrote Smuts.

> What all felt so deeply was that the fight had gone out of the Boers, that the heroes who had stood like a stone wall on the Tugela and the Modder River, who had stormed Spion Kop and Ladysmith and many other forlorn hopes, had lost heart and hope, had gone home and forsaken these great officers. It was not Lord Roberts's army that they feared, it was the utter collapse of the Boer rank and file which staggered these great officers.

On his train at Middelburg, ninety miles east of Pretoria. Kruger was equally despondent. He consulted President Steyn by telegraph, sending a message to his hide-out near Lindley in the eastern Free State suggesting surrender. Steyn was furious. Having lost his own capital two months before, he had embarked on a new phase of the war based in the countryside. He was shocked by the lack of resolve now shown by the Transvaalers and virtually accused them of cowardice. No sooner had the war spread to their own territory, Steyn replied, than they were prepared to conclude a 'selfish and disgraceful' peace. Whether or not the Transvaalers made peace, his own people would fight on to the bitter end. Stung by Steyn's rebuke, Kruger and the Transvaal generals went back to the fray.

With only hours to spare before the British arrived, Smuts rushed to get the government's coin and gold reserves, worth about £500,000, out of Pretoria. When bank officials refused to release the gold, Smuts issued warrants for their arrest, then sent a detachment of fifty police to collect it. The gold was put on one of the last trains to leave Pretoria, with shells bursting around the railway station as it left.

On 5 June, by arrangement with Boer officials, Roberts made a triumphal entry into Pretoria. His army had made the 300-mile march from Bloemfontein in only thirty-four days. With control of both capitals, Johannesburg and the gold mines, Roberts confidently expected the Boers to capitulate. The British were in an unassailable position. Boer morale had collapsed. Thousands of Boer combatants – *hensoppers* or 'hands-uppers' – had already surrendered. Roberts' promise of an amnesty, and protection for all burghers who agreed to take no further part in fighting, prompted thousands more to return home. The war, it seemed, was all but over.

Even though sporadic Boer resistance continued, Roberts assumed it would be dealt with in 'mopping-up' operations. In the eastern Free State, Steyn was harried from one makeshift headquarters to the next; in July, half of the remaining Free State army – 4,500 burghers – was forced to surrender at Brandwater Basin.

In the eastern Transvaal, Kruger's government set up temporary headquarters in long lines of train carriages at a railway halt at Machadodorp. But after Botha's commandos were defeated in the last major set-piece battle of the war, Kruger was forced to retreat further down the line to Nelspruit, sixty miles from the Portuguese border. When Roberts formally announced the annexation of the Transvaal on 1 September, Kruger issued a message of defiance from his railway carriage in Nelspruit, declaring the annexation 'null and void'. But his days in the Transvaal were now numbered. Deneys Reitz caught a final glimpse of him. 'He was seated at a table in a railway saloon, with a large Bible before him, a lonely, tired man . . . bowed in thought.'

As British troops advanced on Nelspruit, Kruger left by train for Delagoa Bay, crossing the border at Komatipoort on 11 September with tears coursing down his cheeks. He was never to return. 'If my departure from Pretoria was a bitter blow to me,' he said in his memoirs, 'my departure under such sorrowful circumstances, from the land to which I had devoted my life was doubly bitter. I saw it swarming with the enemy, who, in his arrogance, was already declaring that the war was over . . . I had to bid goodbye to the men who had stood beside me for so many years and to leave my country and my people, my grey-haired wife, my children, my friends and the little band of lion-hearted fighters . . . But I had no choice.'

On 20 October, Kruger, at the age of seventy-five, left for exile in Europe on board a Dutch warship sent to collect him by Queen Wilhelmina of the Netherlands.

Lord Roberts, too, left the Transvaal, handing over command to his chief of staff, General Kitchener, at the end of November. The war, he proclaimed, was 'practically' over. On his return to England, he was given a rapturous reception. Queen Victoria bestowed an earldom upon him; Parliament voted him £100,000. The celebrations, however, were premature. One phase of the war had ended. Another had only just begun.

41

SCORCHED EARTH

Regrouped into small, mobile units, Boer commandos became adept at guerrilla warfare, sabotaging railway lines, ambushing supply columns, destroying bridges, severing telegraph wires and raiding depots, running rings around British forces with hit-and-run tactics. Their leaders – Louis Botha in the eastern Transvaal; Koos de la Rey and Jan Smuts in the western Transvaal; Christiaan de Wet in the Orange Free State – grew into legendary figures. De Wet's exploits, in particular, confounded the British at every turn. During July and August 1900, the British chased De Wet for six weeks across the Free State and the Transvaal, deploying more than 30,000 troops in a bid to catch him. In November, with British forces in hot pursuit, he briefly captured a British garrison at De Wets Dorp, a Free State village named after his father. In February 1901, he crossed the Orange River into the Cape Colony, hoping to inspire rebellion there, outrunning fifteen British columns sent to capture him for six weeks, before returning to the Free State.

The British high command was totally unprepared for this kind of warfare. Their forces, short of mounted troops, scouts and intelligence, lumbered about the countryside in large numbers but with little effect. 'As for our wandering columns,' wrote Captain March Phillipps, in his book *With Rimington*, 'they have about as much chance of catching the Boers on the veldt as a Lord Mayor's procession would have of catching a highwayman on Hounslow Heath . . . [The Boers] are all around and about us like water round a ship, parting before our bows and reuniting round our stern. Our passage makes no impression and leaves no visible trace.'

Unable to get to grips with Boer commandos, the British high command adopted increasingly brutal tactics towards the civilian population who supported them. Before he left for England, Roberts initiated a policy of collective punishment of civilians living in the vicinity of guerrilla attacks, burning down farms, destroying reservoirs and seizing livestock. 'Unless the people generally are made to suffer for the misdeeds of those in arms against us,' said Roberts in September 1900, 'the war will never end.'

In a letter from Frankfort in the Orange Free State in November 1900, Captain Phillipps wrote:

Farm-burning goes merrily on, and our course through the country is marked as in prehistoric ages by pillars of smoke by day and fire by night. We usually burn from six to a dozen farms a day; these being about all that in this sparsely-inhabited country we encounter. I do not gather that any special reason or cause is alleged or proved against the farms burnt. If Boers have used the farm; if the owner is on commando; if the [railway] line within a certain distance has been blown up; or even if there are Boers in the neighbourhood who persist in fighting – these are some of the reasons. Of course the people living in the farms have no say in these matters, and are quite powerless to interfere with the plans of the fighting Boers. Anyway, we find that one reason or another generally covers pretty nearly every farm we come to, and so to save trouble we burn the lot without enquiry; unless indeed, which sometimes happens, some names are given in before marching in the morning of farms to be spared.

In another letter, written from Kronstadt, he described a particular farm-burning incident:

I had to go myself the other day, at the General's bidding, to burn a farm near the line of march. We got to the place and I gave the inmates, three women and some children, ten minutes to clear their clothes and things out of the house, and my men then fetched bundles of straw and we proceeded to burn it down. The old grandmother was very angry . . . Most of them, however, were too miserable to curse. The women cried and the children stood by holding on to them and looking with large frightened eyes at the burning house. They won't forget that sight, I'll bet a sovereign, not even when they grow up. We rode away and left them, a forlorn little group, standing among their household goods – beds, furniture, and gimcracks strewn about the veldt; the crackling of the fire in their ears, and smoke and flame streaming overhead. The worst moment is when you first come to the house. The people thought we had called for refreshments, and one of the women went to get milk. Then we had to tell them that we had come to burn the place down. I simply didn't know which way to look . . .

Phillipps was struck by the resilience of Boer families facing such destruction: 'Husbands and sons in the hill fighting. Homes in the valley blazing, and they sitting and watching it all, almost always with the same fortitude, the same patience, and the same resolve.' And he described a memorable act of defiance:

At another farm a small girl interrupted her preparation for departure to play indignantly their national anthem at us on an old piano. We were carting people off. It was raining hard and blowing – a miserable, hurried home-leaving; ransacked house, muddy soldiers, a distracted mother saving one or two trifles and pushing along her children to the ox-waggon outside, and this poor little wretch in the midst of it pulling herself to strum a final defiance . . .

He questioned the whole purpose of the campaign:

We can't exterminate the Dutch or seriously reduce their numbers. We can do enough to make hatred of England and thirst for
revenge the first duty of every Dutchman, and we can't effectively reduce the numbers of the men who will carry that duty
out. Of course it is not a question of the war only. It is a question of governing the country afterwards.

Other officers thought the results were justified. Captain R. F. Talbot
of the Royal Horse Artillery wrote in his diary:

I went out this morning with some of my men ostensibly to get
vegetables, but joined the provost marshal and the sappers in a
farm burning party, and we burnt and blew up two farms with
gun-cotton, turning out the inhabitants first. It is a bit sickening
at first turning out the women and children, but they are such
brutes and the former all spies; we don't mind it now. Only those
are done which belong to men who are sniping or otherwise
behaving badly.

Destitute families were at first left to drift through the countryside,
fending for themselves, taking whatever shelter they could get. Some
found refuge on other farms; some made their way to towns; some
were taken in by African kraals. As their numbers grew, the British
authorities decided in September 1900 to set up what initially were
called 'refugee camps'. By December, there were nine such camps. As
well as housing Boer families displaced by Roberts' scorched-earth
tactics, they were used to accommodate the families of *hensoppers* –
surrendered burghers – fearful of reprisal. From the start, the camps
were placed under direct military control.

When Kitchener took over command in December 1900, he
developed more systematically both Roberts' scorched-earth policy
and the wider practice of population clearance from hostile rural
areas. A military engineer of iron resolve, already renowned for his use
of ruthless methods, Kitchener had won fame for his campaign to
crush the Mahdi's Dervish army in the Sudan, and as a reward, had
been raised to the peerage, choosing the title of Kitchener of

Khartoum. He regarded Boer women as being as much of an obstacle in the way of military victory as Boer fighters. 'The women question is always cropping up,' he said five days after assuming command. 'There is no doubt the women are keeping up the war and are far more bitter than the men.' The position of 'women left in farms' continued to exercise him. 'Every farm,' he remarked to one of his generals, 'is an intelligence agency and a supply depot so that it is almost impossible to surround or catch' the enemy. The solution he devised was the mass removal of Boer women and children from farms into what were called concentration camps. Their removal, he believed, would not only deprive Boer fighters of food and intelligence, it would hasten the end of the war by inducing them to surrender. 'It was thought that pressure might be brought to bear on the commandos through their womenfolk and that they would not be able to bear separation from their families,' recalled a British intelligence officer. 'It was apparently expected that the Boers would be prepared to abandon war for the sake of love.'

Another central part of Kitchener's strategy was the construction of a network of fortifications – blockhouses and barbed-wire barricades – strung out across the veld, intended to restrict commando movements and to trap them. Thousands of miles of blockhouse lines were built in the Transvaal and the Free State covering them like a spider's web.

In January 1901, Kitchener embarked on a series of military 'drives' to flush out Boer guerrillas, 'scouring' rural districts bare of all their means of support – horses, cattle, sheep, livestock, crops, women and children. Whole areas were laid waste, left as blackened and desolate patches on the landscape. Thousands of Boer refugees, carrying what few possessions they were allowed to take with them, were dumped into concentration camps. Africans were caught up in the same sweeps and sent to their own concentration camps.

Kitchener's measures had little discernible effect, other than to deepen Boer hatred of the British. 'It is a most difficult problem,' Kitchener remarked in February, 'an enemy that always escapes, a country so vast that there is always room to escape, supplies such as they want abundant almost everywhere.' When Kitchener learned, therefore, that Louis Botha was willing to discuss a possible peace settlement, he pursued the idea vigorously, using Botha's wife as an intermediary to arrange a meeting with him at Middelburg at the end of February.

Nothing came of their talks, however. While Kitchener sought compromise, Milner, given overall charge of the Transvaal and the Orange River Colony, insisted on nothing less than 'unconditional surrender'. There was, he wrote to a friend, 'no room for compromise in South Africa'. What he wanted, he said, was 'to knock the bottom out of the "great Afrikander nation" for ever and ever, Amen'. He adamantly refused to allow a full amnesty for all Boer combatants, in particular for Cape rebels. Kitchener blamed Milner's intransigence over the amnesty issue for the collapse of the talks with Botha. 'Milner's views may be strictly just, but to my mind they are vindictive,' he told St John Brodrick, Britain's new war minister. 'We are now carrying on a war to be able to put two or three hundred Dutchmen in prison at the end of it. It seems to me absurd.'

But in reality, the gulf between the two sides was much wider: the Boers still wanted their independence. Botha's willingness to meet Kitchener in the first place angered President Steyn and many other Free Staters. In June 1901, Boer leaders meeting in the eastern Transvaal agreed a joint statement rejecting British terms: 'No peace shall be made, and no peace proposals entertained which do not ensure our independence, and our existence as a nation, or which do not satisfactorily provide for the interests of our Colonial brothers.'

As Kitchener's military drives swept increasing numbers of 'refugees' into concentration camps, conditions there rapidly deteriorated. Kitchener made no adequate preparations for their welfare. Women and children were given only meagre food rations and minimal shelter; they were often left short of water and basic necessities. Latrine facilities were rudimentary: unemptied buckets stood in the sun for hours. Little medical assistance was provided. As disease and malnutrition took hold, the death rate began to climb.

British ministers were well aware of how dire conditions were. 'Pretty bad reports have been received here of the state of the Bloemfontein laager in [January],' the war minister, Brodrick, cabled to Kitchener. He cited 'insufficient water, milk rations, typhoid prevalent, children sick, no soap, no forage for cows, insufficient medical attention . . .' And he asked Kitchener for a full report to help defend himself from political attack. 'I think I shall have a hot time over these probably in most cases inevitable sufferings or privations – war of course is war . . .' Kitchener replied that he had everything under control and pronounced the inmates to be 'happy'.

It was not until a lone Englishwoman, Emily Hobhouse, made her own investigation that the scandal of the concentration camps reached public attention. A 41-year-old Quaker, Hobhouse travelled to the war zones in January 1901 on behalf of a relief fund, the South African Women and Children Distress Fund, taking twelve tons of clothes and home comforts to distribute to camp inmates. She called first at Bloemfontein, the largest camp in the Orange River Colony, where she found 1,800 people living in tents on the bare veld with 'not a vestige of a tree in any direction, nor shade of any description'. What struck her was not merely the hardship of the place, but the death rate:

I began to compare a parish I had known at home of 2,000 people where a funeral was an event – and usually of an old person. Here some twenty to twenty-five were carried away daily . . . The full realization of the position dawned upon me – it was a death-rate such as had never been known except in times of the Great Plagues . . . The whole talk was of death – who died yesterday, who lay dying today, who would be dead tomorrow.

In her book *The Brunt of the War and Where It Fell*, she detailed her findings of the Bloemfontein camp:

The shelter was totally insufficient. When the 8, 10 or 12 persons who occupied a bell-tent were all packed into it, either to escape from the fierceness of the sun or dust or rainstorms, there was no room to move, and the atmosphere was indescribable, even with duly lifted flaps. There was *no soap* provided. The water supplied would not go round. No kartels [bedsteads] or mattresses were to be had. Those, and they were the majority, who could not buy these things must go without. Fuel was scanty . . . The [food] ration was sufficiently small, but when . . . the actual amount did not come up to the scale, it became a starvation rate.

The soldiers in charge, she said, had little idea of how to cope. In letters home, she accused them of 'crass male ignorance, stupidity, helplessness and muddling'.

From Bloemfontein she travelled to other camps finding similar conditions. By the time she returned to Bloemfontein in April, the numbers there had doubled.

More and more are coming in. A new sweeping movement has begun resulting in hundreds and thousands of these unfortunate people either crowding into already crowded camps or else being dumped down to form a new one, where nothing is at hand to shelter them. Colonel says, what can he do? The General wires: 'Expect 500 or 1000 at such a place.' And he has nothing to send there to provide for them . . . No wonder sickness abounds. Since I left here six weeks ago there have been 62 deaths in camp, and the doctor himself is down with enteric [typhoid]. Two of the Boer girls we had trained as nurses and who were doing good work are dead, too . . .

Appalled by what she had witnessed, Emily Hobhouse sailed back to England in May determined to expose the brutality of Kitchener's scorched-earth policy and the death and suffering occurring in the concentration camps. Her cause was taken up by opposition politicians critical of the war. After meeting Hobhouse, the Liberal leader, Sir Henry Campbell-Bannerman, referred to 'methods of barbarism' that he said the British military were using; in a parliamentary debate, he described the countryside outside the towns as a 'howling wilderness'. Another Liberal politician, David Lloyd George, accused the government of pursuing what was in effect 'a policy of extermination' against women and children. 'When children are being treated in this way and dying, we are simply ranging the deepest passions of the human heart against British rule in Africa,' he told parliament in June. 'It will always be remembered that this is the way British rule started there, and this is the method by which it was brought about.'

The war minister, Brodrick, shrugged off all such criticism. The army's policy of sweeping the countryside, he said, had been forced upon it by guerrilla activity. The camps were necessary to protect families who would otherwise starve on the veld. Conditions in the camps were improving; mortality rates were falling. 'It is urged that we have not done sufficient to make these camps sanitary, and to preserve human life. I deny it altogether.'

As Kitchener's sweeps continued, ever greater numbers were packed into the camps: in August, the camps' population reached 105,000 whites and 32,000 blacks. With epidemics of typhoid and measles raging, the death rate rose month by month: in August, 2,666; in September, 2,752; in October, 3,205. It was not until an official all-ladies commission issued their own damning verdict in December that the government saw fit to take remedial measures. In all, some 26,000 Boers died in concentration camps from disease and malnutrition, most of them children under the age of sixteen – about one tenth of the Boer populations of the old republics. In black concentration camps, where the population eventually rose to 116,000, some 14,000 died, most of them children.

In one last effort to stir up rebellion in the Cape Colony, Smuts crossed the Orange River boundary in September 1901 with a hand-picked commando of 250 Transvaalers. Though previous incursions had met with little success, Smuts was convinced of the potential for rebellion. Even British officials acknowledged that half of the Colony's white population was 'more-or-less' pro-Boer and that the greater part of the Colony was 'in a half suppressed state of secret rebellion'.

For six weeks, Smuts' commando made its way through the mountain ranges of the eastern Cape, clashing repeatedly with British patrols, losing men and horses, struggling through heavy rains. 'By day we were wet and cold, and the nights were evil dreams,' wrote Deneys

Reitz, a member of the commando. 'Dry fuel was almost unprocurable, and after a weary day we had to spend the hours of darkness cowering together to snatch a little sleep on some muddy mountainside, or in an equally sodden valley.' The night of the 'Great Rain' was the worst.

> Our guide lost his way; we went floundering ankle-deep in mud and water, our poor, weakened horses stumbling and slipping at every turn; the rain beat down on us, and the cold was awful. Towards midnight it began to sleet. The grain-bag which I wore froze solid on my body, like a coat of mail, and I believe that if we had not kept moving every one of us would have died. We had known two years of war, but we came nearer to despair that night than I care to remember.

In October, Smuts broke further west, into the open plains of the Karoo, collecting recruits as he went and fetching up in Namaqualand, a remote part of the western Cape of little interest to British forces. He was free to roam about at will, but to no discernible effect. He whiled away the time reading copies of books he managed to acquire along the way, such as Kant's *Critique of Pure Reason* and Überweg's *History of Philosophy*. 'On the whole we were much hampered by want of literature, many of the Boers highly educated,' wrote Smuts, 'and one of the pleasures of capturing an English convoy was the number of English books found among the officers' kit.'

The fortunes of other Boer commanders – De Wet in the Free State, Botha in the eastern Transvaal, De la Rey in the western Transvaal – had meanwhile turned for the worse. Facing overwhelming British numbers and increasingly hemmed in by blockhouse lines, they were confined to areas that Kitchener's scorched-earth programme had reduced to a wasteland. In a despatch to London, Milner described the Free State as 'virtually a desert'. Cattle and sheep had been slaughtered or carried away on such a scale that Boers in the Free State had lost half of their herds, those in the Transvaal, three-quarters. Some 30,000 farmsteads had been destroyed; whole villages had been razed to the ground. Shortly after the end of the war, a rising Labour politician, Ramsay MacDonald, described what he found at Lindley, a Free State village that had periodically served as President Steyn's headquarters:

> It was as though I had slept among ancient ruins of the desert. Every house, without a single exception was burnt; the church in the square was burnt . . . Although taken and retaken many times, the place stood practically untouched until February 1902, when a British column entered it unmolested, found it absolutely deserted and proceeded to burn it. The houses are so separated from each other by gardens that the greatest care must be taken to set every one alight. From inquiries I made from our officers and from our host, who was the chief intelligence officer for the district, there was no earthly reason why Lindley should have been torched . . . The whole journey was through a land of sorrow and destruction, of mourning and hate.

Constantly harassed by British patrols, short of food, arms, ammunition and horses, Boer commandos struggled just to survive. Known as *bittereinders*, they were determined to fight to the last but managed to achieve little, making only occasional forays against the enemy. In March 1902, De la Rey succeeded in capturing a British general, Lord Methuen, and 600 troops, but, having no means of holding them, was obliged to let them return to the nearest British base. A few weeks later when commando delegates from the eastern Transvaal met to consider a peace initiative, their dishevelled appearance shocked Deneys Reitz. 'Nothing could have proved more clearly how nearly the Boer cause was spent than those starving, ragged men, clad in skins or sacking, their bodies covered with sores, from lack of salt and food,' he wrote. 'Their spirit was undaunted, but they had reached the limits of physical endurance.'

Only remnants of the Boer armies that had marched out with such confidence at the start of the war remained in the field. Nearly 7,000 Boer combatants had died. Thousands had been captured and deported to prison camps in Bermuda, Ceylon, India and St Helena to make sure they would not fight again. Thousands more – *hensop-*

pers – had surrendered, passively accepting British rule. Some *hensop-pers* had become 'joiners', agreeing to serve with British forces as guides and scouts. In the Transvaal, they were formed into National Scouts; in the Free State, they were known as the Orange River Colony Volunteers. Many joiners objected to the way Boer commanders insisted on continuing the fight at great cost even though there was no possibility of military success. Among them was Christiaan de Wet's brother, General Piet de Wet, who joined the Orange River Colony Volunteers. By April 1902, some 4,000 Boers were collaborating with British forces.

Kitchener was quick to exploit these divisions within Boer ranks. 'There are already two parties amongst them ready to fly at each other's throats,' he wrote to Brodrick, 'and if the Boers could be induced to hate each other more than they hate the British, the British objective would be obtained.' In the long term there would also be political advantages. 'We shall have a party among the Boers themselves depending entirely on British continuity of rule out here.'

With massive military might at his disposal, Kitchener was keen to wind up the war as rapidly as possible. His army by now numbered 250,000 men. He had built 8,000 blockhouses and 3,700 miles of barbed-wire barricades and was able to conduct drives against Boer commandos on a huge scale. In February 1902, he deployed 9,000 men to form a continuous cordon fifty-four miles long – one man every twelve yards advancing steadily forward – in an attempt to trap De Wet and Steyn, with another 8,000 men stationed along block-house lines and eight armoured cars patrolling the railway. His 'bag' was 300 burghers but De Wet managed to escape. In March, he launched a similar drive against De Wet, this time sweeping up 800 burghers, but still De Wet evaded capture. As well as white troops, Kitchener made increasing use of Africans as scouts, spies and armed guards.

Kitchener also changed his tactics towards Boer civilians – women and children – living in rural areas. While continuing to destroy farms, he instructed his column commanders to leave them where they found them instead of packing them off to concentration camps. The burden of caring for destitute Boer families thus fell on the commandos. Some 13,000 women and children were said to be homeless, wandering across the veld, exposed to the vagaries of the weather and the danger of black attack. Their plight weighed heavily on Boer leaders and became another factor propelling them towards negotiations.

42

THE BITTER END

Given safe passage by the British high command, Boer leaders from the two republican governments gathered at Klerksdorp in south-west Transvaal on 9 April 1902, to review the war situation and to decide whether to open negotiations. The British military provided them with a large tent for the occasion. Among those present were Marthinus Steyn, president of the Orange Free State, Schalk Burger, the acting president of the Transvaal and four Boer generals – Botha, Smuts, De Wet and De la Rey – whom the British had spent months trying in vain to capture. Two days later, ten representatives boarded a special train for Pretoria, taking with them a peace plan to present to Kitchener.

Meeting at Kitchener's headquarters at Melrose House on 12 April, they proposed seven points intended to lead to an 'enduring treaty of friendship'. These included a commercial union with adjoining British territories; votes for uitlanders; equal language rights in schools; and a mutual amnesty. Schalk Burger opened the proceedings; Steyn followed, making clear that he did not accept Britain's annexation of Boer territory. 'Must I understand from what you say that you wish to retain your independence?' asked Kitchener with astonishment. 'Yes,' Steyn replied, 'the people must not lose their self-respect.' Kitchener knew that the Boer peace plan would never be accepted but, keen for negotiations to continue, he forwarded the proposals to London.

On 14 April, Milner joined the talks. As before, he was hostile to the idea of negotiating with the Boers. 'Personally,' he told Chamberlain, 'I distrust all negotiations. This feeling is shared I believe by all our friends in South Africa. But as public feeling at home evidently favours negotiations one must do the best we can.' What he wanted was an unconditional surrender that would give him a free hand to dictate the post-war reconstruction of South Africa. He was also distrustful of Kitchener, resenting his willingness to look for compromise. Kitchener, he complained, was 'extremely adroit in his management of negotiations, but he does not care what he gives away'.

While rejecting the Boer peace plan, the British government put forward its own proposals, requiring the Boers to accept the surrender of their independence. The Boer delegates replied that they had no constitutional authority to negotiate on the basis of surrendering their independence, and they asked for an armistice to enable them to consult with their commandos. To Milner's disgust, Kitchener agreed to a series of local armistices – in his words, a 'go-slow'. In his diary for 17 April, Milner wrote: 'I think it a very bad arrangement . . . Very tired & not a little disgusted to bed.'

On 15 May, sixty delegates elected by the *bittereinder* commandos – thirty from the Transvaal and thirty from the Free State – assembled at Vereeniging, a village on the Vaal River, to decide the fate of their republics. They were deeply divided. The Transvaal delegates were desperate for an end to the war. Botha described the plight of the Transvaal's farming community. In the hundred miles between Vereeniging and Ermelo, he said, there were no cattle, only thirty-six goats and horses that were too weak to move; women were trekking about in a pitiable condition. Moreover, Africans were beginning to act more aggressively towards Boers; in one incident, Boer farmers had been massacred by Zulus in Vryheid. Even worse, the Boers themselves were becoming ever more divided. A growing number were joining the British side as National Scouts. 'If we continue the war, it may be that the Afrikaners against us will outnumber our own men.' There was a danger that in the end Boer fighters would come to be regarded as little more than bandits by their own people. Peace was essential to prevent the Boers from sliding into irreparable ruin. If the war continued, it would end in a defeat so overwhelming that the Boers would have no chance of salvaging anything in negotiations. 'We have heard much talk about fighting "to the bitter end". But what is "the bitter end"? Is it to come when all of us are banished or in our graves? Or does it mean the time when the nation has fought until it can never rise again?'

Schalk Burger put similar arguments: 'Can we let the people be annihilated for the sake of honour and fame for ourselves?' De la Rey echoed Botha's words: 'Fight to the bitter end, it is said. But has not the bitter end come?' He advised:

> I think each one must decide for himself. It must be borne in mind that everything – cattle, goods, money, man, woman and child – has been sacrificed. In my division many people go almost naked. There are men and women who wear nothing more than plain skins on the naked body. Is this not the bitter end?

The Free State delegates, however, were in favour of continuing the war. Foremost among them were De Wet and Steyn. De Wet refused to countenance the surrender of Boer independence. The Free State burghers, he said, were as well able to fight on now as they had been a year before. Harking back to a previous occasion when the *volk* appeared to be in mortal danger, he urged delegates: 'Let us again renew our covenant with God.' Steyn was equally adamant, but, in rapidly declining health, he was forced to withdraw from the deliberations.

At the end of the second day, Frank Reitz, the Transvaal's state secretary, suggested a compromise. He proposed that, provided the republics could keep their independence, they should be prepared to surrender control of foreign relations; agree to internal self-government under British auspices; cede control of Swaziland; and give up the Witwatersrand and its goldfields – 'that cancer in our country', as Botha described it. Armed with this plan, a five-man commission – Botha, De La Rey, De Wet, Smuts and General Barry Hertzog, a former Free State judge – travelled to Pretoria hoping to gain British approval.

The plan, presented to Milner and Kitchener at Melrose House on 19 May, was given short shrift. 'Grant it,' said Kitchener, 'and before a year is over we shall be at war again.' For day after day, the British and the Boers haggled over the terms the British demanded, the Boers striving to hang on to a semblance of independence. The exchanges were further complicated by disputes between Milner and Kitchener. Milner wanted terms that would leave Boer leaders humiliated and destroy their credibility; Kitchener sought terms that would assist post-war reconciliation.

The British made several concessions. Contrary to Milner's previous insistence, they agreed that Cape Afrikaner rebels would be dealt with leniently (they were disenfranchised for five years). More crucially, the British gave way over the issue of black political rights. On the eve of the war, Chamberlain had used Boer maltreatment of blacks and Coloureds as a pretext for intervention. 'The treatment of the natives [in the Transvaal] has been disgraceful,' he told parliament in October 1899, 'it has been brutal; it has been unworthy of a civilized Power.' Both Chamberlain and Milner had declared that the claims of the African and Coloured communities for political rights would be considered sympathetically. 'We cannot consent to purchase a shameful peace by leaving the Coloured population in the position in which they stood before the war,' said Chamberlain. He had been equally insistent on the need for some form of African representation, similar to the franchise available to the Cape's black elite. But in order to assuage Boer opinion, the British backed down. The priority now was postwar reconciliation between the two white groups.

In their original draft proposals, the British had indicated that blacks would be accorded some form of representation after the introduction of self-government. 'The Franchise will not be given to Natives until after the Introduction of Self-Government.' But Smuts re-wrote the clause to read: 'The question of granting the Franchise to Natives will not be decided until after the introduction of self-government'. The

British accepted this amendment. It meant that the white electorates of the Transvaal and the Orange River Colony would be left to decide themselves whether to enfranchise the black population. Given that the republics had never allowed blacks to vote, it was a foregone conclusion, as both sides acknowledged, that blacks would be excluded. As Milner remarked in a private letter: 'You have only to sacrifice "the nigger" absolutely and the game is easy.'

A more contentious issue concerned war debts. Boer leaders wanted funds to compensate burghers whose property they had commandeered for war purposes; otherwise promissory notes they had issued to their followers would not be honoured. Payment of these debts, Botha argued, would 'strengthen our hands by enabling us honourably to terminate this matter'. The British government initially offered a sum of £1 million; Botha asked for £3 million to allow for full compensation. Kitchener openly supported Botha's request and agreed 'that the honour of every officer is affected by these documents'. It was a matter, he told Brodrick, that was 'vital to peace'.

Milner, however, obdurately refused to consider paying 'every debt incurred by every officer of both armies for the purpose of fighting us' and appealed to Chamberlain to back him. He described the Boer request as 'detestable', 'preposterous', and 'an audacious try-on' and claimed his position was being undermined by Kitchener. Kitchener, he said, 'does not always support me even in the presence of Boers'. And he made clear his distaste for the whole business of negotiation. 'My own conviction is that Boers are done for, and that if the assembly at Vereeniging breaks up without peace they will surrender left and right. The men here are either anxious to upset negotiations or bluffing, in reliance on our weakness, probably the latter.'

Chamberlain was unimpressed. 'I do not think a mere question of money should prevent termination of war, which costs more than a million a week . . . There should be some argument more cogent than money cost to justify risking a failure on this point. Can you supply it, and would you go so far as to wreck agreement at this stage upon this one question?'

On 27 May 1902, the British cabinet met to decide the final terms to be offered to the Boers. Henceforth, they would be required to acknowledge King Edward VII 'as their lawful sovereign'. The Transvaal and the Orange River Colony would be run first by a British military administration, then by a civil administration, then by self-government 'as soon as circumstances permit it'. The terms were presented to the ten Boer leaders in Pretoria on 28 May. They were told there would be no further discussion and given three days in which to give their answer, a simple 'yes' or 'no'.

Returning to Vereeniging, they first showed the peace terms to Steyn. Steyn denounced them as a gross betrayal of the Boer cause. 'You have sold out the *volk* for £3 million,' he told them. Amongst the sixty delegates, the arguments raged back and forth once more. The burden of persuading them to surrender rested largely on Botha. Other Transvaalers supported him. De la Rey told delegates that if there was salvation for the *volk* in continuing to fight, he would go along, and if a grave were being dug for the *volk* he would get into it. But there was a real chance that the nation would be driven to surrendering en masse, bringing the war to an end in dishonour and disgrace.

Smuts added his own weight. The *bittereinders* had fought bravely and were prepared to sacrifice everything for the independence of the *volk*, he said; but there was no longer a reasonable chance of success:

> We have moved to stand fast to the bitter end; but let us be men and acknowledge that the end has now come and it was more bitter than we thought it would be. For death itself would be sweeter than the step we must now take . . . No one shall ever convince me that this unparalleled sacrifice that the [Afrikaner] nation has laid upon the altar of freedom will be in vain . . .

However, he went on, independence was not the highest value in the struggle for survival. 'We must not sacrifice the *Afrikaansche volk* on the altar of independence.' Once the chance of maintaining independence had gone, it was the duty to stop the fight. 'We must not run the risk of sacrificing our nation and its future to a mere idea which can no longer be realized.'

The Free Staters remained adamant. 'I shall never put hand on a piece of paper in which I sacrifice my people's independence,' Steyn declared. But he was too ill to continue to participate. After the first day of deliberation, he resigned as president, handing over office to De Wet and parting with some cautionary words of advice:

> If the Transvaalers should decide to make peace and if you should find it futile to resist any further – then give in. We cannot continue the war with a handful of Free Staters. So we are not to blame. We have fulfilled to the letter our agreement with the sister Republic. Without the Transvaal it would be folly for us to continue the struggle on our own.

To avoid a disastrous split, De Wet decided to go along with the Transvaalers. Just after 2 p.m. on Saturday 31 May, the vote was taken: fifty-four delegates agreed to surrender; six voted 'no'.

'How great was the emotion,' wrote the Reverend 'Vader' Kestell, who had served as chaplain to Boer commandos. 'I saw the lips quiver of men who had never trembled before a foe. I saw tears brimming in eyes that had been dry when they had seen their dearest laid in the grave.'

When Smuts explained the peace terms to his own commando, a burgher cried out: 'Jan Smuts, you have betrayed us.'

In Kipling's memorable phrase, the war gave Britain 'no end of a lesson'. It had been provoked by Britain – by a handful of politicians and officials – on the assumption of an easy military victory over a group of backward peasant farmers – a 'tea-time' war that would be 'over by Christmas'. But it had turned into a campaign of humiliating reverses and setbacks, and it had been won only through the deployment of 450,000 imperial troops and the use of scorched-earth tactics. The cost to the British military was 22,000 dead, two-thirds of them from disease and illness. The cost to the British exchequer – originally estimated at £10 million – was £217 million. When it was finally over – after two and a half years – it was not so much a sense of victory that the British felt as a sense of relief. As Kipling wrote:

Me an' my trusty friend 'ave 'ad,
As you might say, a war,
But seein what both parties done
Before 'e owned defeat,
I ain't more proud of 'avin won
Than I am pleased with Piet.

When Boer leaders gathered at Kitchener's headquarters at Melrose House in Pretoria on 31 May 1902 to sign the peace agreement, Kitchener shook their hands, declaring: 'We are good friends now.' For Milner, however, the war was unfinished business. He later told the journalist H. Spenser Wilkinson: 'It has changed its character: it is no longer war with bullets, but war it still is. It is quite true we hold the winning cards, but it is not true we have won the game, and we cannot afford to lose a single trick.'

43

ENVOI

Cecil Rhodes did not live long enough to see the end of the war. In the early months of 1902, his health deteriorated rapidly. He was only forty-eight years old but looked more like a man in his sixties. His diseased heart left him gasping for breath and often wracked with pain. To members of his staff he appeared to be in steep decline. 'His face was bloated, almost swollen, and he was livid with a purple tinge in his face,' wrote Gordon le Sueur, who met him in London in January 1902 shortly after Rhodes returned from a journey to Egypt. 'I realized that he was very ill indeed.'

His last months were dogged not just by ill-health but by a tiresome imbroglio with Princess Radziwill. Their friendship had long since turned sour. Rhodes was infuriated by her persistent attempts to meddle in Cape politics and the insinuations she made to all and sundry that they were intimately involved. Among the acquaintances she took into her confidence while staying at the Mount Nelson Hotel was Leo Amery, a correspondent for the London *Times*. 'Princess Radziwill,' Amery recalled, 'had conceived an infatuation for Rhodes and had come out in the vain hope at vamping him into matrimony.' Radziwill was later to admit that Rhodes resented her constant meddling. 'What can one do with you, Mr Rhodes?' she once demanded angrily. 'Leave me alone!' was his exasperated reply.

When Radziwill appealed to Rhodes for a loan to help her sort out her growing mountain of debts, Rhodes paid her bills at the Mount Nelson Hotel, amounting to more than £1,000, in the hope that she might leave Cape Town and return permanently to London.

But she continued to haunt him. After a luncheon at Groote Schuur on 22 January 1901, they had what Radziwill later described as 'a violent quarrel'. In her own account of what happened, she wrote: 'I had some [papers] which were very compromising for certain reasons and I possessed above all several which, after having been stolen from their legitimate owners, had fallen into my hands . . . I had on this subject a tragical scene with Rhodes. He insisted that I should surrender to him such letters and papers as I possessed. I refused vehemently.' The suspicion was that Radziwill had stolen papers from Rhodes' private office during her visits to Groote Schuur – papers possibly connected with the Jameson Raid – and that she intended to blackmail him. Their encounters came to an abrupt end.

Despite her dire financial straits, Radziwill had decided to launch her own newspaper in Cape Town – a sixpenny weekly she called *Greater Britain*. She rented offices and hired an editor, Frederick Lovegrove, telling him she had enough money to cover publication costs for six months and then intended to 'worm the money from Rhodes' to keep the paper going. But she was soon mired in debt. In June 1901, after purchasing a signed photograph of Rhodes from a bookshop, she began forging his signature on promissory notes and bills. When one promissory note fell due, she forged others, for amounts up to £6,000, trying to keep her creditors at bay, calculating that Rhodes would not dare to move against her.

With a lifetime's experience of sharp business practice, Rhodes prepared his own trap. While keeping his own role hidden from view, he set out to discredit her, to expose her as a forger, in case she decided to disclose whatever incriminating papers were in her possession. In secret, he arranged for a friend, Tom Louw, to advance £2,000 on the latest of her forged promissory notes. At the same time, he issued press announcements warning that certain promissory notes purporting to have been endorsed by him were in fact forgeries, thus preventing Radziwill from obtaining any more money. When Louw's promissory note fell due in September 1901, she was unable to pay up. In October, Louw began legal proceedings against both Radziwill and Rhodes over the £2,000 promissory note. Rhodes, in London at the time, signed an affidavit denying that he had endorsed any promissory notes. Using various intermediaries, he offered Radziwill money if she agreed to return whatever incriminating papers she held, but she refused, convinced that Rhodes would settle her debts rather than 'go into court'.

But Rhodes allowed the legal proceedings to continue. Along with Radziwill, he was formally summoned to appear in the Supreme Court at Cape Town on 6 February 1902. Though he could have given his evidence in England, he insisted on travelling to Cape Town. His doctors in London warned him his heart would not stand the strain. Friends urged him not to put himself at risk over such a trivial matter. 'It is not the money,' he replied, 'but no risk will prevent me clearing my character of any stain in connection with that woman.' He was determined, he said, to defend his honour and upset 'the bona fides' of Radziwill. However, it was not in fact damage to his reputation that worried Rhodes, but the possibility that Radziwill might produce her 'papers' in court. He wanted to bring to bear the full weight of his personal prestige to convince the court to brand the princess a forger.

Accompanied by Dr Jameson, Rhodes set sail for Cape Town. The voyage aggravated his ill-health. He caught a severe cold while at sea, and suffered a bad fall one night while sleeping on a writing table in his cabin in an attempt to catch a cool breeze. He arrived in Cape Town on 4 February, at once puffy-faced and haggard. The heat that summer was oppressive. During the daytime he remained at Groote Schuur, but every evening retreated to a small cottage on the seafront at Muizenberg, seeking relief from breezes blowing off False Bay. One of his aides, Gordon le Sueur, recalled:

Rhodes would wander about the house like a caged animal, his clothes all thrown open, his hand thrust characteristically inside his trousers, the beads of perspiration glistening on his forehead beneath his tousled hair as he panted for breath. Into the darkened drawing room he would go and fling himself upon a couch, then he would start up and huddle himself up in a chair . . . and anon painfully toil upstairs to his bedroom and pace to and fro, every now and then stopping at the window which gave him that wondrous view of Table Mountain.

When the case opened at the Supreme Court on 6 February, Radziwill failed to attend, pleading ill-health. In his evidence, Rhodes disclaimed all knowledge of the promissory notes. 'They are all forgeries,' he said. 'All absolute forgeries.' He explained that he had paid Radziwill's bills at the Mount Nelson Hotel on condition that she should leave the country. 'I paid her bills and she left the country, but she came back again.' Passing judgement, the chief justice, Sir Henry de Villiers, duly declared Louw's promissory note to have been forged, but he declined to initiate criminal proceedings against Radziwill on the grounds that no affidavit charging her with an offence had been lodged.

Rhodes assumed the matter was at an end. But to his astonishment, Radziwill decided to hit back. Furious at being branded a forger, she sued Rhodes for the £2,000 bill which she claimed he had endorsed. 'Damn that woman!' he shouted when his secretary handed him the summons. 'Can't she leave me alone?' Left with no alternative, he drew up an affidavit accusing Radziwill of forgery.

On 28 February, Radziwill was formally charged with uttering a forged document. As Rhodes was too ill to attend the preliminary hearing in court, he gave his evidence to a magistrate at Groote Schuur. Radziwill was present with her lawyer, sitting at the back of a small circle of people gathered in front of the magistrate's desk. Rhodes entered the room dressed in a grey jacket, white flannel trousers and black boots and took his place on a sofa, coughing badly. The proceedings lasted no more than a few minutes. After signing a prepared statement repudiating the promissory notes, Rhodes staggered to his feet and left. Not once did he glance at Radziwill. She was subsequently convicted of twenty-four counts of fraud and forgery and sentenced to two years' imprisonment.

Rhodes spent his last few weeks at his cottage in Muizenberg in the company of friends and aides, his breathing becoming increasingly laboured. Jourdan wrote:

> It was most heartrending to see him sit on the edge of his bed with one limb resting on the floor and the other akimbo in front of him on the bed, at one moment gasping for breath, and at another with his head sunk so low that his chin almost touched his chest. Sometimes in the early morning and towards evening it became quite chilly, but he did not heed the cold. He could not get sufficient fresh air, and, even when those around him were in their overcoats, he sat in front of the open window with his thin pyjamas as his only covering. He was always asking for more fresh air.

Dr Jameson arranged for layers of ice to be placed in the ceiling; an extra window was knocked through the wall to allow for a continuous draught; and Indian-type pankah fans were kept going day and night. But his suffering was unabated.

On his last day, 26 March 1902, his friend, banker and biographer, Lewis Michell, heard him murmur: 'So little done, so much to do.' After a long pause, said Michell, Rhodes began singing to himself, 'maybe a few bars of an air he had once sung at his mother's knee'. In the evening, just before he died, he roused himself and spoke to Jack Grimmer, a favourite aide: 'Turn me over, Jack,' he said, and then fell silent.

It was Jameson who formally announced Rhodes' death to the crowd waiting in the street outside. Standing on the veranda, Jameson solemnly read from a prepared statement. When asked about Rhodes' last words, he replied: 'So little done, so much to do.' This was the version that newspapers recorded. Rhodes would have delighted in this final piece of story-telling about him.

His body was taken to Groote Schuur. Over the Easter weekend, some 30,000 people filed through the oak-panelled hall to view the catafalque. His coffin was then moved to Cape Town to lie in state in parliament where thousands more came to pay their respects. From parliament, the coffin was borne on a gun carriage draped with a Union Jack and the flag of Rhodes' Chartered Company to a funeral service at the cathedral. In his address, the Archbishop of Cape Town urged the congregation to follow Rhodes' great example and dedicate their lives 'to the expansion and consolidation of the British Empire, to the provision of new markets for British merchandise, and to a new country for British colonists'. Then, in another procession, the coffin was taken to the railway station for a journey to the north.

In his will, Rhodes had stipulated that he wanted to be buried in the Matopo Hills in Matabeleland. Riding there with Hans Sauer in 1896, he had come across the granite dome of Malindidzuma – a Sindebele name meaning 'the dwelling place of the spirits'. Rhodes was profoundly impressed by the grandeur and loneliness of the place, calling it 'a view of the world'.

The journey to Bulawayo took five days. The funeral train passed through Kimberley and then Mafeking, skirting the war zone where a British general had just surrendered to Koos de la Rey. At towns along the way, there were guards of honour and military bands playing funeral marches.

From Bulawayo, a procession of Cape carts and horsemen accompanied the coffin to the Matopos. As the coffin was hauled up the granite slope of Malindidzuma, crowds of Ndebele accorded Rhodes a royal salute. At the funeral service, the Bishop of Mashonaland read out a poem about Rhodes composed by Rudyard Kipling for the occasion:

> The great and brooding spirit still
> Shall quicken and control;
> Living he was the land, and dead
> His soul shall be her soul!

In his own tribute to Rhodes, the London editor W. T. Stead described him as 'the first of the new Dynasty of Money Kings which has been evolved in these later days as the real rulers of the modern world'. Rhodes died a rich man, but his estate of £4 million was considerably smaller than that of Beit or Wernher, his old Kimberley partners. Their preoccupation was with wealth. Rhodes' preoccupation had been with power.

Paul Kruger spent his last years in exile in Europe, a lonely figure, increasingly deaf, half-blind and deeply embittered by Britain's conduct of the war. 'The war in South Africa has exceeded the limits of barbarism,' he said on his arrival at Marseilles in November 1900. 'I have fought against many barbarous Kaffir tribes in the course of my life; but they are not so barbarous as the English, who have burnt our farms and driven our women and children into destitution, without food or shelter.' He sought support from European governments, but to no avail; none wanted to pick a quarrel with Britain; the Kaiser declined to meet him. 'Will no one arbitrate?' he demanded of a journalist, Emil Luden. 'Will no one give us a fair hearing, a chance of defending ourselves? We may have done wrongly; we have had our faults, our weaknesses; we declared this war, but our hands were forced – we can prove it! Let someone judge between this England and ourselves. Let someone judge.'

In an article published in the *Pall Mall Gazette*, Luden described her encounters with Kruger at The Hague:

At first sight the impression one gets of him is not prepossessing: a large, heavy face and two great hands on a mass of dark clothing. He does not rise from his ponderous chair unless absolutely necessary. One can see easily how irksome bodily movement has become to this valiant old fighter of battles. He looks up sharply when a stranger enters the room, then his head sinks on his chest again. He has never cultivated 'company manners', and his thoughts are all-absorbing. His hands are quite motionless, held finger-tips against his big loose body . . .

His thoughts form slowly, and are born at last in abrupt travail, throes of words and distress of gesture that are eloquent of passion. For his hands are only motionless when his tongue is passive. As he begins to speak the finger-tips part from each other with a wrench. He throws imaginary weights behind him, strikes the arms of his chair, and drops his hands heavily on his knees. Then, when he has cast his thought forth as only a strong man can, his finger-tips seek their fellows again, his eyes close, and the mask of abstraction is drawn down over the inscrutable face.

On his travels in Europe, Kruger was accorded a far warmer reception by the public than by governments. He was widely regarded as a victim of British bullying, a heroic defender of his small republic against the might of the world's largest empire. Crowds turned out to greet him, waving the Transvaal flag. Dinners and receptions were held in his honour. Shops did a brisk trade in Kruger memorabilia: postcards, busts, medallions, mugs in the shape of his head, plates bearing his effigy. But Kruger had no particular liking for public acclaim; nor did he enjoy small talk.

In England, his reputation remained that of a coarse-mannered peasant, familiar from cartoon drawings for his chimney-pot hat, oyster eyes and shabby clothes, who had obdurately refused to accord Englishmen their rights and had dragged his people into a war against England rather than give way. Facing defeat, he had fled to escape the consequences, taking with him 'millions' in gold. It was a caricature that prevailed long after his death.

When Boer generals signed the peace treaty on 31 May 1902, Kruger broke down at the news, but cast no blame. 'I applied to the generals the text in the Bible, 2 Corinthians Chapter VIII Verse 3: "For to their power, I bear record, yea, and beyond their power they were willing of themselves."

'Nor, in so far as I myself am concerned,' he added, 'will I consent to lose courage because the peace is not such as the burghers wished it. For, quite apart from the fact that the bloodshed and the fearful sufferings of the people of the two Republics are now ended, I am convinced that God does not forsake His people even though it may appear so.'

The death of his wife Gezina in Pretoria a few weeks later left him all the more bereft. He lingered on for two more years, his health steadily failing, devoting much of his time to reading the Bible and retreating into long periods of silence. On his seventy-seventh birthday, he attended a special church service in Utrecht, sitting in the front row flanked by Botha, De Wet and De la Rey. Towards the end of the service, helped by aides, he mounted the pulpit to deliver a short sermon, 'the words falling with difficulty from his trembling lips'. The following winter, Emily Hobhouse visited him at Menton on the French Côte d'Azur. 'Our talk was not long,' she wrote. 'I saw that already his mind was elsewhere and the world had ended for him . . . He wanted so much to know if I had seen his wife and when I told him that I had not been allowed to visit Pretoria before her death, he seemed too disappointed to make further effort.'

In May 1904, Kruger settled in a villa at Clarens on the shores of Lake Geneva. When Smuts and Botha urged him to return to the Cape Colony, he declined. In one of his last letters, he wrote to Botha:

> Born under the British flag, I do not wish to die under it. I have learnt to accept the bitter thought of death as a lone exile in a foreign land, far from my kith and kin, whose faces I am not likely to see again; far from the soil of Africa upon which I am not likely to set foot again; far from the country to which I devoted my whole life in an effort to open it up for civilization and in which I saw my own nation grow.

A few weeks later, he contracted pneumonia and died on 14 July.

In a letter to Emily Hobhouse, Smuts wrote of Kruger: 'He typified the Boer character both in its brighter and darker aspects and was no doubt the greatest man – both morally and intellectually – whom the Boer race has yet produced. In his iron will and tenacity, his "never say die" attitude towards fate, his mystic faith in another world, he represented what is best in all of us. The race that produced such a man *can* never go down, and with God's help it never will.'

In November 1904, Kruger's body was brought back from Europe for burial. On the railway journey from Cape Town, the driver had orders to stop the train whenever a light was shown, and so all through the night it halted to allow small parties of farmers to deliver their wreaths. He was buried next to his wife in Pretoria on Dingane's Day, 16 December.

PART X

44

THE SUNNYSIDE STRATEGY

As the new overlord of the Transvaal and the Orange River Colony, Lord Milner set out to impose on them his own post-war strategy. Moving his headquarters from Cape Town, he chose Johannesburg rather than Pretoria as a base. 'The more I see of Pretoria,' he said, 'the more I am impressed by its unfitness to be the capital of anything.' It was, he said, 'the most enervating place I know'. Chamberlain ruled that Pretoria had to remain the capital. He also had misgivings about allowing Milner to take up residence in Johannesburg because of the predominant influence there of the gold-mining industry. 'My objection is that it necessarily lacks that diversity which in other great cities renders public opinion healthy and impartial.' But Milner got his own way and established himself in a red-tiled villa on the northern outskirts called Sunnyside built for one of the Randlords. To help him run his new fiefdom, he recruited a group of young Oxford graduates who became known, derisively at first, as 'Milner's Kindergarten'. Among them was John Buchan who later used his South African experiences as material for his novels, notably *Prester John*. Buchan served as an assistant private secretary, first dealing with concentration camps for women and children; then the repatriation of Boer prisoners; then land resettlement and agricultural schemes. 'I had to be in some degree a jack-of-all-trades – transport rider, seedsman, stockman, horsecoper, merchant, lawyer, not to speak of diplomatist,' he wrote.

Milner arrived in Johannesburg with decided views about what he intended to accomplish, and dictatorial powers to implement them. Above all, he was determined to convert the Transvaal into a 'thoroughly British' domain where 'British interests, British ideas, British education' would prevail.

He envisaged two principal methods of achieving this goal. The first was large-scale immigration of people of British descent. 'I attach the greatest importance of all to the increase in the British population,' he told the Colonial Office. 'If, ten years hence, there are three men of British race to two of Dutch, the country will be safe and prosperous. If there are three of Dutch to two of British, we shall have perpetual difficulty . . . We not only want a majority of British, we want a fair margin because of the large proportion of cranks that we British generate and who take particular pleasure in going against their own people.'

Milner foresaw little difficulty in ensuring British dominance in towns. The bulk of immigrants would be urban industrial workers, drawn to the Transvaal by the 'vast and immediate expansion of mining and other industrial enterprises' following the end of the war. But he expressed concern about the future of rural areas.

> The majority of the agricultural population will always be Dutch. That does not matter provided that, in most districts, there are a sufficient number of British to hold their own. A mere sprinkling is no use. They only get absorbed and become more Dutch than their neighbours. The only way to achieve this is by large purchases of land on the part of Government with a view to reselling to suitable settlers. Men willing to risk some capital of their own should be preferred, and they should be planted on large or middle-sized farms . . . Our great hope is in getting . . . thousands of settlers of a superior class . . . They will get on all right with the Dutch if they are not too greatly outnumbered . . . A healthy social and political white population would be the following: assuming that 60 per cent

of the white population will be industrial and commercial and 40 per cent agricultural, I should like to see 45 out of the 60 British and 15 Dutch, and 15 out of the 40 British and 25 Dutch. The former proportion will accomplish itself . . . but to make even as much as 2/5ths of the agricultural population British will take some working. It is only to be done by bringing British settlers through Government Agency in considerable numbers.

After five years of peace and beneficent British rule, Milner expected the British population of the Transvaal to rise from 100,000 to 250,000, while the Afrikaner population would increase marginally from 140,000 to 150,000. Only when a loyal majority was ensured could the Transvaal be safely entrusted with a measure of self-government.

The other principal method that Milner intended to use in his campaign to 'anglicize' the Transvaal was a new education system. 'Next to the composition of the population, the thing which matters most is its education.' The key was to make English the chief medium of instruction in state schools. English, Milner told the Colonial Office, should be the language of all higher education. 'Dutch should only be used to teach English and English to teach everything else.' He placed particular emphasis on the need to recruit effective teachers. 'Language is important, but the tone and spirit of teaching conveyed in it is even more important. Not half enough attention has been paid to school reading books. To get these right would be the greatest political achievement conceivable. I attach especial importance to school history books.'

To put these ideas into practice, Milner employed as director of education an ardent imperialist, Edmund Sargant. Teachers were carefully selected for their loyalty to the cause. At interviews conducted by the Board of Education, prospective candidates were asked: 'Are you in sympathy with the intention of the Government to make the Orange River and Transvaal Colonies permanently part of the British dominions?'; and 'Will you use your best endeavours . . . to reconcile all the Boer men, women and children . . . to their new position as citizens of the British Empire?' A large part of the curriculum was devoted to imperial history.

English was duly established as the medium of instruction. The only concession was a provision that allowed parents to request that their children be given fifteen minutes of religious instruction in Dutch each day, and a further three hours per week for the study of the Dutch Bible until the children were confirmed, and thereafter three hours weekly for the study of Dutch literature.

Alongside his initiatives on immigration and education, Milner pursued two other objectives. He planned to install a modern professional bureaucracy and to promote economic development. Modernisation and economic prosperity, Milner believed, would not only stimulate large-scale British immigration; they would destroy the basis of Afrikaner nationalism. Once the Transvaal had acquired a sufficiently British character, it would be allowed to take the lead in establishing a British federal dominion in southern Africa. Although the Orange River Colony was bound to remain an Afrikaner-dominated state, it would have no option but to become part of the federal dominion. 'A thoroughly British Transvaal,' Milner maintained, 'will draw all South Africa after it.' The ultimate aim was to turn southern Africa into 'one Dominion', under one flag with a common government dealing with customs, railways, defence and native policy – 'a self-governing white Community, supported by *well-treated* and *justly governed* black labour from Cape Town to Zambesi'.

Milner threw himself into his great scheme with formidable energy. A massive effort was soon under way to transport Boers back to the land. By the end of the war the bulk of the Boer population had been removed from their homes: 117,000 men, women and children were living in concentration camps; 31,000 burghers were prisoners-of-war, most of them held in camps overseas, as far afield as Ceylon and Bermuda. Returning farmers were provided with seeds, livestock, implements and building materials. A department of agriculture was established for the first time with sections dedicated to veterinary science, soil chemistry, forestry, horticulture and locust control. Schemes were launched to promote improved arable farming and pastoral agriculture. Everything from the police to the courts to local government was organised anew; more railways were constructed; an elaborate system of government schools was created. Development, said Milner, was 'our trump card'. 'Every new railway, every new school, every new settlement is a nail in the coffin of Boer nationalism.'

As for the political future, he was determined that political power should be withheld from the white population until British ascendancy was assured. He set up two 'legislative councils' – one for the Transvaal and one for the Orange River Colony. But they were composed of officials and selected nominees. Among the nominees he appointed to the Transvaal legislative council were two mining magnates, Sir Percy FitzPatrick, the first post-war president of the Chamber of Mines, and Sir George Farrar, the second post-war president; both had been involved in Rhodes' plot to overthrow Kruger, but were newly knighted.

But Milner's grand design soon encountered difficulties. His hopes for economic expansion depended heavily on the fortunes of the gold-mining industry. He looked to the mines to create an 'overspill' – a surplus of revenue that would 'lift' the Transvaal economy; and he cultivated close ties with the Chamber of Mines, giving it 'semi-official status'. But mining expansion in the aftermath of the war proved to be far slower than expected. A principal cause was the shortage of unskilled African labour. Whereas in 1899 the mines had employed 96,000 African workers, in 1903 they managed to recruit only 63,000. A Transvaal labour commission estimated in 1903 that the mines were short of 130,000 men. The main reason for the shortfall was a decision by the Chamber of Mines to reduce wages from their 1899 level of 50 shillings a month to 35 shillings a month. Mining companies insisted that they had to cut labour costs in order to make deep-level mining profitable.

Keen to help solve the problem, Milner struck a hurried deal with the Portuguese administration in Mozambique to supply labour in exchange for a guarantee that half of the Transvaal's import and export traffic would be channelled through the port of Lourenço Marques. But recruitment from Mozambique remained no more than a trickle.

Milner then suggested to Chamberlain the possibility of importing indentured labour from Asia on short-term contracts. Indentured labourers from India had been employed in the Natal sugar plantations since the 1870s. Many had stayed on at the end of their contracts, adding to the mix of South Africa's racial problems. Among whites there was strong local prejudice against imported Asian labour. Chamberlain was well aware of the issue. In a diary entry in January 1903, he recorded: 'Lord Milner would be inclined to favour an experiment in the importation of Chinese labour . . . I consider that such an action would be extremely unpopular and would raise a storm at home [in England].'

But both Milner and the Chamber of Mines continued to press the case for the use of Chinese labour. After Chamberlain resigned in September 1903, Milner found his successor as colonial secretary, Alfred Lyttelton, far more amenable to the idea. In 1904 the British government duly approved the Transvaal Labour Importation Ordinance. To appease white miners, the ordinance included a clause debarring imported labour from more than fifty specified skilled jobs, thus enshrining in statute an industrial colour bar that had been enforced previously almost entirely by custom. It was later applied against African workers. The first contingent of Chinese workers arrived on the Rand in June 1904 on three-year contracts; over the course of the next four years, more than 60,000 followed, forming nearly one third of the total mine labour force. The value of gold output rose sharply, from £12.6 million in 1903 to £27.4 million in 1907.

Though the introduction of Chinese labour helped ease the Rand's labour shortage, it also fuelled local resentment against Milner's regime. Returning uitlanders found little to their liking about his autocratic rule. Within weeks of the peace settlement they began agitating for representative government. Critics attacked the administration as expensive and over-regulating and accused officials imported from England of being aloof, inexperienced and ignorant of South African conditions. They also disliked the way in which Milner allied himself so closely to the interests of mining companies.

Milner was well aware of his unpopularity. 'It is inevitable,' he wrote, 'that a Crown Government should be unpopular in a community like this, and that its accumulated unpopularity must ultimately lead to a change. The whole question is, at what pace the unpopularity accumulates?' His hope was that he would be allowed a period of three or four years before the advent of self-government in which to entrench 'an administration so competent and so imposing' that self-government, when it came, would be unable to destroy it.

But uitlander demands for representation gathered momentum. In November 1904 two political organisations were launched to campaign for political rights. The Transvaal Progressive Association, led by FitzPatrick, Farrar and other directors of gold-mining companies and financial houses, argued for a limited form of self-government that allowed British officials to retain considerable executive power until such time as the British were assured of a majority in a future Transvaal legislature; its members were motivated principally by fear of Afrikaner nationalism. The Transvaal Responsible Government Association, led by prosperous professional men, were critical of many of Milner's policies, including his decision to introduce Chinese labour, and wanted immediate self-government.

Not only did Milner face uitlander opposition but Boer resistance was beginning to stir.

In the bitter aftermath of the war, Boer society seemed destined for decline and oblivion. The war had wrought destruction in many places of a kind that could never be repaired. Numerous Boers had been uprooted from the land altogether. Some ten thousand stayed on for months in concentration camps because they had nowhere else to go. The plight of the Boers was made even worse in 1903 by a record drought; that same year marked the beginning of an agricultural depression lasting six years. A growing number drifted to the towns hoping to find work, but the towns offered no refuge. They were the citadels of British commerce and culture where Boers from the *platteland*, possessing no skills or education, found themselves scorned and despised for their poverty, their country ways and their language.

Even worse, the war had left a legacy of deep divisions within Boer communities. *Bittereinders* who had fought to the end despised *hensoppers* for surrendering and, even more so, joiners who had collaborated with British forces. 'The feelings of hate . . . are deep as the ocean and wide as God's earth,' wrote Eugène Marais, editor of the Dutch newspaper *Land en Volk*, in October 1902. 'We hate these people from the depth of our hearts because they besmirched our honourable name. It is not possible to forgive and even less to forget.' A leading collaborator, Piet de Wet, complained in January 1903: 'We are branded, distrusted and hated.'

But Milner's policy of anglicisation, intended to absorb Boers into the British empire, provoked a mobilisation against it. Rather than submit to Milner's new school system and to his insistence on the use of the English language, Afrikaner leaders in the Transvaal and the Orange River Colony founded their own private schools for what was called Christian-National Education which used Dutch as well as English as the medium of instruction, adhered strictly to Calvinist tradition and promoted a sense of Afrikaner national consciousness among students. At the forefront of the schools campaign were the Dutch Reformed Churches, the most powerful Afrikaner institutions to survive the war intact, determined to preserve Afrikaner culture and religion as much for their own interests as for wider nationalist motives.

Afrikaner writers joined the language campaign, debating the rival merits of Dutch and Afrikaans. Afrikaans still had no standard written form and virtually no literature. In some quarters, it was regarded as a 'kitchen language'. At Stellenbosch in the Cape Colony, the main centre for higher education for Afrikaners, the language used by students in debates, journalism and private letters was generally English. But now the need for their own language and their own literature was seen to be of paramount importance for Afrikaner survival.

A second Afrikaans language movement was soon under way. Organisations were founded in the Transvaal, the Orange River Colony and the Cape Colony to promote the writing of Afrikaans, to convince Afrikaners that it should be used as their written as well as their spoken language, and to campaign for official recognition of it. Writers such as Eugène Marais, Louis Leipoldt and Jan Celliers began to publish poetry of a quality that showed that Afrikaans had a high literary potential. Much of their poetry dwelt on the heroic sacrifices made in *die Tweede Vryheidsoorlog* – the Second War of Freedom – and the suffering that Afrikaners had endured at the hands of the British Empire. 'It is clear to every Afrikaner,' wrote Jan Celliers, 'that only our own literature, steeped in the Afrikaner spirit and intelligible to Afrikaners, through and through in language and content, that only such a language is really calculated to hit the mark here. Who wants to help us build up such a literature for our people? We have a people to serve, we have a nation to educate; we cannot wait.' A *predikant* of the Dutch Reformed Church at Graaff-Reinet, Dr Daniel Malan, later to become a prominent nationalist leader, added his voice to the campaign. 'Give the young Afrikaner a written language which comes easily and naturally to him, and in that way you will have set up a bulwark against the anglicization of our people . . . Raise the Afrikaans language to a written language, let it become the vehicle for our culture, our history, our national ideals, and you will also raise the people who speak it.'

Leading Boer generals, notably Louis Botha and Jan Smuts in the Transvaal and Barry Hertzog in the Orange River Colony, emerged as vociferous critics of Milner's regime. Appalled by Milner's intention to import Chinese labour, they organised a series of protest meetings and sent a telegram to Lyttelton, the colonial secretary, denouncing the plan as 'a public calamity of the first magnitude'. When Lyttelton refused to accept their claim to speak 'on behalf of the great majority of the Boer population', Botha and his colleagues resolved to found a political movement to demonstrate the strength of their support. Above all, they were determined to overcome the fierce divisions that had beset Afrikanerdom.

In January 1905, Botha announced the launch of *Het Volk* – The People – with a 'head committee' which included four Boer generals. Het Volk demanded full self-government for both the Transvaal and the Orange River Colony; an end to restrictions on the public use of the Dutch language; and termination of the Chinese labour system. It also wanted increased relief for thousands of Afrikaners ruined by the war. Het Volk rapidly won the support of the vast majority of Transvaal Afrikaners. In the Orange River Colony, a similar political organisation, *Orangia Unie*, was launched in July 1905 by Barry Hertzog and Abraham Fischer. Far from obliterating the notion of

Afrikanerdom, Milner's measures succeeded only in reviving it. 'Milner has made us a nation,' said one prominent Afrikaner in 1906.

Milner's ambition to reshape southern Africa according to his grand design affected not only the Transvaal and the Orange River Colony but the Cape Colony. The war had divided the British and Afrikaners in the Cape into two hostile camps. Milner was especially distrustful of the Afrikaner Bond, regarding it as a 'rebel party' disloyal to the British cause. Several Bond members of parliament had joined rebel forces in the Cape; others had been outspoken in condemning British war measures such as farm-burning. Parliament had been suspended in 1900 but was due to reassemble once the peace settlement was in place. Milner feared that in the post-war era the Afrikaner Bond might gain control, leaving loyalist parties such as the Progressives in opposition. He considered that in any case the Cape's political system needed to be reorganised to make it easier for the Colony to join a British-run federation, linking it with the Transvaal, the Orange River Colony and Natal. He therefore attempted what was in effect a coup against the Cape constitution.

Acting behind the scenes, he arranged for a petition to be drawn up and signed by Progressive members of parliament asking the British government to suspend the Cape constitution. He was aware that Chamberlain was opposed to any notion of suspension but intended to force his hand. Explaining his plan to the Cape governor, Sir Walter Hely-Hutchinson, Milner said he was 'absolutely convinced . . . of the necessity of intervention from home to put Cape Colony straight and prevent it being a drag on all South African progress'. The initiative, he said, would have to come from loyal colonists, 'supported, if need be, by a popular agitation'. In May 1902, shortly after the signing of the Treaty of Vereeniging, a petition signed by forty-two members of parliament was duly presented to Hely-Hutchinson, who, in turn, presented it to Milner.

Milner's official reply was that, as high commissioner, he was unable to comment on the petition. But he enclosed an unofficial letter to the petitioners, written in his private capacity, authorising that it should be published in Cape newspapers.

Speaking unofficially as to old friends, I may say that I am entirely sympathetic with the desire to preserve the Colony from the disastrous consequences which are likely to result from the resumption of parliamentary and party strife before the bitter passions excited by the war have had even a little time to settle . . . It may well be that an interregnum of non-party government in the Cape may not prevent but promote a return to the normal working of the Constitutional system. I think that such a system is much more likely to make for real freedom, for industrial and commercial development, and for the appeasement of race hatred than an immediate return to the old condition of things.

But Milner's plan miscarried. His support for suspending the constitution caused a rumpus in the Cape. In London, Chamberlain was furious at not being consulted in advance, telling Milner he was 'dismayed', 'seriously embarrassed' and 'deeply hurt'. Milner tried to justify himself in forthright terms:

I think it unfortunate that public opinion in England is capable of regarding it as tolerable that within six months of the end of a struggle for British supremacy in South Africa, the men who have fought for that supremacy at the Cape should be allowed to fall under the control of bitter and treacherous enemies . . . It seemed not only permissible but my plain duty to tell them that, unless they could themselves and through the regular channels, bring their fears and their necessities before the British Government and people, judgement might go against them by default.

Deeply disappointed by the failure of his coup attempt, Milner took some comfort from the results of the Cape elections in February 1904. Helped by the disenfranchisement of 10,000 Cape voters, as punishment for their involvement in rebellion, the Progressives triumphed over the South African Party, an alliance of the Afrikaner Bond and other groups.

The Progressives' election victory also marked a remarkable recovery in the fortunes of Rhodes' old friend Dr Jameson. In the last few years of Rhodes' life, Jameson had striven to escape the notoriety into which he had fallen. Appointed by Rhodes as a director of De Beers, he stood for parliament as a Progressive in a Kimberley constituency in 1900 and was returned unopposed. Making his first appearance in parliament in July, he was met, according to the *Cape Times*, with 'a dead silence'. His biographer, Ian Colvin, a journalist, recorded how the occasion turned into a personal attack: 'Through a dreadful session, while Jameson sat without answering or appearing to notice, a little forlorn-looking, hunched-up figure on one of the back benches, the [Afrikaner] Bond threw poisoned darts of speech and laughter at him from the other side of the House. His talent for getting into uncomfortable places had never been better shown.'

Nevertheless, Jameson persevered. Upon the death of Rhodes, he sought to take up Rhodes' mantle, considering it his 'duty' to finish Rhodes' interrupted work, and moved into Groote Schuur. In 1903, he emerged as leader of the Progressives and a year later found himself prime minister.

It was Jameson whom Rudyard Kipling had in mind when composing his celebrated poem 'If':

If you can make one heap of all your winnings
    And risk it on one turn of pitch-and-toss,
And lose, and start again at your beginnings . . .

Lord Milner left South Africa in 1905 with little to show for his attempts to anglicise the Afrikaner population other than a few thousand British immigrants who had been established on the land and a depth of hostility among Afrikaners greater than anything that had existed before the war. A census in 1904 showed the total white population in the Transvaal to number 300,000; Johannesburg's population had risen from 76,500 before the war to only 83,000; the Witwatersrand's population now numbered 117,000; but the rural population gave Afrikaners an overall majority. In his final speech in Pretoria, Milner complained about the obstruction he faced from opponents, not from Afrikaners, but from British citizens. 'Serious injury' had been done to the 'best interests' of the Transvaal, he said, through 'perpetual fault-finding, this steady drip, drip of deprecation, only diversified by occasional outbursts of hysterical abuse'.

Milner's efforts were soon undone. In Britain, as the tide of jingoism receded, the Anglo-Boer war came to be seen more as a costly and inglorious episode rather than an imperial triumph. In parliament, the Liberal opposition criticised the use of low-paid Chinese labour in the gold mines, claiming it was tantamount to 'Chinese slavery'. What made matters worse was the discovery that Milner had authorised the flogging of Chinese labourers – without reference to magistrates – in cases of violence and unruliness. 'At the time,' Milner told his successor, Lord Selborne, 'it seemed to me so harmless that I really gave very little thought to the matter.'

In January 1906, a Liberal government under Sir Henry Campbell-Bannerman came to office, inclined to grant the Transvaal and the Orange River Colony self-government. General Smuts hastened to London to meet the new prime minister. 'I put a simple case before him that night in 10 Downing Street,' wrote Smuts. 'It was in substance: Do you want friends or enemies?'

Five years after Britain had conquered the Boer republics, at a massive cost in lives, the Transvaal and the Orange River Colony were handed back to Afrikaner leaders. In February 1907, Het Volk won a clear majority over FitzPatrick's Progressives and formed a government under Louis Botha as prime minister. In November 1907, Orangia Unie won all but eight seats in the legislative council and Abraham Fischer became prime minister.

To Smuts, it was 'a miracle of trust and magnanimity'. To Milner, it was 'a great betrayal'.

45

VUKANI BANTU!

While whites were engaged in their own political manoeuvres, the black population was relegated to the sidelines. Black hopes that British rule would lead to improved political rights and status were swiftly shattered. When British troops arrived on the Witwatersrand in 1900, crowds of black workers jubilantly burned their passes, assuming they would not be needed under an enlightened British administration; but pass laws were enforced with even greater vigour. African leaders, such as the Pedi chief, Sekhukhune II, and the Kgatla chief, Lentshwe, who had rendered valuable assistance to British forces during the war, helping to oust Boer commandos from their neighbourhoods, gained little in return. Transvaal Africans who had moved on to deserted Boer farms, hoping that land colonised in the nineteenth century would be restored to them, were swiftly evicted by British troops and police. Writing in the magazine *South African Outlook*, an African contributor expressed the sense of disillusionment felt in rural areas:

> One strong incentive reason that impelled the Natives of the New Colonies to put themselves at the disposal of His Majesty's troops in the late war was that the British Government, led by their known and proverbial sense of justice and equity, would, in

the act of general settlement, have the position of the black races upon the land fully considered, and at the conclusion of the war the whole land would revert to the British Nation, when it would be a timely moment, they thought, for the English to show an act of sympathy towards those who have been despoiled of their land and liberties. Alas! This was not the case. The black races in these colonies feel today that their last state is worse than their first.

Among the black elite there was profound shock that, under the terms of the Treaty of Vereeniging, Britain had agreed to postpone consideration of black political rights until after the introduction of self-government – effectively handing over the decision to white voters. The Transvaal Native Congress complained to the House of Commons in London that, while Afrikaners who had been 'enemies of the King and British principles' had been favourably treated, the interests of Africans who had shown their loyalty by 'hearts and deeds' had been ignored. A petition sent to King Edward VII by the Orange River Colony Native Congress made a similar protest. 'It seemed to [your petitioners] deplorable that before bloodshed ceased the avowed cause of Justice, Freedom and Equal Rights, for which the war had been undertaken should have been so easily abandoned. Your petitioners believed that without some measures of representation in the legislature of this Colony their interests will ever remain in jeopardy.' For years to come, African spokesmen in all four colonies denounced the Treaty of Vereeniging as one of the greatest injustices that had been perpetrated against them.

Lord Milner gave short shrift to African protests. 'A political equality of white and black is impossible,' he said. 'The white man must rule because he is elevated by many, many steps above the black man; steps which it will take the latter centuries to climb, and which it is quite possible that the vast bulk of the black population may never be able to climb at all.' Milner's main concern was to achieve a uniform 'Native policy' that would facilitate the integration of the four colonies in a federation. He believed that the different traditions and laws affecting the African population that each colony maintained represented a serious stumbling block.

The Cape Colony's tradition of adhering to a non-racial franchise had endured for fifty years since the establishment of a parliament. Although the Rhodes administration had raised franchise qualifications with the intention of making access to the voters' roll more difficult for non-whites, any man could vote, regardless of race, provided he was at least barely literate and that he either earned £50 a year or occupied a house and land worth £75 outside communal land in the African reserves. Africans and Coloureds formed a significant part of the electorate: some 10 per cent of registered voters were Coloured; about 5 per cent were African. In 1903, according to an official report, the 8,117 African voters on the register affected the results in seven of the forty-six Cape constituencies, enough to decide the outcome of the election. Moreover, though no Coloured or African man had ever sat in the Cape parliament, they were eligible to stand for election. Coloureds and Africans were also entitled to own land as individuals and to take up any profession or occupation.

The three northern territories had followed a harsher tradition. Although Natal had been granted representative government by Britain in 1856 on the same basis as the Cape Colony, the Natal parliament had imposed so many hurdles on Africans seeking the vote that an official inquiry concluded in 1903 that only two Africans had ever registered as voters and both of them were believed to be dead.

In the Transvaal and the Orange Free State, only whites had political rights. The only relationship tolerated between white and black was that of master and servant. Resolutions were passed from time to time to emphasise the point. As recently as 1899, the Transvaal Volksraad had prohibited Africans from walking on the sidewalks of streets. Africans were excluded from trade and from all skilled work; nor could they own land individually. Only a tiny fraction of land in the Transvaal and the Orange Free State had been set aside for use as African reserves. The vast bulk of the African population 'squatted' on white-owned land working as sharecroppers or labour tenants in exchange for a place to live, raise crops and pasture their cattle.

To help him fashion a uniform native policy, Milner appointed a

South African Native Affairs Commission in 1903 to draw up a blue-print. Its chairman, Sir Godfrey Lagden, a colonial official, and almost all its other members, were English-speaking. Most were regarded as representing 'progressive' opinion on native matters; several were described as 'pro-Native men'. They travelled extensively throughout southern Africa gathering evidence. The report they issued in 1905 was to have a profound effect on South African thinking on race relations.

The main recommendation of the report was that whites and blacks should be kept separate in politics and in land occupation and own-ership on a permanent basis. In order to avoid the 'intolerable situation' in future whereby white voters might be outnumbered by black voters, a system of separate representation should be established for the black population, though political power, of course, would always remain in white hands. Land should also be demarcated into white and black areas with, as the report said, 'a view to finality'. In urban areas, separate 'locations' should be created for African towns-men.

These ideas on the need for segregation between white and black were widely shared at the time, by friends of the black population as well as by adversaries. The Reverend Charles Bourguin, a well-known missionary, produced a paper in Pretoria in 1902 giving support to the policy of keeping races apart. Alluding to increasing tension between white and black, he said: 'If we will avoid disaster I think, as many others, that the best thing for Black and White would be for the Natives to live as much as possible their own life, manage their own affairs, and have their independent institutions under the guidance of sympathetic White administrators.'

The significance of the Lagden Commission was that it elevated practices of segregation commonly employed throughout southern Africa during the nineteenth century to the level of a political doc-trine. Segregation was used by every leading white politician as a respectable slogan and found its way in one law after another on to the statute book.

Facing the juggernaut of white power, the small black elite made strenuous efforts to mobilise political action to protect their interests.

They had emerged from mission schools strongly attached to the ideals of Christianity, wore Victorian attire, adhered to British cultural values and put much faith in what they referred to as a 'white sense of fair play'. Cricket was a favourite leisure pursuit. Detached from traditional society, they were employed as teachers, church ministers, clerks, interpreters and journalists, and aspired to show how easily Africans could adapt to 'white civilisation'. They shared a vision of a non-racial 'civilised' society in which merit counted for more than colour.

In one polite petition after another, elite organisations aired their grievances – over land, pass laws and other discriminatory measures affecting Africans of 'training, character and ability' – and demanded political representation. But they were constantly rebuffed. Responding to a Transvaal petition signed by no less than forty-six chiefs and 25,700 other Africans, Lagden dismissed it, saying it had been 'rapidly engineered by a few half-educated natives who are connected with native newspapers . . . [and] cannot be taken to have been understood by or to represent the natives in general'. More strident calls were sometimes heard. In 1906, an African-owned newspaper in Natal, *Ilanga Lase Natal*, urged Africans to take political action. '*Vukani Bantu!*', it demanded, a phrase in Zulu and Xhosa meaning 'Rise up you people!' Its editor, John Dube, was summoned before the Governor, given a severe reprimand and obliged to publish an apology.

It was in Natal that local grievances erupted into open revolt. Land shortages and a series of natural disasters – drought, locusts and an outbreak of rinderpest that decimated cattle herds – had resulted in widespread poverty. The white quest for ever more land fuelled discontent. After Zululand was incorporated into Natal in 1897, Natal's white rulers allocated large areas of it for white settlement. A Zululand Land Delimitation Commission in 1904 set aside 3.8 million acres for Zulus, much of it 'stony, arid and malarial', and 2.6 million acres for whites, deemed suitable for commercial agriculture. Government instructions prohibited Africans living in 'white' areas from either buying or renting land there, requiring them, in effect, to become labour tenants or move. In Natal itself, half of the black population lived in reserves that were mostly overcrowded and overworked; the other half occupied land leased from white owners, paying relatively high rents, many falling into debt. Increased taxes added to their burden. In September 1905, the Natal government, in financial straits, promulgated a new poll tax due to be paid in January 1906

Though Natal was habitually swept by rumours of African unrest, the authorities regarded their system of 'native administration' as by far the best in southern Africa. 'We rather congratulate ourselves,' a government minister, Frederick Moor, told the South African Native Affairs Commission, 'that our Natives are the best-mannered, and the best behaved, and the most law-abiding people that we have got in South Africa.' When trouble started, the authorities were taken by surprise.

The revolt grew out of a small incident. On 7 February 1906, a group of twenty-seven Africans living on a farm near Byrnetown in the Natal Midlands refused to pay the poll tax. When a police detachment was sent to arrest them, a scuffle broke out; two white policemen were stabbed to death. The reaction of the authorities bordered on panic. On 9 February, they declared martial law over the entire colony and sent a column of the Natal Militia to the Midlands under the command of Colonel Duncan McKenzie. A Natal-born farmer and transport rider, who had served in Rhodesia during the Ndebele and Shona uprisings, McKenzie was a firm believer in ruling native populations through fear. The use of martial law, he said, provided 'a golden opportunity' to inflict 'the most drastic punishment on all leading natives found guilty of treason' and to instil in them 'a proper respect for the white man'. The *Times of Natal* subsequently described him as 'a fanatic . . . whose sole idea is of "keeping top dog" and whose simple cure for most native trouble is systematic and wholesale "walloping the nigger"'.

The first two culprits caught by McKenzie's men were given a summary trial by a drumhead court martial and executed by firing squad. Twelve others captured in March were tried by a regular court martial and shot before assembled chiefs and tribesmen. Long prison sentences were handed out to other participants. As well as dealing with the Byrnetown dissidents, McKenzie spent six weeks marching through Midlands chiefdoms tracking down tribesmen reported to be 'defiant', burning villages and crops, confiscating cattle and deposing chiefs, convinced that he was 'nipping in the bud' a widespread conspiracy against white rule.

But just when it seemed that repression had succeeded in snuffing out tax protests, a more serious episode occurred in the mountains and forests of Nkandla, on the southern border of Zululand. A minor chief from the Weenen district of Natal called Bambatha fled there after falling foul of the authorities. Appointed a chief in 1890, Bambatha had become embroiled with white landlords in a series of disputes over rent defaults. Heavily in debt, he evaded demands for payment of the new poll tax and left for Zululand. In his absence, the authorities installed a new chief. Returning home in April 1906, Bambatha kidnapped the new chief, opened fire on a police detachment sent to investigate and then headed for the Nkandla hills intent on fomenting rebellion, taking with him several hundred followers. Claiming to be acting in the name of Dinuzulu, the son and heir of Cetshwayo, he was joined by a number of prominent chiefs, collected an army of a thousand men and adopted the war-cry and war-badge of the old Zulu kings. For nearly a month, he conducted guerrilla warfare against white troops commanded by Colonel McKenzie until, in June, he was trapped in the Mome Gorge and killed. Once more, it seemed that resistance had been successfully suppressed. On 18 June, Natal's governor, Sir Henry McCallum informed the Colonial Office that there was 'no chance whatever of the rebellion spreading into Natal'.

On that same day, a troop convoy was attacked in Mapumulo, a heavily populated district of Natal bordering on Zululand. The attack marked the start of an uprising by thousands of armed tribesmen, led by their chiefs aggrieved by the poll tax and the arbitrary punishments inflicted on defaulters. The rising was put down with indiscriminate brutality. In all, more than 3,000 were killed; 7,000 were imprisoned; some 700 had their backs 'lashed to ribbons'; villages were razed to the ground and crops destroyed. White casualties, by contrast, were minimal: six white civilians died and eighteen white soldiers were killed in action. Winston Churchill, a junior minister at the Colonial

Office, described Natal as 'the hooligan of the British Empire'. White politicians in southern Africa were equally critical. General Smuts described Natal's 1906 campaign as 'simply a record of loot and rapine'. Britain's high commissioner, Lord Selborne, remarked in private: 'Natal is bankrupt in policy and finance.'

Though the revolt – or the Bambatha rebellion, as it came to be known – was crushed, tension and unrest in Natal and Zululand continued unabated. Rumours persisted that another revolt was being planned. Dinuzulu's name was frequently mentioned. After eight years of banishment abroad, he had been allowed to return to Zululand in 1897. Officially, he was treated as no more than one of eighty-three petty chiefs of Zululand, with authority confined to his own Usuthu clan. But Zulus regarded him as representing the Zulu royal house, the embodiment of their national pride, and looked to him for leadership. The authorities knew that he had been in contact with rebel leaders, including Bambatha, but were uncertain of what role he had played. His name, his war-cry 'Usuthu' and his war emblem had been used during the uprising, but Dinuzulu himself affirmed his loyalty to the government and offered to raise a levy to aid government forces to prove it. His offer was turned down.

In 1907, after the murder of several loyalist chiefs and the discovery that Dinuzulu had given shelter to Bambatha's wife and two children for seventeen months at his headquarters at Nongoma, government officials became convinced that not only was he the mastermind behind the 1906 rebellion, but also that he was planning another uprising. Although the Colonial Office in London considered the evidence against Dinuzulu to be flimsy, the Natal government declared martial law over Zululand once more and mobilised the militia. Dinuzulu was arrested and charged with high treason, incitement to murder, incitement to sedition and rebellion, being an accessory to murder, sheltering rebels, and other lesser charges.

The trial of Dinuzulu on twenty-three charges of high treason opened in Greytown in November 1908. In a letter to his defence lawyer, William Schreiner, the former prime minister of the Cape Colony, Dinuzulu wrote: 'My sole crime is that I am the son of Cetshwayo. I am being killed through ill-will, there is nothing that I have done.' The presiding judge, Sir William Smith of the Transvaal bench, delivered his verdict in 1909. On the charge that Dinuzulu had fomented the rebellion, Smith remarked: 'I think the probabilities of the case are so overwhelmingly against the theory that the prisoner incited Bambatha to commence the rebellion that it seems to me to be incredible . . . If, under the circumstances I find to have existed in this case, the prisoner did incite him to rebel, I should be inclined to say that he deserves to be acquitted on the ground of insanity. As it is, I think he is entitled to be acquitted upon the facts.' On the charge that during 1907 Dinuzulu had conspired to raise a further rebellion, Smith said bluntly: 'I do not find any evidence which would warrant the conclusion that any further insurrection or rebellion was contemplated.' Twenty of the twenty-three charges against Dinuzulu were dismissed. However, on the charge of having harboured rebels during and after the rebellion, Dinuzulu was found guilty and sentenced to four years' imprisonment.

The Bambatha rebellion was the last tribal revolt against white rule in South Africa. In searching for the underlying causes of the rebellion, Natal's white community placed much of the blame on mission-educated Africans stirring up trouble for their own purposes rather than on the harsh impact of white taxes, fines and land-grabbing. Most whites tended to distrust Christian Africans – *kholwa*, as they were known – far more so than 'traditional' Africans whom they believed to be more respectful of white rule. A Natal police commissioner attributed African discontent and the 1906 rebellion to education and missionary influence which, he claimed, 'tends to inculcate an equality between black and white, which is a dangerous doctrine in Natal, and must result in discontent in the subject race'. Natal's governor, Sir Henry McCallum, concurred: 'It seems certain that many of the semi-civilised natives who are the outcome of missionary effort . . . have been, unfortunately, agents for spreading ideas of resistance against constitutional authority.' He blamed, in particular, members of independent African churches – 'Ethiopians', as they were called – who had broken away from the mainstream.

A relatively small number of Christian Africans, in fact, participated

in the rebellion. But the notion nevertheless became deeply embed-
ded among the white community. John Buchan used the idea in his
novel *Prester John*, published in 1910, which was based on events in
Natal. He tells the story of a fanatical black church minister fomenting rebellion in order to revive the empire of Prester John, the
legendary Christian ruler of Ethiopia. The plot is thwarted by a heroic
young Scots storekeeper.

46

THE BLACK ORDINANCE

A different challenge to the racial order was meanwhile under way in the Transvaal, led by Mohandas Gandhi. Since arriving in southern Africa in 1893 at the age of twenty-four, hired by a Durban-based Indian merchant company on a year's contract to assist in a law-suit against an Indian trader in the Transvaal, Gandhi had made it his business to campaign for Indian rights. His initiation into the region's racial milieu had been swift. Travelling by train with a first-class ticket on the journey from Durban to Pretoria, he had been told by a white conductor at Pietermaritzburg to vacate his first-class compartment and move to the baggage car. When he refused to leave, the conductor summoned a police constable who pushed him off the train. Gandhi was left in the waiting room at Pietermaritzburg on a bitterly cold winter's night, with no light, shivering in the cold. 'I began to think of my duty,' he wrote later. 'Should I fight for my rights or go back to India, or should I go on to Pretoria without minding the insults, and return to India after finishing the case? It would be cowardice to run back to India without fulfilling my obligation.'

The next day, on the stage-coach journey to Johannesburg, he was involved in an altercation with another white conductor over seating arrangements. On arrival in Johannesburg, he was refused admission to a hotel. Then on the train journey from Johannesburg to Pretoria, travelling again with a first-class ticket, he was told by a white conductor to remove himself to third class. An English passenger intervened.

The year that Gandhi spent in Pretoria, honing his skills as a lawyer, he described as 'a most valuable experience'. But he was constantly reminded of the inferior status accorded to Indians. Indians were subject to night-time curfews; they were also prohibited from using public sidewalks. Taking one of his customary walks past Kruger's house one day, a policeman pushed and kicked him into the street.

After Pretoria, Gandhi settled in Durban, helping to launch the Natal Indian Congress in 1894 and playing a prominent role in its campaign for Indian political rights. Indians had first come to Natal in 1860, recruited as indentured labourers to work on sugar plantations. By the time Gandhi stepped ashore in Durban in 1893, the Indian community in South Africa numbered 76,000. Most were of humble Hindu origin, but there was also a sprinkling of Gujerati merchants, commonly Muslims, attracted by the prospects of trade. Wealthier, more confident and ambitious than the labourers, they constituted an elite group within the Indian community and were at the forefront of protests over discriminatory measures. Most were based in Natal, but several hundred were resident in the Transvaal.

When the Anglo-Boer war broke out, Gandhi saw an opportunity to impress on the British authorities the loyalty and value of the Indian population. The ambulance corps he organised performed with considerable distinction, often evacuating wounded men under heavy fire, notably at the battle of Spion Kop. Natal's prime minister, Sir John Robinson, publicly thanked Gandhi for 'his timely, unselfish and most useful action' in assembling a corps of 1,100 volunteers. 'All engaged in that service,' said Robinson, 'deserve the grateful recognition of the community.'

There were, however, limits to British gratitude. Indian activists, like Gandhi, expecting that the advent of British rule in the Transvaal would lead to increased rights soon discovered that the British authorities were no more sympathetic to their claims than the Afrikaners had been. Officially, Transvaal law had hitherto excluded 'Asiatics' from citizenship, denied them the right to reside or to own land outside segregated locations, and restricted their trading activities. In practice, Kruger's government had been lax in implementing its own regulations. But British officials proceeded to enforce them with considerable zeal. Milner led the way, supporting white demands for stricter controls. 'South Africa is essentially a white man's country,' he said in 1904. 'The Asiatics are strangers forcing themselves upon a community reluctant to receive them.'

Gandhi still retained hopes that Britain would eventually deliver on its promises of justice and equality for British subjects. He was concerned only with the welfare of the Indian population – and in particular the interests of what Gandhi called 'respectable' Indians, like himself – rather than with the wider issue of civil rights affecting Africans and Coloureds as well. Indeed, he objected to 'the mixing of the Kaffirs' with Indians as vehemently as did the whites. 'If there is one thing which the Indian cherishes more than any other,' he wrote in 1903, 'it is the purity of the type.'

Active in both Natal and the Transvaal, he launched a Durban-based newspaper, *Indian Opinion*, as a vehicle for the Indian merchant class and enrolled as an attorney of the Transvaal Supreme Court, opening offices in Rissik Street in Johannesburg. He helped finance a Johannesburg vegetarian restaurant run by a German woman who, according to Gandhi, was 'fond of art, extravagant and ignorant of accounts'. The restaurant eventually went bust, but it was there that Gandhi met Henry Polak, an English sub-editor on the *Transvaal Critic*. Polak was an admirer of the work of John Ruskin and lent Gandhi a copy of Ruskin's book *Unto This Last*, a treatise on the merits of life based on simplicity and self-reliance. Gandhi read the book on a train journey to Durban. 'The book was impossible to lay aside, once I had begun it,' wrote Gandhi. 'It gripped me. Johannesburg to Durban was a 24-hour journey. The train reached there in the evening. I could not get any sleep that night. I determined to charge my life in accordance with the ideals of the book.' Gandhi proceeded to set up a communal settlement on one hundred acres of land at Phoenix, fourteen miles from Durban, intending, once he had retired as a lawyer, to live there, working as a manual labourer. But he only ever visited Phoenix for brief periods.

When the Bambatha rebellion erupted in 1906, Gandhi offered his services once more to the British authorities. 'I bore no grudge against the Zulus, they had harmed no Indian. I had doubts about the "rebellion" itself. But I then believed that the British Empire existed for the welfare of the world. A genuine sense of loyalty prevented me from even wishing ill to the Empire.' Gandhi was given an honorary rank of sergeant-major and appointed to head an Indian ambulance corps.

Gandhi's expectations of British rule were modest enough. 'What the Indians pray for is very little,' he wrote in a memorandum for the British Indian Association of Johannesburg. 'They admit the British race should be the dominant race in South Africa. They ask for no political power. They admit the principle of restricting the influx of cheap labour . . . All they ask for is freedom to trade, to move about, and to hold landed property . . . And they ask for abrogation of legislation that imposes disabilities on them.'

What galvanised Gandhi and the Transvaal's Indian community into action against the British authorities was draft legislation introduced in 1906 requiring all Asian males over the age of eight to be registered and fingerprinted, and making any Asian who failed to produce on demand a registration certificate liable to arrest without a warrant and to deportation. Gandhi denounced the draft legislation as a 'Black Ordinance', reducing Asians 'to a level lower than the Kaffirs'. At a mass meeting in the Empire Theatre in Johannesburg in September 1906, he called on 'every British Indian in the Transvaal' to be ready to go to prison 'rather than submit to the galling, tyrannous and Un-British requirements' proposed in the legislation. 'Going to gaol is a unique step, a sacred step, and only by doing so can the Indian community maintain its honour,' he told the audience. With a roar of enthusiasm, the 3,000-strong crowd rose and pledged themselves under oath 'not to submit' to the Ordinance and to suffer the consequences.

This new political technique was called at the time 'passive resistance'. But Gandhi disliked the term and, after offering a prize for a better name, settled on *satyagraha*, a Gujerati expression which meant 'soul-force' or 'truth-force' but which was more commonly used to denote non-violent struggle.

Armed with his mandate, Gandhi led a delegation to London to protest to the colonial secretary, Lord Elgin. 'Our lot is today infinitely worse than under the Boer regime,' Gandhi told him. Elgin responded by withholding assent to the 'Black Ordinance', not out of concern for Indian rights, but to evade the issue until the Transvaal was granted self-government and could assume responsibility for the decision.

Shortly after Het Volk won the 1907 election, Louis Botha's government introduced similar legislation subjecting the Asian population to a pass system. Though Elgin had the power to intervene on discriminatory measures, he declined to do so. The British government, he said, felt 'that they would not be justified in offering resistance to the general will of the Colony clearly expressed by its first elected representatives'. Other legislation followed, restricting Asian immigration into the Transvaal.

Returning from England, Gandhi mobilised the Indian community. Despite government threats to impose prison terms or deportation orders on defaulters and to withhold trading licences, by the time the final deadline for registration had expired at the end of November 1907, only 545 applicants out of a possible total of 7,000 or so had come forward.

It fell to Jan Smuts, as Botha's colonial secretary, to deal with the challenge. Smuts decided 'to strike at the head, not at the tail' – to prosecute leading dissidents rather than their followers. The first wave of arrests took place on 28 December 1907. Gandhi and some twenty others were rounded up and summoned before a magistrate's court. 'I had some slight feeling of awkwardness,' Gandhi wrote later, 'due to the fact that I was standing as an accused in the very Court where I had often appeared as counsel. But I well remember that I considered the former role as far more honourable than the latter, and did not feel the slightest hesitation in entering the prisoner's box.' He pleaded guilty and asked the court for the maximum sentence of six months' hard labour and a £500 fine. Much to his disappointment, he received a lighter sentence – two months' simple imprisonment – than most of his companions.

The fear of government reprisal, however, soon took its toll on the protesters. While in prison, Gandhi received 'discouraging' reports from newly arrived colleagues. 'They told me that people were losing courage. The hawkers, they told me, had stopped going their rounds for fear of prosecution for hawking without a licence . . . Those who went to gaol lost their nerve in a few days and some of them hinted they would not go to gaol again.'

With the movement in danger of collapse, Gandhi sought a compromise. In a letter to Smuts on 28 January 1908, he proposed that, if the legislation was repealed, 'Asiatics' would agree to register voluntarily. Smuts replied with a non-committal letter. Two days later, the two men met. Both were destined to have a profound personal impact on the fortunes of the British empire. Though from disparate backgrounds – Smuts was brought up in a staunchly Calvinist home in the fertile farmlands of the western Cape, Gandhi was part of a Hindu family of the Vaishya caste in the arid state of Porbander on the west coast of India – both were British-trained lawyers with a deep admiration for the workings of the British constitution.

No record was taken of what the two men said to each other, but they got on well together; they were of similar age. Gandhi left the meeting a free man and told his followers that he had reached an honourable understanding with Smuts that the Black Act would be repealed and that the Indians could now register themselves voluntarily without suffering any stigma. Smuts, however, denied that he had made any such promise. Though he introduced legislation to validate voluntary registrations, he refused to repeal the Black Act. Whereupon Gandhi accused him of a breach of faith and resumed the campaign.

At a mass meeting in the grounds of a Johannesburg mosque in August 1908, demonstrators burned some 2,000 registration certificates and trade licences. During the campaign, hundreds went to prison, hundreds more were fined. Gandhi himself served two more prison sentences; in Pretoria, he was marched through the streets in handcuffs. But after months of agitation the movement faltered and collapsed. By February 1909, almost all Asian males had taken out registration certificates. During his third spell of prison, Gandhi learned that the British Indian Association was bankrupt and that 'the people have been financially ruined'. Released from prison in May 1909, he

broke down in front of the crowd in Johannesburg which had gathered to greet him.

Gandhi's ideas about the power of non-violent struggle were eventually to become a phenomenon of the twentieth century. But in
South Africa, where he developed them, they were little more than a
footnote to its turbulent history. More momentous events were under
way.

47

THE SPHINX PROBLEM

The impetus towards closer union between the four British colonies of southern Africa accelerated throughout 1908, bolstered by a change of government in the Cape Colony. After four years in office, Jameson's Progressive party was ousted in elections in February by the South Africa Party, a coalition backed by the Afrikaner Bond. The Cape's new prime minister, John Merriman, an English-born anti-imperialist, had long been an outspoken critic of British policy in southern Africa and considered that in the post-war era colonial politicians should be left to manage their own affairs without interference from Britain. In a lengthy exchange of letters after the war, he found common cause with Jan Smuts in the Transvaal and Marthinus Steyn, the former president of the Orange Free State. Like Merriman, Smuts regarded union as a way of diminishing imperial influence. On the eve of Merriman's election campaign, Smuts sent him his best wishes. If Merriman won in the Cape, Smuts wrote, then 'a unique opportunity will present itself for righting the situation in South Africa, an opportunity such as may not recur in our lifetime'. Three governments in the region – the Transvaal, the Orange River Colony and the Cape – would then share a common outlook. 'There is the chance to neutralize all the evil effects of the war, to weld South Africa into a compact South

African nation, and to rid ourselves of the internal discords which always and inevitably invite Downing Street interference.' What Smuts envisaged was a self-governing dominion within the British empire. Steyn, for his part, hoped that closer union would bring together the Afrikaner people in one state, giving them effective control and hastening the prospect of full independence.

In Natal, the white population was generally averse to the idea of a union with other colonies likely to fall under Afrikaner control; they would have preferred to retain a separate British identity. But the Zulu rebellion of 1906 had aroused fears about their ability to maintain their own security, making them more amenable to the idea of closer union for the first time.

British officials encouraged the idea of closer union, hoping that it would help secure British influence through increased British immigration, and compiled a memorandum outlining the benefits that would accrue to the four South African colonies and to Southern Rhodesia. The British high commissioner, Lord Selborne, disclaimed any intention of interfering in their internal affairs, but added: 'What South Africa requires more than anything else is stability – stability in political conditions, stability in economic conditions, stability in industrial conditions . . . But true stability will remain impossible so long as there are five separate governments in South Africa, each developing a different system in all branches of public life and each a potential antagonist of the other, but no one national government with authority to harmonise the whole.'

In May 1908, when representatives of the four colonies met in Pretoria to try to resolve disputes over customs tariffs and railway routes, Smuts pointed to the need for a political solution to their economic differences and proposed a 'national convention' to find a way forward to union. His proposal won unanimous approval.

The convention assembled first in Durban in October 1908, then moved to Cape Town in November. There were thirty delegates, nominated from the ranks of each colonial parliament: twelve from the Cape Colony; eight from the Transvaal; five from the Orange River Colony and five from Natal. Fourteen were Afrikaners; sixteen were of British origin. They included four prime ministers –

Merriman from the Cape; Botha from the Transvaal; Fischer from the Orange River Colony; and Frederick Moor from Natal – and many other prominent figures: from the Orange River Colony, Marthinus Steyn, General de Wet and General Hertzog; from the Transvaal, General de la Rey, Jan Smuts and Sir Percy FitzPatrick; and from the Cape, Starr Jameson. The chairman was the Cape's chief justice, Sir Henry de Villiers. Three delegates from Southern Rhodesia were also invited to attend. But there were no representatives of the black population.

The principal architect was Smuts. He arrived at the convention with a constitutional scheme that he had already cleared with leading delegates from the Cape, the Transvaal and the Orange River Colony. The most contentious issue concerned political rights. Cape delegates were determined to retain their non-racial franchise; the Transvaal and the Orange River Colony delegates were adamant in refusing to allow any form of black representation. The issue had been discussed at length previously in correspondence between Smuts and Merriman. Merriman argued for a limited, uniform franchise, similar to the Cape's system, for reasons of expediency:

> I do not like the natives at all and I wish we had no black man in S.Africa. But there they are, our lot is cast with them by an over ruling providence and the only question is how to shape our course so as to maintain the supremacy of our race and at the same time do our duty.

He contended that the Cape system, fortified by a more stringent educational test, would not mean that blacks would exercise any great weight in elections but that it would provide a necessary 'safety-valve'. To allow no African vote at all would be 'building on a volcano'.
Smuts replied:

> I sympathize profoundly with the native races of South Africa whose land it was long before we came here to force a policy of dispossession on them. And it ought to be the policy of all par-ties to do justice to the natives and to take all wise and prudent

measures for their civilization and improvement. But I don't believe in politics for them. Perhaps at bottom I do not believe in politics at all as a means for the attainment of the highest ends; but certainly so far as the natives are concerned politics will to my mind only have an unsettling influence. I would therefore not give them the franchise . . .

When I consider the political future of the natives in S.A. I must say that I look into shadows and darkness; and then I feel inclined to shift the intolerable burden of solving that sphinx problem to the ampler shoulders and stronger brains of the future.

After heated debate at the convention, a compromise was reached: delegates agreed that each colony should retain its own franchise laws. They also agreed to a safeguard for the political rights of the Cape's Africans and Coloureds, stipulating that any bill altering the Cape's franchise law would require the support of two-thirds of the members of both houses of parliament in a joint sitting. But simultaneously, they proposed that Africans and Coloureds in the Cape should be deprived of the right to sit in the union's parliament; at the insistence of northern delegates, 'only persons of European descent' were to be eligible as members.

By February 1909, the delegates had reached sufficient consensus to sign a draft constitution. They agreed to a unitary rather than federal political system, with a bicameral parliament consisting of a Senate and House of Assembly, a cabinet system of government, and a governor-general as formal head of the executive. The four colonies were to become the provinces of the Union of South Africa, each with its own provincial assembly. Dutch and English languages would be accorded equal recognition. The draft constitution also included provisions to facilitate the eventual incorporation of Southern Rhodesia and the three British territories of Basutoland, Bechuanaland and Swaziland. Politicians on all sides declared that union would not be complete without them; most wanted their immediate transfer to the union.

After its publication on 9 February, the draft constitution gained general approval from the white population. In Natal and the Cape, there were pockets of dissent, but most whites, whatever their misgivings about the details of the draft constitution, considered that union was too valuable a prize to lose. In June, after various amendments had been agreed, the parliaments of the Transvaal and the Orange River Colony gave the draft constitution unanimous consent; in the Cape parliament, only two members dissented; in Natal, voters in a referendum approved it by a three-quarters majority. In July, a delegation from the four governments left for London to obtain the blessing of Britain's parliament.

The reaction to the draft constitution among African and Coloured groups, meanwhile, was overwhelmingly hostile. Cape Africans and Coloureds were appalled that a colour bar curbing their right to sit in parliament was to be introduced for the first time. They also resented the way in which Africans and Coloureds in the three northern colonies were to remain excluded from political representation. Protest meetings were held throughout South Africa. A convention of African groups from all four territories assembled in Bloemfontein in March 1909 and agreed that union was 'essential, necessary and inevitable', but pleaded that the Cape's tradition of a non-racial franchise should be upheld. They looked to the British government to protect their interests.

Their cause was taken up by William Schreiner, the Cape's former prime minister, newly elected to the Cape parliament in 1908 as an independent member. In a letter to Cape Town newspapers, he described the draft constitution as 'narrow, illiberal and short-sighted'. During parliamentary debates, he fought the colour-bar provisions point by point, describing them as 'a blot' on the constitution, introducing amendments at every opportunity, speaking no less than sixty-four times. 'We are in the position of trustees, and the rights of the coloured people should not be bartered away for any benefit which the Europeans may get.' It would be better to stand outside the union than to forsake that trust, he said. Serious consequences would follow 'this wrongdoing' – 'Union without honour is the greatest danger any nation can incur.'

Schreiner was praised by African newspapers as 'our South African Abe Lincoln', but his efforts were to no avail. Only one other member of the Cape parliament voted with him against the draft constitution; ninety-six voted in favour.

Schreiner's last hope rested with the British government. Together with a handful of other white liberals in Cape Town, he drew up an 'Appeal to the Parliament and Government of Great Britain and Ireland', protesting about the proposed Cape colour bar. He argued that since it was Britain that had granted the 'fundamental rights and liberties' of the Cape Colony in the first place, it was Britain's duty now to protect them. He then resolved to travel to London to put the case himself, joining forces with deputations from African and Coloured groups. Gandhi too, newly released from his third spell of prison, set sail for London to make clear Asian opposition to the colour bar. 'The Union should not merely be a union of the White British subjects, but of all British subjects who are domiciled here,' he said.

On arrival in London, the official delegates from South Africa were accorded a warm welcome, provided with cars and office accommodation and praised by the press. General Botha who had won admiration during a visit to London in 1907 as the doughty foe transformed into a trusted ally, was singled out for special attention. 'He is quite the *favoured* Premier,' Merriman's wife, Agnes, wrote home. 'All these people are as keen about the Dutch now just as much as they *hated* them during the War – and it is a mercy Botha takes it all for what it is worth . . . The more I see of Botha the more I like him – he goes his course utterly unmoved – and people are really quite silly about him.' Botha was introduced to Edward VII at a dinner on 22 July, and two days later a state banquet was held at Buckingham Palace for all nineteen delegates and their wives. Abraham Fischer's wife, Ada, found herself sitting next to Lord Milner but managed to make clear her disdain for him. 'I almost pitied the man,' Abraham Fischer wrote to his son, 'he seemed so out of it.'

The Liberal government considered that few changes were needed to the draft constitution. The colonial secretary, Lord Crewe, took the view that Britain was still bound by the decision about the franchise taken at the time of the Vereeniging peace conference in 1902, postponing the issue 'until after the introduction of self-government' – in effect, leaving the matter in the hands of white politicians.

The official delegates themselves were adamant that they expected no British meddling. 'It is my firm conviction,' wrote Sir Henry de Villiers, the head of the delegation, in advance of their arrival in London, 'that no worse blow could have been struck at the cause of sound relations between the races [Boers and British] than this notion of attempting to induce the British Parliament to over-ride the almost unanimous wish of South Africa on a question of native policy.'

Nevertheless, the official delegates were worried about the impact that Schreiner and his Coloured and African colleagues might make on public opinion in Britain and sought to discredit them at every opportunity. Sir Starr Jameson, the first to arrive in London, informed *The Times* that the 'agitation' of the 'extreme negrophilists' was 'doing a great deal of harm to the native people'. Merriman added his voice: 'The present agitation can have nothing but the worst possible effect. It will put the clock back and upset the very friendly liberal policy manifested by those states which do not adopt the Cape policy. I think Mr Schreiner's present mission is one of the most unkind things ever done to the natives.' Botha insisted that the question of political rights for non-whites would 'have to be solved in South Africa by the South Africans', who had always 'shown a spirit of justice and fair play towards the native races' in the past and could be trusted to do so in the future.

When the official delegates met Lord Crewe at the Foreign Office on 20 July, he reassured them that he had no intention of amending provisions concerning the franchise and representation. 'These matters must be settled in South Africa itself,' he said. He insisted, however, that the British government would retain responsibility for administering Basutoland, Bechuanaland and Swaziland; there would be no immediate transfer, he said, 'until we see how the new machine works'. Crewe was worried that once control of the territories had been passed to the union, then Britain's 'power of protest' would vanish. If something went wrong, then 'a terrible responsibility will rest upon us in view of our obligations'. Other than that, Crewe and the official delegates reached rapid agreement on the draft constitution.

When Schreiner's delegation met Crewe on 22 July, the morning after he had finalised matters with the official delegates, he received them courteously and responded sympathetically to their representations, but was otherwise non-committal. Schreiner also found difficulty in arousing public interest in his mission. The British press was almost unanimous in opposing the suggestion that the British parliament should tamper with the draft Act; only the *Manchester Guardian* came out in support.

The South Africa Bill was debated in the House of Lords on 27 July, with all the delegates from South Africa present. Exercising their right as Privy Councillors, Botha, Merriman, Moor and De Villiers sat in the chamber of the House, while other government delegates looked on from the Official Gallery. Above, seated in the Strangers' Gallery were Schreiner, Gandhi and the African and Coloured delegates. Only seven peers participated in the debate; six of them were in favour of accepting the Bill without amendment. The Archbishop of Canterbury said it was justifiable to impose on the native population restrictions and limitations 'which correspond to those which we impose on children', and expressed the hope that 'the larger, sounder, and more Christian principles will in the long run prevail in South Africa as years advance'.

In the debate in the House of Commons in August, a disparate collection of Liberal backbenchers, Irish nationalists and Labour members fought the colour bar, proposing amendments to the Bill. The Labour leader, Keir Hardie, quoted statements by Botha, Smuts and other white politicians to show that they might be intending to destroy the Cape franchise. As a result of economic competition, he said, white opinion was becoming less liberal rather than more liberal. No member of the House, he went on, could justify the colour bar. It was nonsense to maintain that amendments to the colour bar would wreck the union. In its present form it was a Bill to unify the whites and to disenfranchise the non-whites. 'For the first time we are asked to write over the portals of the British Empire: "Abandon hope all ye who enter here."' But none of the amendments received more than a fraction of votes in support.

In summing up, the Liberal prime minister, Herbert Asquith, acknowledged the 'absolute unanimity of opinion in the way of regret' about clauses dealing with the rights of blacks and Coloureds. But he said he believed that the whites would deal with these issues more wisely if they were united than if they were to remain divided between separate colonies. 'Any control or interference from out-side . . . is in the very worst interests of the natives themselves . . . I anticipate that, as one of the incidental advantages which the Union of South Africa is going to bring about, it will prove to be a harbin-ger of a native policy . . . more enlightened than that which has been pursued by some communities in the past.'

EPILOGUE

The Union of South Africa was launched on 31 May 1910 with much good will and with the hope that the Boers and the British might find a way of resolving their differences and merge into a single South African nation. Outwardly there seemed a reasonable prospect of success. South Africa was by far the richest state in Africa, providing one third of the world's gold supply and 98 per cent of the world's diamond production. The new government, led by Louis Botha as prime minister, consisted of prominent figures from both communities committed to a policy of reconciliation. They included two other Boer generals, Jan Smuts and Barry Hertzog, as well as a large contingent of English-speaking South Africans. An election in 1910 showed that an overwhelming number of Afrikaners supported pleas for reconciliation.

Yet fear and resentment of British domination ran deep. Many Afrikaners never accepted the idea of being part of the British empire and mourned the loss of their own republics. Everywhere they were reminded of the presence of British authority. 'God Save the King' became the official anthem. The national flag was a British Red Ensign, with the Union Coat of Arms in a lower corner. The Privy Council in London, rather than the Supreme Court, was the final arbiter in the administration of justice. Moreover, on questions of war and peace, South Africa, under the 1910 constitution, was not a sovereign independent state, but bound by decisions of the British government. Most civil servants were English-speaking; even on the *platteland* English civil servants and teachers played a prominent role. The towns too were British. The British dominated industry, commerce and the mines and controlled the banks and finance houses. They also held an almost complete monopoly of industrial skills and training.

Fearing that the sheer weight of British influence would eventually engulf the Afrikaner people and turn South Africa into a mere appendage of the British empire, a group of Afrikaner leaders began openly to repudiate the policies of reconciliation that Botha and Smuts supported. Among them was Barry Hertzog. Hertzog had accepted the imperial connection only because it served to allay the fears of the English-speaking minority and thereby promoted good relations between the two groups. But he was determined that South Africa should develop a separate and independent identity within the empire, embracing both English and Afrikaners on a basis of complete equality. 'I am not one of those who always have their mouths full of conciliation and loyalty,' he said in 1912, 'for those are idle words which deceive no one.' And in a clear reference to a recent meeting of the Imperial Conference in London that General Botha had attended, he added: 'I would rather live with my own people on a dunghill than stay in the palaces of the British Empire.' Dropped from the cabinet in 1913, Hertzog travelled from village to village in the Orange Free State promoting the Afrikaner cause and leaving in his wake a host of Afrikaner vigilance committees. The following year, with a handful of parliamentary colleagues, he formed a new National Party, demanding that 'the interests of the Union come before those of any country'.

When Botha and Smuts took South Africa into the First World War, at Britain's behest, Hertzog stood against them. 'This is a war between England and Germany,' he said. 'It is not a South African war.' Several of his old Boer war colleagues, including Christiaan de Wet and Koos de la Rey, thought the time was ripe for rebellion and issued a call to arms. In sporadic encounters lasting three months, Afrikaner rebels fought government troops. It was an episode that left yet more bitter memories. In the general election in 1915, the National Party won sixteen of the seventeen Free State seats, as well as seven seats in the Cape and four seats in the Transvaal.

Adding to the anguish of Afrikaner nationalists was an immense social upheaval afflicting the Afrikaner community. Economic change in rural areas, caused in part by the war, in part by the growth of modern agriculture, pitched hundreds of thousands of Afrikaners into an abyss of poverty, precipitating a mass exodus to the towns – *die trek na die stad*. Yet, as Afrikaners found them, the towns were an alien and often hostile world. The language of industry, commerce and the civil service was overwhelmingly English; their own language, derided as a 'kitchen language', was treated with contempt. Lacking skills, education and capital, many were forced to seek work in competition with cheap black labour and to live cheek by jowl in slums on the ragged edges of towns. Urban poverty became as common as rural poverty.

The 'poor white problem', as it was called, was frequently blamed on the evil designs of 'British imperialism' and 'Anglo-Jewish capitalism'. Afrikaner leaders responded by establishing their own social organisations to try to hold the *volk* together through the maelstrom of depression and to preserve their own traditions. One such organisation, launched in 1918, was the *Afrikaner Broederbond*. It began as a small, select society interested principally in the promotion of Afrikaner culture and language. But it was to grow into one of the most formidable organisations in South African history and to become a major factor in determining its fate.

The black population, meanwhile, was subjected to a barrage of legislation designed to relegate it to a strictly subordinate role and to exploit its labour potential. In 1911, the Mines and Works Act barred blacks from skilled industrial jobs. In 1913 the Natives' Land Act laid down the principle of territorial segregation along lines similar to those advocated by the Lagden Commission. Africans were prohibited from purchasing or leasing land in white areas; the only areas where they could lawfully acquire land henceforth were in native reserves which then amounted to about 8 per cent of the country. Africans in the Cape were excluded from the legislation since African land rights there affected voting rights.

The effect of the Natives' Land Act was to uproot thousands of black tenants renting white-owned land – 'squatters' as they were commonly known. Some sought refuge in the reserves, though overcrowding there was already becoming a noticeable feature. Others were forced, after selling their livestock and implements, to work as labourers for white farmers. A whole class of prosperous peasant farmers was eventually destroyed. The impact was particularly severe in the Orange Free State where many white farmers lost no time in evicting squatters in compliance with the law. The plight of these destitute families driven off the land was described by the African writer Sol Plaatje in his account of *Native Life in South Africa*. 'Awakening on Friday morning, 20 June 1913,' he wrote, 'the South African Native found himself not actually a slave, but a pariah in the land of his birth.' Plaatje recorded how travelling through the Orange Free State in the winter of 1913, he found bands of African peasants trudging from one place to the next in search of a farmer who might give them shelter, their women and children shivering with cold in the winter nights, their livestock emaciated and starving. 'It looks as if these people were so many fugitives escaping from a war.'

Although the amount of land reserved for Africans was increased in 1936 from 8 per cent to 13 per cent of the total area of the country, overcrowding caused ruinous conditions. Official reports continually warned of land degradation, soil erosion, poor farming practices, disease and malnutrition. Unable to support their families in the reserves and needing money to pay taxes, more and more men headed for towns in search of work.

The same process of segregation was applied to towns. The Natives Urban Areas Act of 1923 established the principle that the towns were white areas in which Africans were permitted to reside in segregated 'locations' only as long as they served white needs. The Act provided for 'influx controls' regulating the entry of Africans into urban areas through greater use of the pass system. Pass laws, commonly employed since the nineteenth century for a variety of purposes, became an integral part of Native policy. African men were required to carry passes recording permission to work and live in a particular white area. They needed passes for travel, for taxes, for curfews, always liable for inspection by police. Africans deemed to be 'surplus' to labour requirements faced deportation to the reserves.

In 1936, African voters were struck from the common roll in the Cape Province, losing a right they had held for more than eighty years. The practical effect of the legislation – the Representation of Natives Act – was limited. African voters at the time numbered only some 10,000, amounting to no more than 2.5 per cent of the provincial electorate and 1 per cent of the Union's electorate. But the political significance was crucial. As the historian Cornelis de Kiewiet noted: 'To destroy the Cape native franchise was to destroy the most important bridge between the world of two races.'

By the 1930s, the Broederbond had developed into a tightly disciplined, highly secretive group with an elite membership bound together by oath. Its reach extended throughout the country. It had penetrated the civil service and the teaching profession and begun to infiltrate members into 'key positions' in all leading institutions. Its ultimate goal was to establish Afrikaner domination in South Africa – 'baasskap'.

With the help of Afrikaner academics, it fashioned a new, hardened version of Afrikaner ideology. Christian-Nationalism, as it was called, was essentially a blend of the Old Testament and modern politics, influenced in part by the rise of European fascism. At its core was the notion once expounded by Paul Kruger that Afrikaners were members of an exclusive *volk* created by the hand of God to fulfil a special mission in South Africa. Their history, their language, their culture, being divinely ordained, were unique. They were an organic unity from which 'foreign elements' like English-speakers were excluded.

Afrikaner history was portrayed as an epic struggle against two powerful enemies, the British and the blacks, both intent on their annihilation and only prevented from succeeding by divine intervention. 'The last hundred years,' asserted the former *predikant* Dr Daniel Malan, 'have witnessed a miracle behind which must lie a divine plan.'

In the context of the 1930s, the greatest threat to Afrikanerdom was seen to come from British imperialism and its allies in the English-speaking population. In the 1940s, however, nationalist intellectuals became increasingly obsessed with the *swart gevaar* – the black threat to Afrikaner *baasskap* – and turned their political machine to confront this new menace.

An economic boom during the Second World War drew massive numbers of Africans into industrial centres on the Witwatersrand and other urban areas. By 1946 there were almost as many Africans living in urban areas as whites, most of them crammed into slums and shantytowns. Census figures in 1946 reminded whites that they were a declining proportion of the population. Since 1910 the white population had increased by little more than a million to 2.4 million, whereas the non-white population had expanded by nearly 4.5 million to 9 million. The mood of the African population, moreover, was becoming ever more militant.

As prime minister, Jan Smuts struggled to find an effective policy for dealing with the *swart gevaar*. The impression he gave to an increasingly worried white electorate was that his government was beginning to lose control of the black population and, what was worse, lacked the will to restore control.

Malan's National Party, meanwhile, put forward a plan which it claimed provided a permanent solution to the problem: *apartheid*. Only total racial separation, it argued, would ensure white survival. In the 1948 election, the National Party won a narrow victory. 'For the first time since Union,' declared Malan on taking office as prime minister, 'South Africa is our own, and may God grant that it will always remain so.'

At the time, South Africa's racial policies differed in detail rather than in essence from the discriminatory practices employed elsewhere in Africa under European rule. But once in power, Afrikaner nationalists proceeded to construct the most elaborate racial edifice the world has ever seen – a vast apparatus of laws and controls to enforce white supremacy. Under the apartheid system, every facet of African life – residence, employment, education, public amenities and politics – was regulated to ensure their subordination.

In their quest for political rights, the black opposition tried public protests, petitions, passive resistance, boycotts and eventually sabotage, guerrilla warfare and urban insurrection. Their struggle lasted for much of the twentieth century. It was not until 1994, after years of internal strife, that South Africa's first democratic elections were held and Nelson Mandela became president of a democratic government.

CHAPTER NOTES

The material for this book is based on memoirs and reminiscences; on biography and autobiography; on government reports and correspondence; and on the work of several generations of historians. These chapter notes include references to books I found to be of particular interest and value. A more complete list is contained in the Select Bibliography.

Introduction

Recent general histories include those by William Beinart; Rodney Davenport and Christopher Saunders; Robert Ross; Leonard Thompson; Frank Welsh; and Nigel Worden. Early Cape history is covered by Martin Hall; and by Richard Elphick and Hermann Giliomee (eds.). Much has been written about the Cape's slave society including accounts by Robert Ross; Robert Shell; and Nigel Worden; and a collection of essays edited by Nigel Worden and Clifton Crais.

A note on currency values: £1 at the end of the nineteenth century was worth 86 times £1 in 2007.

Part I

Diggers and other residents of the diamond fields produced a variety of reminiscences about the early years there. Some were written years after the events they describe and are not always reliable. Among the first accounts published were those by Charles Payton (1872); Frederick Boyle (1873); and Josiah Matthews (1887); Louis Cohen's entertaining memoir was published in 1911; William Scully followed in 1913; and George Beet in 1931. Marian Robertson unravels the first diamond discoveries in Griqualand. Brian Roberts, in two books, provides an overall history of Kimberley and covers the careers of the diamond magnates. Studies by Rob Turrell and by William Worger give a wealth of detail about the development of the diamond mining industry.

More than thirty biographies and biographical sketches of Cecil Rhodes have been published. Three were in print before his death in 1902. Friends and acquaintances produced eulogies about his achievements. His banker, Lewis Michell, wrote an official biography in 1910. His devoted secretary, Phillip Jourdan, gave his account in 1911. Another aide, Gordon Le Sueur, followed in 1913. Rhodes' architect, (Sir) Herbert Baker, wrote perceptively about him in his memoir published in 1934. The first historian to publish a biography was Basil Williams, the Beit Professor of Imperial History at Oxford. He too fell under Rhodes' spell. In the introduction to his own portrait (1921) he wrote: 'It frankly sets forth . . . the belief that [Rhodes] was, with all his grievous faults, a great man, and that at the root of his imperialism were qualities that have done good service to mankind. His character was cast in a large mould, with enormous defects corresponding with his eminent virtues.' A more critical perspective came from William Plomer in 1933 and from John Flint in 1974. The most comprehensive account of Rhodes' life is Robert Rotberg's *The Founder* (1988). Brian Roberts deals with his entanglement with Princess Radziwill.

Part II

Britain's 'forward' policy in southern Africa is examined by Cornelis de Kiewiet in *The Imperial Factor*; by C. F. Goodfellow; by Ronald Robinson and John Gallagher; and by Deryck Schreuder.

Kruger dictated his *Memoirs* to members of his staff in the form of fragmented notes at the age of seventy-six when he was living in exile in Europe. The notes were then passed to an editor, the Rev. Dr A. Schowalter, who found them far from clear and drew up a long list of questions for Kruger to answer. Schowalter then pieced together the results along with references to official documents. The original Dutch was translated first into German and then into English. Among the biographies that followed are those by Manfred Nathan; D. W. Kruger; Johannes Meintjes; and John Fisher.

Afrikaner history is covered comprehensively by Hermann Giliomee. Leonard Thompson deals with the mythology that grew up around it.

Rider Haggard based his novel *She* – 'She who must be obeyed' – on the legends surrounding Modjadji, the 'rain queen' of northern Transvaal, who was said to possess the secrets of rain-making and hence held the power of life and death over whole communities. The title of Modjadji has been passed down through a line of women rulers since the sixteenth century.

The fate of Sekhukhune's Pedi state is examined by Peter Delius. Zulu history is covered by Donald Morris; John Omer-Cooper; John Laband; and Stephen Taylor. John Cope explores the origins of the Anglo-Zulu war; Saul David provides a brilliant account of the course of the war; and Jeff Guy describes the aftermath.

The first Anglo-Boer war is covered by John Laband; and by Joseph Lehmann.

Part III

Rhodes wrote his 'Confession of Faith' on 2 June 1877 at a time when he appeared to be searching for 'a band of brothers' to join. On that same day he was inducted as a member of the Oxford University Apollo Chapter of the Masonic Order. He did not regard the Freemasons with any solemnity or awe, but joined them for much the same reasons he had joined other exclusive clubs. On the day of his induction he questioned how 'a large body of men can devote themselves to what at times appear the most ridiculous and absurd rites without an object and without an end'.

The missionary Robert Moffat was a sturdy evangelist, but despite his years of effort at Kuruman, he never gained more than seventy communicants. His son-in-law David Livingstone was even less successful. Livingstone's successor, John MacKenzie, appointed himself both the spiritual and political guide of the Tswana, writing about his experiences in Bechuanaland in two books. His career is covered by Anthony Sillery. Kevin Shillington describes the fate of the southern Tswana. Dan Jacobson makes a modern journey along the missionary road, writing of his experiences in *The Electronic Elephant* published in 1995.

Part IV

During the first gold rush to the eastern Transvaal, hundreds of prospectors made the hazardous journey from Delagoa Bay, the nearest port, to the goldfields, crossing a mountain range and then one of the roughest and most disease-ridden bushlands of Africa to get there. Among the new arrivals in 1884 was Percy FitzPatrick, a young Cape Town bank clerk. He worked first as a storekeeper at Pilgrim's Rest, but bored with a humdrum existence took up transport-riding, plying the 'fever' route to Delagoa Bay for two years. Recounting his adventures to his young children years later, FitzPatrick included many tales about his dog Jock, the runt of a bull terrier litter, who became a brave and devoted companion. Encouraged by Rudyard Kipling, FitzPatrick turned the tales into what became a best-selling children's book, *Jock of the Bushveld*.

A dispute over exactly who discovered the main gold reef at Johannesburg continued for many years. There were three contenders: George Harrison, George Walker and George Honeyball, an Englishman who had come from the Australian goldfields. A report by the Historical Monuments Commission in 1941 favoured Harrison, but failed to end the controversy. Eric Rosenthal examines the evidence in his history of the gold mines.

There is also some dispute about the origin of gold on the Witwatersrand. The orthodox theory is that the Witwatersrand Basin, some 210 miles long and 120 miles wide, was the site of an ancient sea around 2.75 billion years ago. Rivers running through gold-bearing hills washed sediments of sand and gravel – along with specks of gold – on to the bed of this sea. They gradually built up a four-mile-thick layer of ore-bearing conglomerate. In 2002, however, researchers from the University of Arizona argued that the gold welled up from the earth's core some three billion years ago, making it more ancient than the Witwatersrand's rock. Their thesis was that the gold surfaced elsewhere, and was gradually washed into the Witwatersrand Basin by ancient rivers.

More than 40,000 tons of gold have been mined on the Witwatersrand, but with considerable difficulty, as the Chamber of Mines explains:

> Imagine a solid mass of rock tilted . . . like a fat 1,200 page dictionary lying at an angle. The gold-bearing reef would be thinner than a single page, and the amounts of gold contained therein would hardly cover a couple of commas in the entire book. It is the miner's job to bring out that single page – but his job is made harder because the 'page' has been twisted and torn by nature's forces, and pieces of it may have been thrust between other leaves of the book.

An estimated 40,000 tons of gold still lie underground.

There are three main contenders after whom Johannesburg was said to have been named: Johannes Meyer, the first government official to bring order to the area; Johann Rissik, head of the surveyor-general's office; and Christiaan Johannes Joubert, the minister of mines.

Geoffrey Wheatcroft covers the careers of the Randlords; Alan Cartwright deals with Beit's Corner House and Rhodes' Gold Fields. Hans Sauer's *Ex Africa* stands out among the memoirs of the time. Jim Taylor observed about the partnership of Beit and Wernher: 'The combination of Wernher and Beit . . . was very successful because Beit had all the initiative and creative faculties, whilst Wernher saw to it that all their enterprises were placed on a sound financial basis with adequate reserves. No crisis ever found Wernher unprepared.'

Rodney Davenport provides a standard history of the Afrikaner Bond; Mordechai Tamarkin examines the relationship between

Rhodes and the Afrikaner Bond. Biographical accounts of other Cape luminaries are also useful: Phyllis Lewsen on John X. Merriman; J. H. Hofmeyr and F. W. Reitz on Jan Hendrik Hofmeyr; Eric Walker on John de Villiers; and James Rose Innes' autobiography.

Part V

Two of the most interesting contemporary accounts of Lobengula and his Bulawayo capital are by Frank Thompson and by John Cooper-Chadwick. Chadwick, a young Irishman, was typical of the adventurers seeking their fortune in southern Africa at the time. After military service with Warren in Bechuanaland, he tried his hand as a prospector, miner, building speculator and surveyor on the Witwatersrand before joining a concession-hunting expedition to Bulawayo. Although only a minor figure, Lobengula liked him and called him 'Charlie'. Fred Selous and Frank Johnson provide other valuable accounts. In *Crown and Charter* John Galbraith examines the early years of the BSA Company. Philip Bonner charts the downfall of the Swazi state.

Part VI

Olive Schreiner began her novel *Undine* at the diamond fields in 1873 at the age of seventeen, but it was not published until after her death. The Schreiner family was deeply split over Rhodes. Olive Schreiner's early infatuation gave way to bitter contempt. Olive traces the course of her relationship with Rhodes in letters to her mother and sister that are reproduced in the biography by her husband, Samuel Cronwright-Schreiner. William Schreiner became a member of Rhodes' cabinet, staying loyal to him until overwhelmed by evidence of his complicity in the Jameson Raid. Eric Walker covers his career. Their mother remained a passionate supporter of Rhodes until the last. Arthur Keppel-Jones provides a detailed history of Rhodesia in its early years.

Part VII

Vivien Allen describes Kruger's Pretoria; Charles van Onselen's essays provide a wealth of detail about the early history of Johannesburg.

C. T. Gordon examines the growing Boer opposition to Kruger's regime.

Much of the evidence about the Rhodes conspiracy and Chamberlain's involvement in it remained hidden until Jean van der Poel's pioneering work was published in 1951. Chamberlain's biographer, James Garvin (1934) claimed that Chamberlain 'had not a shadow of complicity with the Raid'. In 1961, J. S. Marais followed Van der Poel with a magisterial study of the fall of Kruger's regime. Elizabeth Longford's 1982 narrative adds further detail. A number of contemporary accounts are invaluable: Francis Dormer; John Hays Hammond; Carl Jeppe; James Bryce; and Francis Younghusband. Edmund Garrett, editor of the *Cape Times*, in collaboration with E. J. Edwards, his Johannesburg correspondent, pieced together a vivid journalistic account in 1897. Percy FitzPatrick's book is mainly a work of propaganda, but also well documented (1899). Graham Bower wrote several private versions, but his papers were not made available to researchers until 1946. His account was eventually published in 2002. A useful collection of essays, edited by Jane Carruthers, was published in 1996 as a centennial retrospective.

Terence Ranger examines the Ndebele and Shona revolts of 1896–7. Olive Schreiner took her manuscript of *Trooper Peter Halket* to London in January 1897, travelling on board the same boat as Cecil Rhodes who was on his way to face the Select Committee investigating the Jameson Raid. They did not speak to each other. Schreiner feared that Rhodes and the BSA Company would sue for libel. The original edition contained a frontispiece photograph of a row of Africans hanging from trees, with armed and smiling whites posed beside them. Schreiner later told a friend that the only epitaph she would like on her grave was: 'She wrote Trooper Peter Halket'.

Part VIII

Controversy over the causes of the Anglo-Boer war lasted for much of the twentieth century. It started in 1900 with the publication of John Hobson's book *The War in South Africa: Its Causes and Effects* in which he claimed that ultimately Britain had gone to war 'to place a

small oligarchy of mine-owners and speculators in power at Pretoria'.
In essence, he said, the war grew out of a conspiracy by gold
millionaires and Jewish financiers, aided and abetted by British politicians, aimed at making mining operations more profitable. Hobson
developed this theme into a general analysis of the relationship
between capitalism and imperialism in his book *Imperialism: A Study*,
published in 1902. Hobson's work had a profound influence on Lenin
who acknowledged it in his treatise *Imperialism: The Highest Stage of
Capitalism*, published in 1917. It was subsequently used by generations
of Marxist and left-wing writers to illustrate the evil machinations of
capitalism.

Hobson's perspective of the war, however, was limited. He had no
knowledge, for example, of the role played by Milner. He had arrived
in the Transvaal in mid-1899 as a correspondent for the *Manchester
Guardian* at a time when pro-Kruger newspapers such as *The Standard
and Diggers' News* were full of tirades against the mining industry and
the capitalists who ran it. As a result of the Jameson Raid, Kruger and
his colleagues had good reason to assume that a conspiracy to overthrow his regime, organised by mining magnates with the collusion of
British politicians, lay behind uitlander agitation. Smuts believed that
the Jameson Raid was 'the real declaration of war in the great Anglo-
Boer conflict'. The 'four years of truce' that followed were merely an
interim period to allow time for 'the allied aggressors' to find a new
stratagem. In a manuscript entitled 'Memoirs of the Boer War', Smuts
wrote:

> It was the rooted conviction of the Boers generally, a convic-
> tion which was I believe shared by their responsible leaders, that
> the war was at bottom a mine-owners' war, that it had its
> origins in the Jameson Raid – in the firm resolve of the mine-
> owners to get the political control of the Transvaal into their
> hands by fair means or foul, to shape the legislation and admin-
> istration of the country along the lines dictated by their
> economic interests, and to destroy the Boer Government which
> had stupidly proved obdurate to their threats no less than to
> their seductions.

Smuts argued that British politicians and mine-owners used each other to attain their own ends. Lord Salisbury was well aware of this line of argument, telling his colleagues: 'The one dangerous objection that is made to our policy is that we are doing work for the capitalists.'

But when historians later searched government archives and the private papers of politicians and magnates for evidence about the conspiracy theory, there was little to be found. Far from being a united group of conspirators using British politicians to wage war on their behalf, mining companies held disparate views. Most feared that war would disrupt their mining operations and involve potentially heavy losses and possibly long-term damage through flooding and sabotage. What they wanted was not war but reform.

The archive evidence also showed that British ministers, when taking decisions about the Transvaal in 1899, were motivated not by any concern about mining company profits or about ambitions to control the gold trade, but by the need to strengthen Britain's political hold over the Transvaal to reinforce British supremacy in the region. Milner himself claimed responsibility for starting the war. 'I precipitated the crisis, which was inevitable, before it was too late,' Milner told Lord Roberts in June 1900. 'It is not a very agreeable, and in many eyes, not very creditable piece of business to have been largely instrumental in bringing about a big war.'

The historian Iain Smith unravels the issue in his book *The Origins of the South African War*. Andrew Porter provides another valuable account. Smuts' career is covered by W. K. Hancock. Two volumes of Milner's papers were published in the 1930s, edited by Cecil Headlam.

Part IX

The best single narrative of the Anglo-Boer war is given by Thomas Pakenham. Also useful is Bill Nasson's account and the collection of essays edited by Peter Warwick. Warwick also explores the role of the black population. There are a number of outstanding contemporary accounts, notably Deneys Reitz's *Commando* and March Phillipps' *With Rimington*.

When Emily Hobhouse tried to return to the war zones in

October 1901, Kitchener ordered her deportation back to England. In conversation with his aides, he referred to her as 'that bloody woman'. On her death in 1926, her ashes were buried at the foot of a memorial in Bloemfontein, erected in 1913 to commemorate the thousands of Boer women and children who died in concentration camps. At the interment ceremony, Jan Smuts addressed a huge crowd of mourners: 'We stood alone in the world, friendless among the peoples, the smallest nation ranged against the mightiest Empire on earth. At the darkest hour, when our race almost appeared doomed to extinction, she appeared as an angel, as a heaven-sent messenger. Strangest of all, she was an Englishwoman.'

Part X

The postwar period of reconstruction is covered by Leonard Thompson; G. H. L. Le May; and Donald Denoon. John Buchan's memoir includes some notable descriptions of the northern Transvaal. He based his character Peter Pienaar on his own encounters with Afrikaner hunters there. 'I think I must have met the last of the great Boer hunters, whose lives were spent far beyond the edge of civilisation, and to whom the War signified nothing . . . In Pieter Pienaar I have tried to draw the picture of one of those heroes.'

Rudyard Kipling travelled to the Cape at the end of each year from 1900 to 1907 accompanied by 'a complete equipage of governess, maids and children'. In his memoir, *Something of Myself*, he relates how returning by boat to England on one occasion, Dr Jameson joined him, sitting for meals at the Kipling table in the dining room. 'A most English lady with two fair daughters had been put there our first day out, and when she rightly enough objected to the quality of the food, and called it prison fare, Jameson remarked: "Speaking as one of the criminal classes, I assure you it is worse." At the next meal the table was all our own.' Jameson was subsequently knighted.

Shula Marks examines the Zulu rebellion. Gandhi's life in South Africa is covered by Robert Huttenback and by Maureen Swan. Gandhi left South Africa in 1914.

Epilogue

The Union's first census, conducted in 1910, enumerated a population of 5,878,000, with 3,956,000 Africans; 1,257,000 whites, of whom about 700,000 were Afrikaners; 517,000 Coloureds; and 148,000 Asians.

SELECT BIBLIOGRAPHY

Agar-Hamilton, J. A. I. *The Road to the North: South Africa, 1852–1886.* London: 1937

Algar, Frederic. *The Diamond Fields, with Notes on the Cape Colony and Natal.* London: 1872

Allen, Vivien. *Kruger's Pretoria: Buildings and Personalities of the City in the Nineteenth Century.* Cape Town: 1971

Ally, Russell. *Gold and Empire: The Bank of England and South Africa's Gold Producers, 1886–1926.* Johannesburg: 1994

Amery, L. S. (gen. ed.). *The Times History of the War in South Africa, 1899–1902,* 7 vols. London: (1900–1909)

—— *Days of Fresh Air.* London: 1939

Angove, John. *In the Early Days: The Reminiscences of Pioneer Life on the South African Diamond Fields.* Kimberley: 1910

Atkins, James Black. *The Relief of Ladysmith.* London: 1900

Babe, Jerome L. *South African Diamond Fields.* New York: 1872

Baker, Herbert. *Cecil Rhodes, by his Architect.* London: 1934

Beet, George. *The Grand Old Days of the Diamond Fields: Memories of Past Times with the Diggers of Diamondia.* Cape Town: 1931

Beinart, William. *The Political Economy of Pondoland, 1860–1930.* Cambridge: 1982

—— *Twentieth Century South Africa.* Oxford: 2001

Beinart, William and Colin Bundy (eds.). *Hidden Struggles in Rural South Africa: Politics and Popular Movements in the Transvaal & Eastern Cape.* Johannesburg: 1987

Beinart, William, Peter Delius and Stanley Trapido (eds.). *Putting a Plough to the Ground: Accumulation and Dispossession in Rural South Africa, 1850–1930.* Johannesburg: 1986

Beinart, William and Saul Dubow (eds.). *Segregation and Apartheid in Twentieth Century South Africa.* London: 1995

Bell, E. Moberly. *Flora Shaw – Lady Lugard DBE.* London: 1947

Bennett, Will. *Absent-Minded Beggars: Volunteers in The Boer War*. London: 1999

Bickford-Smith, Vivian. *Ethnic Pride and Racial Prejudice in Victorian Cape Town*. Cambridge: 1995

Bickford-Smith, Vivian, Elizabeth van Heyningen and Nigel Worden. *Cape Town in the Twentieth Century: an Illustrated Social History*. Cape Town: 1999

Blake, Robert. *A History of Rhodesia*. London: 1977

Bonner, Philip. *Kings, Commoners and Concessionaires: The Evolution and the Dissolution of the Nineteenth-Century Swazi State*. Cambridge: 1983

Bower, Sir Graham. *Sir Graham Bower's Secret History of the Jameson Raid and the South African Crisis, 1895–1902; Edited with an Introduction by Deryck Schreuder and Jeffrey Butler*. Cape Town: 2002

Boyce, D. George (ed.). *The Crisis of British Power: The Imperial and Naval Papers of the Second Earl of Selborne, 1895–1910*. London: 1990

Boyle, Frederick. *To the Cape for Diamonds: A Story of Digging Experiences in South Africa*. London: 1873

Bryce, James. *Impressions of South Africa*. London: 1898

Buchan, John. *Memory Hold-the-Door*. London: 1940

Bundy, Colin. *The Rise and Fall of the South African Peasantry*. University of California Press: 1979

Burke, E. E. (ed.). *The Journals of Carl Mauch, 1869–1872*. Salisbury: 1969

Butler, Jeffrey. *The Liberal Party and the Jameson Raid*. Oxford: 1968

Butler, W. F. *Sir William Francis Butler: An Autobiography*. London: 1911

Cammack, Diana. *The Rand at War, 1899–1902: The Witwatersrand and the Anglo-Boer War*. London: 1990

Carruthers, Jane (ed.). *The Jameson Raid: A Centennial Perspective*. Johannesburg: 1996

Cartwright, A. P. *The Dynamite Company: The Story of African Explosives and Chemical Industries Limited, 1896–1958*. Cape Town: 1964

—— *The Corner House: The Early History of Johannesburg*. Cape Town: 1965

—— *Gold Paved the Way: The Story of the Gold Fields Group of Companies*. London: 1967

Chapman, Charles. *A Voyage from Southampton to Cape Town . . . and Illustrations of the Diamond Fields*. London: 1876

Chapman, James. *Travels in the Interior of South Africa, 1849–63*. London: 1868

Chilvers, Hedley A. *The Story of De Beers: With Some Notes on the Company's Financial, Farming, Railway and Industrial Activities in Africa, and Some Introductory Chapters on the River Diggings and Early Kimberley*. London: 1939

Churchill, Randolph. *Men, Mines and Animals in South Africa*. London: 1892

Churchill, Winston S. *My Early Life: A Roving Commission, 1874–1908*. London: 1930

Clemens, Samuel Langhorne ('Mark Twain'). *More Tramps Abroad*. London: 1897

Cohen, Louis. *Reminiscences of Kimberley*. London: 1911

Colvin, Ian. *The Life of Jameson*, 2 vols. London: 1922

Comoroff, John L. (ed.). *The Boer War Diary of Sol T. Plaatje: An African at Mafeking*. London: 1973

Cook, E. T. *Edmund Garrett: A Memoir*. London: 1908

Cooper-Chadwick, John. *Three Years with Lobengula, and Experiences in South Africa*. London: 1894

Cope, Richard. *The Ploughshare of War: The Origins of the Anglo-Zulu War of 1879*. University of Natal Press: 1999

Crais, Clifton C. *The Making of the Colonial Order: White Supremacy and Black Resistance in the Eastern Cape, 1770–1865*. Johannesburg: 1992

Cronwright-Schreiner, S.C. *The Life of Olive Schreiner*. London: 1923

—— (ed.) *The Letters of Olive Schreiner, 1876–1920*. London: 1924

Currey, Ronald. *Rhodes: A Biographical Footnote*. Cape Town: 1964

Curtis, Lionel. *With Milner in South Africa*. London: 1951

Davenport, T. R. H. *The Afrikaner Bond: The History of a South African Political Party, 1880–1911*. Cape Town: 1966

Davenport, T. R. H. and Christopher Saunders. *South Africa: A Modern History*, 5th edition. London: 2000

Davey, Arthur. *The British Pro-Boers*. London: 1978

—— (ed.) *Breaker Morant and the Bushveldt Carbineers*. Cape Town: 1987

David, Saul. *Zulu: The Heroism and Tragedy of the Zulu War of 1879*. London: 2004

Davidson, Appollon and Irina Filatova. *The Russians and the Anglo-Boer War*. Cape Town: 1998

De Kiewiet, C. W. *British Colonial Policy and the South African Republics, 1848–1872*. London: 1929

—— *The Imperial Factor in South Africa*. Cambridge: 1937

—— *A History of South Africa, Social and Economic*. Oxford: 1941

De Waal, D. C. *With Rhodes in Mashonaland*. Cape Town: 1896

De Wet, Christiaan R. *Three Years War*. London: 1902

Decle, Lionel. *Three Years in Savage Africa*. London: 1898

Delius, Peter. *'The Land Belongs To Us': The Pedi Polity, the Boers and the British in the Nineteenth Century Transvaal*. London: 1983

Denoon, Donald. *A Grand Illusion: The Failure of Imperial Policy in the Transvaal Colony During the Period of Reconstruction, 1900–1905*. London: 1973

Dormer, Frances J. *Vengeance as a Policy in Afrikanderland: A Plea for a New Departure*. London: 1901

Doughty, Oswald. *Early Diamond Days*. London: 1963

Duminy, A. H. and W. R. Guest (eds.). *FitzPatrick: South African Politician: Selected Papers, 1888–1906*. Johannesburg: 1976

Duminy, Andrew and Bill Guest. *Interfering in Politics: A Biography of Sir Percy FitzPatrick.* Johannesburg: 1987

Eldredge, E. A. and F. Morton (eds.). *Slavery in South Africa: Captive Labour on the Dutch Frontier.* Pietermaritzburg: 1995

Elphick, Richard. *Kraal and Castle: Khoikhoi and the Founding of White South Africa.* Yale University Press: 1977

Elphick, Richard and Hermann Giliomee (eds.). *The Shaping of South African Society, 1652–1840.* Cape Town: 1979

Emden, Paul H. *Randlords.* London: 1935

Etherington, Norman. *Preachers, Peasants, and Politics in Southeast Africa, 1835–1880: African Christian Communities in Natal, Pondoland and Zululand.* London: 1978

First, Ruth and Ann Scott. *Olive Schreiner.* London: 1980

Fisher, John. *That Miss Hobhouse: The Life of a Great Feminist.* London: 1971

—— *Paul Kruger, His Life and Times.* London: 1974

FitzPatrick, J. Percy. *The Transvaal from Within; A Private Record of Public Affairs.* London: 1899

—— *South African Memories.* London: 1932

Flint, John. *Cecil Rhodes.* London: 1974

Fort, G. Seymour. *Alfred Beit: A Study of the Man and His Work.* London: 1932

Fraser, Maryna and Alan Jeeves (eds.) *All that Glittered: The Selected Correspondence of Lionel Phillips, 1890–1924.* Cape Town: 1977

Fraser, Peter. *Joseph Chamberlain: Radicalism and the Empire, 1868–1914.* London: 1966

Fripp, Constance E. and V. W. Hiller (eds.). *Gold and Gospel in Mashonaland, 1888: Being the Journals of 1) The Mashonaland Mission of Bishop Knight-Bruce; 2) The Concession Journal of Charles Dunell Rudd.* London: 1949

Froude, J. A. *Two Lectures on South Africa.* London: 1880

Fry, A. Ruth. *Emily Hobhouse.* London: 1929

Fuller, Thomas E. *The Right Hon. Cecil John Rhodes: A Monograph and a Reminiscence.* London: 1910

Galbraith, John S. *Reluctant Empire: British Policy on the South African Frontier, 1834–1854.* University of California Press: 1963

—— *Crown and Charter: The Early Years of the British South Africa Company.* University of California Press: 1974

Gandhi, M. K. *An Autobiography.* London: 1982

Gann, L. H. *A History of Southern Rhodesia.* London: 1965

Gardner, Brian. *Mafeking: a Victorian Legend.* London: 1966

—— *The Lion's Cage: The Siege of Kimberley.* London: 1969

Garrett, F. Edmund and E. J. Edwards. *The Story of an African Crisis: Being the Truth about the Jameson Raid and Johannesburg Revolt of 1896 Told with the Assistance of the Leading Actors in the Drama.* London: 1897

Garson, Noel. *The Swaziland Question and the Road to the Sea, 1887–1895.* Pretoria: 1957

Garvin, J. L. *The Life of Joseph Chamberlain: Empire and World Policy,* 3 vols. London: 1934

Giliomee, Hermann. *The Afrikaners: Biography of a People.* London: 2003

Gollin, A. M. *Proconsul in Politics: A Study of Lord Milner in Opposition and in Power.* London: 1964

Goodfellow, C. F. *Great Britain and the South African Confederation, 1870–1881.* Cape Town: 1966

Gordon, C. T. *The Growth of Boer Opposition to Kruger, 1890–1895.* Cape Town: 1970

Green, George A. L. *An Editor Looks Back: South African and Other Memories, 1883–1946.* Cape Town: 1947

Griffiths, Kenneth. *Thank God We Kept the Flag Flying: The Siege and Relief of Mafeking, 1899–1900.* London: 1974

Gross, Felix. *Rhodes of Africa.* London: 1956

Guy, Jeff. *The Destruction of the Zulu Kingdom: The Civil War in Zululand, 1879–1884.* London: 1979

Haggard, H. Rider. *Cetywayo and His White Neighbours; or, Remarks on Recent Events in Zululand, Natal and the Transvaal.* London: 1882

—— *King Solomon's Mines.* London: 1885

—— *The Days of My Life: An Autobiography.* London: 1926

Hall, Martin. *The Changing Past: Farmers, Kings and Traders in Southern Africa, 200–1860.* Cape Town: 1987

Hammond, John Hays. *The Autobiography of John Hays Hammond,* 2 vols. New York: 1935

Hancock, W. K. *Smuts: Vol 1, The Sanguine Years, 1870–1919.* Cambridge: 1962

Hancock, W. K. and J. van der Poel (eds.). *Selections from the Smuts Papers,* 7 vols. Cambridge: 1966–73

Harris, David. *Pioneer, Soldier and Politician: Summarised Memoirs of Col. Sir David Harris.* London: 1931

Harris, Frank. *My Life and Loves,* 5 vols. New York: 1925

Headlam, Cecil (ed.). *The Milner Papers: South Africa, 1899–1905,* 2 vols. London: 1931, 1933

Hensman, Howard. *Cecil Rhodes, A Study of a Career.* Edinburgh: 1941

Hillegas, Howard. *With the Boer Forces.* London: 1900

Hobhouse, Emily. *Report of a Visit to the Camps of Women and Children in the Cape and Orange River Colonies.* London: 1901

—— *The Brunt of the War and Where It Fell.* London: 1902

Hobson, J. A. *The War in South Africa: Its Causes and Effects.* London: 1900

—— *Imperialism, A Study.* London: 1902

Hofmeyr, J. H. and F. W. Reitz. *The Life of Jan Hendrik Hofmeyr (Onze Jan).* Cape Town: 1913

Hole, Hugh Marshall. *The Making of Rhodesia*. London: 1926
—— *Lobengula*. London: 1929
Huttenback, Robert A. *Gandhi in South Africa: British Imperialism and the Indian Question, 1860–1914*. Cornell University Press: 1971
'Imperialist' (pseud. J. R. Maguire). *Cecil Rhodes, A Biography and Appreciation, with Personal Reminiscences by Dr. Jameson*. London: 1897
Ingham, Kenneth. *Jan Christian Smuts, The Conscience of a South African*. London: 1986
Innes, James Rose. *Autobiography*, edited by B.A. Tindall. London: 1937
Jackson, Stanley. *The Great Barnato*. London: 1970
Jeal, Tim. *Baden-Powell*. London: 1989
Jeppe, Carl. *The Kaleidoscope Transvaal*. London: 1906
Johnson, Frank. *Great Days: The Autobiography of an Empire Pioneer*. London: 1940
Johnson, R. W. *South Africa; The First Man, The Last Nation*. London: 2004
Johnston, Harry H. *The Story of My Life*. London: 1923
Jourdan, Philip. *Cecil Rhodes: His Private Life by His Private Secretary*. London: 1911
Judd, Denis. *Radical Joe: A Life of Joseph Chamberlain*. London: 1977
Judd, Denis and Keith Surridge. *The Boer War*. London: 2002
Kaye, Helga. *The Tycoon and the President: The Life and Times of Alois Hugo Nellmapius, 1847–1893*. Johannesburg: 1978
Keegan, Timothy J. *Rural Transformations in Industrializing South Africa, The Southern Highveld to 1914*. London: 1987
—— *Colonial South Africa and the Origins of the Racial Order*. London: 1996
Keppel-Jones, Arthur. *Rhodes and Rhodesia: the White Conquest of Zimbabwe, 1884–1902*. McGill-Queen's University Press: 1983
Kestell, J. D. *Through Shot and Flame*. London: 1903
Kestell, J. D. and D. E. Van Velden. *The Peace Negotiations Between Boer and Briton in South Africa*. London: 1912
Kipling, Rudyard. *Something of Myself*. London: 1936
—— *The Definitive Edition of Rudyard Kipling's Verse*. London: 1943
Knight-Bruce, G. W. T. *Memoirs of Mashonaland*. London: 1895
Kochanski, Halik. *Sir Garnet Wolseley: Victorian Hero*. London: 1999
Koss, Stephen (ed.). *The Pro-Boers: The Anatomy of an Antiwar Movement*. Chicago: 1973
Kotzé, Sir John. *Memoirs and Reminiscences*, 2 vols. Cape Town: 1934, 1949
Krikler, Jeremy. *Revolution from Above, Rebellion from Below: The Agrarian Transvaal at the Turn of the Century*. Oxford: 1993
Kruger, D. W. *Paul Kruger*, 2 vols. Johannesburg: 1961–3
Kruger, S. J. P. *The Memoirs of Paul Kruger, Four Times President of the South African Republic, Told by Himself*, 2 vols. London: 1902
Kruger, Rayne. *Good-bye Dolly Gray: The Story of the Boer War*. London: 1959

Kubicek, Robert V. *Economic Imperialism in Theory and Practice: The Case of South African Gold-Mining Finance, 1886–1914*. Duke University Press: 1979

Laband, John. *Rope of Sand: The Rise and Fall of the Zulu Kingdom in the Nineteenth Century*. Johannesburg: 1995

—— *The Transvaal Rebellion: The First Boer War, 1880–1881*. London: 2005

Le May, G. H. L. *British Supremacy in South Africa, 1899–1907*. Oxford: 1965

—— *The Afrikaners: An Historical Interpretation*. Oxford: 1995

Le Sueur, Gordon. *Cecil Rhodes: The Man and His Work*. London: 1913

Leasor, James. *Rhodes and Barnato; The Premier and the Prancer*. London: 1997

Lee, Emanoel. *To the Bitter End: A Photographic History of the Boer War, 1899–1902*. London: 1985

Lehmann, Joseph H. *All Sir Garnet: A Life of Field-Marshal Lord Wolseley*. London: 1964

—— *The First Boer War*. London: 1972

Lewsen, Phyllis (ed.). *Selections from the Correspondence of J.X. Merriman, 1870–1924*, 4 vols. Cape Town: 1960–1969

—— *John X. Merriman, Paradoxical South African Statesman*. Yale University Press: 1982

Livingstone, David. *Missionary Travels and Researches in South Africa*. London: 1857

Lockhart, J. G. and C. M. Woodhouse. *Cecil Rhodes: The Colossus of Southern Africa*. London: 1963

Longford, Elizabeth. *Jameson's Raid: The Prelude to the Boer War*. London: 1982

Lowry, Donal (ed.). *The South African War Reappraised*. Manchester University Press: 2000

MacDonald, J. Ramsay. *What I Saw in South Africa*. London: 1902

Mackenzie, John. *Ten Years North of the Orange River*. Edinburgh: 1871

—— *Austral Africa: Losing It or Ruling It*, 2 vols. London: 1887

Mackenzie, W. D. *John Mackenzie, South African Missionary and Statesman*. London: 1902

Maclennan, Donald. *A Proper Degree of Terror*. Johannesburg: 1986

Macmillan, Mona. *Sir Henry Barkly: Mediator and Moderator*. Cape Town: 1978

Macnab, Roy. *The French Colonel: Villebois-Mareuil and the Boers, 1899–1900*. Cape Town: 1975

Marais, J. S. *The Fall of Kruger's Republic*. Oxford: 1961

Marks, Shula. *Reluctant Rebellion: The 1906–1908 Disturbances in Natal*. Oxford: 1970

Marks, Shula and Anthony Atmore (eds.). *Economy and Society in Pre-industrial South Africa*. London: 1980

Marks, Shula and Richard Rathbone (eds.). *Industrialisation and Social Change in South Africa: African Class Formation, Culture and Consciousness, 1870–1930*. London: 1982

Marks, Shula and Stanley Trapido (eds.). *The Politics of Race, Class and Nationalism in Twentieth Century South Africa*. London: 1987

Marlowe, John. *Cecil Rhodes: The Anatomy of Empire*. London: 1972

—— *Milner: Apostle of Empire*. London: 1976

Marsh, Peter. *Joseph Chamberlain: Entrepreneur in Politics*. Yale University Press: 1994

Martineau, John. *The Life and Correspondence of Sir Bartle Frere*, 2 vols. London: 1895

Mathers, E. P. *Golden South Africa, or the Gold Fields Revisited*. London: 1888

—— *South Africa and How to Reach It*. London: 1889

—— *Zambesia, England's Eldorado*. London: 1891

Matsebula, J. S. M. *A History of Swaziland*. Cape Town: 1972

Matthews, Josiah Wright. *Incwadi Yami; Or Twenty Years' Personal Experience in South Africa*. New York: 1887

Maylam, Paul. *Rhodes, The Tswana, and the British: Colonialism, Collaboration and Conflict in the Bechuanaland Protectorate, 1885–1899*. Westport, Conn.: 1980

—— *A History of the African People of South Africa from the Early Iron Age to the 1970s*. London: 1995

McCracken, Donal P. *The Irish Pro-Boers, 1877–1902*. Cape Town: 1976

—— *MacBride's Brigade: Irish Commandos in the Anglo-Boer War*. Dublin: 1989

McDonald, J. G. *Rhodes: A Life*. London: 1927

Meintjes, Johannes. *De la Rey: Lion of the West*. Johannesburg: 1966

—— *President Steyn: A Biography*. Cape Town: 1969

—— *General Louis Botha: A Biography*. London: 1970

—— *The Commandant-General: The Life and Times of Petrus Jacobus Joubert of the South African Republic, 1831–1900*. Cape Town: 1971

—— *President Paul Kruger*. London: 1974

Mendelsohn, Richard. *Sammy Marks, 'The Uncrowned King of the Transvaal'*. Cape Town: 1991

Menpes, Mortimer. *War Impressions: Being a Record in Colour*. London: 1901

Michell, Lewis. *The Life of the Rt. Hon. Cecil John Rhodes, 1852–1902*, 2 vols. London: 1910

Millin, Sarah Gertrude. *Rhodes*. London: 1933

Moffat, Robert Unwin. *John Smith Moffat, C.M.G., Missionary: A Memoir*. London: 1921

Morris, Donald R. *The Washing of the Spears: A History of the Rise of the Zulu Nation under Shaka and Its Fall in the Zulu War of 1879*. London: 1966

Nasson, Bill. *The South African War*. London: 1999

Nathan, Manfred. *Paul Kruger: His Life and Times*. Durban: 1944

Nimrocks, Walter. *Milner's Young Men: The 'Kindergarten' in Edwardian Imperial Affairs*. London: 1970

O'Brien, Terence H. *Milner: Viscount Milner of St James's and Cape Town, 1854–1925*. London: 1979

O'Connor, Damian. *The Life of Sir Bartle Frere*. London: 2002

Odendaal, André. *Vukani Bantu! The Beginnings of Black Protest Politics in South Africa to 1912*. Cape Town: 1984

Oliver, Roland. *Sir Harry Johnston and the Scramble for Africa*. London: 1957

Omer-Cooper, John D. *The Zulu Aftermath: A Nineteenth-Century Revolution in Bantu Africa*. London: 1966

Orpen, Joseph Millerd. *Reminiscences of Life in South Africa from 1846 to the Present Day*. Cape Town: 1964

Pakenham, Thomas. *The Boer War*. London: 1979

Palmer, Robin. *Land and Racial Domination in Rhodesia*. London: 1977

Palmer, Robin and Neil Parsons (eds.). *The Roots of Rural Poverty in Central and Southern Africa*. London: 1977

Payton, Charles Alfred. *The Diamond Diggings of South Africa: A Personal and Practical Account*. London: 1872

Peires, J. B. *The House of Phalo: History of the Xhosa People in the Days of their Independence*. Johannesburg: 1981

Phillips, Florence. *Some South African Recollections*. London: 1899

Phillips, Lionel. *Some Reminiscences*. London: 1924

Phillipps, L. March. *With Rimington*. London: 1901

Plaatje, Sol T. *The Boer War Diary of Sol T. Plaatje*; edited by John L. Comaroff. Johannesburg: 1973

—— *Native Life in South Africa*. London: 1916

Plomer, William. *Cecil Rhodes*. Edinburgh: 1933

Porter, A. N. *The Origins of the South African War: Joseph Chamberlain and the Diplomacy of Imperialism, 1895–1899*. Manchester University Press: 1980

Porter, Bernard. *Critics of Empire: British Radical Attitudes to Colonialism in Africa, 1895–1914*. London: 1968

Preston, A. (ed.). *Sir Garnet Wolseley's South African Journal, 1879–80*. Cape Town: 1973

Ranger, Terence O. *Revolt in Southern Rhodesia, 1896–97: A Study in African Resistance*. London: 1967

Reitz, Deneys. *Commando: A Boer Journal of the Boer War*. London: 1929

Reunert, Theodore. *Diamonds and Gold in South Africa*. Cape Town: 1893

Rive, Richard (ed.). *Olive Schreiner, Letters 1871–1899*. Cape Town: 1987

Roberts, Andrew. *Salisbury: Victorian Titan*. London: 1999

Roberts, Brian. *Cecil Rhodes and the Princess*. London: 1969

—— *The Diamond Magnates*. London: 1972

—— *Kimberley: Turbulent City*. Cape Town: 1976

—— *Cecil Rhodes: Flawed Colossus*. London: 1987

—— *Those Bloody Women: Three Heroines of the Boer War*. London: 1991

Robertson, Marian. *Diamond Fever: South African Diamond History, 1866–1869*. Cape Town: 1974

Robinson, John (ed.). *Notes on Natal: An Old Colonist's Book for New Settlers.* Durban: 1872

Robinson, Ronald and John Gallagher. *Africa and the Victorians: The Official Mind of Imperialism.* London: 1961

Rosenthal, Eric. *Gold! Gold! Gold! The Johannesburg Gold Rush.* New York: 1970

Ross, Andrew. *John Philip (1775–1851): Missions, Race, and Politics in South Africa.* Aberdeen University Press: 1986

Ross, Robert. *Cape of Torments: Slavery and Resistance in South Africa.* London: 1983

—— *A Concise History of South Africa.* Cambridge: 1999

Rotberg, Robert I. *The Founder: Cecil Rhodes and the Pursuit of Power.* Johannesburg: 1988

Rouillard, Nancy (ed.). *Matabele Thompson: An Autobiography.* London: 1936

Sauer, Hans. *Ex Africa.* London: 1937

Saunders, Christopher and Robin Derricourt (eds.). *Beyond the Cape Frontier: Studies in the History of the Transkei and the Ciskei.* London: 1974

Schreiner, Olive. *The Story of an African Farm.* London: 1883

—— *Trooper Peter Halket of Mashonaland.* London: 1897

—— *Thoughts on South Africa.* London: 1923

—— *Undine.* London: 1929

Schreuder, Deryck M. *Gladstone and Kruger: Liberal Government and Colonial 'Home Rule', 1880–85.* London: 1969

—— *The Scramble for Southern Africa, 1877–1895: The Politics of Partition Reappraised.* Cambridge: 1980

Scully, William Charles. *Reminiscences of a South African Pioneer.* London: 1913

—— *Further Reminiscences of a South African Pioneer.* London: 1913

Selous, Frederick Courteney. *A Hunter's Wanderings in Africa.* London: 1881

—— *Travel and Adventure in South Central Africa.* London: 1893

—— *Sunshine & Storm in Rhodesia.* London: 1896

Shell, Robert C.-H. *Children of Bondage: A Social History of the Slave Society at the Cape of Good Hope, 1652–1838.* Johannesburg: 1994

Shillington, Kevin. *The Colonisation of the Southern Tswana, 1870–1900.* Johannesburg: 1985

Sillery, Anthony. *The Bechuanaland Protectorate.* Cape Town: 1952

—— *John Mackenzie of Bechuanaland, 1835–1899: A Study in Humanitarian Imperialism.* Cape Town: 1971

Simons, Jack and Ray. *Class and Colour in South Africa, 1850–1950.* London: 1983

Smith, Iain R. *The Origins of the South African War, 1899–1902.* London: 1996

—— (ed.) *The Siege of Mafeking.* Johannesburg: 2001

Smuts, J. C. *A Century of Wrong.* London: 1900

SELECT BIBLIOGRAPHY   549

—— *Memoirs of the Boer War*. Johannesburg: 1994

Smuts, J. C. *Jan Christian Smuts, By His Son*. London: 1952

Spies, S. B. *The Origins of the Anglo-Boer War*. London: 1972

—— *Methods of Barbarism? Roberts and Kitchener and Civilians in the Boer Republics, January 1900–May 1902*. Cape Town: 1977

Stead, W. T. *The Last Will and Testament of Cecil John Rhodes*. London: 1902

Stent, Vere. *A Personal Record of Some Incidents in the Life of Cecil Rhodes*. Cape Town: 1924

Stevenson, Edmond Sinclair. *The Adventures of a Medical Man*. Cape Town: 1925

Swan, Maureen. *Gandhi: The South African Experience*. Johannesburg: 1985

Tamarkin, Mordechai. *Cecil Rhodes and the Cape Afrikaners: the Imperial Colossus and the Colonial Parish Pump*. London: 1996

Tatz, C. M. *Shadow and Substance: A Study in Land and Franchise Policies Affecting Africans*. Natal University Press: 1962

Taylor, James B. *A Pioneer Looks Back*. London: 1939

Taylor, Stephen. *The Mighty Nimrod: A Life of Frederick Courteney Selous; African Hunter and Adventurer, 1851–1917*. London: 1989

—— *Shaka's Children: A History of the Zulu People*. London: 1994

Templin, J. Alton. *Ideology on a Frontier: The Theological Foundation of Afrikaner Nationalism, 1652–1910*. Westport: 1984

Thomas, Antony. *Rhodes, The Race for Africa*. London: 1998

Thompson, Leonard. *The Unification of South Africa, 1902–1910*. Oxford: 1960

—— *Survival in Two Worlds: Moshoeshoe of Lesotho, 1786–1870*. Oxford: 1975

—— *The Political Mythology of Apartheid*. Yale University Press: 1985

—— *A History of South Africa*, 3rd edition. Yale University Press: 2001

Trollope, Anthony. *South Africa*, 2 vols. London: 1878

Turrell, Rob. *Capital and Labour on the Kimberley Diamond Fields, 1871–1890*. Cambridge: 1987

Van der Poel, Jean. *The Jameson Raid*. Cape Town: 1951

Van Jaarsveld, F. A. *The Awakening of Afrikaner Nationalism, 1868–81*. Cape Town: 1961

—— *The Afrikaner's Interpretation of South African History*. Cape Town: 1964

Van Onselen, Charles. *Studies in the Social and Economic History of the Witwatersrand, 1886–1914*, 2 vols. Johannesburg: 1982

'Vindex' (pseud. John Vershoyle). *Cecil Rhodes: His Political Life and Speeches, 1881–1900*. London: 1900

Walker, Eric A. *Lord De Villiers and His Times, South Africa, 1892–1914*. London: 1925

—— *W.P. Schreiner: A South African*. London: 1937

Walshe, Peter. *The Rise of African Nationalism in South Africa: The African National Congress, 1912–1952*. London: 1970

Warwick, Peter. *Black People and the South African War, 1899–1902.* Cambridge: 1983

Warwick, Peter and S. B. Spies (eds.). *The South African War: The Anglo-Boer War, 1899–1902.* Harlow: 1980

Weinthal, Leo (ed.). *The Story of the Cape to Cairo Railway and River Route from 1887 to 1922,* 5 vols. London: 1922–26

—— *Memories, Mines and Millions: Being the Life of Sir Joseph B. Robinson.* London: 1929

Welsh, David. *The Roots of Segregation: Native Policy in Colonial Natal, 1845–1910.* Oxford: 1971

Welsh, Frank. *A History of South Africa.* London: 2000

Wheatcroft, Geoffrey. *The Randlords: The Men Who Made South Africa.* London: 1985

Willan, Brian. *Sol Plaatje, South African Nationalist, 1876–1932.* London: 1984

Williams, Basil. *Cecil Rhodes.* London: 1921

Williams, Gardner F. *The Diamond Mines of South Africa: Some Account of their Rise and Development,* 2 vols. London: 1902

Williams, Ralph. *How I Became a Governor.* London: 1913

Williams, Watkin W. *The Life of General Sir Charles Warren.* Oxford: 1941

Wilmot, Alex. *The Life and Times of Sir Richard Southey.* London: 1904

Wilson, Monica and Leonard Thompson (eds.). *The Oxford History of South Africa,* 2 vols. Oxford: 1969, 1971

Wilson, Sarah. *South African Memories: Social, Warlike & Sporting, from Diaries Written at the Time.* London: 1909

Wolseley, Garnet. *The South African Journal of Sir Garnet Wolseley, 1879–1880; Edited with an introduction by Adrian Preston.* Cape Town: 1973

Worden, Nigel. *Slavery in Dutch South Africa.* Cambridge: 1985

—— *The Making of Modern South Africa: Conquest, Segregation and Apartheid.* Oxford: 2000

Worden, Nigel and Clifton Crais (eds.). *Slavery and its Legacy: Breaking the Chains in the Nineteenth Century Cape Colony.* Johannesburg: 1994

Worden, Nigel, Elizabeth van Heyningen and Vivian Bickford-Smith. *Cape Town: The Making of a City.* Cape Town: 1998

Worger, William H. *South Africa's City of Diamonds: Mine Workers and Monopoly Capitalism in Kimberley, 1867–1895.* Yale University Press: 1987

Worsfold, Basil. *Sir Bartle Frere.* London: 1923

Wrench, Evelyn. *Alfred Lord Milner: The Man of No Illusions, 1854–1925.* London: 1968

Wright, Harrison (ed.). *Sir James Rose Innes: Selected Correspondence (1884–1902).* Cape Town: 1972

Younghusband, Francis. *South Africa of Today.* London: 1898

INDEX

PublicAffairs is a publishing house founded in 1997. It is a tribute to the standards, values, and flair of three persons who have served as mentors to countless reporters, writers, editors, and book people of all kinds, including me.

I.F. STONE, proprietor of *I. F. Stone's Weekly*, combined a commitment to the First Amendment with entrepreneurial zeal and reporting skill and became one of the great independent journalists in American history. At the age of eighty, Izzy published *The Trial of Socrates*, which was a national bestseller. He wrote the book after he taught himself ancient Greek.

BENJAMIN C. BRADLEE was for nearly thirty years the charismatic editorial leader of *The Washington Post*. It was Ben who gave the *Post* the range and courage to pursue such historic issues as Watergate. He supported his reporters with a tenacity that made them fearless and it is no accident that so many became authors of influential, best-selling books.

ROBERT L. BERNSTEIN, the chief executive of Random House for more than a quarter century, guided one of the nation's premier publishing houses. Bob was personally responsible for many books of political dissent and argument that challenged tyranny around the globe. He is also the founder and longtime chair of Human Rights Watch, one of the most respected human rights organizations in the world.

• • •

For fifty years, the banner of Public Affairs Press was carried by its owner Morris B. Schnapper, who published Gandhi, Nasser, Toynbee, Truman, and about 1,500 other authors. In 1983, Schnapper was described by *The Washington Post* as "a redoubtable gadfly." His legacy will endure in the books to come.

Peter Osnos, *Founder and Editor-at-Large*

Made in the USA
Lexington, KY
03 October 2013